Dialogue of Love

Dialogue of Love

Confessions of an Evangelical Catholic Ecumenist

EDUARDO J. ECHEVERRIA

WIPF & STOCK · Eugene, Oregon

DIALOGUE OF LOVE
Confessions of an Evangelical Catholic Ecumenist

Copyright © 2010 Eduardo J. Echeverria. All rights reserved. Except for brief quotations in critical publications or reviews, no part of this book may be reproduced in any manner without prior written permission from the publisher. Write: Permissions, Wipf and Stock Publishers, 199 W. 8th Ave., Suite 3, Eugene, OR 97401.

Wipf & Stock
An Imprint of Wipf and Stock Publishers
199 W. 8th Ave., Suite 3
Eugene, OR 97401
www.wipfandstock.com

ISBN 13: 978-1-60608-176-1

Manufactured in the U.S.A.

The Catholic Edition of the Revised Standard Version of the Bible, copyright 1965, 1966 by the Division of Christian Education of the National Council of the Churches of Christ in the United States of America. Used by permission. All rights reserved.

Scripture taken from the HOLY BIBLE NEW INTERNATIONAL VERSION®. NIV®. Copyright© 1973, 1978, 1984 by International Bible Society. Used by permission of Zondervan. All rights reserved.

To DR

Contents

Foreword ix
Introduction xiii

1 The Church in the Gospel 1

2 The One Church of Jesus Christ:
 Unity and Legitimate Diversity 19

3 The Church and the World:
 Anthropological and Ecclesial Foundations 53

4 "The Spirit of Truth":
 On the Sacramental and Epistemological Significance of
 the Holy Spirit 118

5 The God of Philosophy and of the Holy Scriptures 180

Afterword 243
Selected Bibliography 245
Subject/Name Index 259

Foreword

A BRIEF SYNOPSIS OF a true story: Two friends, both seminary professors now teaching in the same state (Michigan), one Roman Catholic and the other Reformed, discover through their education at schools in the other's tradition the rich resources for appropriating and renewing or deepening commitment to their own. The Roman Catholic does advanced degree study at the school that represents the crowning achievement of the Dutch neo-Calvinist tradition in which his friend is born and raised and the encounter deepens his understanding of, commitment to, and practice of his Catholic faith. His friend, raised and trained in the schools of the Dutch neo-Calvinist tradition, completes doctoral study at a leading Roman Catholic university and gains renewed appreciation for the catholicity of his Reformed faith. This is an entirely true story and the two friends are of course the Roman Catholic author of this volume and the Dutch Reformed author of this foreword.

Though excessive autobigraphical reflection is generally a self-serving virus to be avoided in good academic writing, I believe that in this instance my brief account lends credibility to my friend Eduardo's "confession." We are friends but before that we are brothers in Christ who profoundly know that what unites us in our Lord is vastly greater than what still keeps us apart. Neither of us of course knows the future of Christ's church in the world in this coming century, not to mention millennium, but we are equally confident that the gates of hell will not prevail against her. We share the pain of ecclesial division knowing that it pains our Lord and we believe passionately, because we have experienced it deeply, that dialogue across the visible and invisible barriers that exist between Christians is a *gift* to both. We also share the prayerful hope that ecumenical exchanges of gifts such as this volume may be blessed by the God and Father of our Lord Jesus Christ to his full glory and praise.

Read this book with that framework before you. And then, whether you are a Roman Catholic or a Protestant, reflect on its key concerns.

Be reminded (chapter 1) of the seriousness with which our Lord took the unity of his followers (John 17) and let its discomfort stay with you. Be reminded of Rome's acknowledgment of the genuineness of Christian faith and practice outside its fellowship and take seriously the reality of the gospel's power in the lives of the other. Especially for those who teach, follow the author's lead in listening to the best representatives of traditions other than your own, present them fairly and sympathetically, and think of them as he does: as "partners" in a search for truth and thus as a "gift." Whether the author's conviction that the recent statements of the Vatican on church unity (Vatican II's *Unitatis Redintegratio* and John Paul II's *Ut Unum Sint*) in which what is said about the legitimate diversity in unity between the Roman Catholic Church and the Eastern Church "could also be said about the Reformed, particularly neo-Calvinist tradition of historic Christianity," is fully shared in his communion or not, it remains true that a posture that begins with affirming unity will produce greater truth than one that denies it.

Truth and its place in the church is therefore the key issue. If for Roman Catholics the issue is not the salvation of individual persons outside of the Catholic Church but the nature of the church itself and the necessity of ecclesial identity, what then must Protestants do about their easy divisions and all-too frequent schisms? If, as John Paul II has so eloquently set forth in, among other places, *Fides et Ratio*, unity is not a trump card that can be used to downgrade truth then what is the obligation of Protestants who so readily divide over truth to not let doctrinal debates trump the dominical command for unity? One need not follow Rome and the author in believing that Vatican II's formulation that the Church of Christ "subsists in the Catholic Church" (*Lumen Gentium*, no. 8) solves the matter of unity and diversity to appreciate that the extended discussion in the second chapter is not an avoidable luxury for Protestants. Protestant ecclesiology, notably evangelical ecclesiology, is simply not providing the churches with their frames for identity and self-understanding. This is not entirely the fault of evangelical theologians who have tried valiantly in recent years to fill the void;[1] it is the churches themselves who seem indifferent to ecclesiological concerns, preferring pragmatically simply "to be busy doing the work of the Lord."

---

1. See, for example, Bolt, "Evangelical Ecclesiology," *Calvin Theological Journal* 39/2, 400–11.

Avoiding or evading the questions of unity and truth leads to a distortion of our Christian life in the world. Here (chapter 3)—using the Roman Catholic Fr. Romano Guardini (1885–1968) and the Dutch neo-Calvinist philosopher Herman Dooyeweerd (1894–1977)—the author's treatment of the capacity that serious Christian philosophical and social thought has for transcending the modern problematic of individualism versus universalism is instructive. In the final analysis, it all comes down to anthropology. If the church is "the way to become human" can Protestants so easily be satisfied with an "invisible church" that lacks institutional weight and authority? Has Protestantism then not, as American churchman Philip Lee argued a number of years ago, become intrinsically gnostic?[2] We humans are *embodied* creatures; does the fullness of our redemption not require an *embodied*—that is, visible, institutional—church? How else is it possible to be the *body* of Christ? Protestants need to be honest in admitting that Rome has better answers here than we do. The point here is not that there are no answers at all from the Protestant side; the discussion of sacraments (chapter 4) raises questions that Protestants will feel obligated to answer quite differently. None of that, however, takes anything away from the blessing that this book can be to those who accept it as a gift. I know I do. Eduardo my brother and friend, thank you.

John Bolt, PhD
Professor of Systematic Theology
Calvin Theological Seminary
Grand Rapids, Michigan

---

2. Lee, *Against the Protestant Gnostics*.

Introduction

Dialogue does not extend exclusively to matters of doctrine but engages the whole person; it is also a dialogue of love.[1]

Theology has to do with truth. It is not intended merely to inform but rather to communicate truth—truth which makes valid claims upon the other party and therefore can and should be communicated by the informant only in such a way that he identifies himself with this claim to truth. . . . Evidently theological dialogue too is not intended merely to communicate information to the other party of what one thinks oneself, but rather to speak to him that truth which is intended to lay claims upon him.[2]

Ecumenism is really nothing other than living at present in an eschatological light, in light of Christ who is coming again. It thus also signifies that we recognize the provisional nature of our activity, which we ourselves cannot finish; that we do not want to do for ourselves what only Christ, when he comes again, can bring about. On our way toward him, we are on our way toward unity.[3]

I HAVE WRITTEN THIS book as an evangelical Catholic ecumenist.[4] I am an *evangelical* Catholic because I believe that the Gospel, God's free gift of salvation, by which is meant salvation by faith in the saving death and bodily resurrection of Jesus Christ, calls for a response, for personal conversion by the Spirit's power to Jesus Christ as Savior and Lord. I am an evangelical because I believe in the centrality of the Holy Bible as the authoritative Word of God in the faith and life of a committed Christian. I am an evangelical because I

---

1. John Paul II, *Ut Unum Sint*, no. 47.
2. Rahner, "Theology of the Ecumenical Discussion," 30.
3. Ratzinger (Benedict XVI), "Ecumenical Situation," 269.
4. Portier, "Here Come the Evangelical Catholics"; Root, "Catholic and Evangelical Theology"; Beckwith, *Return to Rome*; Tjørhom, *Visible Church-Visible Unity*; Braaten, *Mother Church, Ecclesiology and Ecumenism*; Braaten and Jenson, eds., *Catholicity of the Reformation*.

believe that the gospel is the Good News of Jesus Christ for all men, and hence it is the free gift of God to which I am called to give public witness.

I am an evangelical *Catholic* because I am "committed to the Christological and Trinitarian dogmas of the early church as the permanently normative context for the explication of the Christian faith." I am a Catholic because I am "committed to the constitutive significance of the Church for the reality and the interpretation of the faith."[5] In other words, I am a Catholic because I am committed to the teaching that the existence of the Church belongs to the gospel,[6] that Christian faith and life is ecclesial, sacramental, and liturgical, and that the Church of Christ is one and universal, under the guidance of the Holy Spirit working through the Church's Magisterium, the successors of the Apostles. In the words of the Dogmatic Constitution on the Church, *Lumen Gentium*, "This Church, constituted and organized as a society in the present world, subsists in the Catholic Church, which is governed by the successor of Peter and by the Bishops in communion with him."[7] I am a Catholic because I am committed to the teaching that the Catholic Church *is* the one Church of Christ, and hence that the one gospel is inseparable from this really existing Church, most fully and rightly ordered through time as well as space (as the late Father Richard John Neuhaus phrases it).[8]

Last but not least, I am an evangelical Catholic *ecumenist* because I am "committed to the [God-given] unity of the Church and the reconciliation of divided Christians."[9] I am an ecumenist because the teaching that the Church Jesus Christ founded *is* the Catholic Church, and the concomitant teaching that "many elements of sanctification and truth

---

5. Root, "Catholic and Evangelical Theology," 10–12.

6. Evangelical catholic (Lutheran) Braaten writes: "Evangelical Protestantism is centered in the gospel. This is what the word 'evangelical' means, to be defined by the evangel, the good news of the gospel. But where does the church fit in? Many evangelicals, feeling the insufficiency of a 'gospel reductionism,' are attempting to retrieve more churchly elements from the great tradition. . . . They realize that there is no gospel apart from the church and its sacramental life. . . . There is no such thing as churchless Christianity" ("The Problem of Authority in the Church," 55).

7. Vatican II, *Lumen Gentium*, no. 8. The controversial issue regarding the meaning of the phrase "subsists in" for understanding the identity of the Church founded by Jesus Christ will be discussed in chapter 2.

8. Neuhaus, *Catholic Matters*.

9. Root, "Catholic and Evangelical Theology," 10–12.

are found outside [the Church's] visible confines," impels me to seek the restoration of unity among my separated brethren.[10]

Given my commitment to these teachings, I raise the question for myself that John Paul II rightly asked: "How is it possible to remain divided, if we have been 'buried' through Baptism in the Lord's death, in the very act by which God, through the death of his Son, has broken down the walls of division?"[11] As the pope says elsewhere:

> By fixing our gaze on Christ, the Great Jubilee has given us a more vivid sense of the Church as a mystery of unity. 'I believe in the one Church': what we profess in the Creed has *its ultimate foundation in Christ, in whom the Church is undivided* (cf. 1 Cor 1:11–13). As his Body, in the unity which is the gift of the Spirit, she is indivisible. The reality of division among the Church's children appears at the level of history, as the result of human weakness in the way we accept the gift which flows endlessly from Christ the Head to his Mystical Body. The prayer of Jesus in the upper room—"as you, Father, are in me and I in you, that they also may be one is us" (John 17:21)—is both *revelation* and *invocation*. It reveals to us the unity of Christ with the Father as well as the wellspring of the Church's unity and as the gift, which in him she will constantly receive until its mysterious fulfillment at the end of time. This unity is concretely embodied in the Catholic Church, despite the human limitations of her members, and it is at work in varying degrees in all the elements of holiness and truth to be found in the other Churches and Ecclesial Communities. As gifts properly belonging to the Church of Christ, these elements lead them continuously toward full unity. Christ's prayer reminds us that this gift needs to be received and developed ever more profoundly. The invocation *"ut unum sint"* is, at one and the same time, a binding imperative, the strength that sustains us, and a salutary rebuke for our slowness and close-heartedness. It is on Jesus' prayer and not on our own strength that we base the hope that even within history we shall be able to reach full and visible communion with all Christians.[12]

I was raised Catholic, attended Catholic primary and secondary schools, but I did not respond to the Gospel in a Catholic context.[13] It was

10. *Lumen Gentium*, no. 8.
11. John Paul II, *Ut Unum Sint*, no. 6.
12. John Paul II, *Novo Millennio Ineunte*, no. 48.
13. For a fuller biographical account of my return to the Catholic Church, see "My

at L'Abri Fellowship, Huémoz sur Ollon, Switzerland, forty years ago in the summer of 1970 that I first committed my life to Christ as Lord and Savior, "the Way, the Truth, and the Life" (John 14:6). L'Abri Fellowship, an evangelical Protestant community where people live, study, and work, was founded by Francis A. Schaeffer (1912–1984), along with his wife Edith (1918–), more than a half century ago. It was at L'Abri that I began to understand the Christian faith as a way of life rooted in the truth about reality, about the meaning of life, and communion with God the Father, in Christ, and through the power of the Holy Spirit. It was also at L'Abri that I began to understand that living under the Lordship of Jesus Christ entailed the sanctification of the whole of life, including the life of culture, particularly the intellectual life.[14]

Now, this understanding of the Christian life, which I first learned at L'Abri Fellowship, was deepened in the paths I took on my journey back to full communion with the Catholic Church in 1992. One path was the Augustinian and Reformed or Dutch neo-Calvinist tradition of historic Christianity. Another path, which deepened my understanding of the historic Christian faith, especially the antiquity of the Church, of the Liturgy, of the sacramental life of grace in Christ, particularly of Baptism and the Eucharist, the Church Fathers, and the idea of doctrinal development, I found in the writings of not only John Henry Newman but also John Paul II. I returned to full communion with Mother Church, the Catholic Church—twenty-two years after discovering Christ, by grace, the Lord Jesus led me to discover his Church.

At the start of my journey, however, the path that played a defining role in my understanding of the Christian faith, and is my central interlocutor in this book, is the Reformed tradition of historic Christianity. In other words, that version of confessional Protestant Christianity arising from the Calvinist Reformation in sixteenth-century Europe, in particular, Dutch neo-Calvinism, which refers to a movement within the Augustinian and Reformed tradition that stems from the nineteenth-century Dutch educator, theologian, church leader, and politician Abraham Kuyper (1837–1920). Besides Kuyper, other genial spirits within this intellectual milieu that profoundly influenced my walk with the Lord include

---

Journey Home."

14. See my book, *Slitting the Sycamore*; idem, "Living Truth for a Post-Christian World"; idem, "Christian faith as a way of life" (on the 50th anniversary of L'Abri Fellowship).

Herman Bavinck (1845–1921), Gerritt C. Berkouwer (1904–1996), and Herman Dooyeweerd (1894–1977).¹⁵ All that is good in the neo-Calvinist Reformed tradition—its doctrines of creation, fall into sin, and redemption, its understanding of the relation between nature, sin, and grace, the Lordship of Christ over the whole spectrum of life, the idea and practice of Christian scholarship, its cultural, social, and political theology and philosophy, and so much more—deepened my understanding of, commitment to, and practice of the Christian faith.

My thesis is that the neo-Calvinist theological formulations of some of these issues can stand on their own as important and insightful formulations of the truth, complementing rather than contradicting Catholic formulations. This claim is consistent with the teachings of Vatican II. "Taking up an idea expressed by Pope John XXIII at the opening of the Council, the Decree on Ecumenism mentions the way of formulating doctrine as one of the elements of a continuing reform. Here it is not a question of altering the deposit of faith, changing the meaning of dogmas, eliminating essential words from them, accommodating truth to the preferences of a particular age, or suppressing certain articles of the *Creed* under the false pretext that they are no longer understood today. The unity willed by God can be attained only by the adherence of all to the content of revealed faith in its entirety. In matters of faith, compromise is in contradiction with God who is Truth."¹⁶ John Paul is referring here to the distinction his predecessor made between the *substance* and the *formulations* of the truth in his opening address to Vatican II.¹⁷ John XXIII said, "The deposit or the truths of faith, contained in our sacred teaching, are one thing, while the mode in which they are enunciated, keeping the same meaning and the same judgment, is another."¹⁸ I agree with John Paul that this distinction has genuine ecumenical significance. Of course, philosophical issues of meaning and truth are at stake in drawing on the distinction between the substance and the formulations of truth in order

---

15. A brief history of the Dutch origins of the Christian Reformed Church as well as the history of inter-church relations and ecumenicity in this Church, see Zwaanstra, *Catholicity and Secession*.

16. John Paul II, *Ut Unum Sint*, no. 18.

17. "Pope John's Opening Speech to the Council," 710–19.

18. Ioannes XXIII, "Allocutio habita d. 11 oct. 1962, in initio Concilii," "Est enim aliud ipsum depositum Fidei, seu veritates, quae veneranda doctrina nostra continentur, aliud modus, quo eaedem enuntiantur, eodem tamen sensu eademque sententia."

to defend the idea of legitimate diversity in complimentary theological rather than contradictory expressions of doctrine.[19] I will discuss these issues in conversation with Berkouwer's work on Vatican II in chapter 2 of this book.[20]

Furthermore, like Neuhaus once wrote regarding his own reception into the Church and departure from the Lutheran tradition, I too experienced respect for the Evangelical, Reformed, and Anglo-Catholic traditions, "Nothing that is good is rejected, all is fulfilled."[21] Indeed, I will illustrate in this book the validity of Neuhaus's principle that "Nothing that is good and true is rejected, all is fulfilled" and its corollary of legitimate diversity. In particular, all that is good and true in neo-Calvinism is affirmed in authentic Catholicism—all is fulfilled and perfected. By implication, all that is false is rejected.

Now, although I am a committed Roman Catholic, I have written this book drawing both on confessional Catholicism with its roots in the Augustinian and Thomist traditions and confessional Protestantism with its own roots in the Augustinian and more recent Reformed or neo-Calvinist tradition. It will be evident in this book that I have been philosophically and theologically formed by both traditions. Let me make clear, however, that this book as such is neither an apologetic in defense of the Catholic faith nor an overall assessment of the Catholic Church and the ecumenical movement.[22] Rather, this book is a modest but hopefully faithful attempt to respond to the prayer that Christ offered for the gift and

---

19. John Paul II, *Ut Unum Sint*, nos. 18–19.

20. Berkouwer, *Vatikaans Concilie en de nieuwe theologie*, 5–103. ET: *Second Vatican Council and the New Catholicism*, 11-88. Both sources will be cited throughout this book, first the original, followed by the pagination of the English translation in square brackets [ ]. Berkouwer (1904–1996), renowned Dutch Reformed theologian, holder of the Chair in Dogmatics at the Free University, Amsterdam, and author of a 15-volume work, Studies in Dogmatics, as well as a highly regarded study and trenchant critique of Barth, *Triumph of Grace in the Theology of Karl Barth*, was an officially appointed observer, so-called "Delegated Observer" from other Christian communions, at Vatican II. After his attendance in 1962 at the Council, he published, *Vatikaans Concilie en de nieuwe theologie*, which was almost immediately translated in English. The words "nieuwe theologie" (literally "new theology") in the Dutch title of the book is a clear allusion to the *nouvelle théologie* of de Lubac, et al. One would not know that allusion from the English title, which speaks of "New Catholicism."

21. Neuhaus, "How I Became the Catholic I was."

22. In particular, Whitehead, *New Ecumenism*, is an instructive account of the relationship between the Catholic Church and the ecumenical movement.

promise of the unity of the Church in the Father and Son, "*so that* the world may come to believe that it is thou who has sent me" (John 17:21; Knox translation). The words of John Paul II ring true to my own experience as an evangelical Catholic ecumenist: "Dialogue is not simply an exchange of ideas. In some way it is always an 'exchange of gifts.'"[23] Indeed, John Paul adds, "Dialogue does not extend exclusively to matters of doctrine but engages the whole person; it is also a dialogue of love."[24] May God continue to bless us in this ecumenical exchange of gifts, in this dialogue of love, "so that in all things he may be glorified through Jesus Christ, to whom belong glory and dominion forever and ever. Amen" (1 Pt. 4:11).

Finally, I have structured the chapters of this book in the following way. In the first chapter, I give an overview of the theological argument in recent Catholic teaching supporting the thesis that the Church is an integral part of the gospel, or better put, that the Church belongs to the gospel. In Chapter 2, I consider the question whether Vatican Council II eroded the traditional Catholic doctrine on the full identity of the Church of Christ with the Catholic Church. If not, how are we to understand the ecclesial reality of non-Catholic communions? In particular, do the "many elements of sanctification and truth"[25] that can be found outside the visible boundaries of the Church exist in an ecclesial vacuum? I follow up this analysis with a discussion in the remaining three chapters of this book on some of the issues that continue to divide Christians, particularly those in the Reformed and Catholic traditions, namely, the relation of the Church and the World, the Holy Spirit and his sacramental and epistemological significance, and the relation of Faith and Reason. Why did I pick these topics and not others?[26] For the simple reason that these topics were roadblocks in understanding the Catholic faith and from my experience they still are for many separated brethren who are seeking to move toward full communion with Mother Church, the Catholic Church.

---

23. John Paul II, *Ut Unum Sint*, no. 28.
24. Ibid., no. 47.
25. *Lumen Gentium*, no. 8.
26. For instance, see the topics John Paul II identified in *Ut Unum Sint*, no. 79.

1

The Church in the Gospel

"Homesickness for the una sancta [ecclesia]" is genuine and legitimate only insofar as it is a disquietude at the fact that we have lost and forgotten Christ, and with Him have lost the unity of the Church."[1]

To believe in Christ means to desire unity; to desire unity means to desire the Church; to desire the Church means to desire the communion of grace which corresponds to the Father's plan from all eternity. Such is the meaning of Christ's prayer: "that they may all be one."[2]

VISIBLE CHRISTIAN UNITY, EVANGELISM, AND ECUMENISM

IN THE RECENT PAST, the Southern Baptist Convention put the brakes on official ecumenical talks with the Catholic Church. Rev. R. Philip Roberts, the current president of Midwestern Baptist Theological Seminary, Kansas City, Missouri, was quoted as saying, "We're not ecumenists. We're evangelicals committed to sharing the Gospel."[3] The anti-ecumenical sentiment expressed in this statement is not unique to Southern Baptists like Roberts; one can find it expressed historically and in recent times by all sorts of Christians, Protestant, and Catholic alike. Indeed, Pope Pius XI's 1928 encyclical *Mortalium Animos* ("On Religious Unity") dismisses ecumenical initiatives in the early twentieth century because they fostered, he argued, a dangerous indifferentism and confu-

---

1. Barth, *Church and Churches*, 20.

2. John Paul II, *Ut Unum Sint*, no. 9. Further references to this encyclical will be found parenthetically in the text as *UUS*.

3. "Baptists Halt Ecumenical Talks with Catholics," reported by the Associated Press, March 23, 2001. Online: http://www.independentchristian.org/understand.pdf.

sion about the faith.[4] As Yves Congar remarks, "it might have been feared that an interest in Protestant or Orthodox thought and life could lead to disaffection with regard to the teaching and life of the Church, for dogmatic indifferentism is often the *forecourt of unbelief, or at least tepidity*."[5] Some twenty years later, the Congregation for the Doctrine of the Faith, known then by the name of the Holy Office, issued an Instruction "On the 'Ecumenical Movement', naming as one of the reasons for the Church's early dismissal of the ecumenical movement the following: "that the purity of Catholic doctrine be impaired, or its genuine and certain meaning be obscured. . . . Or, what is worse, that in matters of dogma even the Catholic Church has not yet attained the fullness of Christ, but can still be perfected from outside."[6] This Instruction does say to those who return to the Church that "they will lose nothing of that good which by the grace of God has hitherto been implanted in them, but rather that it will be supplemented and completed by their return."[7] Yet, it cautions Catholics engaged in ecumenical initiatives against giving the impression to those "returning to the Church [that] they are bringing to it something substantial which it has hitherto lacked."[8] Absent here is any sense of reciprocity, a requirement for ecumenical dialogue, as later popes, such as Paul VI and John Paul II, were to say, not to mention the idea that such dialogue "is always an 'exchange of gifts', indeed, a 'dialogue of love'" (*UUS*, nos. 28, 47). Nevertheless, when I read these words of Roberts, I immediately thought that he was making a division where none should exist—between the Gospel of Jesus Christ and authentic ecumenism. "Christ calls all His disciples to unity" (John 17:20–23), the late John Paul II writes in *UUS*. Furthermore, behind this false division is a fundamental failure to recognize the ecclesial dimensions of the Christian faith and life, ruling out

---

4. Pius XI, *Mortalium Animos*, nos. 8–9.

5. Congar, OP, *Dialogue between Christians*, 101. "In addition," Congar writes in 1958, "The Catholic Church is fearful, above all, of fostering in the minds of the faithful the idea that she would be prepared to make concessions, not only on practical points but also in doctrinal matters. She is afraid of favoring a certain doctrinal indifferentism according to which 'all religions are equally good'. Many are already inclined to indifferentism which experience shows to be the forecourt of virtual atheism" (120–21).

6. An Instruction of the Holy Office, "On the 'Ecumenical Movement'," no. 2.

7. Despite the traditional teaching affirming the full identity of Christ's Church with the Catholic Church, in 1713 Clement XI condemns the thesis that "Outside of the Church, no grace is granted," in the "Errors of Paschasius Quesnel," 349, no. 1379.

8. "On the 'Ecumenical Movement'," no. 2.

that the Church is an integral part of the gospel, or better put, that the Church belongs to the gospel.[9]

In the Gospel of John, we read that Jesus himself prayed to his Father, at the hour of his passion, "that all of them may be one" (17:21). What is the nature of this unity? The Church, which is Christ's body, is neither a collection of individuals, nor a sociological subject, for example, a voluntary association of like-minded individuals sharing a belief in Christ and who by virtue of human agreement wants to give corporate expression to that belief. Hence, the unity of Christ's disciples is not that of a mere gathering of people "who first became believers apart from the church and subsequently united themselves."[10] Rather, the Church is the divinely created communion of persons, the reborn (i.e., new) humanity in Christ, who is the New Adam, the religious root of the human race, profoundly described by the Apostle Paul as the "Body of Christ" (in Ephesians and Colossians), with her Head and individual members. The Church is then the religious bond of unity of the reborn human race sharing in the life of God. As the former Joseph Ratzinger, now Benedict XVI, puts it, "For the believer . . . the Church is . . . a truly new subject called into being by the Word and in the Holy Spirit; and precisely for that reason, the Church herself overcomes the seemingly insurmountable confines of human subjectivity by putting man in contact with the ground of reality which is prior to him."[11] The ground of reality that is prior to man is Trinitarian communion, Father, Son, and Holy Spirit, and the "faithful are *one* because, in the Spirit, they are in *communion* with the Son and, in him, share in his *communion* with the Father." In other words, adds John Paul II, "For the Catholic Church, then, the *communion* of Christians is none other than the manifestation in them of the grace by which God makes them sharers in his own *communion*, which is his eternal life" (*UUS*, no. 9).

Furthermore, the Church's unity is not simply a goal or ideal to be sought, or a mere spiritual or invisible unity, contrasted, as Karl Barth put it, with "the multiplicity of the churches as a necessary mark of the visible and empirical." "This entire distinction," adds Barth, "is foreign to the

---

9. Neuhaus, "Catholic Difference," 222. Especially helpful is DiNoia, OP, "Church in the Gospel." See also, Marshall, "Church in the Gospel."

10. Bavinck, *Gereformeerde Dogmatiek* IV, 264. ET: *Reformed Dogmatics*, Vol. 4, 280. Both sources will be cited throughout this book, first the original as *GD*, followed by the pagination of the English translation in square brackets [ ].

11. Cardinal Ratzinger (Pope Benedict XVI), *Deus Locutus Est Nobis in Filio*, 23.

New Testament . . . the Church of Jesus Christ is but one."[12] The fundamental unity of the Church is a gift of God's grace: the grace of communion with the Father through Christ and in the power of the Holy Spirit. Father Neuhaus understands this well: "Our purpose is not to create a unity among Christians that does not already exist. Indeed, we cannot create Christian unity at all. Unity is God's gift, not our creation. . . . In the Catholic view, the problem posed by the division between Catholics and Evangelicals is not that we are *not* united. *The problem, indeed the scandal, is that we are united but live as though we are not.*"[13] The Protestant Reformer John Calvin also understood this point well when he wrote, "there could not be two or three churches without Christ himself being torn apart, and that is impossible."[14] In other words, the Church's unity is a gift of God—visible, historical, temporal, institutional, in short, bodily—belonging to the Church herself, and "this gift needs to be received and developed ever more profoundly."[15] Thus, unity is both a gift and a task.[16] Furthermore, this unity is not a purely spiritual, invisible reality, as if Christ's Church exists nowhere on earth, but rather is concretely embodied. Nor is Christ's Church a confederation of Christian communities, which taken together form the one Church of Christ. On the contrary, as Joseph Cardinal Ratzinger then put it, "The Church of Christ is not something intangible, hidden under the variety of human constructions." Alternatively, says Barth, the multiplicity of the churches cannot be explained "as an unfolding of the wealth of that grace which is given to mankind in Jesus Christ, divinely purposed and therefore normal . . . as branches of the one and the self-same tree." Rather, the Church's unity has a recognizable delineation, truly existing as a bodily Church: "She is one

---

12. Barth, *Church and Churches*, 25.
13. Neuhaus, "Catholic Difference," 187.
14. Calvin, Book IV, I, no. 2, *Institutes of the Christian Religion*.
15. John Paul II, *Novo millennio ineunte*, no. 48.
16. On this, see *One Body through the Cross*, eds. Braaten and Jenson, 16–17. See also, Heim, *Joseph Ratzinger*, "Ratzinger understands Church *unity to be a gift and a task* that the Church has received from the Lord, because it is an essential mark of the one, holy, catholic, and apostolic Church. Yet the visible Church is wounded because, even though she is one, 'the reality of salvation and of being saved, ecclesial reality', exists outside her visible boundaries as well. Thus unity becomes a task, not in the sense of a utopian dream, but rather as a search for truth, for anyone who seeks the truth is, as Ratzinger puts it, 'objectively on the way to Christ and thus also on the way to the communion in which he remains present to history—the Church'" (325; italics added).

in [the confession of] faith, one in the celebration of the sacraments, one in apostolic succession, and one in ecclesial governance."[17] This unity is a present reality bestowed by the Holy Spirit on Christ's body, and Christ cannot be divided. "There is one body and one Spirit," St. Paul states in his Letter to the Ephesians, "just as you were called to the one hope of your calling, one Lord, one faith, one baptism, one God and Father of all, who is above all and through all and in all" (Eph 4:4–7). Given the God-given unity of the Church—one Lord, one faith, one baptism, one Spirit, we can easily understand why Herman Bavinck also says that schisms and discord among Christians "is a sin against God, in conflict with Christ's [high-priestly] prayer [for unity], and caused by the darkness of our minds and the lovelessness of our hearts."[18]

In this connection, Catholic theologian Bruce Marshall remarks, "In baptism the Holy Spirit makes us members of the Church by joining us in love to Christ and, equally, to one another. Paul does not implore the Ephesians to seek by the Spirit's power a unity they presently lack, but to 'maintain the unity of the Spirit in the bond of peace' (Eph 4:3), the very bond that holds together the one body of Christ."[19] In short, just as there is only one God and one Lord, so there is also one Church, one ark, one temple, one house of God, which is the only Bride of Christ, the single Body of Christ.

Moreover, as the Dogmatic Constitution *Lumen Gentium* and the Decree *Unitatis Redintegratio*, as well as the more recent *UUS* (1995) and *Dominus Iesus* (2000), fundamentally affirm, the one Church of Christ subsists in the Catholic Church.[20] The Second Vatican Ecumenical Council teaches the historical continuity between the Church founded by Christ and the Catholic Church. The Church of Jesus Christ exists bodily. Christ himself has willed the Church's existence; and the Holy Spirit has continually renewed her since Pentecost, *ecclesia semper reformanda*, preserving her in her essential identity, which belongs to the concreteness of the Incarnation. The Church is one, absolutely singular, subsisting in the

---

17. *Lumen Gentium*, no. 14, as cited in Ratzinger, "Deus Locutus Est Nobis in Filio," 24.
18. Bavinck, *GD* IV, [316].
19. Marshall, "Who Really Cares about Christian Unity?"
20. This teaching is reasserted most recently by the Congregation for the Doctrine of the Faith, "Responses to Some Questions Regarding Certain Aspects of the Doctrine of the Church." I'll return to discuss this controversial teaching, even among Catholics, in the next chapter.

Catholic Church, existing as a single subject in the reality of history. This means that the Catholic Church is the fully and rightly ordered expression of the Body of Christ in time; in her the fullness of the means of salvation is present. "For it is through Christ's Catholic Church alone, which is the universal help towards salvation, that the fullness of the means of salvation can be obtained. It was to the apostolic college alone, of which Peter is the head, which we believe that Our Lord entrusted all the blessings of the New Covenant, in order to establish on earth the one Body of Christ into which all those should be fully incorporated who belong in any way to the people of God."[21]

Admittedly, this teaching is, to quote Paul VI, "the biggest obstacle on the road to ecumenism."[22] Nevertheless, in words that Fr. Gustave Weigel wrote almost a half a century ago, "If we are to speak to each other, we should know how each partner of the conversation appears to himself. It is antecedently thinkable that the partner in dialogue is in error in his self-evaluation but it is unthinkable that the intercourse would be fruitful if we did not take such self-evaluation into account."[23] Thus, against the background of the Catholic Church's teaching that she is not merely "one part of a divided whole," we can easily understand why the Church rejects "ecclesiological relativism," which is the view that the Church "subsists" intangibly under a variety of human constructions. On this view, according to the then Joseph Ratzinger, "then no Church could claim to possess definitively binding teaching authority, and in this way institutional

---

21. *Unitatis Redintegratio*, no. 3. See also, *Dominus Iesus* (nos. 16–17), "The Catholic faithful *are required to profess* that there is an historical continuity—rooted in the apostolic succession—between the Church founded by Christ and the Catholic Church."

22. Paul VI's 1967 address to the annual assembly of moderators, members, and consultants to the secretariat for Christian Unity, 498.

23. Weigel, SJ, *Catholic Theology in Dialogue*, 76. This point is reiterated by Cardinal Kasper in his July 11, 2007, reply to Protestant reactions to "Responses to Some Questions Regarding Certain Aspects of the Doctrine of the Church." He says, "A first and quick reaction among Protestant Christians to the declaration of the Congregation of the Doctrine of Faith 'Responses to Some Questions Regarding Certain Aspects of the Doctrine on the Church' has been one of irritation. But a second, quiet reading will show that the document does not say anything new. It explains and, in a brief summary, clarifies positions that the Catholic Church has held for a long time. Therefore, no new situation has developed. Nor is there any objective reason for outrage, or the feeling of being offended. Every dialogue presupposes clarity about the different positions. Our Protestant partners are the ones who have recently spoken about an ecumenism of profiles. If this declaration now explains the Catholic profile and expresses what, in a Catholic view, unfortunately still divides us, this does not hinder dialogue, but promotes it."

relativism will lead to doctrinal relativism." "If belief in 'the body' of the Church is taken away," he adds, "the Church's concrete claims regarding the content of faith disappear along with her bodiliness."[24]

Of course we don't have before us yet the full teaching of the Second Vatican Council. The ecclesiology of this Council is that the "Church [of Jesus Christ], constituted and organized in the world as a society, subsists in the Catholic Church, which is governed by the successor of Peter and by the bishops in union with that successor."[25] The Catholic Church in a singularly unique way is the fully and rightly ordered expression of the Church of Jesus Christ in time and space. Yet, there is more. This Council also teaches that "many elements of sanctification and truth" can be found outside the visible boundaries of the Church.[26] Thus, this teaching provides a theological foundation for the Catholic Church's commitment to ecumenical dialogue:

> The Church recognizes that in many ways she is linked with those who, being baptized, are honored with the name of Christian, though they do not profess the faith in its entirety or do not preserve unity of communion with the successor of Peter. For there are many who honor sacred Scripture, taking it as a norm of belief and of action, and who show a true religious zeal. They lovingly believe in God the Father Almighty and in Christ, Son of God and Savior. They are consecrated by baptism, through which they are united with Christ. They also recognize and receive other sacraments within their own Churches or ecclesial communities. Many of them rejoice in the episcopate, celebrate the Holy Eucharist and cultivate devotion toward the Virgin Mother of God. They also share with us in prayer and other spiritual benefits.[27]

So Vatican II teaches that all Christians, all those who are "in Christ," are truly, genuinely, but imperfectly, in communion with the Catholic Church. "In some real way they are joined with us in the Holy Spirit, for to them also He gives His gifts and graces, and is thereby operative among them with His sanctifying power."[28] Elsewhere we read, "It remains true that all who have been justified by faith in baptism are incorporated into

---

24. Ratzinger, "*Deus Locutus Est Nobis in Filio,*" 27.
25. *Lumen Gentium*, no. 8.
26. Ibid.
27. *Lumen Gentium*, no. 15.
28. Ibid.

Christ; they therefore have a right to be called Christians, and with good reason are accepted as brothers by the children of the Catholic Church." "Moreover," the Council Fathers add, "some, even very many, of the most significant elements and endowments which together go to build up and give life to the Church herself, can exist outside the visible boundaries of the Catholic Church: the written Word of God; the life of grace; faith, hope and charity, with the other interior gifts of the Holy Spirit, as well as visible elements. All of these, which come from Christ and lead back to him, belong by right to the one Church of Christ."[29] In other words, although these elements do not exist in an "ecclesial vacuum" (*UUS*, no. 13), because there is ecclesial reality outside the visible boundaries of the Church,[30] they are not "static elements passively present in those Churches and Communities," as John Paul notes (*UUS*, no. 49), or "autonomous and free-floating," in the words of Dominican priest and theologian, Fr. Aidan Nichols. Indeed, "they derive their efficacy from the very fullness of grace and truth entrusted to the Catholic Church."[31] Adds Nichols, "and coming from that source, carry a built-in gravitational pull back—or on!—towards the Church's unity."[32]

This teaching was very important to me in my own journey to full communion with the Catholic Church. It helped me to make sense of the "many elements of sanctification and of truth" that I found throughout my Christian experience—from Evangelical to the Reformed and Anglo-Catholic traditions of historic Protestant Christianity. Indeed, I came to know these elements to be gifts and graces that the Spirit of Christ used as instruments to bring me home to the Church. The inner dynamism of these gifts and graces toward Catholic unity, that essential mark of the Church as Christ willed her to be and which he bestowed on his Church from the beginning, was the guiding force that re-established in my own life true and full communion with the Church (cf. *UUS*, no. 49). In this sense, entering into full communion with the Church essentially involved bringing to fulfillment in my own life a unity already given by God as his gift in founding His Church.

In my own Catholic ecumenical experience, I have always had real fellowship with other Christians who honor the canonical authority of the

---

29. *Unitatis Redintegratio*, no. 2.
30. On this, see Ratzinger, "Deus Locutus Est Nobis in Filio," 28.
31. *Unitatis Redintegratio*, no. 3.
32. Nichols, OP, *Splendor of Doctrine*, 122.

sacred Scriptures, the Word of God, as the standard of faith and morals, who love and openly confess Jesus Christ as Lord and Savior, and as the one Mediator between God and man, who are united by baptism with the one God, the Father, in Christ, and through the power of the Holy Spirit, and who hold the Christian faith to be true. This has served as a common starting point for lively and fruitful ecumenical discussions about the full range of Catholic truth claims, especially the claim that the fullness of the means of salvation, of grace and truth, subsists within the Catholic Church, and nowhere else.

In concluding this first point, I look back to Jesus' High Priestly prayer at the hour of his Passion. His prayer makes clear the basis of his disciples' unity, namely, "that all of them may be one, Father, just as you are in me and I am in you." So Christ's disciples are one in the Spirit, because they are in communion with the Son and, in Him, share in His communion with the Father. Says John the Evangelist, "Our fellowship is with the Father and with His Son Jesus Christ" (1 John 1:3). The communion of Christians, then, is nothing less than our sharing, by grace, in God's own communion, the Holy Trinity, Father, Son and Holy Spirit, which is his eternal life.

Yet, there is more. The Church's unity is at the very heart of the proclamation of the Gospel, not only in the sense that it belongs to the very essence of Christ's body, and Christ cannot be divided. But also, and in particular, because disunity is a grave obstacle for proclaiming the Gospel credibly and authentically. The world will not believe that God himself is an eternal fellowship of love, Father, Son, and Holy Spirit, and that He has chosen us to share by grace in that fellowship unless it sees some manifestation in Christians of that fellowship. The world will not believe that God so loved the world that He gave His one and only Son that whoever believes in Him shall not perish but have eternal life (John 3:16), unless it sees in Christians some evidence of God's love rather than division. The world will not believe, as Francis Schaeffer once put it, "that Jesus' claims are true, that Christianity is true, unless the world see some reality of the oneness of true Christians."[33]

The Church's full and visible unity, then, is not some appendix to the Gospel, or something we can opt for if we so desire. Again, looking back to Christ at the hour of his passion, he prays to the Father, "May they all also be in us so that the world may believe that you have sent me . . . I in them

---

33. Schaeffer, *Mark of the Christian*, 14. See also, Marshall, "Disunity of the Church."

and you in me. May they be brought to complete unity to let the world know that you sent me and have loved them even as you have loved me" (John 17:21, 23). In short, lack of unity compromises our Christian witness to the world, contradicting the Gospel truth that Christians have the missionary mandate to live, proclaim, and defend. Hence, as John Paul II rightly urges, "ecumenism is not only an internal question of the Christian communities" (*UUS*, no. 99). "At the same time," John Paul adds, "it is obvious that the lack of unity among Christians contradicts the Truth which Christians have the mission to spread and, consequently, it gravely damages their witness" (*UUS*, no. 98). In the words of Pope Paul VI, "May the Holy Spirit guide us along the way of reconciliation, so that the unity of our Churches may become an ever more radiant sign of hope and consolation for all mankind" (Letter of January 13, 1970, cited in *UUS*, note 158).

ECUMENICAL DIALOGUE

Undoubtedly, some Christians, Protestant and Catholic alike, have generally opposed the ecumenical movement and inter-confessional dialogue because of concerns regarding the compromising of truth. For example, the June 1996 Southern Baptist Convention Resolution on Baptists and Ecumenism states, "True Biblical unity can only be realized in the bond of truth, and never at the expense of Biblical truth."[34] John Paul II agrees that the "obligation to respect the truth is absolute" (*UUS*, no. 79), but unlike the SBC who apparently does not see its way clear to adhere consistently to this obligation and engage in such dialogue without compromising the truth, John Paul holds that one can uphold the absolute obligation to respect the truth without compromise and hence without putting the brakes on the ecumenical movement. Indeed, the Catholic Church, in particular, holds that "full [visible] communion of course [would] have to come about through the acceptance of the whole truth into which the Holy Spirit guides Christ's disciples," says John Paul (*UUS*, no. 6). Thus the Church's vision of visible unity "takes account of all the demands of revealed truth" (*UUS*, no. 79). Thus, she seeks to avoid all forms of reductionism or facile agreement, false irenicism,[35] and indifference to the

---

34. This resolution is online: http://www.sbc.net/resolutions/amResolution.asp?ID=459.

35. "The manner and order in which Catholic belief is expressed should in no way become an obstacle to dialogue with our brothers. It is, of course, essential that doctrine be clearly presented in its entirety. Nothing is as foreign to the spirit of ecumenism as a

Church's teaching. John Paul II correctly writes, "Love for the truth is the deepest dimension of any authentic quest for full communion between Christians" (*UUS*, no. 36). In other words, he adds, "The unity willed by God can be attained only by the adherence of all to the content of revealed faith in its entirety. In matters of faith, compromise is in contradiction with God who is Truth. In the Body of Christ, 'the way, and the truth, and the life' (John 14:6), who would consider legitimate a reconciliation brought about at the expense of the truth? . . . A 'being together' which betrayed the truth would thus be opposed both to the nature of God who offers his communion and to the need for truth found in the depths of every human heart" (*UUS*, no.18). In short, "Authentic ecumenism is a gift at the service of truth" (*UUS*, no. 38).

Accordingly, the journey, already begun, toward re-establishing full visible unity among all the baptized requires us to continue and deepen the inter-confessional dialogue, whose positive results already makes it possible "to identify the areas in need of fuller study before a true consensus of faith can be achieved" (*UUS*, no. 79). These five areas are:

> 1) [T]he relationship between Sacred Scripture, as the highest authority in matters of faith, and Sacred Tradition, as indispensable to the interpretation of the Word of God; 2) the Eucharist, as the Sacrament of the Body and Blood of Christ, an offering of praise to the Father, the sacrificial memorial and Real Presence of Christ and the sanctifying outpouring of the Holy Spirit; 3) Ordination, as a Sacrament, to the threefold ministry of the episcopate, presbyterate and diaconate; 4) the Magisterium of the Church, entrusted to the Pope and the Bishops in communion with him, understood as a responsibility and an authority exercised in the name of Christ for teaching and safeguarding the faith; 5) the Virgin Mary, as Mother of God and Icon of the Church, the spiritual Mother who intercedes for Christ's disciples and for all humanity (*UUS*, no. 79).

Chapter 4 of this book considers the aspect of sacramental efficacy in Baptism and thus I do look carefully at that second area of division that the pope identifies in the above passage. But because my main interlocutor in this book is representative neo-Calvinist thinkers from the Dutch Reformed tradition of Western Christianity, I have chosen to focus

---

false conciliatory approach which harms the purity of Catholic doctrine and obscures its assured genuine meaning. At the same time, Catholic belief needs to be explained more profoundly and precisely, in ways and in terminology which our separated brethren too can really understand" (*Unitatis Redintegratio*, no. 11).

on areas other than the ones he identifies. Thus, in chapter 3, I examine certain points of difference between these thinkers and the Catholic tradition regarding the relationship of the Church and the world. In chapter 4, in addition to the question of sacramental efficacy, I give an analysis of the epistemological significance of the Holy Spirit. Finally, in chapter 5, I will consider the question regarding the relation of nature and grace, the idea of Christian philosophy, and certain epistemological issues regarding the relation of faith and reason. These are issues that continue to divide thinkers in the Reformed and Catholic traditions.

There remains to say something, albeit briefly, about the nature and purpose of dialogue as expressed in *UUS*, nos. 21–40.[36] Most important, an interior conversion of the heart, indeed, repentance, is required as a precondition for engaging in ecumenical dialogue. Why this summons to conversion? "*Christian unity is possible,*" says John Paul, "provided that we are humbly conscious of having sinned against unity and are convinced of our need for conversion" (*UUS*, no. 34; see also no. 82). Of course the fault of past divisions belongs *on both sides*, and hence, as Karl Barth explains, "we have to deal with [divisions among Christians] as we deal with sin, our own and others', to recognize it as a fact, to understand it as the impossible thing which has intruded itself, as guilt which we must take upon ourselves, without the power to liberate ourselves from it. We must not allow ourselves to acquiesce in its reality; rather we must pray that it be forgiven and removed, and be ready to do whatever God's will and command may enjoin in respect of it."[37] In this light, we can understand why an examination of conscience is required for authentic dialogue; confessing our sins, repentance, putting ourselves, by God's grace, in that "interior space where Christ, the source of the Church's unity, can effectively act, with all the power of his Spirit, the Paraclete" (*UUS*, no. 35). The journey of ecumenical dialogue is thus an ongoing "dialogue of conversion," *on both sides*, trusting in the reconciling power of the truth which is Christ to overcome the obstacles to unity. The ground motive of this dialogue for reconciliation is "*common prayer with our brothers and sisters who seek unity in Christ and in His Church*" (*UUS*, no. 24). "Prayer is the 'soul' of the ecumenical renewal and of the yearning for unity," adds John Paul II, "it is the basis and support for *everything the [Second Vatican*

---

36. On this, see the "Doctrinal Note on Some Aspects of Evangelization," especially section IV on the ecumenical implications of the Church's teaching on evangelization.

37. Barth, *Church and Churches*, 26. See also, *Unitatis Redintegratio*, no. 3.

Council] defines as 'dialogue'" (*UUS*, no. 28). In short, prayer is the heart of spiritual ecumenism.

Yet, there is more: following the lead of the recent doctrinal note on some aspects of evangelization from the CDF, I distinguish three dimensions to the work of ecumenism: listening, theological discussion, and witness/proclamation.[38] Listening is an essential prerequisite to ecumenical theological discussion. Listening means letting your interlocutor speak for himself. Let me give an example of listening. In the graduate course that I teach on theological method at Sacred Heart Major Seminary, Detroit, I regularly assign a research paper on topics in ecumenical theology, say, the theology of the Eucharist. I urge the students to listen to John Calvin[39] and other reformed thinkers such G. C. Berkouwer and Herman Bavinck,[40] letting them speak in their own words, as to their understanding of Eucharistic presence, and not to bring to their reading of these authors from the outset the dilemma of symbol or reality. If they do, they will neither be in a favorable position to understand and, in turn, discuss the theological views of Calvin and Berkouwer nor will they find agreement that at times is hidden under disagreement.

Furthermore, inseparably united with listening and theological discussion is the necessity of comparing and contrasting different theological viewpoints, critically examining disagreements that are obstacles to full visible unity with the Church, and hence dialogue—with the two dimensions of listening and theological discussion—is a means for resolving doctrinal disagreements and determining whether the beliefs of our interlocutor are true or false (*UUS*, no. 35). Sometimes dialogue is made more difficult, indeed, impossible, when our words, judgments, and actions manifest a failure to deal with each other with understanding, truthfully and fairly. "When undertaking dialogue, *each side must presuppose in the other a desire for reconciliation, for unity in truth*" (*UUS*, no. 29). For this to happen, we must be not only intellectually responsible, exercising intellectual virtues such as open-mindedness, fairness in

---

38. On this, see the "Doctrinal Note on Some Aspects of Evangelization," no. 12.

39. Calvin, *Institutes*, Book IV, Chapter XVII, nos. 1–50, especially no. 10.

40. Berkouwer, *De Sacramenten*, 271–326. ET: *The Sacraments*, 188–296, particularly chapters 10 and 11, on Eucharistic presence, "Symbol or Reality," and "Real Presence," respectively. Both sources will be cited throughout this book, first the original, followed by the pagination of the English translation in square brackets [ ].
See also, Bavinck, *GD* IV, 441–74, 515–63 [461–95, 540–85].

evaluating the arguments and positions of others, intellectual humility, insight into persons, problems, doctrinal accounts, and communicative, rather than primarily polemical, knowing your dialogue partner's confessional background, seeing the positive in his tradition, and the like. In addition, dialogue must be deepened in order to engage the other person in a relationship of mutual trust and acceptance as a fellow Christian, responsive to him in Christian love, recognizing the "other as a *partner*" (*UUS*, no. 41). "You shall love your neighbor as yourself" (Gal 5:14), and in St. Paul's words, "especially those who are of the household of faith" (Gal 6:10). Thus: we must speak the truth in love (Eph 4:15). Put differently, as Martin Buber once wrote, "'Real dialogue takes place when each of the partners is really concerned with the others in their existence and in their particular character and turns to them with the intention that a living mutuality may be created.'"[41] And, as Yves Congar adds, "The prerequisite for any dialogue is to accept the other as 'other', to admit that he may have some contributions to make and to keep one's mind open to it."[42] That is, ecumenical dialogue must exhibit both charity toward the other and a thirst for truth in evaluating his beliefs. Charity has to do with how we should approach and relate to other persons, as subjects, when we engage then in dialogue, and the latter should be grounded in fidelity to the truth.

Finally, again following the recent doctrinal note regarding some aspects of evangelization, there is the dimension of witness and proclamation. That is, the Church teaches that "each Catholic has the right and duty to give the witness and full proclamation of his faith." "With non-Catholic Christians," the document adds, "Catholics must enter into a respectful dialogue of charity and truth, a dialogue which is not only an exchange of ideas, but also of gifts, in order that the fullness of the means of salvation can be offered to one's partners in dialogue. In this way, they are led to an ever deeper conversion in Christ."[43]

In sum, with the words of Yves Congar, "*ecumenism works on the scale of history*. Polemics are good enough for opposing argument with argument; it only takes a few hours. For the plenitude that ecumenism requires, however, a maturation is necessary which involves long periods of time." Congar adds, enlisting the words of John Henry Newman

---

41. As cited by Congar, *Dialogue between Christians*, 56–57.
42. Ibid., 57.
43. "Doctrinal Note on Some Aspects of Evangelization," no. 12.

and Etienne Gilson, respectively expressing what it means to work on a historical scale: "What I aim at is not immediate conversions, but to influence, as far as an old man can, the tone of thought in the place, with a view to a distant time when I shall no longer be here." "When their conclusions are opposite, adversaries must be given the necessary time to understand one another better, to understand themselves better, and so to meet at a still undetermined point which is certainly situated beyond their present positions."[44] Against the background of Congar's point about doing ecumenical work in historical perspective, I think we can helpfully distinguish between the Church's ultimate ecumenical goals of full visible unity and, given what is practically possible now between Christians, her proximate goal of dialogue and reconciliation.

FULL UNITY IN LEGITIMATE DIVERSITY

In his 2005 Apostolic Journey to Cologne on the occasion of the 20th World Youth Day, Benedict XVI held an ecumenical meeting in which he, like his predecessor John Paul II, reaffirmed the teaching of Vatican II that the communion of all particular Churches and communities with the Church of Rome, the one and only Church, indeed, with the Bishop of Rome, the Successor of the Apostle Peter, the visible sign and guarantor of unity, is a necessary condition for full visible unity, a unity that Christ bestowed upon his Church from the beginning. Significantly, however, Benedict quickly adds that this "unity does not mean what could be called an ecumenism of return: that is, to deny and reject one's own faith history. Absolutely not! It does not mean uniformity in all expressions of theology and spirituality, in liturgical forms and in disciplines."[45]

What does Benedict XVI mean? Note well that Benedict here distinguishes between "unity" and "uniformity." In the pope's understanding of Church unity, he is following Vatican II by not requiring "uniformity" in four distinct and specific areas of the Church's life: theology, spirituality, liturgical forms, and discipline. He is referring here to the council's "Decree on Ecumenism," *Unitatis Redintegratio*: "All in the Church must preserve unity in essentials. But let all, according to the gifts they have received enjoy a proper freedom, in their various forms of spiritual life and discipline, in their different liturgical rites, and even in their theological

---

44. The citations in this paragraph are from Congar, OP, *Ecumenism*, 31–32.
45. Benedict XVI, *God's Revolution*, 85.

elaborations of revealed truth. In all things let charity prevail. If they are true to this course of action, they will be giving ever better expression to the authentic catholicity and apostolicity of the Church."[46] In other words, there is legitimate theological diversity, say, between Augustine, Aquinas, John Henry Newman, Hans Urs Von Balthasar, Henri De Lubac, and others. Of course there are necessary affirmations of Christian faith that are taught by the Church to be true and that are constitutive of Christian identity. In other words, there is a unity of faith, a doctrinal unity, that is present among the legitimate differences of these theologians, manifested in the different ways of presenting those affirmations, in the different contexts and conceptualities used in which to understand and communicate them. On the matters of spirituality, liturgy, and discipline, Fr. Brian Harrison correctly notes that the Church has never required uniformity. In matters of *spirituality*, Harrison says, "Differing schools of asceticism, ancient and modern, Eastern and Western, have always constituted part of the richness and true catholicity of the Church." In matters of *liturgical* form, one can point to "the wide variety of liturgical rites, Eastern and Western, approved from ancient times by all the successors of Peter." Last, in matters of *discipline*, "the approved lack of uniformity over the centuries has perhaps been more evident" than anywhere else. "Canon law has always allowed for innumerable variations between particular and universal law, and at present the differences in disciplines between the Latin-rite Church and the Oriental Churches are so significant as to require two separate codes of canon law."[47]

Thus, if the restoration of unity among all Christians, according to Catholic teaching, is full communion with the visible Church, the one Church and one Church only that Christ founded, then reunification with the Church is the ultimate goal of the ecumenical movement. Yes, on the one hand, Benedict wholeheartedly affirms this goal of returning home to

---

46. *Unitatis Redintegratio*, no. 4.

47. As cited by Blosser, "Papa Ratzi on the 'ecumenism of return.'" See also, Cardinal Kasper, "Canon Law and Ecumenism." As an example of full unity in legitimate diversity, see the recent "Note of the Congregation for the Doctrine of the Faith about Personal Ordinariates for Anglicans entering the Catholic Church" (October 20, 2009): "In this Apostolic Constitution the Holy Father has introduced a canonical structure that provides for such corporate reunion by establishing Personal Ordinariates, which will allow former Anglicans to enter full communion with the Catholic Church while preserving elements of the distinctive Anglican spiritual and liturgical patrimony." Online: http://212.77.1.245/news_services/bulletin/news/24513.php?index=24513&lang=en.

the Catholic Church. But, on the other hand, it is precisely because he also wholeheartedly affirms that "many elements of sanctification and truth" exist outside the Church's visible boundaries that he stresses a mutual exchange of gifts, dialogue between Catholics, Protestants, and Orthodox, which aims at the reconciliation of communities rather than simply returning to the Church, if that means absorption and disowning one's own Christian heritage. The pope does not speak of a simple "return" to the Church as an ecumenical demand for non-Catholics when that is taken to mean, as Yves Congar rightly states, "absorption or annexation by the Catholic Church, as if they themselves had no contribution to make to us as full and as 'catholic' a realization as possible of Christianity."[48] In other words, our separated brethren have a real contribution to make to the fuller realization of the Church's unity and to the fullness of understanding, and living, of Catholic truth. As Benedict put it recently in St. Peter's Square, "The Week of Prayer for Christian Unity thus reminds us that ecumenism is a profound dialogic experience, a mutual listening and speaking, knowing one another better. It is a task that all can undertake, especially in regard to spiritual ecumenism, based on prayer and on sharing what is possible for the time being among Christians."[49]

In this connection, we do well to acknowledge that the Fathers of Vatican II wrote, "Catholics must gladly acknowledge and esteem the truly Christian endowments for our common heritage which are to be found among our separated brethren. It is right and salutary to recognize the riches of Christ and virtuous works in the lives of others who bearing witness to Christ.... Nor should we forget that anything wrought by the grace of the Holy Spirit in the hearts of our separated brethren can contribute to our own edification. Whatever is truly Christian is never contrary to what genuinely belongs to the faith; indeed, *it can always bring a more perfect realization of the very mystery of Christ and the Church*."[50]

In my own life, as I said earlier, I can personally testify to the gifts and graces of God's Spirit among the Evangelical, Reformed, and Anglo-Catholic traditions that I experienced before coming into full communion with the Catholic Church. Indeed, I still continue to respect and appreciate and, what is more, draw upon these traditions in my theological and

---

48. Congar, *Dialogue between Christians*, 114.
49. Benedict XVI, Angelus, St. Peter's Square.
50. *Unitatis Redintegratio*, no. 4; italics added.

philosophical teaching and writing, not because they add to the fullness of truth that belongs to the Catholic Church but rather to its articulation of that truth. It is in this sense that I understand the meaning of the phrase, "full unity in legitimate diversity" within the Church (*UUS*, no. 57). "Legitimate diversity," adds John Paul, "is in no way opposed to the Church's unity, but rather enhances her splendor and contributes greatly to the fulfillment of her mission" (*UUS*, no. 50).

Unitatis Redintegratio and *Ut Unum Sint* emphasize the legitimate diversity between the Eastern Churches and Roman Catholic Church. But what it says in those documents about legitimate diversity in theological expressions of doctrine could also be said about the Reformed, particularly neo-Calvinist, tradition of historic Christianity, in my judgment. "'It is hardly surprising if sometimes one tradition has come nearer than the other to an apt appreciation of certain aspects of the revealed mystery or has expressed them in a clearer manner. As a result, these various theological formulations are often to be considered as complementary rather than conflicting'. Communion is made fruitful by the exchange of gifts between the Churches [and ecclesial communities] insofar as they complement each other" (*UUS*, no. 57).[51] Philosophical issues of meaning and truth are at stake in discussing legitimate diversity in complementary theological rather than contradictory expressions of doctrine (cf. *UUS*, nos. 18–19), which I now turn to discuss in the next chapter.

---

51. On the contribution of German Catholic theologian, Möhler (1796–1838) to the understanding of unity and diversity, Congar writes: "For Möhler, the church is a living reality. On the one hand it is made up of living subjects, who give and express faith and love in a limited, imperfect fashion; on the other hand, it is an organism given life by the Holy Spirit. Now life is not uniformity, monotony; it requires diversities, which it harmonizes. When it comes to the church, what is needed is not uniformity but universality, that is to say, the unity of diversity which constitutes an organic totality.... The *Gegensätze* are contrasted positions which express different aspects of reality. When they are held in the living unity of the church which embraces them, each one is corrected by at least a potential openness to the complementary aspect. They interpenetrate in such a way that they have a mutual relationship. These are diversities in unity. Heresy arises when a subject or group is isolated (Möhler calls this egoism) and develops its *Gegensatz* outside communion with the others. It then turns this into a *Widerspruch*, a contradiction. The restoration of unity does not come about by a reconciliation of contradictions among themselves" (*Diversity and Communion*, 151).

2

The One Church of Jesus Christ

Unity and Legitimate Diversity

> *The question of whether there are real Christians outside of the Church ["extra ecclesiam"] is not the ultimate problem that Rome is wrestling with. The personal possession of saving grace on the part of outsiders is not in the crucible. Rather the focus of the question is on the nature of the Church and of whether the Christian reality of those outside the Church can be expressed in some ecclesial sense.*[1]

TRUTH AND ITS FORMULATIONS

"MOTHER CHURCH REJOICES" ARE the words that began Pope John XXIII's inaugural address ("*Gaudet Mater Ecclesia*") on October 11, 1962, the first day of the Second Vatican Council, in St. Peter's Basilica.[2] The pope explains his reasons for calling the Council in this address. To begin with, this Council is called to be "a solemn celebration of the union of Christ with His Church, and hence lead to the universal radiation of truth." The truth is that "Christ is ever resplendent as the center of history and of life. Men are either with Him and His Church, and then they enjoy light, goodness, order, and peace. Or else they are without Him, or against Him, and deliberately opposed to His Church, and then they give rise to confusion, to bitterness in human relations, and to the constant danger of fratricidal wars." Furthermore, the pope describes the context in

---

1. Berkouwer, *Vatikaans Concilie en de nieuwe theologie*, 247 [200]. I modified the English translation of this passage because the translator missed some of the nuances in the original Dutch text.
2. "Pope John's Opening Speech to the Council."

which this Ecumenical Council is situated as one where the Magisterium of the Church must take "into account the errors, the requirements, and the opportunities of our time" if it is to present "in exceptional form" its authority "to all men throughout the world." Regarding the errors of our time, fallacious teaching, opinions, and dangerous concepts, John's appeal is that the Church "meets the needs of the present day by demonstrating the validity of her doctrine rather than by issuing condemnations." In this contrast lies the meaning of the word pastoral. The Council is called to be pastoral in outlook rather than condemnatory. Still, as the then Joseph Ratzinger explains, "'Pastoral' should not mean nebulous, without substance, merely 'edifying'—meanings sometimes given to it. Rather what was meant was positive care for the man of today who is not helped by condemnations and who has been told for too long what is false and what he may not do. Modern man really wishes to hear what is true. He has, indeed, not heard enough truth, enough of the positive message of faith for our time, enough of what the faith has to say to our age."[3] In this connection, we can easily appreciate why John states that the "greatest concern of the Ecumenical Council" is "that the sacred deposit of Christian doctrine should be guarded and proclaimed more efficaciously."[4] What is expected of the Council regarding doctrine, particularly in order to guard and proclaim the teachings of the Church more efficaciously?

The pope replies to this question: "to transmit the doctrine, pure and integral, without any attenuation or distortion, which throughout twenty centuries, notwithstanding difficulties and contrasts, has become the common patrimony of men."[5] To carry out this task faithfully and respon-

---

3. Ratzinger, *Theological Highlights of Vatican II*, 23. Ratzinger continues: "'Pastoral' should not mean something vague and imprecise, but rather something free from wrangling, and free also from entanglement in questions that concern scholars alone. It should imply openness to the possibility of discussion in a time which calls for new responses and new obligations. 'Pastoral' should mean, finally, speaking in the language of Scripture, of the early Church Fathers, and of contemporary man. Technical theological language has its purpose and is indeed necessary, but it does not belong in the kerygma and in our confession of faith" (23–24).

4. "Pope John's Opening Speech to the Council," 713. All the quotations in the next several paragraphs are from this opening speech. In certain instances, such as the present, I will cite the original Latin. "Quod Concilii Oecumenici maxime interest, hoc est, ut sacrum christianae doctrinae depositum efficaciore ratione custodiatur atque proponatur," in Ioannes XXIII, "Allocutio habita d. 11 oct. 1962, in initio Concilii."

5. The Latin text unequivocally expresses John's concern with transmitting doctrine "integram, non imminutam, non detortam."

sibly this Council is also called to engage in "a wider and more objective understanding" of the Church's opportunities in terms of "the present, to the new conditions and new forms of life introduced into the modern world which have opened new avenues to the Catholic apostolate." This understanding involves discerning the signs of the times,[6] and overcoming the mentality of those people who, "although they are full of fervor and zeal, are by no means equipped with an abundant sense of discretion and measure, seeing in the modern era nothing but transgression and disaster, and claiming that our own age has become worse than previous ones." The pope explicitly distances himself from "those prophets of doom, who are always announcing some ominous event, almost as if the end of the world were upon us." By contrast, John expresses his conviction, "In the present order of things, Divine Providence is leading us to a new order of human relations which, by men's own efforts and even beyond their very expectations, are directed toward the fulfillment of God's superior and inscrutable designs. And everything, even human differences, leads to the greater good of the Church." Indeed, the pope seems persuaded that the modern turn of events holds new, unprecedented possibilities for liberties of faith and the free action of the Church.

What is striking in the pope's speech is his conviction that the only way for the Church to guard and proclaim the truth of Christian teaching more efficaciously is for her understanding of these teachings to undergo a fitting measure of renewal. Renewal is not about bringing the Church "up to date" by the standard of credibility to the modern mind, or by the standard of relevance to current problems. Renewal isn't even first and foremost about realizing the unity of all Christians, indeed, of the entire human race. Rather, John XXIII emphasizes that the dynamics of renewal stems from the following: "The Church's solicitude to promote and defend truth derives from the fact that, according to the plan of God, who wills all men to be saved and to come to the knowledge of the truth (1 Tim 2:4), men without the assistance of the whole of revealed doctrine can-

---

6. The phrase, "signs of the times," does not occur in the opening address, but it is found in John XXIII's official call to convoke the Council with the Apostolic Constitution, *Humanae salutis*, Christmas Day, 1961. Notwithstanding the moral and spiritual crisis of our time, John wished to affirm his own continued trust "in our Savior, who has not left the world which He redeemed." He adds, "we make ours the recommendation of Jesus that one should know how to distinguish the "signs of the times" (Matt 16:4), and we seem to see now, in the midst of so much darkness, a few indications which auger well for the fate of the Church and of humanity" ("Pope John Convokes the Council," 704).

not reach a complete and firm unity of minds, with which are associated true peace and eternal salvation." It is in this perspective that the pope expresses his disappointment that "the entire Christian family has not yet fully attained this visible unity in truth, and hence the duty of the Church to work actively so that there may be fulfilled the great mystery of that unity, which Jesus Christ invoked with fervent prayer from His heavenly Father on the eve of His sacrifice." It is, therefore, understandable, John continues, on the basis of the "renewed, serene, and tranquil adherence to all the teaching of the Church in its entirety and preciseness" that "the Christian, Catholic, and apostolic spirit of the whole world expects a leap forward toward a doctrinal penetration and a formation of conscience in faithful and perfect conformity to the authentic doctrine. But this should be elaborated and presented according to the forms of inquiry and literary expression proper to modern thought." Thus John XXIII is calling for a suitable restatement, a fitting measure of renewal in our understanding, of Catholic teaching, of the *depositum fidei*.

This, too, is the understanding of John Paul II who has written insightfully on the responsibility, not only of effectively communicating the truths of the Christian faith to a given culture, but also, indeed emphatically, on the primacy and priority of Christian revelation as epistemically basic, or normative, for the theological task of renewal and a deepened understanding of the faith.

> As an understanding of Revelation, theology has always had to respond in different historical periods to the demands of different cultures, in order to communicate the content of faith to those cultures with the appropriate formulation of doctrine. Today, too, theology faces a dual task. On the one hand, she must be increasingly committed to the task entrusted to her by the Second Vatican Council, the task of renewing its specific methods in order to serve evangelization more effectively. How can we fail to recall in this regard the words of Pope John XXIII at the opening of the Council? He said then: "It is imperative, as many sincere members of the Christian, Catholic and Apostolic faith earnestly desire, that this doctrine should be more widely and deeply known and that souls should be instructed and formed in it more completely. It is vital that the same certain and unchangeable doctrine to which we owe faithful obedience should also be understood more profoundly and presented in a way which meets the needs of our time." On the other hand, theology must direct its attention to the ultimate

truth that Revelation entrusts to it, never content to stop short of that goal. Theologians should remember that their work is a response to the "dynamism which exists in the faith itself" and that the proper quest of its enquiry is to be: "Truth, the living God, and his plan for salvation revealed in and through Jesus Christ."[7]

Most important, John XXIII points out that this restatement and renewal in understanding is only possible, all the while maintaining to transmit the pure and integral truth of doctrine, without any attenuation or distortion, because "the deposit or the truths of faith, contained in our sacred teaching, are one thing, while the mode in which they are enunciated, keeping the same meaning and the same judgment, is another."[8] Much has been made of the pope's distinction between "substance and expression," some even arguing that what we have here is the rejection of a "non-historical orthodoxy," meaning thereby "the wholly perfect and absolute expression of faith, in which it suffices to rest firmly and securely."[9] With this alleged rejection, the pope was now taken by some to be implying that past statements of the Church were wholly historically conditioned such that new ways of expressing the substance of the faith would have to be found.

Berkouwer is right, however, "It would be reckless to pull far-reaching conclusions out of Pope John's statement [regarding the distinction between truth and formulations of truth] and to brand it with the mark of strong progressive theological outlook." The pope's words as such do

---

7. John Paul II, *Fides et Ratio*, no. 92.

8. "Est enim aliud ipsum depositum Fidei, seu veritates, quae veneranda doctrina nostra continentur, aliud modus, quo eaedem enuntiantur, eodem tamen sensu eademque sententia," Ioannes XXIII, "Allocutio habita d. 11 oct. 1962, in initio Concilii," 792. This translation from the Latin of the opening address is from Grisez, *Way of the Lord Jesus*, Vol. 1, 502. For commentary and discussion of the ramifications of this passage for the Catholic view of the unchangeability and changeability of dogma, see Berkouwer, *Vatikaans Concilie en de nieuwe theologie*, 61–104 [57–88]. For a brief summary of Berkouwer's view on the influence of the *nouvelle théologie* of Henri de Lubac, et al., for the issue of unchanging truth and its changeable formulation, and unchanging content and a changeable form, see his small book, *Recent Developments in Roman Catholic Thought*. Significantly, Berkouwer is persuaded "that there is an undeniable, powerful influence [in contemporary Roman Catholic thought] coming from Biblical theology in this new theology [*nouvelle théologie*]" (42).

9. This is how Novak, in a very early phase of his career, describes what he calls "non-historical orthodoxy" and contrasts it with historical consciousness in his book, *Open Church*, 66.

not, adds Berkouwer, "give us justification for supposing that a confessional watering-down or relativizing of dogma is taking place in Rome."[10] Rather, given John's conviction to transmit the pure and integral truth of doctrine, without any attenuation or distortion, it seems plausible to argue that the pope was hoping to express the truths of faith in a way revealing possibilities for a rediscovery of communion with separated brethren.[11] Admittedly, the pope's distinction between truth and its formulations presupposes something like the claim that Herman Bavinck made late in the nineteenth century, namely, "No one claims that content and expression, essence and form, are in complete correspondence and coincide. The dogma that the church confesses and the dogmatician develops is not identical with the absolute truth of God itself."[12] And so, yes, pared down for my purpose here, the pope's distinction between the truth and its formulations is of ecumenical significance because it "implied that the Church's *formulation* of the truth could have, for various reasons, actually occasioned *misunderstandings* of the truth itself."[13] In other words, the pope's distinction, rightly understood, need not bring the truth of the Church's dogmas into uncertainty. To quote Berkouwer again, "The Church has been constant in *truth at its deepest intent*, even though it [the Church] has not been elevated above historical relativity in its *analysis of the rejected errors*."[14] The Church's universal truth claim regarding the exclusive identity of the Church of Christ with the Catholic Church entailed the rejection of ecumenism. It seemed that the acceptance of the latter entailed the errors of doctrinal indifferentism and hence ecclesiological relativism. The Fathers of Vatican II rejected that entailment and saw a way of rejecting these errors without rejecting ecumenism. This is a clear example of Berkouwer's point. Put differently, appreciating the ecumenical significance of the distinction between truth and its formulations does not sacrifice the immutability or permanence of dogmatic truth, say, regarding Catholic ecclesiology. It simply brings

---

10. Berkouwer, *Vatikaans Concilie*, 19–20, 22 [23, 25].

11. Congar, *Dialogue Between Christians*, 129.

12. Bavinck, *Gereformeerde Dogmatiek*, I, 7. ET: *Reformed Dogmatics, Prolegomena*, Volume I, 31–32. Both sources will be cited throughout this book, first the original, followed by the pagination of the English translation in square brackets [ ].

13. Berkouwer, *Vatikaans Concilie*, 20 [23–24].

14. Ibid., 52 [49].

with it the "immense advantage of dissipating prejudices and correcting false interpretations."[15]

Although he expresses Berkouwer's point somewhat differently, this, too, is Ratzinger's view: "The really hard cases of division are only those in which one or more of the parties is convinced that they are not defending their own ideas but are standing by what they have received from revelation and cannot therefore manipulate. The aim of [ecumenical] dialogues is then to perceive how positions that are apparently opposed may be compatible at a deeper level and, in doing so, of course, to exclude everything that derives only from certain cultural developments."[16] Thus, the distinction between truth and its formulations does not ask us to renounce anything that God has revealed and the Church has infallibly declared to be true. Rather, this distinction makes it possible "For the Church's deepest intentions [to declare a universal truth] . . . simply [to] be brought to clearer expression in a new formulation."[17] Furthermore, a new formulation must not contradict the revealed truth; rather, it must "keep the same meaning and the same judgment." In the next section of this chapter, I shall illustrate the ecumenical significance of this distinction in an analysis of Ratzinger's claim that the Council found a way within "the logic of Catholicism for the ecclesial character of non-Catholic communities . . . without detriment to Catholic identity."[18]

Surely then the interpretation of the pope's distinction that undermines the permanence of the truth of dogma is questionable, and could only be given when the phrase, "keeping the same meaning and the same judgment," is omitted as seems to have regularly happened in the translation of his opening address.[19] This phrase is a clear allusion to the

---

15. Congar, *Dialogue between Christians*, 129.

16. Ratzinger, "On the Ecumenical Situation," 256.

17. Berkouwer, *Vatikaans Concilie*, 50 [48]. See also, Ratzinger, "On the Ecumenical Situation," 257–258.

18. Ratzinger, *Principles of Catholic Theology*, 232.

19. I agree with Grisez that "this statement of Pope John's has often been mistranslated and misrepresented." "Est enim aliud ipsum depositum Fidei, seu veritates, quae veneranda doctrina nostra continentur, aliud modus, quo eaedem enuntiantur, eodem tamen sensu eademque sententia." Grisez continues, "He is making clear that the propositional truths of faith are distinct from linguistic expression. The phrase, "keeping the same meaning and the same judgment," usually is omitted by those who misinterpret this statement, because it would block the misinterpretation" (*Way of the Lord Jesus*, I, 502). There seems to be some controversy about whether the original text had been tampered

fifth-century theologian, Vincent of Lérins, that development of Church teaching must always be understood "in accord with the 'same doctrine, in the same meaning, and in the same judgment' with what has preceded it (*in eodem scilicet dogmate, eodem sensu eademque sententia*)."[20] Vatican I cites St. Vincent when it teaches that the "meaning of sacred dogmas that has once been declared by holy Mother Church, must always be retained; and there must never be any deviation from that meaning on the specious grounds of a more profound understanding. Let, then, understanding, knowledge, and wisdom increase as ages and centuries roll along, and greatly and vigorously flourish, in each and all, in the individual and the whole church: but simply in its own proper kind, that is to say, in one and the same doctrine, one and the same sense, one and the same judgment."[21] The Fathers of the Council state this point succinctly

---

with and censored. Some writers, such as Hebblethwaite, claim that this phrase was later added (cf. *Pope John XXIII, Shepherd of the Modern World*, 432). Hebblethwaite's claim has been refuted decisively by Fr. Chapping, SJ, in his critical review of the book, "Pope and Journalist," 528: "'Oportet ut haec doctrina *certa et immutabilis, cui fidele obsequium est praestandum*, ea ratione pervestigetur et exponatur, quam tempora postulant nostra. Est enim aliud ipsum depositum Fidei, *seu veritates, quae veneranda doctrina nostra continentur,* aliud modus, quo eadem enuntiantur, *eodem tamen sensu eademque sententia*'. In italics are the words that did not appear in the draft by the Pope, neither in the Italian text published, *without censure*, by the *Osservatore Romano*, on October 12, 1962. The Latin text with its additions (quoted not without inaccuracies by Mr. Hebblethwaite on 432) is the text the Pope had in front of him while reading the speech; the official publication in the *Acta Apostolicae Sedis* and the *Acta Synodalia Concilii Vaticani II* is thus *not censoring*. Did the Pope disagree with the additions put into the Latin version of his speech? If he during its public reading did omit these words, then we have a strong indication; Mr. Hebblethwaite says the Pope did and invites us to check the Archives of Vatican Radio. Well, I found out that the Pope did *not* omit these words. . . . [Note 26: Information given by Rev. Pasquale Borgomeo, General Director of Vatican Radio (Letter of April 3, 1986, accompanied by a tape!), to whom I express my gratitude.] Why is Mr. Hebblethwaite stating something that is not true?" Furthermore, this phrase, "keeping the same meaning and the same judgment," is not omitted in the Dutch and German translations of the opening speech. Besides the English translation, it is omitted in the Spanish. It is also missing in *Gaudium et Spes*, Pastoral Constitution on the Church in the Modern World (no. 62).

20. Vatican Council I, Dogmatic Constitution *Dei Filius* on the Catholic Faith (1870), Chapter IV, "Faith and Reason." For a commentary on this Vatican text, see Lonergan, *Method in Theology*, Chapter 12, Doctrines, Section 9, The Permanence of Dogmas, 320–324. For an insightful analysis and application of Vincent of Lérins criterion that development needs to be always "*eodem sensu eademque sententia*," see Guarino, "Tradition and Doctrinal Development."

21. Vatican Council I, Dogmatic Constitution *Dei Filius* on the Catholic Faith (1870),

in the third canon of Chapter IV, Faith and Reason: "If anyone says that, as knowledge progresses, at times a sense is to be given to dogmas propounded by the Church, different from that which the Church has understood and understands: let him be *anathema*."[22] Clearly, then, in light of Vatican I's teaching and its corresponding third canon, we can understand the import of the pope's distinction between truth and its formulations, that is, truths of revelation and their linguistic expression, propositions and sentences, content and context. The chief aim of such distinctions is to come to an ever better understanding of the same dogma, keeping the same meaning, the same judgment, about the truth of that dogma.[23] This point needs further explaining.

We are language users: asking questions, making requests, giving commands, expressing emotions, and much else. But none of these can be asserted or denied and hence are not either true or false. Only propositions make assertions about what is (or is not) the case, which means that only they are the logical entities that can be true or false. Indeed, every proposition is either true or false. Furthermore, a proposition is true if what it says corresponds to the way objective reality is; otherwise, it is false. Of course human beings speak in sentences to communicate propositions, but they are not the same thing as propositions. Propositions are nonlinguistic entities. That is, the same proposition, or same meaning, is the message having many and varied expressions in different languages or in the same language. Moreover, the truth of a proposition is closely connected with its meaning. Bernard Lonergan explains that "meaning of its nature is related to what is meant, and what is meant may or may not correspond to what is in fact so." "If it corresponds," Lonergan adds, "the meaning is true. If it does not correspond, the meaning is false." Lonergan then correctly notes the implication of denying the correspondence view of truth, namely, that a proposition is true if what it says corresponds to what is in fact the case; otherwise, it is false.

> To deny correspondence is to deny a relation between meaning and meant. To deny the correspondence view of truth is to deny that, when the meaning is true, the meant is what is so. Either de-

---

Chap. IV, Faith and Reason, 809.

22. Ibid., Canon 3, 811.

23. On the distinction between content/context, see Cardinal Dulles, SJ, *Craft of Theology*, 108. See also Fr. Guarino's extensive analysis of the importance of this distinction in, *Foundations of Systematic Theology*, 141–208.

nial is destructive of the [Catholic] dogmas.... If one denies that, when the meaning is true, then the meant is what is so, one rejects propositional truth. If the rejection is universal, then it is the self-destructive proposition that there are no true propositions. If the rejection is limited to the dogmas, then it is just a roundabout way of saying that all the dogmas are false.[24]

It seems obvious that John XXIII is, then, distinguishing in his opening address between the propositional truths of faith and their linguistic expressions. This seems even more obvious in light of the point he makes (referring us to Vincent of Lérins) that the linguistic expressions, or formulations, of the truths of faith must keep the same meaning and the same judgment—if one grasps what a proposition means one knows what that proposition is asserting to be true, and because it is true, Lonergan correctly remarks, the proposition "tells us of things as in fact they are." In other words, he adds, "realism [about truth] consists in this, that the truth that is acknowledged in the mind corresponds to reality."[25] On the one hand, propositions are, if true, always and everywhere true; their linguistic formulations, on the other hand, the different ways of expressing these propositional truths, that is, may vary in our attempts to come to a clearer and more accurate communication of these revealed truths, but these formulations do not affect the truth of the propositions. To quote Lonergan again, "what God has revealed and the church has infallibly declared, is true. What is true, is permanent: the meaning it possessed in its own context can never be denied truthfully." Thus, he adds, "When a truth is more fully understood, it is still the same truth that is being understood."[26] In the words of John Paul II:

> The Word of God is not addressed to any one people or to any one period of history. In the same way dogmatic statements, while reflecting at times the culture of the period in which they were defined, formulate an unchanging and ultimate truth. The question therefore arises as to how the absolute and universal nature of truth can be reconciled with unavoidable historical and cultural conditioning of the formulae in which truth finds its expression. The claims of historicism [which denies the enduring validity of truth] cannot be defended. However the use of the discipline of

---

24. Lonergan, "The Dehellenization of Dogma," 14–15, 16, respectively.
25. Lonergan, *Way to Nicea*, 128.
26. Lonergan, *Method in Theology*, 323, 325, respectively.

hermeneutics, which is not closed to metaphysics, is capable of showing how it is possible to move from the historical and contingent circumstances in which the sacred texts developed to the truth which they express, a truth transcending those circumstances. Man is able to express truths that transcend the normal use of words in language that is both historical and circumscribed. Truth can never be confined to time and culture: it is known within history, but also goes beyond history.[27]

Because the revealed Word of God is true, meaning thereby that it tells us of things as in fact they are, whatever is true, is permanent, enduringly valid, or transcendent. The reason why John Paul can confidently claim that the permanence of the meaning of dogmas can be reconciled with the unavoidable historical and cultural conditioning of the formulae in which that meaning is expressed is because the meaning of a dogma is a transcendent truth, in particular, a revealed mystery. As Lonergan says, "It is not a human truth but the revelation of a mystery hidden in God. . . . It presupposes (1) that there exist mysteries in God that man could not know unless they were revealed, (2) that they have been revealed, and (3) that the church has infallibly declared the meaning of what has been revealed."[28] In short, the permanence of the truth of dogmas is grounded in the fact they disclose revealed mysteries.[29] Furthermore, on this view, "the meaning of the dogma is not apart from a verbal formulation, for it is a meaning declared by the church. However, the permanence attaches to the meaning and not to the formula."[30] That is, Lonergan adds, "What permanently is true, is the meaning of the dogma in the context in which it was defined. To ascertain that meaning there have to be deployed the resources of research, interpretation, history, dialectic," in short, hermeneutics.[31] Moreover, this point, too, has ecumenical significance. For, as John Paul II puts it, "the element which determines communion in truth is *the meaning of truth*. The expression of truth can take different forms" (*UUS*, no. 19).

Of course Berkouwer is correct in remarking that the distinction between absolute and universal affirmations of faith and their linguistic ex-

---

27. John Paul II, *Fides et Ratio*, no. 95.
28. Lonergan, *Method in Theology*, 323.
29. Ibid., 326.
30. Ibid., 323.
31. Ibid., 326.

pressions cannot be used "as a magician's wand to clear up every burning question."[32] Berkouwer's concern is that truth and its expression can never be so easily separated. Granted, truth is known within history, as John Paul states in the above passage. Thus, Berkouwer urges us to consider the undeniable fact that "*form* is given to faith the moment the Church puts it into words. And the moment form is given to faith a hermeneutical problem arises that creates an honest need for consideration of the background and the orientation of a given confession." In other words, to ascertain the meaning of the truths of revelation, of doctrinal truths, we need to understand the *context* in which they were expressed. "To insist that there is a direct, verbal clarity in the statements of the past, apart from historical context and the need for hermeneutical principles of interpretation, is to betray an ignorance of Church history."[33] In other words, to understand the meaning of dogmatic statements—let us remember that their meaning is permanent because they are expressions of truths—we need to understand the context in which they are made.

Notwithstanding this important qualification introduced by Berkouwer, we cannot reduce everything to hermeneutics. But that is precisely what happens without the proposition/sentence distinction: some wrongly conclude that truths of faith are *not* more than their linguistic expressions. Some have abandoned the importance of the concept, "keeping the same meaning and the same judgment," for understanding propositional truth, wrongly concluding then that the Christian faith is "open to diverse and incompatible interpretations to complete [its] meaning at different times and place."[34] This has resulted in a relativistic view of truth itself—what is true for some would not be true for others.[35] Put differently, abandoning the content/context distinction threatens us with "hermeneutical anarchy," to borrow a phrase from Aidan Nichols. "For," adds Nichols, "if the content/context distinction is irredeemably naïve, then with a change of context—so imperious logic demands—a change in con-

---

32. Berkouwer, *Vatikaans Concilie*, 99 [84].

33. Ibid., 89 [78].

34. Grisez, *Way of the Lord Jesus*, vol. 1, 496.

35. On this, see the widely read and commented upon address by the then Cardinal Ratzinger, now Pope Benedict XVI, "Relativism." For a more fully developed critique of relativism, see his *Truth and Tolerance*. Relativism is one of the main points of criticism in *Dominus Iesus*. See also, "On the Interpretation of Dogmas," for the International Theological Commission's rejection of what the document calls "dogmatism relativism."

tent necessarily follows."[36] The specter of epistemic relativism also raises its head when emphasis on the limitations and historical conditionedness of human reason leads to a lack of confidence in its ability to make truth known—keeping the same meaning and same judgment. It is a short but fateful step from this epistemic relativity to relativism in regard to truth itself. Once again, we face relativism when emphasis on the variability of linguistic and conceptual formulations of the truths of faith implies that "dogmatic formulas . . . cannot signify the truth in a determinate way, but can only offer changeable approximations to it, which to a certain extent distort or alter it." In this connection, given the indeterminate way that dogmatic formulations "point to" (as some vaguely put it) to the truths of faith, "truth is like a goal that is constantly being sought by means of such approximations"[37] but never actually attained. Now, when doctrinal truth itself is felt to be unattainable, we can understand why some, misguidedly, "attempt to replace 'orthodoxy' by 'orthopraxy'—there is no common [Christian] faith any more (because truth is unattainable), only common praxis."[38] To avoid the slide into relativism, I think we need to say that the dogmatic formulations satisfactorily and faithfully express the truths of revelation even if not exhaustively.[39] Says John Paul II correctly, "Faith

---

36. Nichols, OP, "Relaunching Christian Philosophy," 58.
37. *Mysterium Ecclesia*, no. 5.
38. Ratzinger/Benedict XVI, *Spirit of the Liturgy*, 155.

39. Furthermore, there is the question regarding the permanence and validity of the language and concepts (e.g., consubstantial, hypostasis, person, nature, substance, and many others) employed in doctrinal definitions, creeds (e.g., Niceno-Constantinopolitan, Chalcedon), and the like. In note 112 of *FR*, John Paul II cites Pius XII who replied to this question in his 1950 Encyclical Letter *Humani generis* (no. 16), "It is clear that the Church cannot be tied to any and every passing philosophical system. Nevertheless, those notions and terms which have been developed through common effort by Catholic teachers over the course of the centuries to bring about some understanding of dogma are certainly not based on any such weak foundation. They are based on principles and concepts deduced from a true knowledge of created things. In the process of deduction, this knowledge, like a star, gave enlightenment to the human through the Church. Hence it is not astonishing that some of these concepts have not only been employed by the Ecumenical Councils, but even sanctioned by them, so that it is wrong to depart from them." John Paul II comments on this passage, "It is no easy matter dealing with this argument since we must reckon seriously with the varied meanings the words have been accorded in differing ranges of cultures and periods of time. Even so the history of human reflection clearly demonstrates that in and through the progress and variety of cultures *certain basic concepts have preserved both their universal validity for knowledge and the truth of the propositions they express* [italics added]. Were it otherwise, philosophy and

clearly presupposes that human language is capable of expressing divine and transcendent reality in a universal way—analogically, it is true, but no less meaningfully for that." "Were this not so," the pope adds, "the Word of God, which is always a divine Word in human language, would not be capable of saying anything about God. The interpretation of this Word cannot merely keep referring us to one interpretation after another, without ever leading us to a statement which is simply true; otherwise there would be no revelation of God, but only the expression of human notions about God and about what God presumably thinks of us."[40] Accordingly, the Christian must be a theological realist, a metaphysical realist, insisting that his knowledge of God is partial but true, and that his predication about God is realist, genuinely referring to God, and not instrumentalist, that is, not a mere symbolic vehicle for expressing religious experience.[41]

In this connection, we should note that the International Theological Commission urges us to consider that "no clear-cut separation can be made between the content and form of the statement." Nevertheless, the Commission adds: "The symbolic system of language is not mere external apparel, but to a certain extent the incarnation of a truth. This is the case, against the background of the incarnation of the eternal Word, especially with regard to the proclamation of faith by the Church. Of its nature, that proclamation takes concrete form by way of articulation and thus as a real, symbolic expression of the content of faith, contains and makes present what it designates. Therefore the images and concepts (employed in that proclamation) are not arbitrarily interchangeable." It continues to explain why the language and concepts employed in doctrinal definitions and creeds have permanent validity:

> The study of the history of dogma makes it clear that in dogmas the church has not just adopted already given conceptual system. Rather it has subjected pre-existing concepts, deriving for the most part from sophisticated discourse of the day, to a process of purification as well as of redefinition and new definition, thus

---

the sciences would be unable to engage in mutual interchange nor could they be understood outside the cultures where they were first conceived and worked out. There remains, therefore the hermeneutical question, but it can be solved" (*Fides et Ratio*, no. 96).

40. John Paul II, *Fides et Ratio*, no. 84.

41. John Paul II urges that "metaphysics . . . plays an essential role of mediation in theological research. A theology without a metaphysical horizon could not move beyond an analysis of religious experience, nor would it allow the *intellectus fidei* to give a coherent account of the universal and transcendent value of revealed truth" (ibid., no. 83).

creating a speech which suits its message. One recalls, for example, the distinction between essence (nature) and hypostasis as well as the development of the concept of person, which in this form did not exist in Greek philosophy, but was the result of reflection on the reality of the Christian mystery of salvation and on biblical language.... As a community of faith, the church is a community in spoken confession (of that faith). Consequently, unity in those fundamental verbal expressions of faith belongs to the unity of the church diachronically and synchronically. *And those expressions are not revisable if one does not wish to lose sight of the "reality" manifested in them.* However, in a multiplicity of ways in which it is proclaimed that "reality" must be appropriated ever anew and given further expression. For this an occasion and obligation are provided by Christianity's taking root in other cultures. *The truth of revelation nevertheless remains always the same "not only in its real substance (content), but also in its decisive linguistic formulations."*[42]

Of course distinguishing between the truths of faith and their linguistic expression allows for doctrinal development—faith seeking understanding of the content of divine Revelation. As Germain Grisez puts it, "[T]he Church always can bring such fresh truths from the riches of revelation. Since every such new truth is an aspect of the one truth revealed by God in the Lord Jesus, no authentic development of doctrine ever can contradict what the Church believed and taught in earlier times and other places."[43] This is precisely what canon 3 of chapter IV (Faith and Reason) of Vatican I excludes: "If anyone says that, as knowledge progresses, at times a sense is to be given to dogmas propounded by the Church, different from that which the Church has understood and understands: let him be *anathema*."[44] As we shall now show, this canon holds also for the issue regarding the identity of the Church of Jesus Christ with the Catholic Church. The question of identity has been heavily debated because of the controversial claim that Vatican II rejected the equation—the full identity—between the Church of Christ and the Catholic Church by virtue of recognizing the ecclesial status of non-Catholic churches and communities. Ratzinger has consistently contested this claim for the past forty years after Vatican II. A 1984 interview summarizes his view:

42. "On the Interpretation of Dogmas," 12–13.
43. Grisez, *Way of the Lord Jesus*, vol. 1, 496.
44. *Dei Filius*, Canon 3, 811.

The Second Vatican Council specifically states that the only Church of Christ "subsists in the Catholic Church, which is governed by the successor of Peter and by the bishops in communion with him." As we know, this "subsists" replace the earlier "is" (the only Church "is" the Catholic Church) because there are also many true Christians and much that is truly Christian outside the Church. However, the latter insight and recognition, which lies at the very foundation of Catholic ecumenism, does not mean that, from now on, a Catholic would have to view the "true Church" only as a utopian idea that may ensue in the end of days: the true Church is reality, an existing reality, even now, without having to deny that others are Christian or to dispute the fact that their communities have an ecclesial character.[45]

Here the question we must address is not only how the subsistence of the one Church of Jesus Christ in the Catholic Church may be seen as the foundation for recognizing the ecclesial character of non-Catholic communities, but also why this view does not undermine the traditional doctrine on the full identity of Christ's Church with the Catholic Church.

RATZINGER, THE CHURCH'S IDENTITY, AND ECUMENISM

"[The] spiritual awakening, which the bishops accomplished in full view of the Church, or, rather, accomplished *as* the Church, was the great and irrevocable event of the Council." In short, "the true event" of the Council, adds Ratzinger, is "the awakening of the Church. If we keep this in mind we will be full of gratitude for what God has chosen to set in motion through that seemingly so simple old man, good Pope John."[46] This phrase, "awakening of the Church," is a clear allusion to the opening words of Fr. Romano Guardini's book, *Vom Sinn der Kirche* (1922): "A process of immense significance has begun: The Church is awakening in people's souls." In fact, Ratzinger later refers to Guardini's phrase in his 1985 article, "The Ecclesiology of the Second Vatican Council," and remarks that "Vatican II was the fruit of this awakening; it expressed in its documents and presented to the whole Church as a patrimony the knowledge that had matured through faith during the four decades from 1920 to 1960, which were so full of ferment and hope. . . . This statement by Guardini was very carefully formulated, for what mattered to him was

---

45. Ratzinger, "Luther and the Unity of the Churches," 118–19.
46. Ratzinger, *Theological Highlights*, 132.

precisely the fact that the Church was now being recognized and experiences as something interior that does not stand opposite us like some sort of equipment but, rather, is alive within us. . . . We ourselves are the Church; she is more than an organization, she is an organism of the Holy Spirit, a living thing that encompasses all of us from within. This new awareness of Church found verbal expression in the term 'Mystical Body of Christ.'"[47] In a nutshell, perhaps we can describe the Church as awakening to her "evangelical presence in history," recovering her evangelical identity as a world Church for the dawning history of humanity.

With this Council, Karl Rahner correctly notes, the Church is self-consciously entering "the period in which the sphere of the Church's life is in fact the entire world." [48] One final word, this time by Yves Congar, describing the conciliar event that is Vatican II: "The great power of the datum of Vatican II has to do with the fact that it represents a moment when the Church's collective consciousness was concentrated on the act of experiencing its faithfulness to Jesus Christ and his Spirit in confessing and celebrating its faith."[49] In this act of confessing and celebrating the faith, the Church had then been called to a renewal so as to regain its evangelical clarity. The "measure of the renewal is Christ," says Ratzinger, "as Scripture witnesses him." "And," he adds, "if the renewal seeks to think through and to speak the Gospel of Christ in a way understandable to contemporary man—i.e., in a contemporary fashion . . . , then the objective is precisely that Christ may become understood."[50] How was the Church to deepen her self-understanding of the Gospel of Christ, of her spiritual awakening to the evangelical presence of Christ in history, so as to guard and proclaim that Gospel more faithfully, clearly and efficaciously? Part of the answer to this question is found in Ratzinger's reflections throughout the years, starting with his early reflections during Vatican II, on the question of Catholic-Protestant ecumenism.

My purpose, therefore, is not to give an overall account of Ratzinger's ecclesiology, but rather to consider his response to the issue of the relationship between the *one* Church of Jesus Christ that subsists in the Catholic Church, on the one hand, and the *plurality* of Churches on the

47. Ratzinger, "Ecclesiology of the Second Vatican Council," 13.

48. Rahner, SJ, "Towards a Fundamental Theological Interpretation of Vatican II," 15.

49. Congar, OP, "Last Look at the Council," 239.

50. Ratzinger, *Theological Highlights*, 2.

other. "The Catholic Church dares and must dare to take the paradoxical position of attributing to herself in a unique way the singular form, 'the Church,'" says Ratzinger, "despite and in the midst of the plurality she has accepted."[51]

The Second Vatican Council made a courageous step forward toward the unity of all Christians, according to Ratzinger.[52] Indeed, the movement toward ecumenism, Ratzinger explains, "is the genuinely ecclesiological breakthrough of the Council," and, significantly, is an important illustration of the hermeneutics of continuity and renewal. The Council found a way within "the logic of Catholicism for the ecclesial character of non-Catholic communities . . . without detriment to Catholic identity."[53] Constitutive of Catholic ecclesial identity is that the Church of Jesus Christ is a *single* reality. Ratzinger adds, "this one and only Church, which is at once spiritual and earthly, is so concrete that she can be called by name." That is, she is "constituted and organized in this world as a society," and "subsists in the Catholic Church, which is governed by the successor of Peter and the bishops in union with that successor."[54] "This declaration of the Second Vatican Council," states a 1973 intervention of the Congregation for the Doctrine of the Faith, "is illustrated by the same Council's statement that 'it is through Christ's Catholic Church alone, which is the general means of salvation, that the fullness of the means of salvation can be obtained' [*Unitatis Redintegratio*, no. 3], and that same Catholic Church 'has been endowed with all divinely revealed truth and with all the means of grace' [no. 4], with which Christ wished to enhance His messianic community."[55] Yet, although Vatican II does not differenti-

---

51. *Das neue Volk Gottes: Entwürfe zur Ekklesiologie*, 149, as cited in Heim, *Joseph Ratzinger*, 309.

52. Ratzinger, *Principles of Catholic Theology*, 370.

53. Ibid., 232.

54. *Lumen Gentium*, no. 8. The Council does not always says that the Church of Jesus Christ subsists in the Catholic Church. In *Orientalium Ecclesiarum*, which was promulgated the same day as *Lumen Gentium*, the document states: "The Holy Catholic Church, which *is* [est] the Mystical Body of Christ, is made up of the faithful who are organically united in the Holy Spirit by the same faith, the same sacraments and the same government" (no. 2; italics added).

55. *Mysterium Ecclesiae*, no. 1. This, too, is the position of Rahner. He wrote: "The Catholic Church cannot think of herself as one among many historical manifestations in which *one and the same* God-man Jesus Christ is made present, which are offered by God to man for him to choose whichever he likes. On the contrary she must necessarily think of herself as the one and total presence in history of the one God-man in his truth

ate between the Church of Jesus Christ and the Catholic Church, it also stated in the same context of *Lumen Gentium* and elsewhere that "many elements of sanctification and truth" are found outside the visible boundaries of the Church.[56] Ratzinger explains:

> No translation can fully capture the sublime nuance of the Latin text in which the unconditional equation of the first conciliar drafts—the full identity between the Church of Jesus Christ and the Roman Catholic Church—is clearly set forth: nothing of the concreteness of the conciliar concept of the Church is lost—the Church is there present where the successors of the Apostle Peter and of the other apostles visibly incorporate her continuity with her source; *but this full concreteness of the Church does not mean that every other Church can be only a non-Church.* The equation is not mathematical because the Holy Spirit cannot be reduced to a mathematical symbol, not even where he concretely binds and bestows himself.... The working of the Holy Spirit is admittedly not clear, but it can be trusted: the equation is valid even though it cannot be stated be stated mathematically.[57]

In this passage Ratzinger affirms the identity between the Church of Christ and the Catholic Church but rejects the view that non-Catholic churches can be only a non-Church. How are we to understand the nature of this identity? How can Ratzinger affirm full identity and yet account for the *ecclesial* status of non-Catholic churches and communities? Most important, can one affirm extra-Catholic *ecclesial* reality without denying by implication the full identity between the Catholic Church and Christ's Church?

As Reformed theologian Berkouwer puts this question, "The question of whether there are Christians outside of the Church is not the ul-

---

and grace, and as such as having a fundamental relationship to all men. She is conscious of herself as making abidingly present that which derives authoritatively and juridically, even from the aspect of historical succession, from *that* Church which Jesus Christ gathered about himself as the community of those who believe in him.... For this reason the Catholic Church cannot simply think of herself as one among many Christian Churches and communities on an equal footing with her.... And the Church cannot accept that this unity is something which must be achieved only in the future and through a process of unification between Christian Churches, so that until this point is reached it simply would not exist" ("Church, Churches and Religions," 40–41).

56. *Lumen Gentium*, no. 8. See also, Vatican II, *Unitatis Redintegratio*, no. 3.

57. Ratzinger, *Principles of Catholic Theology*, 230–231; italics added to the last clause.

timate problem that Rome is wrestling with. The personal possession of grace on the part of outsiders ["extra ecclesiam"] is not in the crucible. The question rather focuses on the nature of the Church and of whether the Christian reality of outsiders can be given expression in some ecclesial sense." Again, adds Berkouwer, "The decisive question is not whether Rome acknowledges other Christians as real Christians. The decisive question at this point is whether Rome will acknowledge other churches *as real churches*. Voices at the Council were heard asking that non-Catholic 'fellowships' be granted the *title* of Church. But even if this were done, the question would still persist as to the significance and extent of this semantic concession. Would it be only a recognition that non-Catholic groups are *analogous* to the Church? Or would it be a real recognition of them as genuine churches? *If the latter, Rome could be shaking its own dogmatic structure to the foundation*."[58] A similar question was raised by Edmund Schlink (1903–1984), who was a leading German Lutheran theologian, a prominent figure in the modern ecumenical movement, and, like Berkouwer, an official observer at the Second Vatican Council.[59] Rome faces a dilemma, stresses Schlink, in recognizing non-Catholics as Christians while not recognizing non-Catholic churches as genuine churches. The Catholic Church is the fully and rightly ordered expression of the Body of Christ. The fullness of the means of salvation is found only in her, and that fact implies that the one true Church is the Roman Catholic Church alone. Says Schlink, "From this assumption there results only the possibility of summoning the non-Roman Christians to return to the Roman Church." "Strictly speaking," adds Schlink, the question of ecumenism for Rome "is thus not a question here of the union of divided Churches but of a subjection by which these other communities first become Churches."[60]

---

58. Berkouwer, *Vatikaans Concilie*, 247, 250 [200, 202]. Bavinck raised a similar objection in 1901. Writing in *GD* IV, Bavinck stated, "Rome can recognize sects alongside itself but not churches" (299 [314]). "Sect," in Bavinck's sense, means a voluntary association of individual persons (280 [264]), which are expressive of an individualistic and anti-institutional mentality, and hence, according to Rome, is not a church. Now that half a century later Rome has come to admit that at least some communities not in union with the Catholic Church are in some sense truly particular Churches, how does this admission impact the Catholic Church's claim to be exclusively identical with the Church of Christ?

59. Schlink, "Themes of the Second Vatican Council," 296–329.

60. Ibid., 323–24.

In sum, Schlink is arguing that the ecumenical aim of Rome is *absorption* of the non-Roman churches. But then, he asks, "What is the meaning then of Roman Catholic ecumenism? What is the meaning of addressing non-Roman Christians as 'separated brethren' instead of as 'heretics' and 'schismatics' as in the past? What is the meaning of the praise given to the spiritual fruits' to be found in non-Roman Churches, and what's meant by 'accepting the witness of their devotion . . . and theological insights'? Is not all this an effort aimed at absorption? Is not this kind of ecumenism, as some Protestant Christians suspect, merely a continuation of the Counter-Reformation with other, more accommodating methods?"[61] In other words, Schlink is asking whether Catholic ecumenism is not only just more of the same old "ecumenism of return" but also are the "elements of sanctification and truth" found outside the visible boundaries of the Church *only* elements in a "*churchless void*" (as the recent intervention of the Congregation for the Doctrine of the Faith phrases it[62]) or are they *ecclesial* elements?[63]

In response to Schlink, Ratzinger sketches his own Catholic vision of the aim of the ecumenical movement. He begins by rejecting Schlink's assumption that the "existing Churches" are various expressions of the one, not-yet-existent, Church, and the implication then that none of the "existing Churches" can claim to be *the* Church. The acceptance of Schlink's assumption by a Catholic would amount to his conversion to Protestantism. Of course, then, this Protestant concept of the Church and hence of the ecumenical movement is unacceptable to the Catholic Church. Ratzinger writes,

---

61. As cited in Ratzinger, *Theological Highlights*, 69–70.

62. Congregation for the Doctrine of the Faith, Commentary on the Document "Responses to Some Questions." The Congregation's answer is negative: "It does not follow [from recognizing the presence of ecclesial elements proper to the Church of Christ in the non-Catholic Christian communities] that the identification of the Church of Christ with the Catholic Church no longer holds, nor that outside the Catholic Church there is a complete absence of ecclesial elements, a '*churchless void*.'"

63. Congar writes, "We would have to say that the Catholic Church has ceased to see and above all to commend union purely in terms of 'return' or conversion to itself. It has learnt something; it has become converted to ecumenism. We have abandoned the attitude which made Maynard say: 'After all, Rome does not want any of us except as fuel for its ecclesiastical machine'; that was in 1938. We have made progress since" (*Diversity and Communion*, 161–62).

> Ever since the days of primitive Catholicism which reaches back to the time of the New Testament, it has been considered essential to believe that *the* Church really exists, although with shortcomings, and that this has been reflected concretely in the visible Church which celebrates the liturgy. The Catholic is convinced that the visible existence of the Church is not merely an organizational cover for a real Church hidden behind it, but on the contrary that, for all its humanity and insufficiency, the visible Church is the actual dwelling place of God among men, that it is *the* Church itself. To that extent Professor Schlink's contention that there exists an identification of the Catholic Church with the Church of Jesus Christ is valid.[64]

Thus, adds Ratzinger, "the true Church is a concrete reality, an existing reality, *even now*," but that constitutive feature of Catholic identity does not imply that others outside the Church are not Christians or "dispute the fact that their communities have an ecclesial character."[65] They don't exist in an ecclesial vacuum. True, they exist in real communion with *the* Church, the Catholic Church, but they are "true particular churches"[66] only in some *analogous* sense since they remain in "imperfect communion" with that Church.[67] The Council describes these "true particular churches" as "positive ecclesial entities" (as Ratzinger phrases it[68]), and, in addition, says Ratzinger, since "uniformity and unity are not identical," this means that "a real multiplicity of Churches must be made alive again within the framework of Catholic unity."[69] I shall return below to explain the sense in which these other communities have an ecclesial character as well as the sense in which Catholic teaching recognizes unity and a plurality of Churches.

Now, in the aftermath of the Council, the dogmatic structure of the Church's foundation was severely shaken (as Berkouwer phrases it) because of the common impression that the Council, in stating that the Church of Christ "subsists" in the Roman Catholic communion, rather than simply saying that the Church Jesus Christ founded *is* (*est*) the

---

64. Ratzinger, *Theological Highlights*, 71.
65. Ratzinger, "Luther and the Unity of the Churches," 119; italics added.
66. *Dominus Iesus*, no. 17.
67. *Unitatis Redintegratio*, no. 3.
68. Ratzinger, *Theological Highlights*, 75.
69. Ibid., 72.

Catholic Church, was somehow implying that the former is wider and more inclusive than the latter. If so, that is, if the Church of Christ extends beyond the Catholic Church, how can the logic of Catholicism allow for the *ecclesial* character of non-Catholic communities without detriment to the first principle of Catholic ecclesial identity, namely, that the *one* Church of Jesus Christ subsists in the Catholic Church?

One thing is for sure: the first principle of Catholic ecclesial identity logically excludes the view that understands the Catholic Church to be "one part of a divided whole." On this view, nowhere on earth does the Church of Jesus Christ actually exist. Rather, it is an eschatological reality, ideal or goal, as Christopher Malloy puts it, "for which Christians must hope and labor but which does not or cannot have a concrete, 'subsisting' realization in history."[70] As the Dutch neo-Calvinist theologian Herman Bavinck puts it, "No one church, no matter how pure, is identical with the universal church. In the same way no confession, no matter how refined by the Word of God, is identical with the whole of Christian truth. . . . The one, holy, universal church that is presently an object of faith, will not come into being until the body of Christ reaches full maturity."[71] Ratzinger rejects this view: "Christ's Church really exists, and not just scraps of her. And she is not a never-to-be-attained utopia; on the contrary, she is concrete. This is precisely what the *subsistit* means."[72]

This first principle also logically excludes the so-called "branch theory of Christianity," which may be understood as the view that the Church of Christ is a confederation of all Christian communities that taken together to form the one Church of Christ. "Wherefore, the Christian

---

70. Malloy, "*Subsistit In*," 9. Ratzinger makes the same point in his *Church, Ecumenism & Politics*, 118. The Congregation for the Doctrine of the Faith makes the same point in *Mysterium Ecclesiae*, no. 1: Much less are [the Christian faithful] free to hold that, today, the Church of Christ does not really subsist anywhere, so that it is considered to be only the goal that should be sought by all churches and communities." I am indebted to Malloy's article for helping me to understand the phrase "subsistit in." Also helpful is the magisterial study by Heim, *Joseph Ratzinger*, especially 305–330. In addition, very helpful is Fr. O'Connor, "The Church of Christ and the Catholic Church" (1983), 248–63.

71. Bavinck, "The Catholicity of Christianity and the Church," 250–51. See also, Bavinck, *Gereformeerde Dogmatiek* IV, 299–300 [314–16], especially 315: "A true church in an absolute sense is impossible here on earth; there is not a single church that completely and in all its parts, in doctrine and in life, in the ministry of the Word and sacrament, meets the demand of God."

72. "Cardinal Ratzinger answers the main objections raised against the Declaration *Dominus Iesus*."

faithful [meaning here 'Catholics'] are not allowed to suppose that the Church of Christ is nothing other than a certain sum total of churches and ecclesial communities, indeed divided but to some extent united as one."[73] Ratzinger objects to this view: not only does it obscure the integral unity of the visible and invisible aspects of the Church but also it neglects the contradictory reality of human sin that is reflected in the contradiction of division among Christians, indeed, in ecclesial division. "Because sin is a contradiction, this distinction between *subsistit* and *est* is, in the end, something that cannot be entirely explained logically. Reflected in the paradox of the distinction between the uniqueness and the concrete existence of the Church, on the one hand, and, on the other, the continuing existence of a concrete ecclesiastical entity outside of the one active agent is the contradictory element of human sin, the contradictory element of schism."[74] In short, because of sin we may not simply regard the multiplicity of churches as a reflection of the abundance of the Church's rich *depositum fidei*. Rather, we read in the opening paragraph in Vatican II's decree on ecumenism, *Unitatis Redintegratio*, "Such division openly contradicts the will of Christ, scandalizes the world, and damages the holy cause of preaching the Gospel to every creature."[75]

Another possibility that is excluded understands "subsists" to mean that the Church subsists in many particular churches, both Catholic and non-Catholic churches, in their own way. In 1985, the Congregation for the Doctrine of the Faith rejected the view that the Church of Christ subsists in other Christian churches as well as in the Catholic Church. "But the Council had chosen the word *subsistit*—subsists—exactly in order to make clear that one sole 'subsistence' of the true Church exists, whereas

---

73. *Mysterium Ecclesiae*, no. 1, as cited in Malloy, "*Subsistit In: Nonexclusive Identity or Full Identity*," 18, note 60. The confederation view of the Church's unity was already rejected by Leo XIII, *Satis Cognitum* ["On the Unity of the Church"], no. 4. See also, Pius XI, *Mortalium Animos*, no. 6.

74. Ratzinger, "The Ecclesiology of the Constitution *Lumen Gentium*," 148.

75. *Unitatis Redintegratio*, no. 1. See, on this, Bavinck, *GD* IV, "Nor can it be denied that the endless divisions of the confessors of Christ offer the world an occasion for pleasure and scorn and give it a reason for its unbelief in the One sent by the Father, inasmuch as it does not see the unity of believers in Christ (John 17:21). As Christians we cannot humbles ourselves deeply enough over the schisms and discord that have existed all through the centuries in the church of Christ. It is a sin against God, in conflict with Christ's [high-priestly] prayer [for unity], and caused by the darkness of our minds and the lovelessness of our hearts" (300–1 [316]).

outside her visible structure only *elementa ecclesiae*—elements of the Church—exist; these—being elements of the same Church—tend and conduct toward the Catholic Church (*Lumen Gentium*, no. 8). The decree on ecumenism expresses the same doctrine (cf. *Unitatis redintegratio*, nos. 3–4), and it was restated precisely in the declaration *Mysterium Ecclesiae* (no. 1)."[76] Ratzinger refers to this rejected view in the Congregation's notification as "ecclesiological relativism," meaning thereby that in a real sense the Church is "something intangible, hidden under the variety of human constructions." He objects to this view not only because this institutional relativism leads to a denial of the bodily concreteness of the Church, "identified through the confession of faith, the sacraments, and apostolic succession." But also, says Ratzinger, "If the Church only 'subsists' intangibly under the various 'Churches', then no Church could claim to possess definitively binding teaching authority, and in this way institutional relativism will lead to doctrinal relativism."[77] Furthermore, because these various Churches "contradict one another," adds Ratzinger, being all Churches in their own way, then the Church of Jesus Christ, "is a collection of contradictions and cannot offer people clear direction."[78] Moreover, Ratzinger then polemically remarks, on this view, "subjectivism is canonized: then everyone would invent his own Christianity and in the end his personal taste would be decisive."[79]

Rather, in speaking of the Church of Jesus Christ "subsisting in" the Catholic Church, Vatican II, says Ratzinger, in keeping with the first principle of Catholic ecclesiology, meant the very opposite of any ecclesiological relativism. He explains, the "subsistit formula" means "that *the Church of Jesus Christ exists*."[80] The Church exists in itself as an independent, concrete agent, and not in something else. The core meaning of concreteness

---

76. Congregation for the Doctrine of the Faith, "Notification on the Book 'Church, Charisma and Power' by Father Leonardo Boff." The view rejected by the Congregation as a valid interpretation of Vatican II is repeated by Pannenberg, "Ecumenical Tasks in Relationship to the Roman Catholic Church." Pannenberg says "While the word 'is' implies the exclusive identity with the church of Christ, the phrase 'subsists in' could be taken to mean the one church of Christ can 'subsist' in other churches besides the Roman Catholic Church" (163–64).

77. Ratzinger, "*Deus Locutus Est Nobis in Filio*, 26–27.

78. "Cardinal Ratzinger answers the main objections raised against the Declaration *Dominus Iesus*."

79. Ibid.

80. Ratzinger, "*Deus Locutus Est Nobis in Filio*," 27.

is uniqueness, since "the view that *subsistit* should be multiplied fails to do justice to the particular point intended."[81] As Ratzinger puts it in one early reflection, "the Catholic Church, even while allowing the usage [of the plural 'Churches'], must nevertheless insist on giving herself the singular designation 'the Church' in a uniquely meaningful way."[82] In short, adds Ratzinger, "the identification of the Catholic Church with the Church of Jesus Christ is valid."[83] The Church of Jesus Christ is visible, historical, temporal, institutional, in a nutshell, bodily. Christ Himself has willed the Church's existence; and the Holy Spirit has continually renewed her since Pentecost, *ecclesia semper reformanda*, preserving her in her essential identity, which belongs to the concreteness of the Incarnation. The Church is one, absolutely singular, an independent, self-contained subject subsisting in the reality of the Catholic Church throughout history. To quote Ratzinger again:

> The word *subsistit* derives from ancient philosophy, as it was later developed among the Scholastics. . . . *Subsistere* is a special case of *esse* [existence]. It refers to existence in the form of an individual subject. That is exactly what it means here. The Council wanted to say that the Church of Jesus Christ, as a concrete subject in the world, is found in the Catholic Church. This can only occur in a single instance, and thus the notion that *subsistit* could be multiplied precisely misses the meaning of the term. With the term *subsistit*, the Council wanted to express the singularity and non-multiplicability of the Church of Christ, the Catholic Church; the Church exists as a single subject in the reality of history. But the difference between *subsistit* and *est* also embraces the drama of ecclesial division: for while the Church is only one and really exists, there is *being* which is from the Church's *being*—there is ecclesial reality—outside the Church.[84]

This explanation of the meaning of the word "*subsistit*" carefully explicates the claim that the one Church of Christ subsists in the Catholic Church, but how does it help us understand the extra-Catholic *eccle-*

---

81. Ratzinger, "Ecclesiology of the Constitution *Lumen Gentium*," 147.
82. Ratzinger, "Catholicism after the Council," 21.
83. Ratzinger, *Theological Highlights*, 71.
84. Ratzinger, "*Deus Locutus Est Nobis in Filio*," 27–28. For a slightly different translation of this quoted passage, see Ratzinger, "Ecclesiology of the Constitution *Lumen Gentium*," 147.

sial reality without denying by implication the full identity between the Catholic Church and Christ's Church.

Yes, there is extra-Catholic ecclesial reality; indeed, the Council Fathers wrote "some and even very many of the significant elements and endowments which together go to build up and give life to the Church itself, can exist outside the visible boundaries of the Catholic Church: the written word of God; the life of grace; faith, hope and charity, with the other interior gifts of the Holy Spirit, and visible elements too." These non-Catholic churches "have been by no means been deprived of significance and importance in the mystery of salvation. For the Spirit of Christ has not refrained from using them as means of salvation."[85] But it is precisely with respect to these elements of sanctification and truth existing outside the Catholic Church's visible boundaries that the notion of "subsistit" finds its most significant meaning. The root meaning of "subsistit" is derived from the neo-scholastic understanding of "substance" and the latter is defined in terms of the concept "*subsistere.*" "From *subsistere*: then substance is a thing that subsists in itself, that *is* in itself, having no need of something else in which to exist. This ... definition considers substance absolutely, in itself, as to its mode of being, that is, its ontological sufficiency, by virtue of which it exists in itself and not in something else."[86] In short, substance is something standing on its own, in itself, and for that reason it means independence in existence. By contrast, properties can be distinguished from a substance by virtue of not standing on their own; rather, they exist in another, being a property of some substance, inhering in it, being supported by it. In other words, substance "stands under" and sustains properties in their being and itself is a source of activity. These properties are in a way beings but they are not self-subsistent. Maximilian Heinrich Heim applies the distinction between substance and properties to the relation between the Catholic Church and extra-Catholic ecclesial reality. He writes:

> The Church of Jesus Christ is present, in an ultimate density of her reality, in the Catholic Church. Moreover, the term "subsis-

---

85. *Unitatis Redintegratio*, no. 3. "But even if in spite of [obstacles to full ecclesiastical communion] it remains true that all who have been justified by faith in baptism are incorporated into Christ; they therefore have a right to be called Christians, and with good reason are accepted as brothers by the children of the Catholic Church" (no. 3).

86. Fernandez, "Metaphysica Generalis," 770, as cited by Heim, *Joseph Ratzinger*, 314–15, note 457.

tence" implies that ecclesiality in all its possible forms *has its basis* in the Catholic Church as the authentic realization of Christ's foundation. And this very subsistence, which is her own, makes it possible for her to support the "elementa plura sanctificationis et veritatis" [many elements of sanctification and truth] that can be found outside her boundaries. But this mean simultaneously that the elements (outside the Catholic Church) do not exist in the manner of subsisting but, rather—expressed philosophically— exist *in alio*, which means, therefore, that they are dependent on the Catholic Church for their continued existence, since they can *be* only through her.[87]

Or as Ratzinger put it above, "for while the Church is only one and really exists, there is *being* which is from the Church's *being*—there is ecclesial reality—outside the Church." Yet, while there is "extra-Catholic ecclesial reality," that is, those many elements of sanctification and truth affirmed by the council, they "should be understood not as self-standing but as both grounded in and oriented towards the Catholic Church."[88] These many elements, which as "gifts proper to the Church of Christ, impel towards Catholic unity."[89] Elsewhere we read, "All these things, which come from and lead to Christ, pertain by right to the one Church of Christ."[90]

In connection with affirming that there are many elements of sanctification and truth outside of the visible society of the Catholic Church, we must ask whether "non-Catholic ecclesial communities and churches have one relation to the Catholic Church and another relation to the Church of Christ?"[91] This question arises from the view that interprets the presence and work of the Church of Jesus Christ in the Catholic Church and in extra-Catholic ecclesial reality as a matter of degrees. Yes, Christ's Church exists fully in the Catholic Church alone but she also exists, in lesser and varying degrees, outside her visible society, in other Christian churches and communities.[92] Therefore, on this view, "the Church of Christ [not

87. Heim, *Joseph Ratzinger*, 315–16.
88. Malloy, "*Subsistit In*," 27–28.
89. *Lumen Gentium*, no. 8.
90. *Unitatis Redintegratio*, no. 3: Latin: "haec omnia, quae a Christo proveniunt et ad ipsum conducant, ad unicam Christi Ecclesiam *iure* pertinent."
91. Malloy, "*Subsistit In*," 13.
92. This view is expressed, among others, by Willebrands: "the *subsistit in* allows emphasizing both the conviction that the one and genuine church of God is found in

only] can exists elsewhere [than the Catholic Church], though not fully," but also those non-Catholic churches and communities are used by the Holy Spirit as means of salvation by or of themselves *independently* of the Catholic Church, that is, as separated churches and communities.[93] That conclusion means that they have one relation to the Catholic Church and another relation to Christ's Church.

This conclusion is the very opposite of what the Church teaches, namely, that these many elements of sanctification and truth are present in extra-Catholic ecclesial reality to the extent of their union with the Catholic Church. The "Decree on Ecumenism" clearly states, they "derive their efficacy from the very fullness of grace and truth entrusted to the Catholic Church." O'Connor explains: "The elements [of separated churches and communities] are operative here and now because they belong by right to the Church and *presently* derive their efficacy from the plenitude of grace entrusted to the Catholic Church. In other words, the ecclesial elements are elements of the Catholic Church presently operative in the separated Churches and Communities because of their real, although imperfect, unity with the Catholic Church."[94] Clearly, then, the ecclesiological breakthrough of Vatican II—recognizing the existence of extra-Catholic ecclesial reality outside the visible boundaries of the Catholic Church—has not resulted in the rejection of the first principle of Catholic ecclesial identity.

There remains to ask, how, then, does Ratzinger think of unity and diversity in the Catholic Church. This question is especially important

---

the Catholic Church and the certitude that it nonetheless extends, though lacking its fullness, beyond the Catholic Church" ("Vatican II's Ecclesiology of Communion," 32). We find a more recent expression of it in Tjørhom, *Visible Church-Visible Unity*; idem, "A Question of Balance," especially 197–98.

93. Malloy, "*Subsistit In*," 28–32. See also, O'Connor, "The Church of Christ and the Catholic Church," 259.

94. O'Connor, "The Church of Christ and the Catholic Church," 259. Regarding the claim that the Church of Christ subsists only in the Catholic Church, Cardinal Dulles writes in "Vatican II: The Myth and the Reality": "This reading [of Ratzinger] coheres well with the full teaching of the council. Certain endowments of the church can, to be sure, exist in other Christian communions, bringing their members into 'imperfect communion' with the Catholic Church (*Unitatis Redintegratio*, the Decree on Ecumenism [1964], No. 3). Non-Catholic communities that have a genuine apostolic ministry and a valid Eucharist are properly called churches, but they should not be reckoned as constituent parts of the one and catholic church in which the true religion subsists" (*Dignitatis Humanae*, the Declaration on Religious Freedom [1965], No. 1).

when we in consider that the goal of ecumenical dialogue is *visible* unity. The Decree on Ecumenism clearly states that this goal is visible unity, a visible structured unity (as Ola Tjøhom phrases it), with the Catholic Church.

> Today, in many parts of the world, under the influence of the grace of the Holy Spirit, many efforts are being made in prayer, word and action to attain that fullness of unity which Jesus Christ desires. The sacred Council exhorts, therefore, all the Catholic faithful to recognize the signs of the times and to take an active and intelligent part in the work of ecumenism . . . to promote Christian unity. . . . Such actions, when they are carried out by the Catholic faithful with prudent patience and under the attentive guidance of their bishops, promote justice and truth, concord and collaboration, as well as the spirit of brotherly love and unity. The results will be that, little by little, as the obstacles to perfect ecclesiastical communion are overcome, all Christians will be gathered, in a common celebration of the Eucharist, into the unity of the one and only Church, which Christ bestowed on his Church from the beginning. This unity, we believe, subsists in the Catholic Church as something she can never lose, and we hope that it will continue to increase until the end of time.[95]

I have argued in this section of this chapter that there exists a true plurality of churches. True, they exist in real communion with *the* Church, the Catholic Church, but they are "true particular churches"[96] only in some *analogous* sense because they remain in "imperfect communion" with that Church.[97] But affirming the existence of true particular churches does not mean, according to Ratzinger, that the ecumenical goal is mutual recognition and hence a "reconciled denominationalism," meaning thereby an approach "which allows the churches to maintain their denominations or even parochial identities and so to 'remain as they are.'"[98] What then of the validity of the ecumenical formula of "reconciled diversity" in the light of the notion of legitimate diversity? This question was posed to the then Joseph Cardinal Ratzinger on the occasion of the publication of *Dominus Iesus* in an interview published on September 22, 2000, in the *Frankfurter*

---

95. *Unitatis Redintegratio*, no. 4.
96. *Dominus Iesus*, no. 17.
97. *Unitatis Redintegratio*, no. 3.
98. Tjørhom, *Visible Church-Visible Unity*, 74.

Allgemeine Zeitung.⁹⁹ He replied sharply, "I accept the concept of a 'reconciled diversity', if it does not mean equality of content and the elimination of the question of truth so that we could consider ourselves one, even if we believe and teach different things." Adds Ratzinger, "To my mind this concept is used well, if it says that despite our differences, which do not allow us to regard ourselves as mere fragments of a Church of Jesus Christ that does not exist in reality, we meet in the peace of Christ and are reconciled to one another, that is, we recognize our division as contradicting the Lord's will and this sorrow spurs us to seek unity and to pray to Him in the knowledge that we all need His love." Ratzinger rejects here a model of unity—reconciled diversity—that no longer recognizes the necessity of overcoming the mutual opposition of the various doctrinal systems. In contrast, the Catholic Church's ecumenical vision means many worshipping communities that all are nonetheless visibly one, in other words, *full unity with the Catholic Church in legitimate diversity*.

The concept of full unity in legitimate diversity makes sense once we grasp the difference between *unity* and *uniformity*.¹⁰⁰ They are not identical, and hence the Council, says Ratzinger, came to recognize that "a real multiplicity of Churches must be made alive again within the framework of Catholic unity."¹⁰¹ Thus, says Ratzinger, "What Catholics mean [by full unity in legitimate diversity] is that a multiplicity of Churches exists within the framework of the *one* and visible Church of God, each of which represents the totality of the Church. In close communion with one another they help build up, within the framework of a unity born of a vigorous multiplicity, the one Church of God."¹⁰² So the aim of the ecumenical movement, as Catholics see it, is the attainment of full unity in legitimate diversity, of a plurality of churches *within the one* Church of Christ, which Catholics identify with the Catholic Church.

---

99. "Cardinal Ratzinger answers the main objections raised against the Declaration *Dominus Iesus*." For an analysis of the ecumenical formula of "reconciled diversity," Congar writes: "The problem with the . . . theme [of reconciled diversity] is that it starts from the division which is expressed in the diversity of confessions and not from the reality of the undivided church which carries within itself a fullness to which, in all truth, its dogmatic or theological formulas give only very imperfect expressions" (*Diversity and Communion*, 151).

100. Ratzinger, *Theological Highlights*, 72.

101. Ibid.

102. Ibid., 71.

This unity of true particular churches with the Catholic Church arises from the concreteness of the joint sharing in the Word and Body of Jesus Christ. At first glance this doesn't seem sufficient for unity. Yet, although Ratzinger doesn't unpack here in this early reflection the meaning of a joint sharing in the Word and Body of Jesus Christ, I think we can assume that he means full, corporate sacramental union with the Catholic Church. Furthermore, this understanding presupposes the visible sacramental structure of the Catholic Church, a structure that is grounded in the communion of bishops among themselves and together with the pope, which was instituted as such by the Lord. So as Ratzinger says elsewhere, "[T]he communion of the *Body* of Christ," full unity in legitimate diversity, is "the communion of his body in the corporeal reality of the community of bishops of all places and times."[103] That joint sharing the Word and Body of Jesus Christ entails full, sacramental union with the Catholic Church is evident from Ratzinger's reply to those Protestants who pressure the Catholic Church "to allow intercommunion based on their understanding of the Lord's Supper." Says Ratzinger, "Since for us the twofold mystery of the Body of Christ—the Body of Christ as Church and the Body of Christ as sacramental gift—is one and the same sacrament, [then] to tear the corporeality of the sacrament out of the context of the Church's corporeality would mean trampling on both the Church and the sacrament."[104]

In this light, we can understand Ratzinger's reply to Edmund Schlink's charge that Catholic ecumenism ultimately amounts to an ecumenism of return and hence to the absorption of the other non-Catholic Churches and ecclesial communities. Ratzinger says that "as long as unity was identified with uniformity, the Catholic goal [of full unity in legitimate diversity] could not help but appear to non-Catholic Christians as complete absorption into the present form of the Church." But there are legitimate differences in theology, spirituality, discipline, and liturgy. "Whatever is truly Christian is never contrary to what genuinely belongs to the faith; indeed, it can always bring a more perfect realization of the very mystery of Christ and the Church."[105] Indeed, regarding the legitimate variety of theological expressions, "It is hardly surprising, then, if sometimes one

---

103. Ratzinger, "Luther and the Unity of the Churches," 114.
104. Ratzinger, "On the Progress of Ecumenism," 137.
105. *Unitatis Redintegratio*, no. 4.

tradition has come nearer to a full appreciation of some aspects of a mystery of revelation that the other, or has expressed them better." "In such cases," the Council adds, "these various theological formulations are often to be considered complementary rather than conflicting."[106] This thesis brings us back to the first section of this chapter, namely, to the distinction between truth and its formulations—propositions of faith and their linguistic expressions—as a way of advancing ecumenical dialogue.

Most Catholics—Ratzinger is writing this early reflection in 1966—are a long distance away from accepting the idea of full unity in legitimate diversity. Catholic renewal is required here and this is something that cannot be accomplished in a day. "This requires a process of opening up, which takes time." So what is practically possible now is a long way off from the Church's ecumenical goal, and hence given that limitation, "the Catholic Church has no right to *absorb* the other Churches. The Church has not yet prepared for them a place of their own, but this they are legitimately entitled to." "However," adds Ratzinger, the Catholic "can hope that the hour will come when 'the Churches' that exist outside 'the Church' will enter into its unity."[107] This model of unity, although not realized through uniformity and absorption, does not stop at the mere claim of the mutual recognition of the different confessional traditions. That model would shake the dogmatic foundation of the Church's Catholic identity—the Catholic Church considers herself as *the* Church of Christ. Rather, then, essential to ecumenism is "a hermeneutics of union that sees the confession of faith as that which unites. . . . The guarantee of unity is a Christianity of faith and fidelity that lives the faith as a decision with a definite content but precisely for that reason is always searching for unity, lets itself be constantly purified and deepened as a preparation for

---

106. Ibid., no. 17.

107. Ratzinger, *Theological Highlights*, 73. This hope for visible unity, full-communion agreement, in accord with the Council's document on ecumenism (*Unitatis Redintegratio*), is surely the impulse behind the formation of the Pontifical Council for Promoting Christian Unity (PCPCU) after the Second Vatican Council. It was John XXIII's desire that the involvement of the Catholic Church in the contemporary ecumenical movement be one of the Council's chief concerns. At present, the PCPCU is engaged in an international inter-confessional dialogue with each of the following Churches and World Communions: the Orthodox Church, the Coptic Orthodox Church, the Malankara Churches, the Anglican Communion, the Lutheran World Federation, the World Alliance of Reformed Churches, the World Methodist Council, the Baptist World Alliance, Disciples of Christ, and some Pentecostal groups. The Council also seeks to promote meetings with Evangelicals.

it and, in so doing, helps the other recognize the common center and to find himself there by the same process of purification and deepening."[108] Along with Ratzinger, with "confidence in the power of the Holy Spirit, we hope also for the unity of the Church and dedicate ourselves to an ecumenism of faith."[109]

In the next three chapters, I will engage the Dutch neo-Calvinist tradition on several issues that for more than one century have been at the center of their disputes with the Catholic tradition. The first issue continues in the area of ecclesiology. I will focus my attention, in chapter 3, on the critical differences between these two traditions on the question of the Church's relation to the world. In chapter 4, I give an extensive analysis of the doctrine of the Holy Spirit, drawing out his significance for the sacramental life of grace and the certainty of faith. I conclude the book, in chapter 5, by considering the call of some neo-Calvinists, but not all, regarding the so-called "dehellenization of the Gospel" and the abandonment of scholasticism. In this connection, I'll examine issues of difference and similarity regarding the relation between nature, sin and grace, Christian philosophy, natural theology, and language about God. Again, similarity and difference between representative thinkers of the Catholic and neo-Calvinist traditions will be highlighted. This ecumenical dialogue with my neo-Calvinist brethren is carried out with the words of John Paul II in mind: "Dialogue is not simply an exchange of ideas. In some way it is always an 'exchange of gifts.'"[110]

---

108. Ratzinger, *Principles of Catholic Theology*, 202–203.
109. Ibid., 203.
110. John Paul II, *Ut Unum Sint*, no. 28.

3

The Church and the World

Anthropological and Ecclesial Foundations

It will be the mission of the coming age once more to envisage truly the relation between the Church and the individual. If this is to be achieved, our conceptions of society and individual personality must once more be adequate. And self-consciousness and the sense of organic life must be brought into harmony, and the inherent interdependence of the Church and the individual must again be accepted as a self-evident truth. Every age has its special task. And this is equally true of the development of the religious life. To see how the Church and the individual personality are mutually bound together; how they live the one by the other; and how in this mutual relationship we must seek the justification of ecclesiastical authority, and to make this insight once more an integral part of our life and consciousness is the fundamental achievement to which our age is called.[1]

THE DILEMMA OF INDIVIDUALISM AND UNIVERSALISM

ESPECIALLY SINCE MAX WEBER (1864–1920) and Ernst Troeltsch (1865–1923), social theory, in its reflections on the relation between the Church and society, has subjected the Christian faith to the dilemma

---

1. Fr. Guardini, *Church and the Catholic*, 45–46. This volume contains two of Guardini's books. My concern is solely with the first, which is an English translation of Guardini's original German book, *Vom Sinn der Kirche*, 32. In general, both sources will be cited throughout this chapter in the text, first the original (hereafter *VSK*), followed by the pagination of the English translation in square brackets [ ]. Almost as important to my analysis in this paper of Guardini's anthropology/ecclesiology is the understanding of the Church that he formulated once again at the end of his life—in the year (1964) when Vatican II promulgated *Lumen Gentium*, the Dogmatic Constitution on the Church—in *Church of the Lord*. For a good anthology of Father Guardini's writings, see *Essential Guardini*.

of individualism or universalism.² On the one hand, individualism, or in other words, social atomism, is the "belief that the individual has a primary reality whereas society is a second-order, derived or artificial construct."³ It makes no difference whether the individualism in question is of a functionalist or substantialist sort. The former construes institutional communities such as the Church and the family from elementary forms of social interaction. The latter absolutizes the individual as a self-contained substance, with such communities deriving from consenting autonomous individuals forming social contracts and being merely a collection of self-contained individuals. In either case only the individual human being is real whereas institutional communities are second-order, derived, or artificial constructs. On the other hand, universalism is the view according to which an institutional totality such as the state or the church is everything; it is an all-inclusive whole, incorporating all types of societal relationships as its parts. Corresponding to individualism and universalism, according to Troeltsch, are two independent sociological types, which he calls sect and Church types, and which he claims is inherent to the "religious sociological basic scheme of Christianity." As Herman Dooyeweerd puts it, "according to Troeltsch, individualism and universalism lie hidden in an inner tension in the basic religious idea of Christianity."⁴

The Dutch neo-Calvinist philosopher Dooyeweerd radically disagrees with Troeltsch's thesis that the dilemma of individualism versus universalism is inherent to Christianity, as does the Catholic philosopher/theologian Fr. Romano Guardini (1885–1968). I make clear in this chapter that both Guardini and Dooyeweerd hold that the Catholic and Calvinist traditions, as understood by them, transcend the dilemma of individualism versus universalism, and hence the sociological types of sect and Church-institute. There are, of course, also important differences between Dooyeweerd and Guardini that I will highlight and critically

---

2. Troeltsch, *Social Teaching of the Christian Churches*, Vols.1 and 2, 23–37, 461–67, and 993–94. Weber, *Die Protestantische Ethik und der 'Geist' des Kapitalismus*, 93–95.

3. I am following here the definition of individualism found in the celebrated study by Robert N. Bellah, et al., *Habits of the Heart*, Glossary, entry on "Individualism," 334.

4. Dooyeweerd, *De Wijsbegeerte der Wetsidee*, III, 472. ET: *New Critique of Theoretical Thought*, Vol. III, 247. Both sources will be cited (except in those instances when the English edition contains material not found in the earlier Dutch edition) throughout this chapter, first the original as *WdW*, followed by the pagination of the English translation in square brackets [ ].

analyze in this chapter. An analysis of those differences will make for an interesting and fruitful exercise, I believe, in ecumenical theology and dialogue.

I turn first to focus on Guardini's assessment of the problem-situation that Catholics faced in the first quarter of the twentieth century regarding the relationship between the Church and the individual. In particular, Guardini's position is well expressed in the epigraph to this chapter, describing the problem-situation he thinks the Church faces and which he originally described in 1922 in his marvelous study, *Vom Sinn der Kirche*. His study examined the relation between the Church and the individual, and hence between Christian anthropology and ecclesiology. I shall argue, in the last section of this chapter, that Guardini's study and hence his analysis of the problem-situation has lost none of its relevance in the almost eighty-five years since it was first written, especially for the *new evangelization*.[5]

PROBLEM-SITUATION
SUBJECTIVISM, INDIVIDUALISM, UNIVERSALISM

In the high Middles Ages, which stretches from the late eleventh century to the beginning of the fourteenth century, there is the growth of subjectivity in religion, that is, of thinking of oneself as an individual before God, as one having a personal calling in Christ, which flows from his radical conversion, in short, an interior life developed.[6] Guardini writes,

---

5. Other sources helpful to my study of Guardini's thought and which I draw on in this chapter are the following: Cardinal Dulles, SJ, *Models of the Church*; Monsignor Giussani, *Why the Church?*; Olsen, *Beginning at Jerusalem*; Heim, *Ratzinger*. Ratzinger/Benedict XVI, *Church, Ecumenism, & Politics*; idem, *Pilgrim Fellowship of Faith*; John Paul II, *Catechesis on the Creed*, IV, *Church, Mystery, Sacrament, Community*; Cardinal Journet, *Theology of the Church*; Bavinck, GD IV, 258–421 [273–440].

6. Olsen, *Beginning at Jerusalem*, 96–98. See also, Taylor, *Varieties of Religion Today*: "First, the emphasis on religion as personal is consonant with a major direction of change through the last several centuries in Latin Christendom. From the high Middle Ages, we can see a steadily increasing emphasis on a religion of personal commitment and devotion over forms of centered on collective ritual. We can see this both in devotional movements and associations, like the Brethren of the Common Life in the fifteenth century, and in the demands made by church hierarchies and leaders on their members.... From that point on, the pressure to adopt a more personal, committed, inward form of religion continued, through the preaching of the mendicant friars and others, through the devotional movements mentioned above, reaching a new stage with the Reformation.... But this movement toward personal, committed, inward didn't exist only in the Protestant

"Naturally much in this individualism is necessary and true." My criticisms of this individualism, he adds, "are directed solely against a false one-sidedness which impoverishes human life; against subjectivism, not against the subjective" (*VSK*, 4, note 1 [15]). Guardini is not especially clear about the onset of this false one-sidedness, of subjectivism and individualism of the modern age.[7] But he is clear about the effect it has on religious life as a whole.

Epistemologically, Guardini notes that in the modern period "religion was considered as something which belonged to the subjective sphere—it was simply something within a man, a condition of his soul" (*VSK*, 2 [12]). Adds Guardini, "there was no genuine belief in the existence of objective religious realities. This subjectivism dominated religious life all through the second half of the nineteenth century and during the beginning of the twentieth. Man felt imprisoned within himself" (*VSK*, 2 [13]). In short, human subjectivity became the basis and center of all meaning, value and reality, and with man's experience assuming the role of determining what will be acceptable as valid, as true.[8] "This attitude was also making its influence felt in the religious sphere.... The individual was sure only of that which he personally experience, perceived, and yearned for, and on the other hand of the concepts, ideas, and postulates of his own thought" (*VSK*, 4 [14]). That this attitude—the logic of modern subjectivism: "Only accept what rings true to your own inner Self"[9]—is still making its influ-

---

churches. There was a parallel development in the Counter-reformation, with the spread of different devotional movements, and the attempts to regulate the lives of the laity according to more and more stringent models of practice.... To take my religion seriously is to take it personally, more devotionally, inwardly, more committedly.... This kind of understanding has deep roots, of course, in our religious tradition. When the psalmist, speaking for God, tells us to set aside our offering of bulls and sheep and to offer instead a contrite heart (e.g., Psalm 51), we are already on the road to our contemporary notion of personal religion" (9–12).

7. Schmitz is very helpful in this regard "St. Thomas and the Appeal to Experience," 47 (1992): 1–20. See also, Taylor, *Varieties of Religion Today*.

8. Schmitz, "St. Thomas," 9–11.

9. Taylor, *Varieties of Religion Today*, 101. Similarly, see Cardinal Kasper, "Timeliness of Speaking of God." In any case, the so-called return of religion does not simply lead back to Christian faith in God, and it does not on any account fill the empty church pews.... Sometimes what is termed a return to religion is a religiosity without God, a religion-like atheism (J.B. Meta). It can lead to a vague, diffuse, free-floating, religiosity, a syncretistic do-it-yourself, what-you-will religiosity which narcissistically seeks the divine not above us but in us" (297).

ence felt in a very practical way even ninety years later is evident from what Father Joseph Komonchak has written:

> I think what Charles Taylor describes as the "new individualism" is very widespread in our culture and even among Catholics. This is the tendency to reduce religion to one's own very personal, even private, spirituality ("following your bliss," "be true to your own inner Self"), which then becomes the criterion by which to decide what tradition, if any, to follow, what community, if any, to enter, what beliefs to hold, if any. As Taylor argues, this is an almost perfect exemplification of William James definition of religion as "the feelings, acts and experiences of individual men in their solitude, so far as they apprehend "theologies, philosophies and ecclesiastical organizations may secondarily grow." This seems to me different from the often deplored "cafeteria Catholicism" (although it may be one if its inspirations), that is, picking and choosing among church teachings; that at least allowed that there were church teaching. For those whom I am describing it is nearly incomprehensible that one's spirituality might need itself to be tested against any external reality or authority. If this phenomenon is as widespread as Taylor thinks it is, then it may be that many of the disputes about doctrines or worship or morality that so often occupy Catholics are rather missing the point: there are many people claiming to be Catholic who couldn't care less.[10]

We don't have the full picture yet of Guardini's assessment of religion in the modern period. It is not only epistemological subjectivism—the real locus of religion is in experience—that plays a vital role but also individualism—individual experience, and *not* in community life. "Religious life was thus individualistic, disintegrated, and unsocial. The individual lived for himself. 'I and my Creator' was for many the exclusive formula. The community was not primary; it took the second place. It no longer was a natural reality which existed from the first by its own right. It [community] has to be though out, willed, and deliberately set up. One individual, it was believed, approached another, and went into partnership with him. But he was not from the outset bound up with a group of his fellows, the member of an organize community, sharing its common life. There was indeed no community, merely a mechanical organization, and this is the religious sphere. How little in Divine worship were the faith-

---

10. Fr. Komonchak, "Dealing with Diversity and Disagreement."

ful aware of themselves as a community! How inwardly disintegrated the community was" (*VSK*, 4 [15])!

What does the Church look like to those who affirmed the real locus of religion to be in experience? Well, then, the importance of the faith (*fides quae* affirmed in biblical, creedal, or doctrinal formulations) of the Church, her sacramental and liturgical life, is diminished, if not eventually eradicated. The faith of the Church is understood as the "outer limit," as the boundary of the individual sphere of experience. "It has, in other words," says Guardini, "been thought of as a thing exterior from which men might receive life, not a thing into which men must be incorporated that they may live with its life." In other words, the Church comes to be thought of as "exterior," of the highest importance but still a mere "external means" serving the salvation of individual Christians. Alternatively, the Church comes to be regarded as the boundary of this [individual] sphere, and perhaps even as its opponent. In any case the Church was felt as a power fettering personality and thereby restricting the religious life. And this external regulation appeared either beneficent, or inevitable, or oppressive, according to the disposition of the individual." "Consequently," adds Guardini, "the Church was of necessity experienced not as a self-justified religious reality, but as the limiting value of the subjective; not as a living body, but as a formal institution" (*VSK*, 1, 4 [11–12, 14–15]). The upshot of this understanding of the relationship between the Church and the individual Catholic is that although he still probably lives *in* the Church, he is less and less *living the Church and its faith* to the extent that he affirms the absolute validity of his subjective religious experience—as Joseph Komonchak and others, like Charles Taylor, have argued.[11] In sum, as Walter Cardinal Kasper says, "It [the Church] will tend not to be seen as *Lebensraum*—a space in which to live," which is the very point that Guardini was making almost eighty-five years ago.[12]

At the root of this religious subjectivism is a faulty anthropology—religious individualism—in which man asserts "his own independence at the expense of the objective community," resulting in a failure to understand "his profound dependence upon the entire social organism." "Consequently," argues Guardini, "the modern man's consciousness of

---

11. Cardinal Kasper, "Church as the Place of Truth," 129–47, and for the consequence of assigning absolute validity to the principle of subjectivity, see 141. See also, Taylor, *Varieties of Religion Today*, 3–29.

12. Kasper, "The Church as the Place of Truth," 141.

his own personality is no longer healthy, [because] no longer organically bound up with the conscious life of the community." It is no wonder then that this "unhealthy personality" "cannot help feeling the Church to be, with her claim to authority, a power hostile to himself" (*VSK*, 31–32 [45]). Such individuals "view her only as a power which confronts them and which, far from having any share in their most intimate, vital purpose, actually threatens or represses it. Man's living will cannot accept a Church so conceived. He must either rise in revolt against her, or else submit to her at the costly price of salvation" (*VSK*, 32 [46]). No one could deny the continuing relevance of this analysis of the effects that religious individualism has had on the life of the Church.

Does Guardini turn to universalism to counteract the negative influence of religious individualism? As I said above, universalism is the view according to which an institutional totality such as the state or the church is everything; it is an all-inclusive whole, incorporating all types of societal relationships as its parts. In particular, does he ascribe a universalistic position to the institutional Church? No, Guardini does not turn to universalism as an antidote, because "the nature of the community as Catholicism understands and realizes it, is not such that individual personality has to struggle for self-preservation against it." The community, adds Guardini, "is not a power which violates personal individuality, as Communism does, or any other variety of the totalitarian state." Thus, Guardini does not embrace universalism because it is a totalitarian ideology that poses a constant threat to the human person. And as to whether Guardini construes the Church along universalistic lines, he responds:

> On the contrary, Catholic community presupposes from the outset and requires the free individual personalities as its components. In particular the Church is a community of beings, which are not simply members and instruments of the whole, but at the same time are microcosms revolving on their own axes, that is, individual personalities. Mere individuals can constitute only herds or human ant heaps; community is a mutual relationship of personalities. This is an ethical requirement, for morality demands a free intercourse. It also results from the very structure of being, for it is only when units with their individual centres, their own *modus operandi* and a life of their own, come together, that there can arise that unity, unique in its tension and flexibility, stable, yet rich in intrinsic possibilities of development, which is termed a community (*VSK*, 26 [38]).

Thus, Guardini's Catholic understanding of community seeks, on the one hand, to maintain the integrity of the human person, that unique, inalienable dignity that is his as a personal subject—"Personal unity, the dignity and sublimity of the self, can never be given away" (*VSK*, 86 [106])[13]—a conception differing from every type of individualism essentially because from the start of his existence man is a member of a community and hence his very nature is social (cf. *VSK*, 27 [39]). On the other hand, Guardini writes, "[T]he community is not a mere feeble social restriction or state [or Church!] bondage, but something fundamentally different. It differs as does living being with its innumerable aspects from an artificial construction without flesh and blood. For the community realizes that it is made up of individuals, each one of which constitutes a self-contained world and possesses a unique character. This is a fundamental truth which it is most important to understand thoroughly. Unless it is grasped the Catholic view of the Church, indeed of society as such, must be unintelligible." In sum, adds Guardini, "We must not get our sociological principles either from Communism, State Socialism, or individualism. For all these tear the living whole to pieces to exaggerate one portion of it. All are false and diseased" (*VSK*, 27 [40]).

Thus, Guardini is attempting to forge a "third way" in Catholic social theory, particularly regarding the relationship between the individual and the Church. "The Catholic conception of society and of individual personality starts on the contrary—like all Catholic teaching—not from isolated axioms or one-sided psychological presuppositions, but from the integrity of real life apprehended without prejudice. In virtue of his nature man is both an individual person and a member of society. Nor do these two aspects of his being simply co-exist. On the contrary, society exists already as living seed in man's individuality, and the latter in turn is necessarily presupposed by society as its foundation, though without prejudice to the relative independence of both these two primary forms of human life" (*VSK*, 27–28 [40]). Significantly, Guardini recognizes and experiences that the fundamental structure of human life—society is as primary and as necessary as individuality—has been deeply shattered by original sin. Thus: "One of two things must happen. Either the power of community will burst all bounds, swamp the free personality of the indi-

---

13. See also, *VSK*, 77 [96]: "The community must be so constituted that the dignity and inner freedom of the individual personality remain possible within it. For free personality is the presupposition of all true community."

vidual, and strip him of spiritual dignity, or else the individual personality will assert itself victoriously, and in the process sever the organic bonds with the community" (*VSK*, 77 [96]). This is the dilemma of individualism versus universalism. Both views are wrong, says Guardini, because individuals and social communities exist in a mutual correlation. In other words, neither can exist without the other: neither is ontologically basic to the other because neither was ever the source of the other.[14] In the next section, I argue that Guardini overcomes this dilemma by developing his claims that "[t]he community is just as primary a fact as individual existence. And the task of building up the community is just as primary and fundamental as that of perfecting personality" (*VSK*, 8 [18]).

OVERCOMING THE DILEMMA

Guardini breaks with the "egocentric predicament" characteristic of the epistemology of modernity that isolates man from the world, other selves, and God. Man is taken to be an enclosed consciousness over against the world, as it were. "Man is felt imprisoned within himself." It is easy to understand why, on this view, man feels trapped in his isolated consciousness, and hence the question arises, "how do I get out of it?" Says Guardini, "[t]hat is why from Kant onwards, and particularly in the more recent idealism, the problem of knowledge became so urgent—indeed for many it constituted the whole of philosophy! The man of this age considered the very existence of an [external] *object* as doubtful. He was not directly and strongly conscious of the reality of things" (*VSK*, 12 [27]). What, then, in the terms of this epistemology, is man directly and strongly conscious of?

Ideas in the mind of the isolated thinking subject are the direct object of his conscious awareness, and these ideas serve as the basis for inferring what the real world of perceptual objects, and other selves, in short, the external world, must be like. On this view, the perceptual world is not directly given to us, it is only an inference from ideas, and in this way it is alleged that we can indirectly know these external objects. A longstanding criticism of this theory of knowledge, which Guardini seems to share, is that it is doomed to failure, leaving the knower locked in his own mind, a mental cabinet we can never get out of, as it were, and hence

---

14. Helpful here with this succinct formulation of mutual correlation is Clouser, *Myth of Religious Neutrality*, 282.

in the egocentric predicament, because he is unable to know whether his ideas have any relationship at all to reality, because he cannot transcend the veil of ideas.

By contrast, Guardini affirms that contemporary thought in the first half of the twentieth century is undergoing a profound change. It is not at all clear whether Guardini is referring here to the phenomenological critique of modernity's epistemology. Be that as it may, it is clear that Guardini thinks that we first experience things, speak about them directly, articulating things and features and relationships. In particular, according to Guardini, reality is no longer taken to be an inference from "ideas in the mind," but rather man has a primary experience of reality, of things, of the reality of the soul and of God, of other human beings. In short, none of these are first and foremost inferred entities, the product of arguments, but concretely experienced realities.

> We are conscious of reality as a primary fact. It is no longer something dubious from which it is advisable to retreat upon the logical validity which seems more solid and more secure. Reality is as solid, indeed more solid, because prior, richer and more comprehensive. . . . The consciousness of reality has burst upon mankind with the force of a new and a personal experience. Our age is literally rediscovering that things exist, and moreover with an individuality incalculable, because creative and original. The concrete, in its boundless fullness, is being once more experienced. . . . It is experienced as freedom and wealth—I am real, and so also is this thing which confronts one in its self-determined abundance! And thought is a living relation between myself and it. . . . A great awakening to reality is in progress. And it is an awakening moreover to metaphysical reality [the reality of the soul and the existence of God].

And of particular relevance to the theme of this chapter, is the experience that

> [c]ommunity is admitted just as directly. The attitude of withdrawal into the barred fortress of self no longer passes, as it did twenty years ago, for the only noble attitude. On the contrary, it is regarded as unjustifiable, barren and impotent. Just as powerful as the experience that things exist and the world exists, is the experience that human beings exists. Indeed, the latter is by far more powerful, because it affects us more closely. There are human beings like myself. Each one is akin to me, but each one is also a separate world of his own, of unique value. And from this

realization springs the passionate conviction that we all belong one to another; are all brothers. It is now taken as self-evident that the individual is a member of the community. The latter does not originate through one man attaching himself to another, or renouncing part of his independence. The community is just as primary a fact as individual existence (*VSK*, 6–8 [16–19]).

So we have the two poles of religious life: the subjective pole of the self and the objective pole of an already formed community, which is the Church. "The Church then is a society essentially bound up with individual personality; and the individual life of the Christian is of its very nature related to the community. . . . There would be no Christian personality, if it did not at the same time form part of the community, as its living member." And in a complete rejection of individualism, with its attendant idea that the church is a voluntary society,[15] a sect,[16] Guardini writes, "The soul elevated by grace is not something anterior to the Church, as individuals originally isolated formed an alliance. Those who hold this view have failed completely to grasp the essence of Catholic personality." Furthermore, in a critique of universalism, Guardini adds, "[n]or does the Church absorb the individual, so that his personality can be realized only when he wrenches himself free from here. Those who think this do not know what the Church is." In sum, [w]hen I affirm the 'Church', I am at the same time affirming individual 'personality', and when I speak of

---

15. Guardini, *VSK*, 26–7 [39]: "And Christian personality is not so constituted that it is only as an afterthought associated with others to form a community. Its membership of the community does not originate in a concession made by one individual to another. It is not the case that individuals by nature independent of one another conclude a contract, by which each sacrifices a part of his independence, that by this concession he may save as much of it as possible. That is the view of society held by individualism. Personality as Catholicism understands it, looks in every direction, and thus *a priori* and of its very nature is social, and man's entire being enters into society."

16. Later in this chapter, I'll return to discuss the specific nature of the basic sociological type that Troeltsch calls "sect-type." For the moment it suffices to hear Dooyeweerd who rightly says, "Troeltsch considers this sect-type as the sociological consequences of the second or individualistic factor in the religious sociological basic scheme of Christianity. One aspect of Jesus' teaching is this radical individualism which emphasizes the eternal and infinite value of the individual personality as a child of God. All differences in social position lose their meaning in comparison with this value of the individual person, who has direct communion with God *without* the intermediary of any institution" (*WdW*, III, 474 [529] italics added). Of course Fr. Guardini rejects the "sect-type" understanding of Christianity, as does Dooyeweerd.

the interior life of the Christian, I imply the life of the Christian community" (*VSK*, 28–29 [41]).

Most significant, at least regarding the community, is that the Church is not understood by Guardini as the "outer limit," that which limits personal faith, or as he puts it, "merely the boundary of the subject to which religion in the strict is confined" (*VSK*, 13 [25]). Rather, the objective and already formed community that is the Church—by its dogma, its liturgy, and its authority—is not about limitations as such, but more about the life-giving presupposition of the Christian life, the way to become human. For that individual the Church "is the living presupposition of his personal existence, the essential path to his own perfection. And he is aware of profound solidarity between his personal being and the Church" (*VSK*, 32–33 [46]). "She is the way to personality." In other words, adds Guardini, "The more resolutely an individual acknowledges himself for what he is, and at the same time endeavors to become and to work out that which God has destined for him by his individual nature, the more powerfully can the Church affect him and complete the personality to which she can raise him.... The more unreservedly I live in the Church, the more completely I shall become that which I ought to be" (*VSK*, 35 [49]).

But how does an individual come to see the Church as the living presupposition of his personal existence? How does he come to knowledge of that deep solidarity between his personal being and the Church? In 1922 Guardini wrote in the opening sentence of *Vom Sinn der Kirche*: "A religious process of incalculable importance has begun—the Church is coming to life in the souls of men." What did Guardini mean here? I think he meant that the Church was now being recognized and experienced as an interior reality, alive within us, rather than some sort of largely external institution, leaving the individual cold and arousing no response in his heart. The then Joseph Ratzinger, now Pope Benedict XVI, whose reflections on Guardini's phrase I just summarized, continues by saying: "Whereas until then the Church had been viewed mainly as a structure and an organization, now it dawned on Catholics: We ourselves are the Church; she is more than an organization, she is an organism of the Holy Spirit, a living thing that encompasses all of us from within. This new awareness of Church found verbal expression in the term 'Mystical Body of Christ'. In this formulae is expressed a new and liberating experience of the Church."[17] Elsewhere Guardini writes, "That stupendous Fact that is the Church is once more becoming a living reality" (*VSK*, 14 [26]).

Sadly, however, we must agree with Cardinal Kasper who writes: "Today we are unfortunately bound to say that in the souls of many believers the church is dying. These believers still probably live *in* the church, but they are less and less *living the church* and its faith."[18] And yet, I would argue that we should see this reality as an opportunity to respond to the late John Paul II's call for the new evangelization, calling men to conversion, repentance, and the forgiveness of sin, to faith, to respond to the Gospel of Jesus Christ. In particular, we should see this reality as an opportunity to give an answer to the question, "Why the Church?" Or as Guardini puts it, "what is the Church's significance for the personal being and life of the man who makes his membership a living reality, for whom the Church is his very life" (*VSK*, 21 [33])?

We have been talking about the Church but we have yet to set out the main lines of Guardini's ecclesiology. What is the Church, then, according to Guardini? The redemptive purpose of the Kingdom (basileia) of God, as far as humanity is concerned, is the Church (ekklesia). "She is the Kingdom of God in mankind. . . . The Church is the human community reborn into God's Kingdom" (VSK, 21 [33]).[19] In short, the Church, according to Guardini, is the new and reborn humanity in Christ, a universal community centered on him, who is the Head of that regenerated human race, which is his Body. The Church as a living reality is a dynamic unity of contrasts, not contradictions, says Guardini, possessing subjective and supra-personal objective sides, which are differentiated from each other, but which require each other. Guardini insists on unity-simultaneous-with-distinctness in his understanding of the Church.

> The Church is the supra-personal, objective aspect of the Kingdom of God—although of course she consists of individual persons. The Kingdom of God, however, has a subjective side as well. That is the individual soul, as God's grace takes possession of it in that private and unique individuality by which it exists for itself. The Church embraces a man as he reaches out beyond himself to his

---

17. Ratzinger, "Ecclesiology of the Second Vatican Council," 13–14.
18. Kasper, "Church as the Place of Truth," 141.
19. Later in this chapter I'll address the question of the relationship between the Kingdom of God and the Church. For now, it is clear that Guardini understands the Church, the Body of Christ, to be the soteriological goal of the Kingdom.

fellows, capable and desirous of forming in conjunction with them a community of which he and they are members. The individual personality, however, is also based upon itself, like a globe which revolves around its own axis. And, as such, also, God's grace takes possession of it (VSK, 22–23 [35–36]).

Significantly, Guardini emphasizes that the subjective and the objective sides of the Church are contrasts in a unity, not separable from each other, but two aspects of the same fundamental mystery of grace that is the Kingdom of God as the Church. This emphasis is motivated by his need to avoid any individualistic misreading of his ecclesiology: "By this I do not mean that there exists in human beings a sphere which lies outside the Church. That would be too superficial a notion. It is truer to say that the whole man is in the Church, with all that he is. Even in his most individual aspect he is her member, although only in so far as this individuality and its powers are directed to the community. His whole being belongs to it; it is in its social reference—his individuality as related to his fellows and incorporated in the community. But the same individuality has an opposite pole. His powers are also directed inwards to build up a world in which he is alone with himself. In this aspect also he is the subject of God's grace. For God is the God of mankind as a whole. As such He is concerned with the supra-personal, the community, and its members jointly find in Him the social Deity of which human society has need. But He is also the God of each individual. This is indeed the supreme and fullest revelation of His life—that for each individual He is 'his God.'" In sum, "There is only one Kingdom of God; only one divine possession of man by the Father, in Christ, through the Holy Ghost. But it develops along the two fundamental lines of organic development. And it manifests itself in accordance with the two fundamental modes of human nature—in man as he is self-contained and asserts himself as an individual, and in man as he merges in the community which transcends his individuality" (VSK, 23–25 [36–38]).

Guardini's view of the Church as a unity of opposites[20] rises above the dilemma of individualism versus universalism. Both views are wrong, says Guardini, because individuals and social communities exist in a mu-

---

20. Guardini insists that the relationship between the subjective and objective, the personal and the supra-personal, is "not a contradiction, but a contrast." It is "a unity of contrasts which are differentiated from each other, yet postulate each other" (*VSK*, 24, note 1 [36, note 1]).

tual correlation in which neither can exist without the other: neither is basic to the other because neither was ever the source of the other.[21]

On the one hand, the supra-personal life of the community that is the Church cannot be individualistically constructed out of elementary interrelations between human individuals, which is the chief claim of individualism. On the other hand, the community does not allow of an opposition of the individual's own experience and action to that of the others; for the community is the living presupposition of his own personal existence, the essential path to his own perfection. "The Church then is a society essentially bound up with individual personality; and the individual life of the Christian is of its very nature related to the community. Both together are required for the perfect realization of the Kingdom of God" (VSK, 28 [401]).

The critical point in any Christian view of the Church is the question what position is to be ascribed to the Church as an organized institution. As Dutch neo-Calvinist theologian Herman Bavinck puts it, "To say that Christ has founded a church without any organization, government, or power is a statement that arises from principles characteristic of philosophical mysticism but takes no account of the teaching of Scripture, nor of the realities of life."[22] Similarly, Guardini rejects the view that has its roots in modern subjectivism and individualism, a view, as Monsignor Luigi Giussani describes it, which sees the Church "lived *exclusively* as an interior, personal, and intimate interpretation of God."[23] As Guardini says, this is a view in which "men speak of the Church, saying that she is not an objective reality, having an unmistakable form in history, but [rather] that she is something purely interior, a relationship between those who believe in Christ." He continues describing the view that he opposes because it pits the Church as an interior reality of communion with Christ—"I need no visible institution. Christ knows me and I know him. That is sufficient."[24]—against the Church as an organized institution: "They maintain that Jesus never thought of a Church in the sense of an objectively historical realization and structure, of authority, office and regulation; that He desired [instead] a communion of the redeemed,

---

21. Clouser, *Myth of Religious Neutrality*, 282.
22. Bavinck, *GD* IV, 393 [412].
23. Monsignor Giussani, *Why the Church?*, 73.
24. Guardini, *Church of the Lord*, 88.

but one that would continually grow through the breath of the Spirit, the opening of men's hearts, and the realization of the brotherhood of man and the universal fatherhood of God, and which would exist in reality insofar as this experience was realized."[25] Of course the Church is more than an organized institution, as Guardini understands it; it is first and foremost a Mystical Communion with the living Christ, but also a Sacrament, a Herald of the Gospel, and a Servant.[26] "There is a community of spirit and spiritual life—the mystical Body of Christ. Through Baptism the individual is born into, into new, supernatural life common to all live by it" (*VSK*, 80 [99]).

Still, it is beyond doubt that the visible Church, the bodily, historical, organized institution, in its inner nature, is *not* to be viewed apart from the *corpus Christi mysticum*, the Church as Mystery, but also Rock[27], says Guardini, Sacrament, Body of Christ, and People of God, which is the radical communion of reborn humanity in Jesus Christ. "The Church is a 'mystery' because," says Guardini, "in her essential nature, she did not arise out of psychology or sociology or any historical necessity, but was founded by Christ and born through the descent of the Holy Spirit. She is permeated by all that we term the world and history, but in her essence she lives by the Cross of Christ and the action of the Spirit. She proclaims the truth of the Holy God, which leads man to salvation but 'passes all understanding' [Phil.4:7]."[28]

The Church in its transcendent religious sense is the religious root of the human race. According to Dooyeweerd, this religious root "disclosed the transcendent bond of unity of the latter [human race] in the creation, the fall into sin, and redemption by Jesus Christ, the Head of the reborn

---

25. Ibid.

26. On these aspects of the one Church, see Cardinal Dulles, SJ, *Models of the Church*, chapters 2–6.

27. Guardini, *Church of the Lord*, 10–11: "The Church is a 'rock' because Christ willed it so (Matt 16:18). She is not the effect of experiences, changing as these change, nor is she the expression of psychological needs and cultural situations at any given time. Rather, over against all which is merely subjective, she is the objective message from God. In spite of all her relations to the times, she is firm and unshakeable in her distinction between truth and error. She despises neither history nor the individual, but respects man and his conscience. For only truth and the demands for truth imply genuine reverence, whereas permissiveness and carelessness constitute weakness, which does not dare to expect of man the recognition of the majesty of the self-revealing God. Indeed, these are fundamentally a contempt for man whose dignity consists in the very fact that he exists by truth."

28. Ibid., 10.

human race, who in the mystery of the Incarnation is truly God and truly man" (*NC*, III, 214; italics added; *WdW*, III, 147). Now, before turning to consider Fr. Guardini's answer to the question—Why the Church?—in the next section of this chapter, I shall examine Dooyeweerd's valuable critique of Ernst Troeltsch's two sociological types, which the latter calls sect and Church-institution types. There are three reasons for taking up Dooyeweerd's critique: first, I think it deepens Guardini's criticism of the dilemma of individualism or universalism, and how the understanding of the Church as the religious root of the human race rises above that dilemma; second, Dooyeweerd has a sophisticated theory of institutions that strengthens, I believe, Guardini's account of the relationship between Church and society; and third, enacting a conversation between Dooyeweerd and Guardini is not only fascinating but is also a valuable exercise in ecumenical theology. Dooyeweerd charges the Catholic tradition's view of the Church with universalism.[29] Universalism is the view according to which an institutional totality such as the state or the church is everything; it is an all-inclusive whole, incorporating all types of societal relationships as its parts. In response, I shall show the weakness of Dooyeweerd's own ecclesiology as well as rebut that charge of universalism.

THE INSTITUTIONAL CHURCH-TYPE AND THE SECT-TYPE

At the start of this chapter, I explained that the German social theorist, Ernst Troeltsch argues that two independent sociological types, which he calls sect and church types, are inherent to the religious sociological basic scheme of Christianity. According to Troeltsch, Christianity is caught in the dilemma of individualism or universalism. In the previous section, I developed the main outline of Romano Guardini's response to this

---

29. In the revised edition (*NC*, 1955) of Dooyeweerd's *WdW* (1936), he argues that "Troeltsch's church-type is nothing but a scientifically untenable generalization of a typical Roman Catholic social form." "It is impossible that such an ideal type can do justice to the different Church-formations issued from the Reformation," adds Dooyeweerd, "*let alone that it should be able to account for all facets of the modern Roman Catholic view of the Church*" (*NC*, III, 531; italics added). This qualification regarding Roman Catholic ecclesiology was absent twenty-years earlier. Unfortunately, Dooyeweerd doesn't say what those facets of the modern Roman Catholic view of the Church might be, nor does this qualification temper his judgment about Roman Catholic ecclesiology. Thus, he sticks to his 1936 charge that Catholic ecclesiology is universalist and hence doesn't rise above the dilemma of individualism versus universalism. I refute this charge in this chapter.

charge. I now want to turn to another Christian critic of Troeltsch, the Dutch neo-Calvinist philosopher Herman Dooyeweerd.

TROELTSCH'S METHODOLOGY

In the first place, Dooyeweerd criticizes Troeltsch's methodology of "ideal type," which the latter appropriated from Max Weber and used throughout his study on the social teachings of Christianity. According to Weber's definition, "an ideal type is formed by the one-sided *accentuation* of one or more points of view" according to which "*concrete individual* phenomena . . . are arranged into a unified analytical construct" (*Gedankenbild*); in its purely fictional nature, it is a methodological "utopia [that] cannot be found empirically anywhere in reality."[30] Those analytical constructs, such as "sect-type" and "Church-type," are "ideal types"—as Dooyeweerd says, "a relatively arbitrary construction of the human mind"—but, as generalizing concepts, they nevertheless attempt to explain tendencies, trends or traits of the concrete history of different social relationships. And although Dooyeweerd doesn't deny the explanatory value of Troeltsch's use of this methodology,[31] he rejects this typological method as such because it presupposes a historicist view of temporal reality. In other words, historicism denies in principle that the different types of modern social relationships such as marriage, family, State, and Church, "are founded in constant structural principles [of the order of creation] which determine their inner nature." "From the absolutized historical viewpoint it [Troeltsch's methodology] can discover nothing but individual transitory cultural phenomena involved in a continuous change and development" (*NC*, III, 82). This makes Troeltsch's method unacceptable, because, given

---

30. Weber, "Objectivity in Social Science and Social Policy," 90. Lonergan gives a helpful definition of "ideal-type": "The ideal-type, then, is not a description of reality or a hypothesis about reality. It is a theoretical construct in which possible events are intelligibly related to constitute an internally coherent system. Its utility is both heuristic and expository, that is, it can be useful inasmuch as its suggests and helps formulates hypotheses and, again, when a concrete situation approximates to the theoretical construct, it can guide an analysis of the situation and promote a clear understanding of it" (*Method in Theology*, 27).

31. Indeed, notwithstanding Dooyeweerd's appreciation that "Christian thought brought a real gain to the philosophy of human society by contributing new and permanent ideas, he writes: "With Troeltsch, we must frankly admit that the Christian theory of society, as it developed in the High Middle Ages, in a more or less closed form, must not be viewed as more Christian than it really was" (*WdW*, III, 149 [216]).

that those "ideal types" are "mere subjective schemes of thought," they are unable to get at the "internal individuality-structures of the communities concerned" (*WdW*, III, 475 [530]).[32] That is so because Troeltsch is not only a historicist, but also an "anti-realist" about social forms, that is, he is against the idea that social forms like the church, marriage and family, the state, are grounded in a normative creation order.

Dooyeweerd, by contrast, is a social realist who regards communities to be as real as individuals. This, too, is the view of Romano Guardini who, we recall, took the community to be just as primary a fact as individual existence. Thus, to be a social realist means you hold that organized institutional communities such as the state, the Church, and natural communities such as marriage and family, are real social wholes, real in themselves, having their own nature or essence and ends, given a normative creation order. Consequently, such communities are not just "fictitious entities," as individualism would have it, constructed by either a contract between self-contained individuals or from "a complex of elementary forms of social interaction, and synthesized by human consciousness to a unity" (*WdW*, III, 174 [239]).

SOCIAL REALISM

The social realist thinks that social communities are to be considered real in an ontological sense. Given Dooyeweerd's social realism, as I have just defined it, he understands a "community" to be a durable social unit. Dooyeweerd writes: a community is a "more or less durable societal relationship which has the character of a whole joining its members into a social unity, irrespective of the degree of intensity of the communal bond." The Church is such a community. Furthermore, he distinguishes "inter-individual or inter-communal relationships," by which he means relationships "in which individual persons or communities function in coordination without being united in a solidary whole" (*NC*, III, 177). And of course, within the Church there are inter-individual relationships,

---

32. Dooyeweerd writes, "Thus the inner nature of the temporal Church-institution is replaced by a schematic subjective 'ideal type'. Such a type is thought to be derivable from a particular moment of the 'religious-sociological basic scheme' of the historical phenomenon 'Christianity', and its rational subjective effects in historical development. The 'ideal type' is then imposed on the phenomena as *the* church-type and used to interpret all real church-formations as historically determined nuances of one and the same basic sociological schema" (Ibid.).

even deep friendships, among the members of the Church community; also, the Church as a community relates to other communities like the family, the state, schools, businesses, charitable organizations, and so forth.

Moreover, Dooyeweerd distinguishes "organized communities" and "natural communities." "If a community is typically founded in a historical power-formation which is organized, we speak of an *organized community*." He adds: "The organization provides a community that lacks a natural foundation with a more or less continuous existence, whereby it becomes independent of the duration of life of its individual members." The Church is an organized community because it is historically founded—"The whole temporal Church-institution is founded in the historical power of Christ as the Incarnate Word. . . . This typical historical foundation of the institutional *ecclesia visibilis* explains why it is not *of all times*. . . . [Thus] as an *actual formation* the Church-institution could only appear after Christ's Incarnation, death and resurrection" (*WdW*, III, 485 [539]).[33] Indeed, adds Dooyeweerd, "Christ himself gave this historical power its first provisional organization in the institution of the apostolic office and the sacraments: 'Therefore go and make disciples of all nations, baptizing them in the name of the Father and of the Son and of the Holy Spirit' [Matt 28:19]. By his Word through the mouth of his apostles He has ordained the basic structure of the institutional Church-organization" (*WdW*, III, 482–482 [537]).

"Unorganized communities, on the other hand, have a *typical biotic foundation*. They are *natural communities*; and since they lack a typical historical foundation they are to be found at all times, though they may show very different social forms" (*NC*, III, 178–179). These communities are not simply the free creation of human planning and formation. Marriage and the family are prime examples of natural communities. Finally, he refers to "institutional communities," meaning thereby both natural and organized communities "which by their inner nature are destined to encompass their members to an intensive degree, continuously

---

33. Ibid., "In the Old Testament there was a people of the Covenant, isolated from the other nations. In this people of the Covenant, kingship, priesthood and the prophet's office were sharply distinguished from each other and foreshadowed Christ's kingship, priesthood and prophetic office. There was already an "*ecclesia visibilis*" as the temporal manifestation of the "*ecclesia invisibilis electorum*," but there was no *institutional Church* as a typical societal institution of regenerating grace in the community of Christian faith."

or at least for a considerable part of their life, and in such a way independent of their will" (*NC,* III, 187). Thus, paring down the significance of Dooyeweerd distinctions for our purpose here, we might say that the visible Church, according to Dooyeweerd, is an organized, institutional community. Of course, Dooyeweerd's view of the Church is not one-sidedly institutionalist, meaning thereby "a system in which the institutional element is treated as primary."[34] "It is beyond doubt that the latter, in its inner nature," says Dooyeweerd, "is not to be viewed apart from the *corpus Christi* in its transcendent religious sense as the radical communion of reborn mankind in Jesus Christ" (*WdW,* III, 148 [215]).

This social realism, along with an understanding of the Church as an organized, institutional community, is also Guardini's view of St. Paul's teaching in the New Testament. According to Guardini, St. Paul uses a concept employed by ancient law to describe the state, namely, the concept of the *corpus*. This concept refers to "the objective, organic unity, in which the individuals are the members, a unity that does not depend upon the will or the experience of the individual but subsists objectively in itself." With the help of this concept he constructed the idea of the *soma Christou,* the Church as the body of Christ (1 Cor 12:12ff). Guardini continues, "She is that great unity in which every individual is a member, and Christ is the head. This unity exists really and objectively in itself, founded and constituted, resting upon the apostles and their successors, expressing itself in valid doctrine, binding regulations and liturgical acts." And in an explicit turn against what Troeltsch called "sect-type," which Guardini, and also Dooyeweerd, do not actually regard as a Church, he adds, "[t]he term for it is not 'gathering' or 'congregation', as modern individualism translates the Greek word *ekklesia,* but 'Church'. In every congregation the Church is present, but she herself and as such is more than the community of kindred souls meeting here and now, unless we give the word 'congregation' a meaning which transcends the ordinary one and take it to signify the union of all baptized believers, founded by Christ and constituted in the apostles. But this would be only a difference in terminology."[35]

---

34. Dulles, *Models of the Church,* 35.
35. Guardini, *Church of the Lord,* 88–89.

What is, then, the explanatory import of these distinctions for rising above the dilemma of individualism or universalism, according to Dooyeweerd?

> While sociological universalism is to be understood as an overestimation of the communal relationships, the absolutization of the inter-individual relationships is characteristic of the individualist view of human society. The latter will always seeks to construe society from its supposed "elements," *i.e.*, from elementary interrelations between human individuals. From this standpoint the reality of communities (especially of organized communities) as societal unities is generally denied. The latter are only considered as fictitious entities resulting from subjective synthesis of manifold inter-individual relations in human consciousness. . . . As soon as it is attempted to construe a community from elementary relations between individuals, the whole dissolves itself into a plurality of elements and its structural principle is lost to sight (*NC*, III, 182–183).

For Dooyeweerd, as well as for Guardini, individuals and social communities exist in a mutual correlation in which neither can exist without the other: neither is basic to the other because neither was ever the source of the other. Against this background, I can now turn to analyze Dooyeweerd's critique of Troeltsch's basic sociological types, church-type and sect-type; the former corresponds to universalism and the latter to individualism.

CHURCH-INSTITUTE TYPE

Dooyeweerd's description of Troeltsch's first sociological type, the Church-type, is worth quoting in full.

> As an organized community the Church is a supra-individual institution ("*Anstalt*"), an organized permanent institution of grace and redemption. One becomes a member of this community at birth, and is immediately in the circle of its sacramental miraculous power ("*Wunderkreis*") at baptism. The official organization remains the bearer of the treasure of grace, independently of accidental personal unworthiness on the part of the office-bearers. These institutional traits make it possible to compromise with the existing "worldly ordinances"; for notwithstanding all the faults and defects of the persons, the sacred character and the divine nature of the institution remain unaltered. Through its inherent

miracle-working power the Church will conquer the world according to the divine promise. The Roman Catholic hierarchical institution is the purest embodiment of this type, which naturally implies the universalistic ideal to subject all existing secular temporal societal relationships to its own authority. These relationships are incorporated into the Church as a lower, previous stage of the Christian community of grace. But now it is necessary to relativize the absolute evangelical standards. For this purpose the latter are combined with the Stoic and Aristotelian conceptions of the *lex naturalis*. So Troeltsch's theoretical church-type is the incarnation of the universalistic synthesis between the "supra-natural Christian religion of grace" and the "natural" societal order.... Sociologically the church-type in some form or other always aims at an "ecclesiastically cultural unity." In this culture the institutional Church takes the charge of the whole of "natural" society, both in its political and non-political structures. This sociological type is considered to be the necessary consequence of the universalistic factor in the sociological basic scheme of Christianity, which aims at conquering and renewing the world. . . . In this universalistic conception the Church-institution is absolutized to the perfect Christian society (*WdW*, III, 472–473, and 453 [528, 511] italics added).

The meaning of this lengthy passage requires unpacking. Troeltsch is making several points here, according to Dooyeweerd's description of the basic sociological type, church-institution. He largely agrees with Troeltsch, despite his strong objection that this type is an unscientific generalization elevating the Roman Catholic conception of the Church to the model of the Church-institute, and hence this type is unable to get at the internal structural principle of that institute.

In the first place, the notion of the Church in this type is strongly, even exclusively, institutionalist, according to Dooyeweerd. Let us call this concept of the Church "institutionalism," following Avery Cardinal Dulles, meaning thereby "a system in which the institutional element is treated as primary."[36] A corollary of this institutionalism is the idea that the Church is essentially a society—"a 'perfect society' in the sense that it is subordinate to no other and lacks nothing required for its own institutional completeness."[37] He charges Catholic ecclesiology with universalism because it, says Dooyeweerd, identifies the institutional Church with

---

36. Dulles, *Models of the Church*, 35.
37. Ibid., 34.

the visible body of Christ. This universalistic conception of the Church institution is the erroneous starting point of the Catholic theory of society, alleges Dooyeweerd and, before him, Bavinck.[38] Several points must be made here.

(1) Dooyeweerd distinguishes the Church as the Kingdom of Christ in the hearts of men, of the members of a new and reborn mankind, that is, the Church in its central religious sense as the "body of Christ," from the temporal Church-institute, and he thinks that the Catholic tradition is reductionistic because it identifies, he alleges, the Church exclusively with its institutional elements.[39] Bavinck also objects in a more articulate way about the equation of the Church of Jesus Christ with the Roman Catholic Church as institution: "For since Christ imparts all grace only by means of the office and sacraments of the church, the teaching church, the Roman Catholic Church as institution, is the only mediatrix of salvation, the custodian and distributor of all grace to all people, the only ark of salvation for all humanity."[40] But, Bavinck adds, "One can only give a good definition of the church if one guards against equating the gathering of believers with its organization as an institution."[41] Why? Pared down for my purpose here, Bavinck's objection amounts to this: with the Catholic emphasis on the hierarchical structures of the Church, and in consequence with the "teaching church" (*ecclesia docens*), the laity, the so-called "listening church" (*ecclesia audiens*), according to Bavinck, is completely dependent, passive, an accident,[42] almost an appendix of the Church, with the highest virtue of the laity being, in consequence, "belief in what the church believes, obedience to the hierarchy, and submission to the pope." The prime result is clericalism. This means the loss not only of the "laity *as a people*,"[43] but also of the whole Church "as being under

---

38. Bavinck, "Catholicity of Christianity and the Church," especially 228–42. See also, *GD* IV, 267–69, 290 [284–86, 304]. Bavinck's contemporary, Abraham Kuyper, makes the same objection as Bavinck, namely, that Rome "wholly identified the visible Church with the Church as an institution," in Vol. II, *Encyclopaedie der Heilige Godgeleerdheid*, 345–346 (ET: 391–92).

39. See Dooyeweerd, *WdW*, III, 453 [216–17, passim].

40. *GD* IV, 268 [285].

41. *GD* IV, 290 [304].

42. I say "accident" because Bavinck claims that the "'teaching church', the objective institution of salvation, would still remain the true church even if all its members were unbelievers and ungodly people" (*GD* IV, 269 [285]).

43. Taylor, "Clericalism," 169.

the Word, and in living subjection to the gracious authority of her Lord, in communion with Christ."[44]

There is some truth in Dooyeweerd's and Bavinck's point. As Avery Cardinal Dulles notes, "Catholic theology in the Patristic period and in the Middle Ages, down through the great scholastic doctors of the thirteenth century, was relatively free of institutionalism. The strongly institutionalist development occurred in the late Middle Ages and the Counter Reformation, when theologians and canonists, responding to attacks on the papacy and hierarchy, accented precisely those features that the adversaries were denying."[45] Notwithstanding that point, Dooyeweerd's and Bavinck's overemphasis on the institutional in the Catholic notion of the Church overlooks, as Dulles adds, that "the institutional model of the Church has rarely been advocated in its purity." "Even the schema of Vatican I and the encyclicals of Leo XIII and Pius XII," Dulles explains, "for all their insistence on the Church as a 'perfect society', never identified the society exclusively with its institutional elements. They tempered the institutional with more spiritual and organic conceptions, such as those of the communion of grace or the Body of Christ."[46] In this connection, consider, for instance, Leo XIII who in his 1896 Encyclical Letter, *Satis Cognitum*, wrote: "The Church is so often called in Holy Writ a *body*, and even the *body of Christ*—'Now you are the body of Christ' (1 Cor 12:27)—and precisely because it is a body is the Church visible: and because it is the body of Christ is it living and energizing, because by the infusion of His power Christ guards and sustains it, just as the vine gives nourishment and renders fruitful the branches united to it."[47]

Indeed, adds Dulles, "After a period of strong institutionalism in ecclesiology, the theology of the Church as Mystical Body began to revive in the middle of the nineteenth century. In the early twentieth century ecclesiology was revitalized by a return to biblical and patristic sources."[48] Similarly, we find Romano Guardini, in 1922, already arguing that the Church is not primarily, and certainly not, exclusively, an institution.

---

44. Berkouwer, *Conflict met Rome* 40. ET: *The Conflict with Rome*, 29. I cite Berkouwer in this context to show that Bavinck's criticism against Roman Catholics (made fifty years earlier than Berkouwer's) has been made time and again by the Dutch neo-Calvinists.

45. Dulles, *Models of the Church*, 36.

46. Ibid., 45–46.

47. Leo XIII, *Satis Cognitum*, no. 3.

48. Dulles, *Models of the Church*, 51–52.

Indeed, he regards the notion of the Church as a "perfect society" to be deficient, because the Church is viewed largely as a structure and organization, in comparison with her being understood and experienced as an interior reality. "It is that which is expressed by St. Paul's concept of the *corpus Christi mysticum* [mystical body of Christ], of which the individual is a member, or, as we would say in modern parlance, of which every believer is a cell (1 Cor 12:12). The individual felt that he lived by the Church, that the Church lived in him, that between her and him there existed a relationship like that between a living part of the organism and the whole. Every believer stood in this relationship and so lived in a communion which was more intimate and rich than that which had been expressed by the ecclesiastical concept of membership in the 'perfect society.'"[49] Dooyeweerd charged Troeltsch with the defect of not taking into account all "facets of the modern Roman Catholic view of the Church" (*NC,* III, 531), but it seems that Dooyeweerd himself suffers from the same defect.

As far as Bavinck's specific objection is concerned, he has a real point that needs attending to even if only briefly here.[50] I agree with Berkouwer who wrote sixty years ago that the authoritative foundation of the Church's teaching "is found in the living actuality of true faith according to the Scripture, in subjection of the hearts to the Lord of the church, and by ceaseless prayer and listening to his Word."[51] In this light, we must say that the obedience of the Church is not a responsibility that the laity alone possesses in respect of the hierarchy. Rather, such obedience is a responsibility that the Church as a whole—hierarchy, laity, and religious—possess with respect to the Word of God, and as such then it is prior to the differentiation of the Church into a teaching and listening part. As Hans Urs von Balthasar puts it: "Ecclesial obedience is in its origin and in truth the obedience of the Church to her Lord; this is why thinking with the Church [*sentire cum Ecclesia*] means feeling in oneself this obedience of the Church." That is, "the more the individual himself, especially the layman, takes on ecclesial responsibility, the more deeply he feels with the Church, indeed, on an ever deeper level, he feels himself *to*

---

49. Guardini, *Church of the Lord,* 5.

50. I briefly address the question of authority in this paragraph, but Bavinck's point also has implications for a theology of the laity, which I also address briefly below.

51. Berkouwer, *Conflict met Rome,* 40 [29].

be the Church."[52] Furthermore, Balthasar adds, "the hierarchical Church . . . can receive the commission to guide her members only out of her own submission to the Lord and Spirit who guides her, and the only way for her to carry out this charge is to mediate this spirit of service to her members."[53]

(2) Dooyeweerd distinguishes the Church as "institution" and the Church as "visible body of Christ," and he criticizes Catholic ecclesiology for identifying the institutional Church with the visible body of Christ. This distinction is not the same as the theological distinction between the Church as the Kingdom of Christ in the hearts of men, of the members of a new and reborn mankind, that is, the Church in its central religious sense as the "body of Christ," and the temporal Church-institute. Rather, in Dooyeweerd's view both "institution" and "visible body of Christ" are *visible* entities. Bavinck makes the same point in distinguishing the Church as "institute" and the Church as "organism." Says Bavinck, "For both 'institution' and 'organism' describe the church in terms of its visible aspect." Of course neither Dooyeweerd nor Bavinck deny that the visible manifestations of the church as institute and organism in the visible realm "have an invisible spiritual background." "For office and gift, the administration of the Word and the sacraments, brotherly love and communion of the saints," adds Bavinck, "are all grounded in the operations of the glorified head of the church through the Holy Spirit."[54]

Significantly, although they use different terms, Dooyeweerd speaking of the visible body of Christ (only one of its manifestations being the institutional church) and Bavinck of the church as organism, both of them regard these terms as the broader category. This is so, they claim, because the visible body of Christ, or church as organism, manifests itself in *all*

---

52. Balthasar, *Razing the Bastions*, 94, 93.

53. Ibid., 95, 94. Vatican II says in *Dei Verbum*, the Dogmatic Constitution on Revelation, some important things regarding the submission of the Magisterium (teaching office) to the Word of the Lord: "The task of giving an authentic interpretation of the Word of God, whether in its written form or in the form of Tradition, has been entrusted to the living teaching office of the Church alone. Its authority in this matter is exercised in the name of Jesus Christ. *Yet this Magisterium is not superior to the Word of God, but is its servant.* It teaches only what had been handed on to it. At the divine command and with the help of the Holy Spirit, it listens to this devotedly, guards it with dedication and expounds it faithfully. All that it proposes for belief as being divinely revealed is drawn from this single deposit of faith" (no. 11; italics added).

54. *GD* IV, 290 [305].

societal relationships of which the "Church institution" is only one. "It is evident that the '*ecclesia visibilis*' in this universal sense cannot be identical with the temporal Church institution.... The temporal revelation of the '*corpus Christi*', in its broadest sense ... embraces all the societal structures of our temporal human existence."⁵⁵ Consequently, given that the "visible body of Christ" is not limited to the Church as "institution," because the former embraces all structures of human society, according to Dooyeweerd, then all temporal societal structures are *equivalent* to one another in light of the Church in its central religious sense as the "Body of Christ." Still, inconsistently, Dooyeweerd wants to acknowledge "the completely exceptional position of the institutional Church as a particular [mediator] of regenerating grace." Indeed, he adds, laying "full emphasis on the thought that in its institutional manifestation the Church is the *mother* of our faith in Christ Jesus. In truth: The light of eternity will always glow in the sanctuary of this particular Christian community" (*WdW*, III, 470 [525]).

Now, with all due respect to Dooyeweerd, it is not at all "evident" that we must distinguish between "Church institution" and "visible body of Christ." In the New Testament, the institutional Church *is* the visible body of Christ. As Reformed theologian John Frame rightly argues:

> [W]e must question the legitimacy of the above distinction between church institute and visible body of Christ. We do not find it in Scripture. Ephesians 4 speaks of the "body" and explains that that body grows through the gifts which God has given to each member. At the head of this list of gifts are "apostles," prophets," "evangelists," "pastors and teachers." These are the men whom God has appointed "for the perfecting of the saints unto the work of ministering, unto the building up of the body of Christ" (vs. 12). In this passage, the apostles, prophets, evangelists and pastor-teachers are the leaders and edifiers, not merely of the "church-institution," but of the "body of Christ" itself. This passage knows of no distinction between the two.⁵⁶

---

55. That Bavinck agrees with this broader understanding is implied in his description of the church as organism and the claim that the church is still visible outside the institution, its offices and ministries, the Word and sacraments, and church government: "For every believer manifests his or her faith in witness and walk in every sphere of life, and all believers together, together with their faith and lives, distinguish themselves from the world" (*GD* IV, 290 [305]).

56. Frame, *Amsterdam Philosophy*. See also, Douma, *Kritische Aaantekeningen bij de Wijsbegeerte der Wetsidee*. ET: *Another Look at Dooyeweerd*.

(3) Of course, even if one rejects Dooyeweerd's distinction between church as institute and the visible body of Christ that does not deny that other institutions such as the Christian family, school, business, and voluntary associations such as the Knights of Columbus and the Fellowship of Catholic Scholars, and others, are legitimate and important signs and manifestations of the Kingdom of God. Christians who are "one in Christ" will demonstrate the truth and love of the Gospel in *all* areas of life and that is, indeed, because "Christ is Lord." This is the important truth behind Dooyeweerd's distinction.

However, the question still remains whether insisting on the manifestation of the Kingdom of God in all areas of life makes the school, family, or business into visible forms of the body of Christ coordinate with the institutional Church? The answer must be negative. Dooyeweerd has put us before a false dilemma: either a universalist conception of the Church-institute or all temporal societal structures, including the Church-institute, are equivalent to one another.[57] We can avoid the horns of this dilemma by rejecting the parity between the institutional Church and all other societal structures. The institutional Church *is* the visible body of Christ, the bride of Christ, and she has received her central place in world history "from Christ, as the true and the only King of the Church" (*WdW*, III, 484 [538]). Indeed, the Church is the concentration point of the Kingdom of God because, as Dooyeweerd himself says, the "whole temporal Church-institution is founded in the historical power of Christ as the Incarnate Word" (*WdW*, III, 482 [537]). "Its historical task," he adds, "revealed by Christ himself, is to gain the spiritual dominion over all nations and peoples" (*WdW*, III, 482 [537]). We cannot measure then the "completely exceptional position of the institutional church," as Dooyeweerd suggests only with respect to its "*temporal* value" (*WdW*,

---

57. Douma, *Kritische Aaantekeningen bij de Wijsbegeerte der Wetsidee*, 22. Douma argues against Dooyeweerd's view that it is "very difficult to class the Church within a series of structures of equal value" once we consider "what the Scriptures say about the Church." He adds, "The Church gathers the believers in Christ's name. She is the mother of the believers and bears children for Christ. She is 'the pillar and bulwark of the truth' [1 Titus 3:15]. To her the Words of eternal life are entrusted. She has the testimony of Jesus Christ. She also has the mandate to make use of the keys of the kingdom of heaven. All this [does not apply] to everything which bears the stamp of 'Christian'—a Christian school, a Christian philosophy, or a Christian political party. It applies to the one, holy, universal Christian Church, which is being gathered in this world by Word and Spirit, using office-bearers, worship services, sacraments and many other concrete instruments" (20 [16]).

III, 481 [535]). For the institutional Church occupies a "position between time and eternity" (*WdW*, III, 482 [537]). "The Church's historical world-dominion," and hence its singularly unique position as the *concentration point* of the Kingdom of God, adds Dooyeweerd, "is radically distinguished from any other meta-historically qualified organization of power. Its sole qualification is the unshakeable power of Christ's Word and Spirit" (*WdW*, III, 482 [537]). In short, we avoid the universalist conception of the Church, because all of life is not ecclesiastically controlled. Still, that Church, which is invested by Christ himself with his unshakable power and Spirit, has spiritual authority for the whole of life. That is why, as Father Guardini says, "[S]he truly is the One and the All" (*VSK*, 14 [26]).

(4) The institutional Church is the concentration point of the Kingdom, but we need to distinguish, not separate, the Kingship of Christ and the Church. The redemptive purpose of the Kingdom of God, as far as humanity is concerned, is the Church. As Aloys Grillmeier states in his commentary on Chapter 1 of Lumen Gentium:

> Those who are members of the Church of Christ are enabled to enter into the most intimate union with God and into a deeper fellowship with men, one not founded merely on the usual basis of human relationships but also on the unifying force of the self-communication of God in Christ and the Spirit. And here we can see at once an essential characteristic of the salvation bestowed in Christ. To enter the Church is to be accepted really, though for the present only initially and invisibly, into the eschatological family of the children of God, of which the centre is God and Christ, the unifying bond the Holy Spirit. *Since mankind has no other goal than this Church in which all is fulfilled*, the Council must bring out as clearly as possible the universal significance of this sign of salvation [italics added].[58]

But the italicized portion of the concluding sentence is true only when we are speaking of the Kingdom's redemptive goal for humanity. Yes, the Church is "the seed and beginning of that kingdom on earth," indeed; it is "the kingdom of Christ already present in mystery."[59] There are several points to make here. First, severing the Kingdom of God from its concentration point in the institutional Church has resulted in

---

58. Grillmeier, Dogmatic Constitution on the Church, Chapter 1, Mystery of the Church, 140.

59. *Lumen Gentium*, nos. 5, 3, respectively.

much contemporary theology in a reductive sense of the mission of that Kingdom, says John Paul II, "inasmuch as [ideas about salvation and mission] are focused on man's earthly needs." "In this view, the pope adds, "the Kingdom tends to become something completely human and secularized; what counts are programs and struggles for a liberation which is socio-economic, political and even cultural, but within a horizon that is closed to the transcendent. . . . Such a view easily translates into one more ideology of purely earthly progress."[60] There is a second point to make: the Kingdom of God is broader than the Church. It is the plan of God that is realized in and through Christ, encompassing the whole of creation. Indeed, as Guardini writes, "the purpose of Christ [is] to win reality, with all that the word implies, for the Kingdom of God" (VSK, 39 [54]). Herman Ridderbos explains, "[The Kingdom of God] has a much more comprehensive content. It represents the all-embracing perspective, it denotes the consummation of all history, brings both grace and judgment, has cosmic dimensions, [and] fills time and eternity."[61] In my view, and arguably the view of the Second Vatican Council, the Kingdom of God is not identical with the Church because the realization of that Kingdom is an enactment of the great divine work of redemption in its recapitulation—fulfillment and consummation—of all the fallen creation in Christ. "In a word," as John Paul II wrote, "the Kingdom of God is the manifestation and the realization of God's plan of salvation in all its fullness."[62] In all its fullness, I would say, refers to the restoration or renewal of creation "in the redemptive plan and in the redemptive power of Jesus Christ."[63] That this, too, is the teaching of the Council is clear from the following passages. For instance, regarding the vocation of the laity:

> But the laity, by their very vocation, seek the kingdom of God by engaging in temporal affairs and by ordering them according to

---

60. John Paul II, *Redemptoris Missio*, no. 17. Pope Benedict XVI makes the same point in his widely read, *Jesus of Nazareth*, 53–54: "A secularist reinterpretation of the idea has gained considerable ground, particularly, though not exclusively, in Catholic theology. . . . 'Kingdom,' on this interpretation, is simply the name for a world governed by peace, justice, and the conservation of creation. It means no more than this. This 'Kingdom' is said to be the goal of history that has to be attained. This is supposedly the real task of religions: to work together for the coming of the 'Kingdom.'"

61. Ridderbos, *Coming of the Kingdom*, 354.

62. John Paul II, *Redemptoris Missio*, no. 15.

63. Congar, OP, *Jesus Christ*, 176, but see also the entire chapter, The Lordship of Christ over the Church and the World, 167–219.

the plan of God.... They are called there by God so that by exercising their proper function and being led by the spirit of the gospel they can work for the sanctification of the world from within.... It is therefore his [layman] special task to illumine and organize [temporal] affairs in such a way that they may always start out, develop, and persist according to Christ's mind, to the praise of the Creator and the Redeemer.[64]

Furthermore, regarding the relation between Christ and culture:

The good news of Christ constantly renews the life and culture of fallen man. It combats and removes the errors and evils resulting from sinful allurements which are a perpetual threat. It never ceases to purify and elevate the morality of peoples. By riches coming from above, it makes fruitful, as it were from within, the spiritual qualities and gifts of every people and of every age. *It strengthens, perfects, and restores them in Christ. Thus by the very fulfillment of own mission the Church stimulates and advances the human and civic culture.*[65]

More generally, the Council makes crystal clear the cosmic significance of Christ in creation and redemption:

[T]he Church has a single intention: that God's kingdom may come, and that the salvation of the whole human race may come to pass. For every benefit which the People of God during its earthly pilgrimage can offer to the human family stems from the fact that the Church is "universal sacrament of salvation," simultaneously manifesting and exercising the mystery of God's love for man. For God's Word, by whom all things were made, was Himself made flesh so that as a perfect man He might save all men and sum up all things in Himself. The Lord is the goal of human history, the focal point of the longings of history and civilization, the center of the human race, the joy of every heart, and the answer to all its yearnings. He it is whom the Father raised from the dead, lifted on high, and stationed at His right hand, making Him judge of the living and the dead. Enlivened and united in His Spirit, we journey toward the consummation of human history, one which fully accords with the counsel of God's love: "To re-establish all

---

64. *Lumen Gentium*, no. 31, but see also no. 36. For a fuller development of the Church's teaching on the mission of the Laity, see *Apostolicam Actuositatem*. See also, the insightful 1881 essay of Herman Bavinck on the all-encompassing character of the Kingdom of God, "Het Rijk Gods, Het Hoogste Goed," 28–56.

65. *Gaudium et Spes*, no. 58; italics added.

things in Christ, both those in the heavens and those on the earth (Eph 1:10)."[66]

Returning to Dooyeweerd's description of Troeltsch's Church-institute type, his criticism of that type as universalistic also addresses the question of the authority of the Church in temporal matters.[67] Dooyeweerd criticizes this type because it implies that all societal relationships must be ecclesiastically controlled. In a nutshell, that is his criticism. Dooyeweerd writes elsewhere that the universalist conception of the Church is in this Troeltschian type described by analogies taken from political society, particularly the classical Greco-Roman view of the State as the perfect whole of human society inclusive of public religion. This gives the notion of the church-type a universalistic tendency to subject all existing temporal societal relationship to the Church's own authority. This universalistic conception of the Church institution gives "the temporal authority of the Church dominion over the souls of the believers, and . . . guarantee[s] the temporal Church the supremacy over the whole of societal life, including the temporal government" (*WdW*, III, 453 [511]). Thus, "The 'church-type' must necessarily have 'universalistic tendencies,' and strive after 'ecclesiastical unity of culture', under the leadership of grace" (*WdW*, III, 476 [531]).

We need to get some clarity on the authority of the institutional Church in temporal matters. I think we can reject the concrete historical ideal[68] of the old Christendom—the ecclesiastical unity of culture—without abandoning the thesis that the Church of Jesus Christ that subsists in the institutional Church has authority in all areas of human life. The question is, "What kind of authority does the Church have?" In replying to Dooyeweerd, then, I want to ask, "What is the appropriate way of understanding the Church's authority in temporal matters?" Following Father Henri de Lubac, I shall distinguish three models of how to relate the authority of the institutional Church and temporal matters—inclusive of all domains of activity, either theoretical or practical: philosophy, the arts,

---

66. Ibid., no. 45.
67. De Lubac, SJ, "The Authority of the Church in Temporal Matters," 199–221. This article appeared in the *Revue des sciences religieuses* (1932). The supplement ("The Church's Intervention in the Temporal Order," 222–233) to this article is a lecture Fr. de Lubac gave at the Union d'études catholiques sociaux, Lyon, 1931.
68. Maritain, *Integral Humanism*, 127: "What do I mean by 'concrete historical ideal'? It is a *prospective image* signifying the particular type, the specific type of civilization to which a certain historical age tends."

sciences, politics, law, the courts, economic life, indeed, the whole spectrum of culture—direct power, indirect power, and directive power.[69]

The model of direct power holds that "the Church has real political authority, a certain temporal jurisdiction."[70] De Lubac explains: "The theory called 'direct power' had its staunchest representative in Giles of Rome and its most celebrated expression in the bull *Unam Sanctam* of Boniface VIII at the beginning of the fourteenth century.... According to the direct-power theory, the pope, vicar of Jesus Christ, who unites all power in his Person, is the supreme head of both the spiritual and temporal orders. Directly, he exercises only spiritual power, but those who preside over the temporal order are juridically his delegates, his responsible lieutenants. Thus, it is the pope's responsibility to appoint them, judge them and, if necessary, depose them."[71] Now, there is no space here to consider the reasons—biblical, theological, and philosophical—why this theory has been universally abandoned.[72] I do wish to say, however, that Dooyeweerd himself abandons this theory because it confuses the differences in the nature of authority possessed by the Church and the State, respectively. I also want to remark that abandoning the theory of direct authority—meaning thereby possessing a jurisdiction over temporal matters—is an entirely different matter from holding that the Church has

---

69. De Lubac, "Church's Intervention in the Temporal Order," 223.

70. De Lubac, "Authority of the Church in Temporal Matters," 203.

71. De Lubac, "Church's Intervention in the Temporal Order," 223. That the theory of direct power is what Dooyeweerd critically rejects, see *NC*, III, 511–12; *WdW*, III, 453–54.

72. De Lubac, summarizes some of the key reasons for its universal abandonment in "The Authority of the Church in Temporal Matters," 210–11: "Moved by the best intentions, theologians who claim that the Church has a jurisdiction over temporal matters do not notice the harm they do to her. By making hopeless claims that do not correspond to any right, they keep alive in many sincere men a wariness, even a hostility, that is invincible. Even more seriously, they do not notice that they are tempting the Church, just as Satan tempted Christ in the desert. Believing that they are justified in spreading her empire, they are ready to expose her (if that were possible) to the loss of sacred authority, to lower her—even if only temporarily and under the holiest of pretexts—to the rank of the powers of the world. Because making civil power a mere instrument of spiritual power demeans the Church as well as humiliates the State. Do not call this liberalism. The scandal provoked by such a doctrine has nothing in common with the one that will always be provoked by the mystery of the Cross."

authority in temporal matters—which, Father de Lubac notes, "for a true Catholic, raises no questions."[73]

The model of indirect power can be treated very briefly. Why? The significant difference between these this model and the former is that the theory of indirect power claims that the Church has temporal jurisdiction in special circumstances, in very particular and rare cases, for the good of religion, of a spiritual good such as the salvation of souls. Notwithstanding that qualification, this theory assumes that the Church has real political authority, and hence a certain temporal jurisdiction. Now, critics such as Father de Lubac argue that "the refutation of the direct-power theory strongly undermines the theory of indirect power."[74] Here, on this point, de Lubac and Dooyeweerd are in agreement; the institutional Church has no direct or indirect political authority, and hence no temporal jurisdiction. However, Dooyeweerd seems to take that to mean that the institutional Church has *no* authority whatsoever in temporal matters.[75] Consider the following:

> The [Roman Catholic] Church reserves for itself the binding interpretation of "natural morality," to which the Christian magistrate is as bound as any individual church member. In fact, [she] delimits the boundaries of the autonomy of the Christian state. Thus, when Leo XIII and Pius XI wrote their encyclicals *Rerum novarum* [1891] and *Quadragesimo anno* [1931], they offered directives not merely for the "specifically Christian" side of the social and socio-economic issues of the modern day; they also explained the demands of "natural law" and "natural morality" for these problems. On both counts, then, the Roman Catholic Church demands that a Christian government subject itself to ecclesiastical guidance. The

---

73. Ibid., 205.

74. Ibid.

75. Of course Dooyeweerd affirms that the "Christian religion struck a decisive blow at the very foundation of the entire ancient of human society." In particular, "In contrast to the absolutistic idea of the Roman Empire, the proclamation that God must be obeyed rather than man was indeed a radical innovation. For the first time, fundamental limitations were imposed upon the competence of the State-authority, limitations both with respect to the new Church-institution and to the natural family-life of the Christians, who laid claim to the freedom of a Christian education of their children; limitations above all with respect to the spiritual centre of personal human life, which was conceived of a being independent of any temporal societal condition of the individual person" (*NC*, III, 214, 216).

state is autonomous only in giving concrete form to the principles of natural law in the determination of so-called positive law.[76]

Zeroing in on Dooyeweerd's key objection: the temporal authority of the Magisterium extends to interpreting the specific precepts of the natural moral law, and hence the state is bound to these interpretations. The Church oversteps its legitimate authority, according to Dooyeweerd, by demanding that a government subject itself to ecclesiastical guidance. He sees this demand as proof of the universalistic tendencies of the Catholic view of the Church. Although it isn't entirely clear from the above passage, Dooyeweerd's reference to the "'specifically Christian' side of the social and socioeconomic issues of the modern day" is further proof, he claims, of the Church's universalistic tendencies inasmuch as the call of the Christian faithful, that is, the "*normal vocation* of the laity," as Charles Taylor puts it,[77] to engage those issues in light of Christian principles is mediated through the authority of the Church. Of course, Dooyeweerd firmly accepts that the Christian faithful *qua* faithful—as *a people of God*—have such a calling. He simply rejects the claim that this calling is mediated through the authority of the institutional church. His objection amounts to a rejection of a false clericalism.

On this matter, I agree with Dooyeweerd's objection. Significantly, so does Vatican II. In the Dogmatic Constitution on the Church, Christ's lay faithful are called "to engage in temporal affairs and directing them according to God's will." That is, the Council Fathers add, "the faithful who by Baptism are incorporated into Christ, are placed in the People of God, and in their own way share the priestly, prophetic and kingly office of Christ, and to the best of their ability carry on the mission of the whole Christian people in the Church and the world."[78] In short, "The apostolate of the laity is a sharing in the salvific mission of the Church. Through Baptism and Confirmation all are appointed to this apostolate by the Lord himself."[79] Yes, they are called by virtue of their Baptism to share in the threefold mission of Christ—Priest, Prophet-Teacher, King.[80]

76. Dooyeweerd, *Vernieuwing en bezinning om het reformatorische grondmotief.* 127; ET: *Roots of Western Culture*, 131.

77. Taylor, "Clericalism," 174.

78. *Lumen Gentium*, no. 31.

79. Ibid., no. 33.

80. For a rich development of the teaching of Vatican II's *Lumen Gentium* on the calling of the laity, see John Paul II, *Christifideles Laici*, nos. 8–17. See also, Congar, OP,

Most important, the purpose of this calling is *not* to subject the temporal order to "the hegemony of the Church," that is, "seeking to bring the entire world under the submission of the church," as Bavinck puts his objection to the Catholic Church.[81] This, too, is Dooyeweerd's objection formulated in the above passage: the church is striving after an ecclesiastically unified culture. As opposed to what? Well, as opposed to understanding the Christian faith itself to be a "leavening agent in everything," that is, Bavinck adds, "an immanent, reforming reality . . . that purifies and sanctifies everything."[82] But Vatican II agrees with Bavinck and Dooyeweerd. That is clear from the following passage that is worth quoting at length:

> The faithful must, then, recognize the inner nature, the value and the ordering of the whole of creation to the praise of God. By their secular activity they help one another achieve greater holiness of life, so that the world may be filled with the spirit of Christ and may the more effectively attain its destiny in justice, in love and in peace. The laity enjoy a principal role in the universal fulfillment of this task. Therefore, by their competence in secular disciplines and by their activity, *interiorly raised up by grace*, let them work earnestly in order that created goods through human labor, technical skill and civil culture may serve the utility of all men according to the plan of the creator and the light of his word. May these goods be more suitably distributed among all men and in their own way may they be conducive to universal progress in human and Christian liberty. Thus, through the members of the Church, will Christ increasingly illuminate the whole of human society with his saving light.[83]

In this light, we can reject Dooyeweerd's conclusion that the Church demands the government itself to be subject to her concrete directives because she is seeking to further her goal of establishing an ecclesiastically unified culture. Having rejected that goal, as the Catholic Church does,

---

Lay People in the Church.

81. Bavinck, "Catholicity of Christianity and the Church," 236, 231.

82. Ibid., 231, 229.

83. *Lumen Gentium*, no. 36. I italicize the words, "interiorly raised by grace," in order to emphasize that the understanding of the relation between nature and grace in *Lumen Gentium* is *not* the dualistic view Bavinck (and, typically, neo-Calvinists like Dooyeweerd and Berkouwer) ascribes to Catholicism. On that view, grace is an "add-on" or a "supplement" to nature, to the structures of reality, to our humanity, rather than being an "immanent, reforming reality" that transforms, restores, and renews a fallen creation.

does not imply, however, the rejection of the claim that the institutional Church is an authoritative interpreter of the natural moral law and hence may confront the power of the State with the abiding objectivity of that law for the purpose of "contributing to the sanctification of the world, as from within like leaven."[84] Dominican theologian Aidan Nichols nicely formulates the Church's message to legislators and public officers.

> Evangelization of the State power means its confrontation with the abiding objectivity of the natural moral law, itself an expression of the divine Wisdom and the measure of all positive law on earth. Human beings govern—whether as law-makers or legislators, law-enforcers or rulers, or law-adjudicators or judges—only by participation in a higher law, by sharing in the care of divine providence for the common good, as by reference to moral truth people build characters that can fit them for life everlasting. No state is excused from the worship of God and obedience to a moral law both integral to that worship and the only stable foundation for human rights. Woe to that State that accepts the seduction of the serpent in the garden, "Ye shall be as gods" [Gen 3:5], and seeks to establish the "natural measures of good and evil."[85]

Furthermore, it is not the state as such that is subject to the Church's directive power, but rather the consciences of men who govern and whose governance is subject to the objectivity of the natural moral law. What then is directive power? The Church articulates objective and general norms for life in society. Those norms are aimed at guiding men's action in concrete and particular social and cultural situations. The Church operates from *within* the temporal order, addressing herself to men's consciences, the governing agents of, say, the State, so that they might take up their calling to live out the power of the Gospel, to live and work for the salvation of the world *in* the world. As Father de Lubac says, "Temporal matters that, in this sense, are the objective of the Church's power cannot be reduced to the political domain. They include all domains of activity that are specifically human or natural, either theoretical or practical: philosophy, the arts, even the sciences, as well as politics, the economy and diverse forms of social organization." He continues:

> Since the supernatural is not separated from nature, and the spiritual is always mixed with the temporal, the Church has eminent

---

84. *Lumen Gentium*, no. 30.
85. Nichols, OP, "Integral Evangelization," 76–77.

authority—always in proportion to the spiritual element present—over everything, without having to step out of her role. *If this is not true, then we might as well admit that the Church has no authority over anything,* that she can speak only in the abstract. She must not limit herself to outlining absolute principles, to proclaiming doctrine and ethics from "above the fray." When circumstances require it, she must be able to make decisions—that is, either approve or condemn, *hic et nunc*—about concrete activities where doctrine and morality are involved.[86]

Father de Lubac is, then, more helpful than Dooyeweerd in answering the question regarding the appropriate way to understand the Church's authority in temporal matters; namely, he defends the *directive power* of the institutional Church's authority to address all the dimensions of human life.

> The *principle*, it seems to me, is very simple. The authority of the Church is entirely spiritual and is exercised only on consciences. But it does not follow that there are areas of thought or human activity, however, profane it may appear, where the Faith and morality guarded by the Church cannot in one way or another, one day or another, be involved. *Christianity is universal not only in the sense that all men have their Savior in Jesus Christ but also in the sense that all of man has salvation in Jesus Christ.* Since the destinies of Christianity were placed in the hands of the Church, the Church is catholic—that is, universal—in that nothing human can remain alien to her. And it is hard to see why "politics" should be an exception to this principle. As we have said, this was the teaching of Leo XIII in his encyclical *Immortale Dei*, and, in general, it suffices to justify the Church's interventions in response to the claims of a certain "liberalism."[87]

There is one final point to make, and this time it is about the claim that the universalistic tendency of Troeltsch's Church-institute type is embedded, says Dooyeweerd, "within the cadre of the scholastic basic motive of nature and supra-natural grace." "In the High Middles-Ages the

---

86. De Lubac, "Authority of the Church in Temporal Matters," 214–15; italics added.

87. De Lubac, "Church's Intervention in the Temporal Order," 230. Regarding the words of *Immortale Dei*, Leo XIII's 1885 Encyclical Letter: "'Everything that is sacred in human affairs, everything that is connected with the salvation of souls and the worship of God, either inherently or by its relationship to the spiritual domain, comes under the jurisdiction of the power and judgment of the Church' [no. 14]. These words of Leo XIII in the encyclical *Immortale Dei* are categorical."

Aristotelian theory of the organized communities was accommodated to the Christian conception of the human race, reborn in Christ, and profoundly described by the Apostle Paul, as the 'body of Christ', with its Head and Individual members. This synthesis was performed by Thomas Aquinas within the cadre of the scholastic basic motive of nature and supra-natural grace. Such a procedure must result in a partial subversion of the Christian view [of human society] by Greek immanence philosophy" (*NC*, III, 214).[88] Dooyeweerd elaborates:

> [J]ust as the State is the perfect society in the natural sphere, the Church-institution is the *societas perfecta* in the supra-natural sphere of grace. And, in accordance with Thomas' conception of the relation between nature and grace, the State is subordinate to the Church, which alone can elevate natural life to the supra-natural level of perfection. So the universalist view of human society, already expressed in the pre-Thomistic idea of the Holy Roman Empire, acquires its typical elaboration within the new scholastic basic motive of nature and supra-nature (*NC*, III, 220).

We have already dealt above with Dooyeweerd's objection that a universalist conception identifies the visible body of Christ with the institutional Church. I have also dealt with his claim that this conception necessarily implies that all Christian organizations must be ecclesiastically controlled. Dooyeweerd's remaining claim is that the universalist conception is rooted in a construal of the relation of nature and grace, of the natural and supernatural, of creation and redemption, such that the natural realm is not perfected *in its natural order*, but rather is sacramentally elevated into the supernatural order of things. This too is Bavinck's view of the Catholic tradition.[89] On this construal of the relation between nature and grace, this is the only way that natural affairs can be brought into contact with the grace of God. Thus, rather than elevating and transfiguring, say, marriage, *in its own order*, that is sanctifying it from *within*, restoring the original order of creation disturbed by sin, it is hallowed extrinsically, that is, by being rendered a sacrament that "adds on" the

---

88. Dooyeweerd does not speak, in the 1936 *WdW*, III, 146–47, of the "scholastic basic motive of nature and supra-natural grace." The problem of nature and grace, particularly Dooyeweerd's interpretation and criticism of Scholasticism in general and St. Thomas in particular, requires more substantial treatment than I can give it here in this paper. I attend to the question of nature and grace in some detail in my book, *Slitting the Sycamore*.

89. Bavinck, "Catholicity of Christianity and the Church," 230–31, 236.

plus-factor of supernatural grace, through an external connection to the institutional Church.

Although there is no denying that some Catholics have interpreted the relation between nature and grace in the extrinsic way that Bavinck suggests, not all have. Indeed, some, such as Henri de Lubac, have been critical of interpreting the notion of "elevation" and "perfection" as one in which the supernatural is "added on" to the natural realm. Briefly, it seems to me that de Lubac rightly understands the relation between nature and grace as one in which elevation involves the natural realm being restored, renewed, transfigured in its own order, from within. As Father de Lubac says:

> In general, the law of the relationship between nature and grace is the same everywhere. Grace seizes nature from the inside and, far from lowering it, lifts it up to have it serve its ends. It is from the interior that faith transforms reason, that the Church influences the State. The Church is the messenger of Christ, not the guardian of the State. The Church ennobles the State, inspiring it to be a Christian State (one sees in what sense) and, thus, a more human one. . . . Just as grace does not come from the outside to diminish and mutilate human nature but, on the contrary, affects it from the interior so that it is elevated and transfigured, the Church, messenger of Christ's grace, influences humanity and, in particular, civil society from within. She does not become society's guardian. Rather, she ennobles it, inspiring it to become Christian—and thus, more human. The Church's most important action by far, as positive as it is diffuse, takes place without a specific intervention: by her very existence and through all of her faithful members, she reveals the ideal introduced into humanity by the Christian revelation.[90]

Consider also the interpretation of the sacrament of marriage in the theology of nature, sin, and grace as we find it expressed in the *Catechism of the Catholic Church*. Marriage belongs to the order of creation. "God himself is the author of marriage. The vocation to marriage is written in the very nature of man and woman as they came from the hand of the Creator. Marriage is not a purely human institution. . . . Holy Scripture affirms that man and woman were created for one another. . . . The Lord himself shows that this signifies an unbreakable union of their two lives by recalling what the plan of the Creator has been 'in the beginning.'"

90. De Lubac, SJ, "Authority of the Church," 212; idem, "Church's Intervention in the Temporal Order," 230–31.

Marriage is also under the regime of sin. Yet, "the disorder we notice so painfully does not stem from the *nature* of man and woman, nor from the nature of their relations, but from *sin*." Despite the impact of sin on marriage, "the order of creation persists." But to heal the wounds of sin upon marriage, grace is needed to transform and restore marriage to God's original creational intent. "In his preaching Jesus unequivocally taught the original meaning of the union of man and woman as the Creator willed it from the beginning. . . . By coming to restore the original order of creation disturbed by sin, he himself gives the strength and grace to live marriage in the new dimension of the Reign of God." Grace permeates marriage, on this view, from within so that it is restored to functioning properly according to God's original normative intent in creating it. *Pace* Dooyeweerd, on this Catholic understanding of the relation between nature and grace, creation and redemption, the latter term in each couplet is "an immanent, reforming reality" (as Bavinck phrases it).[91] Yes, "the order of creation and the order of redemption, the world and the Church, must always remain distinct," rightly says Hans Urs von Balthasar, "still we [need to] hear anew the words about Christ as the Alpha and Omega of creation—he who recapitulates in himself everything in heaven and on earth and indeed was chosen for this before the world began: namely, to bring back to the Father the [fallen] world that was created through him, for him, and in him."[92]

SECT-TYPE

Regarding Troeltsch's sect-type, I shall be very brief, because we already presented Guardini's criticism of this type, and Dooyeweerd's critique is the same. I begin this brief analysis here with Dooyeweerd's description of this type. It, too, is worth quoting at some length:

> The sect-type explicitly relinquishes the idea of the Church as an institution of grace and redemption independent of the personal qualities of its officers; consequently it also abandons the universalistic social ideal of world government by the spiritual authority of a hierarchically organized clergy. A sect prefers a voluntary community to an institution, because it a condition of a real communion of believers that the latter join deliberately of their own

---

91. Bavinck, "Catholicity of Christianity and the Church," 229.
92. Balthasar, *Razing the Bastions*, 102.

free will. Such is compatible only with an associational form of organization. This implies that everything depends on the personal dignity of the cooperating individuals. The sect community does not incorporate any one at his birth but exclusively on account of his personal conversion. This community is not Christian or sacred because of the objective guarantee of an institution, with its sacraments of grace, but because of the personal Christian attitude of life of the individual members. Consequently the sect-type can only form small groups. Such a small community wants to derive its social ideal exclusively and purely from the Gospel and Christ's commandment of love, without stooping to any compromise with existing secular ordinances. . . . Troeltsch considers this sect-type as the sociological consequence of the . . . individualistic factor in the religious sociological basic scheme of Christianity. One aspect of Jesus' teaching is this radical individualism which emphasizes the eternal and infinite value of the individual personality as a child of God. All differences in social position lose their meaning in comparison with this value of the individual person, who has direct communion with God without the intermediary of any institution (*WdW*, III, 473–474 [529]).

Individualism and nominalism are primary features of this sect-type. This congregation is individualistic because it is based on the personal qualities of converted individuals; a "sect" is the simple gathering together of those who as individuals have accepted the Gospel and who voluntarily choose to share their life of faith. It is also nominalistic because it denies that communities are as real as individuals. Hence, the sect-type is a form of anti-realism regarding the existence of communities. Dooyeweerd has one basic criticism of the sect-type, namely, a "sect" is *not* a Church (*WdW*, III, 477 [532]).[93] A "sect," in the sense of *congre-*

---

93. Dooyeweerd is quick to acknowledge, however, "without any reserve that the rise of sects is often an indication of a process of decay in the Church institution." In a similar vein, the Catholic tradition acknowledges so-called "ecclesial movements," which are really renewal movements, in the Church. The then Joseph Ratzinger, now Benedict XVI, wrote in his address, "The Ecclesial Movements: A Theological reflection on their place in the Church": "For me personally it was wonderful experience when, in the early 1980s, I first came into close contact with movements such as the *Neocatechumenal Way*, *Communion and Liberation* and the *Focolare Movement*, and so experienced the energy and enthusiasm with which they lived their faith and the joy of their faith . . . That was the period in which Karl Rahner and others were speaking of a winter in the Church; and, indeed, it did seem that after the great flowering of the Council, spring has been reclaimed by frost, and that the new dynamism had succumbed to exhaustion." Of course Ratzinger concluded his address by recognizing the need for the 'discernment of spirits'

gatio fidelium, that is, as a group of converted individuals, reverses the proper theological order of things: the Church is *convocatio before* being a *congregatio*, meaning thereby that it is of God, that it is God himself who is calling the community together, it is God who unites those people who are "his own," in short, that this community is gathered together by God.[94] Bavinck also makes this point: "From the days of Tertullian onward all Christians not only called the church a gathered community (*coetus*) but also the mother of believers (*mater fidelium*). In this respect, Protestants agree with Catholics, and even Calvin himself very strongly emphasizes it." And, rejecting the sect-type, Bavinck adds, "In their opinion, this was true, not because the church freely and independently organized itself into an institution and gave itself a government of its own, but because Christ had so arranged it. The institution of the church, at least according to the Reformed confession, is absolutely not a product of the believing community but the work of Christ himself."[95] Yet, extremely valuable though Bavinck's point be, there remains to ask whether there is something about the logic of Protestantism, even in Bavinck's self-understanding, that is inherently ordered to seeing the church as an association of individuals and hence to its being "fragmented into innumerable sects and small churches, assemblies, and conventicles," as Bavinck himself puts this point. Indeed, Bavinck adds, "In the Protestant principle there is . . . a

---

in the matter of the new movements. In John Paul II's 1990 encyclical *Redemptoris missio*, he makes reference to "a new development . . . the rapid growth of 'ecclesial movements' filled with missionary dynamism, which represent a true gift from God both for the new evangelization and for missionary activity. . . . I therefore recommend that they be spread, and that they be used to give fresh energy, especially among young people, to the Christian life and to evangelization" ("Church Movements," 176–77). See also Ker, "The Radicalism of the Papacy," 49–68. Unfortunately, I cannot give in this chapter the attention that these ecclesial movements deserve.

94. Especially helpful here in understanding the difference between "*convocatio*" and "*congregatio*" is Giussani, *Why the Church?*, 81–87.

95. Bavinck, *GD* IV, 311–12 [331]. Elsewhere Bavinck writes: "The church is not just an arbitrary association of people who wish to worship together but something instituted by the Lord, pillar and ground of truth," in "Catholicity of Christianity and the Church," 248.

church-dissolving element as well as a church-reforming one."[96] What is the root of this "church-dissolving" element within Protestantism?[97]

My brief answer to this question here is that Protestantism separated the doctrinal sources of authority in the Church—Scripture, Creeds, and Confessions—from the teaching authority of the Church, and hence from an episcopacy, giving to all men "the freedom to understand that Word," and by implication, the Creeds and Confessions, "personally as he interprets it." Bavinck explains this freedom: "Morally, of course, we are bound in this connection to Christ, and we will all have to give an account of how we have understood the word of Christ and put it into practice. But vis-à-vis our fellow humans and fellow Christians, we are completely free." Of course the Catholic Church has, on this score, consistently charged "Protestantism with individualism, subjectivism, and sectarianism." Bavinck adds, in rejoinder, that this charge reflects the weakness of Rome "inasmuch as it must maintain itself by hierarchical means." Admittedly, says Bavinck, "It is perfectly true that, if the Word is the mark of the Church and is put into all men's hands, by that very token everyone has received the right to make judgments concerning the church and, if one sees fit, to separate from it. But we must completely respect this freedom, and no state or church must curb it."[98] This understanding of freedom unleashed upon the Church a "church-dissolving" element within Protestantism and, over time, has resulted in its suicide. Indeed, with this emphasis on freedom Bavinck abandons the official and public teaching office of the Church grounded in an authentic episcopacy. But that is exactly what is needed to counteract that "church-dissolving" element and so that we can distinguish between true and false reform in the Church. Therefore, the task of this teaching office is to implement the authority of the normative

---

96. Bavinck, "Catholicity of Christianity and the Church," 249. There is no space here to discuss the church-reforming dynamism of the ecclesial movements in the Catholic Church, "which," as Ratzinger puts it, "are always sweeping through her . . . reinstating and reapplying the universalist aspect of the [Church's] apostolic mission and the radical dimension of the gospel and thus serving to promote the spiritual life and truth of the local Churches" ("Church Movements and their Place in Theology," 194).

97. Catholics have argued that this "church-dissolving" element of Protestantism belongs to its logic, and hence the fracturing of Protestantism innumerable sects and small churches, assemblies, and conventicles is simply the outworking of its logic. Berkouwer critically evaluates this argument in his earliest book on Roman Catholicism, *De Strijd om het Roomsch-Katholieke Dogma*, 79–99.

98. Bavinck, *GD* IV, [318].

sources—Scripture, Creeds, and Confessions—of the faith by listening to these sources devotedly, guarding them with dedication, and expounding them faithfully.[99] In short, "Neither orthodoxy nor episcopacy alone can deal with the crisis of authority in the church. Orthodoxy without episcopacy is blind; episcopacy without orthodoxy is empty."[100]

Earlier I took note of Guardini's criticism of the sect-type interpretation of the Pauline concept of *corpus*. He wrote: "[t]he term for it is not 'gathering' or 'congregation', as modern individualism translates the Greek word *ekklesia*, but 'Church'. In every congregation the Church is present, but she herself and as such is more than the community of kindred souls meeting here and now, unless we give the word 'congregation' a meaning which transcends the ordinary one and take it to signify the union of all baptized believers, founded by Christ and constituted in the apostles. But this would be only a difference in terminology."[101] Dooyeweerd develops his criticism of the sect-type along similar lines.

> According to the Biblical view of the latter [Church] the foundation of our salvation is solely to be sought in Christ Jesus and not in ourselves. *He* is the firm ground on Whom the temporal Church relationship is built. . . . This is why the concept "association" does not suit the institutional Church. The true Christian Church, in its institutional manifestation, is not built by men. Christ builds His Church by His Word and His Spirit, and not out of "converted individuals" but in the line of the Covenant. The Church members are members of one body sanctified in Christ alone. . . . This "*congregatio*" is an outcome of the divine Covenant and not an assembly of mere individual believers. The Covenant embraces the believers with their children, although the latter may later on prove to be unbelievers who do not wish to belong to the *ecclesia visibilis* in its institutional sense. If we break with the thought of the Covenant in the temporal organization of the Church, we open the door to the individualistic sect-type (*WdW*, III, 477–478 [532–533]).

My analysis of Dooyeweerd's discussion of Troeltsch's basic sociological types, Church-institute type and sect-type has, I believe, sharpened and deepened our understanding of the dilemma of individualism and

---

99. Braaten, *Mother Church, Ecclesiology and Ecumenism*, 96. I am very indebted to Braaten's understanding of the relationship between orthodoxy, magisterium, and episcopacy.

100. Ibid., 97.

101. Guardini, *Church of the Lord*, 88–89.

universalism. By engaging Dooyeweerd's ecclesiology, we have come to a better grasp of how to rise about that dilemma. Notwithstanding my appreciation of Dooyeweerd's ecclesiology, however, at several point I have had to resist Dooyeweerd's efforts to relativize the singularly unique place of the institutional Church. The institutional Church is the *concentration point* of the Kingship of Christ. The institutional Church *is* the visible body of Christ, and so the Church is the place where we come to know the fullness of Truth. Indeed, Guardini calls the Church a "community of truth" because she "effects . . . the common possession [of] those supreme supernatural realities of which faith makes us conscious. They are the foundations of the supernatural life, for all the same—God, Christ, grace, and the work of the Holy Spirit" (*VSK*, 78 [96-97]). Furthermore, "The Church is 'the truth in love' [Eph 4:15], as St. Paul so magnificently describes it. She is truth, in the deepest sense of living truth, essential truth. . . . But it is a fullness of truth which is love . . . It is a light, which is at the same time a glowing heat, a treasure which cannot be contained in itself but must communicate itself to others. . . . The Church is love. She is truth, which communicates itself" (*VSK*, 86 [104]). Because the Church is the house of truth, the actual, specific place of truth, the truth and the Church belong together. Father Guardini explains why the Church is the one and only source of all saving truth:

> In the Church, however, we must acknowledge not simply the religious value in the abstract, nor the mere fact that it is closely knit with the human element, but that it is bound up with this, and only this particular historic community. The concrete Church, as the embodiment of the religious value, demands our allegiance. And even so, we have no said enough. The truth of Christianity does not consist of abstract tenets and values, which are "attached to the Church." The Truth on which my salvation depends is a Fact, a concrete reality. Christ and the Church are that truth. He said: "I am the truth." But. . . the Church is herself Christ, mystically living on, herself the concrete life of truth and the fullness of salvation wrought by the God-man; and . . . the values of salvation cannot be detached from her and sought, but are once and for all embodied in her as an historical reality (*VSK*, 37-38 [52-53]).

In this passage, we find an adumbration of Father Guardini's answer to the question, "Why the Church?" We turn now to look more closely at the sense in which the Church is the place of Truth and, by implication, the home of freedom.

WHY THE CHURCH?
THE WAY TO BECOME HUMAN

The institutional Church is the *concentration point* of the Kingship of Christ. In that light, we should proclaim that Jesus Christ and the Church belong together, according to Father Guardini. Furthermore, the truth of Jesus Christ has an objective form, and that is the Catholic Church. Says Guardini, "These lectures have not attempted to establish by scientific reasoning, but state as my firm conviction, that the sphere of Catholic faith—the Church—is not merely one alternative among many, but religious truth, pure and simply, the Kingdom of God. The Church is not something belonging to the past, but absolute reality, and therefore the answer to every age, including our own, and its fulfillment" (*VSK*, 94 [114]). The institutional Church that is the Catholic Church is the fully and right ordered expression of the body of Christ. Thus, faith in the Church is the step into true life, and affirming the truth of the Church's teaching, its dogma, is the step into true freedom.

THE CHURCH IS THE PLACE OF TRUTH

What is the nature of man? Man is a truth-seeker. As John Paul II explains in his 1998 Encyclical Letter, *Fides et Ratio*: "It is of the nature of man to pursue the truth. This search is not simply concerned with the discovery of specific truths which depend on events or on particular sciences; man is not interested in the true good solely in relation to his own individual interests. His enquiry is directed towards a higher truth which is capable of shedding light on the meaning of life: therefore we are dealing with the sort of search which culminates only in the Absolute."[102] Now, according to Guardini, God is the absolute reality and truth, and "the Church is the spiritual locality where the individual finds himself face to face with the Absolute" (*VSK*, 43 [58]). The Church is the place in which truth is known.[103] But the claim that Church is the actual, specific place of where

---

102. John Paul II, *Fides et Ratio*, no. 33.

103. Similarly, Ratzinger writes, "The Church community is required as the historic condition for the activity of reason, but the Church is not identical with the truth. She does not determine or construct the truth; rather, she herself is determined and built up

truth is known is, as Cardinal Kasper puts it, "a thesis which for many people is no less foolish and scandalous."[104] Yet, I believe that Guardini provides a defense of that claim by raising the question regarding the fullness of man's true humanity, a fullness that he has lost, and that an age sunk in relativism makes it difficult for us to regain. Let me briefly explain Guardini's argument.

Shortly after the First World War, Guardini describes profound changes occurring at many levels: political structures, social and economic order, artistic vision, science, and philosophy. These profound changes have made us "more acutely conscious of what in truth is always happening—that the attitude of the soul towards itself, its environment, and the first principles of being, is continually shifting." "The forms of human life," Guardini adds, "economic, social, technical, artistic and intellectual, are seen to be in a state of steady, if slight, transformation" (*VSK*, 44 [59]). We now live in a time—Guardini is writing in 1922—where the thought of modern man is relativist. This did not happen all of a sudden. Centuries of criticism have worn away all fixed belief and the recognition and experience of living in perpetual flux now "forces itself on the mind with an evidence from which there is no escape." Indeed, "a sense of transitoriness and limitation takes possession of the soul. It realizes with horror how all things are in flux, passing away. Nothing any longer stands firm" (*VSK*, 44 [59]). The upshot of this experience is that man has become "uncertain and vacillating" such that he is spiritually and intellectually impoverished, and hence "[h]e cannot overcome error by truth, evil and weakness by moral strength, the stupidity and inconstancy of the masses by great ideas and responsible leadership, or the flux of time by works born of the determination to embody the eternal values" (*VSK*, 45 [59]). And this spiritual and intellectual poverty is, adds Guardini, "accompanied by a colossal pride." He explains:

> Man is morbidly uncertain and morbidly arrogant. The nations are confused by pride, parties are blinded by self-seeking, and rich and poor alike are the prey of an ignoble greed. Every social class deifies itself. Art, science, technology—every separate department of life considers itself the sum and substance of reality. There is despairing weakness, hopeless instability, a melancholy consciousness of being at the mercy of blind irrational force—and

---

by it as the space in which truth is known" ("Theology and Church Politics," 155).

104. Kasper, "Church as the Place of Truth," 138.

> side by side with these a pride, as horrible as it is absurd, of money, knowledge, power, and ability. Impotence and pride, helplessness and arrogance, weakness and violence—do you realize how by the continued action of these vices true humanity has been lost? We are witnessing a caricature of humanity. In what then does humanity in the deepest sense of the term consist? To be truly human is to be conscious of human weakness, but confident that it can be overcome. It is to be humble, but assured. It is to realize man's transience, but aspire to the eternal. It is to be a prisoner of time, but a freeman of eternity. It is to be aware of one's powers, of one's limitations, but to be resolved to accomplish deeds of everlasting worth (*VSK*, 45 [60–61]).

From Father Guardini's description in the above quotation it is evident that man is internally self-conflicted. How then does he regain his true humanity? What role does the Church play in awakening him to that loss? The Church awakens him to several tensions at the very foundation of his nature and his desire for self-transcendence: radical dependency in light of the Unconditioned; being temporal in light of the Eternal; and being finite in light of the Infinite. This awakening effects in him the realization that, given his dependencies, he yearns "for a life free from the countless dependencies of life on earth, an existence inwardly full." Furthermore, in the awareness of being temporal, he realizes that he is "destined to life without end." And in his awareness of his finitude in the very depths of his being, he realizes that "the Infinite alone can satisfy him" (*SK*, 45 [61]). In other words, man's dependency, temporality, and finitude—the marks of creatureliness—are signals of transcendence. Humanity in its deepest sense, complete humanity, searches for a resolution of the tensions at the root of his awakening to this self-transcendence. But how then does he regain the fullness of his humanity, and is the Church's role just limited to making him aware of that tension? The answer to this question is that the Church accomplishes the resolution of this tension, effecting this self-transcendence in truth (dogma), goodness (morality), and with God Himself (liturgy), and hence she has a necessary role to play in transforming man to his true humanity. Guardini explains:

> [S]he resolves it for him by the mystery of his likeness to God and of God's love, which bestows of its fullness that which totally surpasses the nature. He is not God, but creature, yet he is God's image and therefore capable of apprehending and possessing God. *Capax Dei*, as St. Augustine says, able to grasp and hold the Absolute. And God

Himself is love. He has made the creature in His own image. It is His will that this resemblance should be perfected by obedience, discipline, and union with Himself. He has redeemed man, and by grace has given him a new birth and made him god-like. But all this means that God has made man for His living kingdom. But observe this encounter with the Absolute, in which man faces the Infinite and sees clearly what he is, and what It is; but which at the same time awakens the longing for this Absolute Godhead—this fundamental experience of Christianity, truth, humility, yearning love, and confident hope in one, is the moment in which for the first time in the spiritual sense man become truly human. This transformation of a creature into man in the presence of the Absolute is the work of the Church (*VSK*, 47 [62]).

Guardini is very specific about how this transformation is accomplished. When man is uncertain and hesitant where truth is concerned, the Church comforts him with dogma, which is an objective, generally valid truth of universal importance for the whole of human life—"truths unconditionally valid, independently of changing historical conditions" (*VSK*, 48 [63]). Of course, Guardini's understanding of the nature and importance of dogma goes against the grain of how even some Christians understand Christianity. "Modern people do not expect religion to constitute a structure of doctrine, but to furnish a kind of personal screen on which they can project sympathetic images devised by themselves.... They reject the notion of religion as an objectively true set of beliefs and practices, and instead select their own collection of beliefs, and designate the result 'Christianity'. ... In such a view of things, there is no need for Christianity to teach fixed or permanent dogma—anyone can believe anything, provided the central myths can be celebrated in a manner which elevates the individual's sense of 'spiritual' beauty."[105]

Guardini's view is antithetical to this one. Rather, he makes God's Word revelation his starting point and approaches dogma in the attitude of faith. God's Word Revelation is that which makes divine truth known to us, that is, "Truth divinely guaranteed and unconditional." "If he honestly assents to it," adds Father Guardini, "he becomes 'human'" (*VSK*, 48 [63]). The mission of the Church touches the very foundation of all human society. God's Word Revelation reveals to man the religious root and center of human nature in its creation, fall into sin and redemption by Jesus Christ.

---

105. Norman, *Secularization*, 20, 24.

Man lost true self-knowledge because he lost the true knowledge of God. But confronted by Truth divinely guaranteed and unconditional, "he has a correct valuation of himself." Guardini elaborates:

> His judgments are clear, free and humble. But at the same time he is aware that there is an Absolute, and that it confronts him here and now in its plenitude. By his faith he receives the Absolute into his soul. Humility and confidence, sincerity and trust unite to constitute the fundamental disposition of a thought adequate with the nature of things. Henceforward the unconditional organizes the believer's thought and his entire spiritual life. Man is aware of something which is absolutely fixed. This becomes the axis upon which his entire mental world turns, a solid core of truth which gives consistency and order to his entire experience. For it becomes the instinctive measure of all his thinking even in the secular sphere, the point of departure for all his intellectually activity. Order is established in his inner life. Those distinctions are grasped without which no intellectual life is possible—the distinction between certainty and uncertainty, truth and error, the great and the petty. The soul becomes calm and joyful, able to acknowledge its limitations yet strive after infinity, to see its dependence, yet overcome it. This is what is meant by becoming human (*VSK*, 48–49 [63–64]).

Man is also transformed with respect to the moral life. Our culture—Guardini is speaking of 1922!—is relativistic regarding morality. Not only are ideals, standards of goodness, and individual and social moral codes fluctuating and unstable, but also "effort is this crippled, and the will, powerless when important decisions must be made, will in compensation give a free rein to arbitrary impulse in some particular sphere." In response to this moral subjectivism and relativism, man is confronted by the Church with "a world of absolute values, an essential pattern of unconditional perfection, an order of life whose features bear the stamp of truth." In sum, Guardini adds, "It is the Person of Christ. It is the structure of values and standards which He personified and taught, and which lives on in the moral and hierarchical order of the Church" (*SK*, 49 [64]). Here, too, man's humanity is transformed and deepened, but now in the area of moral thought and practice. "Man is confronted with what is unconditionally valid. He faces and acknowledges his own essential limitation." Others who experience this limitation might remain pessimistic about closing the moral gap between what man does and what he ought to do.

But his interior life is transformed by the Person and Work of Christ, and thus, having recognized his limitation, "at the same time he sees that he can attach his finite life at every point to God's Infinite Life, and fill it with an unlimited content. He there finds rest. He rejoices in the fact that he is a creature, and still more that he is called [in Christ] to be a 'partaker of the Divine Nature' [2 Pt. 1:4]. His inner life becomes real, concerned around a fixed centre, supported by eternal laws. His goal becomes clear, his action resolute, his whole life ordered and coherent—he becomes human" (*VSK*, 49 [65]).

Lastly, the fullness of our humanity is discovered in the Liturgy. "The liturgy is creation, redeemed and at prayer, because it is the Church at prayer." The believer grows "'unto the measure of the age of the fullness of Christ' [Eph 4:13]. Living the liturgy does not mean the cultivation of literary tastes and fancies, but self-subjection to the order established by the Holy Spirit Himself; it means being led by the rule and love of the Holy Spirit to a life in Christ and in Him for the Father" (*VSK*, 18 [30]). In the Church's Liturgy man comes face to face with the true God, with the Father, in the Son, and through the power of the Holy Spirit, and man becomes truly man. Through the liturgy we participate in the mysteries of the divine saving plan. As Guardini puts this point in his study, *The Spirit of the Liturgy*:

> Here, too, the liturgy is our teacher. It condenses into prayer the entire body of religious truth. Indeed, it is nothing else but truth expressed in terms of prayer. For it is the great fundamental truths which above all fill the liturgy—God in His mighty reality, perfection, and greatness, One and Three in One; His creation, providence, and omnipresence; sin, justification, and the desire of salvation; the Redeemer and His Kingdom; the four last things. It is only such an overwhelming abundance of truth which can never pall, but continue to be, day after day, all things to all men, ever fresh and inexhaustible.[106]

THE CHURCH IS THE ROAD TO FREEDOM

"The knowledge of pure truth is the fundamental factor of spiritual emancipation. 'The truth shall make you free' [John 8:32]."[107] In the Gospel of

---

106. Guardini, *Spirit of the Liturgy*, 24.
107. Ibid., 209.

John, Jesus is addressing himself to the Jews who had believed him. He said, "If you hold to my teaching, you are really my disciples. Then you will know the truth, and the truth will set you free." Jesus follows up his address to them by elaborating his message of gospel freedom proclaiming the truth that "everyone who sins is a slave to sin. . . . So if the Son sets you free, you will be free indeed" (John 8:34, 36). What then is freedom? What sort of man, exactly, is the free man?

These questions are meant to probe to the ultimate depth of freedom. "It is that the man who is truly free is open to God and plunged in Him. This is freedom for God and in God" (*VSK*, 57 [72]). So this freedom is not merely about negative freedom, that is, a freedom from external constraint, the absence of obstacles or barriers, possessing the power to choose, according to one's own will, among several possible courses. Instead, Father Guardini is concerned with man's positive freedom—interior freedom—to live in conformity with the pattern of his being, and hence with what God's willed him to be.

Essential to Guardini's notion of humanity is the doctrine of creation: "Each of us possesses a pattern of his being, the divine idea, in which the Creator contemplated him. It comprises not only the universal idea of human nature, but everything besides, which constitutes this particular individual. Every individual is unique, and a unique variety of human nature." Furthermore, "When this unique quality of a man's individual being is allowed to emerge, and determines all his existence and activities; when he lives from the centre of his own being, not, however, putting an artificial restraint upon himself, but naturally and as a matter of course, he is a free man." In sum, Guardini adds, "He is free who lives in complete harmony with the divine idea of his personality, and who is what his Creator willed him to be" (*VSK*, 55 [70]). Thus, the freedom of the subjective person to do as he pleases is overruled by the freedom of the responsible person to act as he must. The man of God who then possesses positive freedom acts rightly "not because a compulsion is upon him, but because he himself is resolved upon it; not merely as the laborious and painful application of principles, but because the impulse and volition of his own nature impel him, and because the very heart of his personality is thereby fulfilled—and thus not otherwise is free" (*VSK*, 57 [72]).

Yet, there is more to freedom, and Guardini links this more with the power of the Church to emancipate man from his many-sided bondage that impedes his development. For instance, there is intellectual bondage that threatens to enslave the soul—philosophical theories, political slogans, human ideals of perfection, psychological fashions. In short, the intellectual environment, current opinions, customs and traditions, reigning worldviews that grip man's intellectual life impede his capacity to see things as they are, the fullness of objective reality. In this instance, man's intellectual freedom is clouded by mistrust, narrowed by prejudice, bias, distorted by passion, inattention, oversight, unreasonableness, and irresponsibility—all of which lead one to mistake the false for the true. Man's judgments are deeply permeated by the influences of his personal characteristics, his stage of development, and his experiences, indeed, by the noetic effects of sin.

Of course, Guardini isn't suggesting for one moment that man's thought and judgments are merely products of his environment—cultural, social, or otherwise. "No reduction of thought and valuation to psychological and sociological processes is implied," says Guardini. "Their nucleus is intellectual, but it is embedded in those processes. Thought has an objective reference," he adds, "and is always striving to realize it more purely, that is to say, to grasp more perfectly objective truth. It has an objective content, this very truth—and becomes more perfect as this content becomes richer and more distinct" (*SK*, 62–63 [79]). Still, the knowing agent is not an abstract *cogito*, a transcendental ego, in short, an abstract, logical subject, *but a living man.*

> In the function of thinking all his other activities and states participate, fatigue, for example, and energy strung to the tensest pitch, joy and depression, success and failure. The experience of every day proves that our intellectual productivity, the direction of our thoughts and the nature of our conclusions, are influenced by the vicissitudes of daily life. Our psychological states may assist, hamper or completely prevents acts of knowledge, strengthen or weaken the persuasiveness of arguments. Desire, love, anger, a longing for revenge, gratitude—anyone who is honest with himself must admit how enormously the force of an argument, apparently purely logical, fluctuates in accordance with his prevalent mood, or the person who puts it forward. Even the climax of the cognitive process—the evidence, the subjective certainty of a judgment, a conclusion, a structure of reasoning—is to an enormous extent subject, as you can see for yourselves, to the influence of psychological states and the external environment. It is a strange chapter in practical epistemology (*VSK*, 62 [78]).

This "chapter" in practical epistemology has become a multi-volume work, as it were, in the twentieth century with the influence of *perspectivism*, namely, the view that we always only have access to "the-way-things-are," that is, to objective reality, through a particular perspective—we perceive the world through the lens of our particular commitments, or within varying "horizons" of interpretations. Perspectivism raises the epistemological challenge of the relativity of human knowledge. Does that mean we can never know the true nature of things? Because this is not an essay about Guardini's epistemology, I can only issue disclaimers preventing some possible misunderstandings of his position. Guardini doesn't deny at all that there is an objective reality with a nature independent of what we all conceive and believe. He does not deny that one can attain true belief concerning that objective reality. Nor does he deny that one can attain knowledge of that objective reality. Nor does he deny that we are justified in accepting some beliefs and in rejecting others. Guardini's only point is that truth or objective reality is made manifest to the knower through "the character and state of mind of the aspirant to truth" (as Cottingham phrases it). In other words, Cottingham adds, "the truth yields itself only to those who are already to some extent in a state of receptivity and trust," indeed, freedom.[108] Man's "determination to possess truth, reality, the whole, is ready for the sacrifice which alone will lay the way open, ready 'to lose his soul, in order to save it' [Matt 10:39]. If this is his disposition, he will experience the Church as the road to freedom. Of her nature the Church is beyond and above these bonds, and he who 'surrenders his soul to her, in her shall win it back', but free, emancipated from its original narrowness, made free of reality as a whole" (*VSK*, 69 [86]). This is the Christian transcendence-standpoint in a nutshell.

The Christian transcendence-standpoint, as Guardini just described it, is only to be found in belonging to the central religious community of mankind, that is, the new and reborn humanity in Christ, which is the Church as the people of God, "constituted in her identity as a historic subject by reference to Jesus Christ and the Spirit."[109] One of the fruits of the Christian transcendence-standpoint is that freedom in Christ—who, being the fullness of God's Revelation, is the Truth—releases us from the intellectual bondage that is a result of the noetic influence of sin in our

---

108. Cottingham, *The Spiritual Dimension, Religion, Philosophy and Human Value*, 139.
109. "Select Themes of Ecclesiology," 275.

fallen selfhood. This divine gift of freedom enables man to "respond to the true nature of things with the integrity of his own nature and in the unique fashion of his divinely ordained individuality" (*VSK*, 56 [71]). And such freedom cannot be acquired through more philosophy, or self-training, or an alternative cultural environment. Says Guardini, "Here once more we encounter the mission of the Church—she, and she alone, conducts us to this freedom" (*VSK*, 57 [72]). "Man can be set free only by a power that opens his eyes to his own inner dependence and raises him above it," adds Guardini, "a power that speaks from the eternal, independent at its centre of all these trammels. It must hold up unswervingly to men the ultimate truths, the final picture of perfection, and the deeper standards of value, and must not allow itself to be led astray by a passion, by any fluctuations of sentiment, or by any deceits of self-seeking. This power is the Church. . . . The Church clears the path to freedom. . . . [S]he shows man truth seen in its essence, and a pure image of perfection to his nature" (*VSK*, 63 [79]). Man receives the gift of transcendent freedom in Christ from the Church, a gift which frees our insight into the fullness of truth, enabling us to abide in the Truth. What is the nature of the Church that she is able to give this gift as we participate in her life?

Before we give Father Guardini's answer to that question below, I shall turn to an even more fundamental challenge that he addresses. A corollary of the epistemological challenge raised by perspectivism is this: perspectivism arises from the fact that reality itself is a complex, rich unity that can be viewed from a variety of perspective; it manifests a diversity of aspects, such as the cultural, ethical, legal, social, economic, confessional, logical, sensory, biotic, and others. This perspectivism raises the question of relating these pluralistic perspectives to each other. How does man grasp reality in all its diversity if he can only have access to things through a particular perspective? All human knowledge is, and has always been partial, provisional, and, consequently, plagued by error. Thus, man "must correct his own vision of the world by the knowledge of others, complete his own insights by those of other men, and thus stretch out beyond himself to the whole of reality." But how does he know the "whole of reality" if his vision of things is always perspectival, partial, fragmented?

Guardini faces this question head on. He writes, "He must acknowledge, and to very core of his being, that reality includes all its possible aspects, is all-round. He must recognize that this reality can be grasped only by a subject equally comprehensive in his knowledge, his valuations and his activities; and that he himself does not possess this comprehensiveness, but is fragmentary, the realization of one possibility of human nature among a host of others. He must recognize the errors which this one-sidedness produces, and how they narrow the outlook and distort the judgment" (*VSK*, 68 [85]). If not man, who then is that subject that makes it possible for man to experience the whole of reality? That subject is the "transtemporal subject," namely, the Church.[110] "The whole of reality, experienced and mastered by the whole of humanity—such, from our present standpoint, is the Church. The problems with which we are faced here involve experience as a whole. No part of it may be detached from the whole. Ever partial question can be correctly envisaged only from the standpoint of the whole, and the whole only in the light of a full personal experience. *For this, however, a subject is required which itself is a whole, and this is the Church*" (*VSK*, 69–70 [87]). But this answer only raises the question once again, but now with respect to the Church herself: How does the Church know the "whole of reality," the totality of truth? Surely, her vision of things is always perspectival, partial, fragmented? What then is the nature of the Church that grounds the Christian-transcendence standpoint?

We saw earlier in this chapter that the Church is, according to Guardini, divinely constituted in her identity by reference to the trinitarian mystery revealed by Jesus Christ and the Spirit as the new people of God, as Christ's Body and Spouse. In this context, Guardini is now stressing the epistemological significance of the Church in knowing the whole of reality, the totality of truth. He writes: "The Holy Ghost is at work in the Church, raising her consistently above the limits of the merely human. Of Him it is said that He 'searcheth all things' ['even the deep things of God'] [1 Cor 2:10]. He is alone the Spirit of discipline and abundant life. To Him 'all things are given' [see John 16:13]. He is enlightenment and Love. He awakens love, and love alone sees things as they are. He 'sets in order charity' and causes it to become truth with a clear vision of Christ and His Kingdom. He makes us 'speaks the truth in love'" [Eph 4:15]. Our belonging to the Church brings us a share in her transcendence, knowledge and truth, discipline, abundant life, clarity of vision, interior freedom, and love. In what sense, then, is the Church transcendent, or eternally abid-

---

110. The reference to the Church as a "transtemporal subject" is from Ratzinger.

ing, as Guardini also says, above space and time, and not rooted in particular local conditions or particular historical periods, raised above the limits of the merely human, and yet able to enter into relation with every age? From one point of view, Guardini answers this question by arguing that the Church is wholly universal and inclusive, in truth, catholic, being the new and reborn humanity in Christ embracing in her communion men of diverse races, ages, characters, social class, professions, and so forth. Thus, the Church's vision of things isn't always perspectival, partial, fragmented. He explains:

> She is the one living organism which is not one-sided in its essential nature. Her long history has made her the repository of the entire experience of mankind. Because she is too great to be national her life embraces the whole of humanity. In her men of diverse races, ages, and characters think and live. Every social class, every profession and every personal endowment contribute to her vision of the whole truth, her correct understanding of the structure of human life. All the stages of moral and religious perfection are represented in the Church up to the summits of holiness. And all this fullness of life has been molded into a tradition, has become an organic unity.... The fundamental questions of man's attitude to life have been the meditation of centuries; so that the entire domain of human experience has been covered and the solution of its problems matured. Institutions have had to be maintained through vicissitudes of period and civilization, and have reached a classical perfection. Consequently, even from the purely natural point of view, the Church represents an organic structure of knowledge, valuation and life, of the most powerful description (*VSK*, 70–71 [88]).

Yet from another point of view, the core of Guardini's answer to this question is that "the substance of her doctrine, the fundamental facts which determine the structure of her religious system and the general outlines of her moral code and her ideal of perfection, transcend time." The Church is able to release us not only from the "tyranny of the temporal," but also from a perspectivalism that keeps our vision of reality fragmentary, one-sided, narrow, and hence distorted, because she possesses the standard of abiding truth in Christ, who, as John Paul II writes, being the fullness of God's Revelation, is "the criterion of both truth and salvation."[111] Indeed, the Church knows that "all the treasures of wisdom

---

111. John Paul II, *Fides et Ratio*, no. 23.

and knowledge" are hidden in Christ (Col 2:3). Indeed, says Guardini, "The Church is the whole of reality, seen, valued, and experience by the entire man" (*VSK*, 69 [86]). In sum:

> If man obeys and accepts the fundamental sacrifice of self-surrender and trusts himself to the Church; if he extends his ideas to the universal scope of Catholic dogma, enriches his religious sentiment and life by the wealth of the Church's prayers, strives to bring his conduct into conformity with the lofty, complete pattern of perfection, a pattern, moreover, which moulds the private life of the spirit presented by here communal life and her constitution, then he grows in freedom. He grows into the whole, without abandoning what is distinctively his own. . . . This is the meaning of '*sentire cum Ecclesia*' [thinking with the Church]—the way from one-sidedness to completeness, from bondage to freedom, from mere individuality to personality (*VSK*, 71–72, 73 [89, 90]).

MAN IS THE WAY OF THE CHURCH
ROMANO GUARDINI AND THE *NEW EVANGELIZATION*

Perhaps the most central theme in the almost twenty-seven-year pontificate of the late Pope John Paul II is the *call to the new evangelization*, that is, to the revitalization of the Christian faith at the heart of Western culture. This vital call for renewal is, in truth, an expression of the Church's missionary nature to preach the Gospel throughout the world, bringing the Gospel to all men, indeed, to the whole spectrum of human life, transforming creation from within and making it new—the plan of creation, fall, redemption, and the consummation of all creation in Christ. I believe that John Paul urged us to carry out the new evangelization as "integral evangelization"—to use a term of Aidan Nichols that nicely captures the full scope of this call.[112] As Nichols describes his understanding of integral evangelization, "I understand an evangelization that addresses all the dimensions of the person-in-society that Christian wisdom can help to flourish."[113] John Paul adds to this, "The men and women of today, like those of every time and place, are yearning for salvation. They wish *to rediscover the truth of God's dominion over creation and history, to encounter his self-revelation, and to experience his merciful love in all*

---

112. Helpful to me in answering this question is Nichols, OP, "Integral Evangelization," 66–80.

113. Ibid., 68.

the dimensions of their lives. The great truth to be proclaimed to this and every age is that God has entered human history so that men and women can truly become children of God."[114] Furthermore, John Paul calls for a *new* evangelization, for integral evangelization, because Western culture has become missionary territory as it increasingly is more estranged from its Christian roots.[115] Moreover, the new evangelization includes not only a call to conversion, to respond to the Gospel, but also to the renewal of contemporary civilization and culture, society, politics, economics, indeed the whole spectrum of life. John Paul was convinced, as he put it, "A faith that does not become culture is a faith not fully accepted, not entirely thought out, not faithfully lived."[116]

In this concluding portion of this chapter, I want to formulate four theses in response to the question, "What can Romano Guardini teach us about how the Church is to deepen its understanding and response to the new evangelization of Western culture?" Given his major position that the Christian faith is essentially ecclesial, and that belonging to the Church community is the living presupposition for becoming fully human, how does Guardini's position help to strengthen the Church's doctrinal, moral, and liturgical identity for the sake of today's task of evangelizing the present? In particular, how does his Christian anthropology help us to address the current cultural climate where the following is happening: the personal unity, the dignity, and transcendence of the self has been eroded (as our possibilities for self-making have greatly expanded), the severance of human roots (as the self becomes unanchored from truth, goodness, and beauty), and the fracturing of human bonds (as individual self-fulfillment becomes ever more relentless and our sense of identity and belonging is not supported by communities)?[117]

1. *The Church is the new and reborn humanity, the people elected and called by God, in Christ, and through the power of the Holy Spirit. She is the human community reborn into the Kingdom of God.*

---

114. John Paul II, *Springtime of Evangelization*, 39.

115. John Paul II, *Tertio Millennio Adveniente*, no. 57.

116. John Paul II, Letter instituting the Pontifical Culture for Culture, as cited in *Towards a Pastoral Approach to Culture*, no. 1.

117. Especially helpful to me in understanding these aspects of the current culture is Leithart, *Solomon among the Postmoderns*.

What then is the relationship between the Church (*ekkelsia*) and the Kingdom (*basileia*)? The Church is the fruit of the revelation of the Kingdom of God, of that great divine work of salvation, which became present and was fulfilled in Christ. The Kingdom is inconceivable without the Church, because the latter, as far as humanity is concerned, is the soteriological goal of the former. Yet, as John Paul II teaches, although the one is inseparable from the other, given that the Church is the concentration point of the Kingdom, its seed, sign, and instrument, they are *not* identical.[118] The Kingdom of God represents the all-embracive perspective of God's plan of salvation—the plan of creation, fall, redemption, and the consummation of all creation in Christ. This consummation has cosmic dimensions, embraces the structures of reality, all of history, bringing both grace and judgment, and filling time and eternity. Insisting on unity-simultaneous-with-distinctness of the relation of Church and Kingdom is fundamentally important in order to understand the full scope of the new evangelization as *integral evangelization*. Evangelization is integral because the Church proclaims to man the way to become human—as Romano Guardini puts it—in all the dimensions of man's existence. She is to proclaim the Lordship of Christ in all aspects of human living, and hence to the renewal of society as informed by the mind of Christ's Church. Of course, although the work of the Kingdom is broader in scope than the institutional Church, this work, says John Paul, "remains incomplete unless it is related to the Kingdom of Christ present in the Church and straining towards eschatological fullness."[119]

> 2. *True self-knowledge is dependent on the true knowledge of God, in Christ, through the Holy Spirit, to the Father. How is this true self-knowledge to be gained? In Catholicism, with its understanding of the relation between the Church and the individual, this central knowledge comes to life within us in the experience of the Church, which is the Mystical Body of Christ, mediated by her dogma, her moral teaching, her liturgy, and her sacramental life, operating in the hearts of the faithful, in the religious center of their existence by the power of the Holy Spirit, and which must reveal itself in the whole of our temporal life.*

---

118. John Paul II, *Redemptoris Missio*, nos. 17–20. See also, Ratzinger/Benedict XVI, *Jesus of Nazareth*, 46–63.

119. Ibid., no. 20. On the eschatological character of the Church, see also Guardini, *Church of the Lord*, 97–108.

For authentic Catholicism, the Church is the living presupposition of man's own personal existence, not a power hostile to himself, because she reveals to man the essential path to his goal, the ultimate end of human life: God calls us to his own beatitude. The Church does not fetter, she frees. Says Father Guardini, "For 'the Word was made Flesh' (John 1:14), and the Church is simply Christ, living on, as the content and form of the society He founded." "'The Church' means that God has entered human history; that Christ, in His nature, power and truth, continues to live in her with a mystical life" (*VSK*, 40, 38 [54, 52]). In this light, we can understand that of first importance to the new evangelization in proclaiming the saving truth of the Gospel is the revivification of ecclesial faith in the lives of men. Otherwise, men will still probably live *in* the Church, but will less and less be *living the Church and its faith (fides quae)*. Accordingly, by God's grace we are placed within the Church, and make her our starting point so that we gain "direct insight into the centre of reality which is the privilege of the genuine Catholic" (*VSK*, 32 [46]). To achieve this revivifying, the primary responsibility of the Church is the doctrinal and spiritual formation of her own members. "The minds of the Church's members [must] be not only alert to contemporary culture but also well-stocked with maturely reflected and apologetically honed dogmatic truth."[120] To appeal away from the Church, consequently, would be to cut oneself off from the source of the reality of divine revelation and salvation, and hence to commit epistemological suicide, as Aidan Nichols once put it.[121] Thus, there exists a profound solidarity between man's personal being and the Church. "But to be truly Catholic is the real, indeed the only genuine form of human existence, its way of life dictated at once by man's deepest nature and by divine revelation" (*VSK*, 53 [68])." The more unreservedly he lives in the Church, the more completely does he become what he ought to be—he experiences the Church as the actual, specific place of truth and as the road to freedom, the one, singularly unique way to be become truly and fully human. This message should be at the heart of the new evangelization.

3. *The Church is the locus and mediation of Trinitarian presence and knowledge, of truth and freedom, being the one, singularly unique way to become truly and fully human. As the fundamental community of*

---

120. Nichols, "Integral Evangelization," 70.
121. Nichols, *Shape of Catholic Theology*, 246.

truth, it has epistemic, ontological,1 and theological depth; it is the most effective resistance to relativism, skepticism, and nihilism.

The Church calls man to become truly and fully human, to become what he ought to be—to be reconciled with the Father, in Christ, and through the communion of the Holy Spirit, because face to face with the true God, man becomes truly man. "This is the covenant communion of life and understanding," the Mystical Body of Christ, "established with us by the gracious divine initiative through the saving revelation made in Jesus Christ."[122] The Church's mission of the new evangelization offers him the gifts of truth and freedom. She is the locus and mediation of the unconditionally valid truths of dogma—creation, fall into sin, and redemption in Jesus Christ—indeed, of God's Grace and Truth, of God Gift of himself. The Church is the locus and mediation of the Good, God's own Beatitude, which is the source of every good and of all love. Here, too, the Church offers man a "world of absolute values, an essential pattern of unconditional perfection, [and] an order of life whose features bear the stamp of truth.... His inner life becomes real, concentrated around a fixed centre, supported by eternal laws. His goal becomes clear, his action resolute, his whole life ordered and coherent—he becomes human" (*VSK*, 49 [64–65]). The Church is the locus and mediation of the liturgy, which is our sacramental entry into the mysteries of the divine saving plan, the redeeming acts of God in history. The Church is the locus and mediation of "one of the supreme treasures of life"—of freedom, especially of the ultimate depth of freedom, freedom for God and in God. The Church is the locus and mediation of the fullness of truth, that is, the comprehensiveness, the vast vision, of our Catholic faith—solid yet open, consistent yet dynamic, unconditionally true yet constantly growing in insight on the basis of Holy Scripture read in the Living Tradition of the Church. A more effective outworking of the new evangelization requires a greater degree of unity of all these elements—dogma, morality, and liturgy—in Catholic theological culture. "That is a major *desideratum* if we are to practice evangelization and catechesis on the foundation of a manifestly self-identical faith."[123]

4. *The epigraph to this chapter states the mission of the coming age, indeed its special task, to be the proper understanding of the relation between the Church and the individual. In order to accomplish this task, we need to*

---

122. Nichols, "Integral Evangelization," 71.
123. Ibid., 72.

> rise above the dilemma of individualism versus universalism. Both views are wrong because individuals and social communities exist in a mutual correlation in which neither can exist without the other: neither is basic to the other because neither is ever the source of the other.[124]

The heart of every individualist theory is the claim that individuals are more basic realities than communities. By contrast, the heart of every collectivist theory sees every person as dependent upon, and thus literally a *part* of, some all-inclusive social whole. Against both individualism and universalism, Guardini writes: "Both the Church and individual personality are necessary. Both, moreover, exists from the first; for neither can be traced back to the other. And if anyone should attempt to ask which of the two is the more valuable in the sight of God, he would see at once that it is a question which cannot be asked. For Christ died for the Church, that He might make her, by His Blood, 'a glorious Church, not having spot or wrinkle' [Eph 5:27]. But he also died for every individual soul . . . The Church and the individual personality—both, then, are equally primordial, equally essential, [and] equally valuable" (*VSK*, 29 [42])." Yet, the epigraph to this chapter also speaks of seeking the justification of ecclesiastical authority in this mutual relationship between the Church and the individual. On this matter, Guardini writes that "there is a profound difference between these two expressions of the Kingdom of God." He explains in a passage with which I will conclude this chapter of my book:

> Priority of rank belongs to the Church. She has authority over the individual. He is subordinated to her; his will to hers, his judgment to hers, and his interests to hers. The Church is invested with the majesty of God, and is the visible representative in face of the individual and the sum total of individuals. She possesses—within the limits imposed by her own nature and the nature of individual personality—the power which God possess over the creature; she is authority. And, however aware the individual may be of his direct relation to God, and as God's child know that he is emancipated from "tutors and governors," and that he enjoys personal communion with God, he is notwithstanding subject to the Church as to God. "He that heareth you, heareth me" [Luke 10:16]. "Whatsoever thou shalt bind upon earth, shall be bound also in heaven" [Matt 16:19]. It is a profound paradox which nevertheless is alone in harmony with the nature of life, and, as soon as the mind's eye is focused steadily upon it, self-evident (*VSK*, 29–30 [42–43]).

---

124. Again, helpful here with this succinct formulation of mutual correlation is Clouser, *Myth of Religious Neutrality*, 282.

4

"The Spirit of Truth"

On the Sacramental and Epistemological Significance of the Holy Spirit

"Spiritus Sanctus non est Scepticus"[1]

INTRODUCTION

"AND IT IS THE Spirit who bears witness, because the Spirit is truth" (1 John 5:6). This verse is just one of many in the Johannine literature where the Spirit is called by Jesus the Spirit of truth.[2] Thomas G. Weinandy explains why: "The Spirit is the Spirit of truth because he testifies to the truth. God's word is truth. Jesus as the Word of God is the truth of God (the source of all truth) to which God's Spirit of truth

---

1. The full quote from Luther (1483–1546) in Latin is: "Spiritus Sanctus non est Scepticus, nec dubia aut opinions in cordibus nostris scripsit, sed assertions ipsa vita et omni experientia certiores et firmiores" (cited in Berkouwer, *De Heilige Schrift*, I, 225, note 392). For an English translation, see Luther's Works, Vol. 33, 24, "The Holy Spirit is no skeptic, and the things he has written in our hearts are not doubts or opinions, but assertions—surer and more certain than all experience and even life itself."

2. Jesus refers to the Holy Spirit as the "Spirit of truth" in the following verses of the Gospel of John: "And I will pray the Father, and He will give you another Helper [Counsellor], that He may abide with you forever—the Spirit of truth" (John 14:16f.). "But when the Helper comes, whom I shall send to you from the Father, the Spirit of truth who proceeds from the Father, He will testify of Me" (John 15:26). Also in John we find Jesus saying, "I still have many things to say to you, but you cannot bear them now. However, when He, the Spirit of truth, has come, He will guide you into all truth; for He will not speak on His own *authority*, but whatever He hears He will speak; and He will tell you things to come" (John 16:12f.).

bears witness."[3] In general, the Holy Spirit has a many-sided role. He was promised by Jesus as the Comforter, Advocate, Counselor,[4] indeed, the Spirit of truth, who leads the Apostles and the Church into the truth. He is the witness to Christ, glorifying him (John 14:17; 15:26; 16:14), convicting men of sin, righteousness, and judgment (John 16:8–11), regenerating them (John 3:3), for with him who is the giver of life is the love and power of a "new creation" (Rom 8:22; 2 Cor 5:17; Col 3:10; Gal 6:15; Eph 2:15), and evoking from men the response that Christ is Lord (1 Cor 12:3). Furthermore, the Spirit assures men of their adoption as sons of God and of their heavenly inheritance (Rom 8:14; 2 Cor 1:22; 5:5; Eph 1:13; 4:30). He also makes known all the things believers have received from God (1 Cor 2:12; 1 John 2:20; 3:24; 4:6–13), and in the Church is the source of all spiritual gifts and Christian virtues (1 Cor 12:8–11; Gal 5:22).[5] Furthermore, the Holy Spirit leads the Church toward a deepened understanding of revealed truth. This explains the significance of Jesus' words: "When the Spirit of truth comes, he will guide you into all the truth" (John 16:13). Commenting on this verse, John Paul II writes, "He watches over the teaching of that truth, over its preservation and over its application to changing historical situations. He stirs up and guides the development of all that serves the knowledge and spread of that truth, particularly in scriptural exegesis and theological research. These can never be separated from the guidance of the Spirit of truth nor from the Magisterium of the Church, in which the Spirit is always at work."[6]

In particular, however, the Holy Spirit has epistemological significance. For example, the Holy Spirit works, epistemically, not only as a witness to the truth of the Gospel (see, e.g., John 15:26–27; Acts 5:32; Rom

---

3. Weinandy, OFM Cap., *Father's Spirit of Sonship*, 48.

4. Jesus calls the Spirit "another *paraclētos* (paraclete)" (John 14:6), another like himself. "The word *paraclētos* has often been translated as "comforter" or "counselor" here (the ESV prefers "Helper"), but there is no one word in English that accurately captures its meaning" (Letham, *Holy Trinity*, 58). On the meaning of *paraclētos*, see also *Catechism of the Catholic Church*, no. 692.

5. Bavinck, *Gereformeerde Dogmatiek*, I, 563. ET: *Reformed Dogmatics, Prolegomena*, Vol. I, 593. Both sources will be cited throughout this chapter and the next, first the original, followed by the pagination of the English translation in square brackets [ ].

6. John Paul II, *Catechesis on the Creed*, Vol. III, *Spirit, Giver of Life and Love*, 24; see also, 346–350. See *Dei Verbum*, no. 8: The apostolic faith "develops in the Church with the help of the Holy Spirit. For there is a growth in the understanding of the realities and the words which have been handed down."

8:16), but also he makes a person inwardly certain of that truth (see, e.g., 1 Thess 1:5). In short, the Holy Spirit has an epistemic role to play: the truth of divine revelation known is known in faith not only by the Spirit's internal illumination or testimony but also he makes a man inwardly certain of that truth. The *Catechism of the Catholic Church* teaches, "'No one can say 'Jesus is Lord' except by the Holy Spirit' [1 Cor 12:3]. 'God has sent the Spirit of his Son into our hearts, crying, *Abba!* Father!' [Gal 4:6]. This knowledge of faith is possible only in the Holy Spirit."[7] Elsewhere the *Catechism* states, "Believing is possible only by grace and the interior helps of the Holy Spirit."[8]

Vatican Council I (1869–1870) affirms the epistemological significance of the internal testimony of the Holy Spirit (*testimonium Spiritus Sancti internum*): "Now, although the assent of faith is by no means a blind movement of the mind, yet no one can accept the gospel preaching in the way that is necessary for achieving salvation without the inspiration and illumination of the Holy Spirit, who gives to all joy and ease in accepting and believing the truth."[9] In order to avoid misunderstanding from the outset of the Spirit's epistemic works, let me make it clear that the internal testimony of the Holy Spirit is, first, *neither* the cognitive source of Christian truth about God *nor*, second, does he work a blind, without reason, and ungrounded faith in the heart.

Following Herman Bavinck, I shall make a threefold distinction in my account of divine revelation.[10] On the first point, then, God is the

---

7. *Catechism*, no. 683.

8. Ibid., no. 154.

9. Vatican I, *Dogmatic Constitution Concerning the Catholic Faith*, Chapter 3, Faith, 445.

10. Bavinck, *GD* I, 10–214 [182–86]. For a further description of these terms, see Muller, *Dictionary of Latin and Greek Theological Terms*, 245–246, 297–298. Such distinctions as Bavinck makes are at work in Aquinas, *In Boet. De Trin.* 3,1, and 4, in Aquinas, *Faith, Reason and Theology*, 69, "So also in the faith by which we believe in God there is not only the accepting of the object of assent, but something moving us to the assent. This is a kind of light—the habit of faith—divinely imparted to the human mind.... It is clear, then, that faith comes from God in two ways: by way of an interior light that leads to assent and by way of the realities that are proposed from without and that had as their source divine revelation." In commenting on the words of Romans 1:19, "God made it [what can be known about him] manifest to them," Aquinas speaks of God's activity in creating as that of a teacher "proposing exterior signs of his wisdom" (Sir. 1:10) but also uniquely "conferring an interior light by which a person actually knows" (*Super Epistulas S. Pauli Lectura* [Rome: Marietti, 1953], *Ad Romanos* §116). St. Thomas's comments on

principium essendi of our knowledge of him: all knowledge of God has its source in God himself. Furthermore, the principle by which we know (*principium cognoscendi*) is the self-revelation or self-communication of God to man. The self-revelation or self-communication of God is the *principium cognoscendi*, which is to be distinguished again as the external cognitive foundation (*principium cognoscendi externum*) and the internal principle of knowing (*principium cognoscendi internum*), otherwise called *verbum externum* and *internum*, *revelatio*, and *illuminatio*.

The external cognitive foundation of faith is the objective revelation of God, with two dimensions of God's act in revealing himself: consisting not only of deeds, in nature, history and culture, culminating in Jesus Christ, but also in words, in the communication of truths. As Vatican II describes this objective revelation of God's self-communication: "This plan of revelation is realized by deeds and words having an inner unity: the deeds wrought by God in the history of salvation manifest and confirm the teaching and realities signified by the words, while the words proclaim the deeds and clarify the mystery contained in them."[11]

Regarding the internal principle of knowing, this refers to the illuminating work of the Holy Spirit by which God moves and assists someone to believingly accept and understand the objective revelation of God. In short, the internal principle of knowing has to do with the personal appropriation of the divine self-communication in words and deeds culminating in Christ. Thus, the illuminating work of the Holy Spirit "does not disclose to us any material truths that are hidden from the 'natural' [unspiritual] person. It only gives us a spiritual understanding of these same things, one that is different and deeper. Paul expressly states that the Spirit makes known to us the things objectively granted us by God in Christ (1 Cor 2). The Spirit whom believers receive is the Spirit of Christ, who takes everything from Christ and is received from the preaching of the gospel (John 14:17; Acts 5:32; Gal 3:2; 4:6; 1 John 2:20, 24, 27). But the truths themselves are known to us from other parts of Scripture; they are only subjectively sealed by the witness of the Holy Spirit."[12]

Romans are cited in Francis Martin, *Feminist Question*, 7, note 16. Fr. Martin also works, in his account of divine revelation, with the distinction between *principium cognoscendi externum* and *principium cognoscendi internum* (see 4–7).

11. *Dei Verbum*, no. 2.
12. Bavinck, *GD* I, 654 [594].

The second point raises the perennial question of the relation between faith and reason, and the corresponding issue of how to understand that "believing is possible only by grace and the interior helps of the Holy Spirit," on the one hand, "but it is no less true that believing is an authentically human act" on the other.[13] Believing is an authentically human act not only because it is an act of the intellect and human freedom but also the Gospel of Jesus Christ is the answer to the question that is human life. "Above all the Church knows that her message is in harmony with the most secret desires of the human vocation, restoring hope to those who have already despaired of anything higher than their present lot. Far from diminishing man, her message brings to his development light, life, and freedom."[14] Still, although the assent of faith is by no means a blind impulse of the mind, no one can "assent to the Gospel message," as is necessary to obtain salvation, "without the illumination and inspiration of the Holy Spirit, who gives to all joy in assenting to the truth and believing it."

What, then, is the epistemic work of the Holy Spirit, given not only the limits of human reason to grasp the truth of the mysteries of faith that man cannot reach by his own efforts, but also the noetic influences of sin, particularly manifested in resistance to this truth? For what, after all, is the work of the Holy Spirit in overcoming resistance to the truth? More to the point, what is the epistemological significance of the internal testimony of the Holy Spirit (*testimonium Spiritus Sancti internum*), as Bavinck phrases it, "concerning the ground of our faith, the certainty of our salvation, the rootedness of our hope in eternal life?"[15] Bavinck is right that the question regarding the certainty of faith is not only of theological but also of practical importance, vital to faith's knowledge of God and to the life of faith.[16]

The goal of this chapter is, then, to give an account of the works of the Holy Spirit, especially with respect to his sacramental significance and the epistemological question regarding the certainty of faith. I will work my way up to that sacramental and epistemological by laying a foundation in the late Pope John Paul II's theology of the Holy Spirit, particularly

---

13. *Catechism*, no. 154.
14. *Gaudium et Spes*, no. 21.
15. Bavinck, *Certainty of Faith*, 10. This book was first published in Dutch as *De Zekerheid des Geloofs*. See also, Warfield, "Review of *De Zekerheid des Geloofs*."
16. On the certainty of faith, see *Catechism*, no. 157.

as he developed it in his 1986 Encyclical Letter, *Dominum et Vivificantem*, the Lord and Giver of Life.[17] My chapter has three parts. First, I'll set out John Paul's doctrine of the Trinity and the identity of the Holy Spirit within the eternal life and communion of the Triune God. Second, the Holy Spirit's work in calling and regeneration, as the giver of life, and the use of sacramental means in the work of salvation is discussed. In this section, I interact with Bavinck and Berkouwer's critique of a Catholic sacramental theology. Third, I set forth a biblically and theologically sound epistemology of the Holy Spirit, which serves an indispensable role in knowing the truth of God. Here, too, I engage Bavinck in an ecumenical conversation.

SPIRIT AND TRINITY

"The mystery of the Most Holy Trinity is the central mystery of Christian faith and life. God alone can make it known to us by revealing himself as Father, Son, and Holy Spirit"[18] The Calvinist theologian B.B. Warfield put this mystery simply: "when we have said these three things, then—that there is but one God, that the Father and the Son and the Spirit is each God, that the Father and the Son and the Spirit is each a distinct person—we have enunciated the doctrine of the Trinity in its completeness."[19] This confession of the triune God is the orthodox faith of the Church professed in the Creed that is called Nicene-Constantinopolitan from the name of two Councils—of Nicaea (AD 325) and Constantinople (AD 381).[20] In this section, I will address briefly three questions regarding the Trinity, especially the identity of the Holy Spirit within the eternal life and

---

17. Extremely helpful here is Volume III of John Paul II, *Catechesis on the Creed*. See also, *Catechism*, nos. 232–267, 638–747. Instructive, even though I cannot give it the attention it deserves, is Kuyper's treatise, *Work of the Holy Spirit*.

18. *Catechism*, no. 234; cf. also, no. 261.

19. Warfield, "Biblical Doctrine of the Trinity," 36. Cardinal Kasper rightly notes, "The church's doctrine of the Trinity has obviously never made the completely absurd claim that is constantly attributed to it, namely that 1=3. The attribution would be correct only if the doctrine claimed that 1 person equaled 3 persons, or that 1 divine substance equaled 3 divine substances; that is, if it claimed that God is both unity and trinity in one and the same respect. Such a claim would violate the principle of contradiction.... But what the doctrine of the Trinity asserts is that in God there is a unity of substance and a trinity of persons or a unity of substance in a trinity of persons" (*God of Jesus Christ*, 234).

20. Dünzl, *Brief History of the Doctrine of the Trinity in the Early Church*, especially 49–59, 123–31, for a salient account of the significance of these councils.

communion of the Triune God.[21] First, how is the mystery of the Trinity revealed in biblical revelation? Second, how has the Church articulated the doctrine of the Trinity? Third, how does the Father fulfill his plan of salvation, of creation, fall into sin, redemption, and sanctification, in and through the divine missions of the Son and the Holy Spirit?

How, then, is the mystery of the Trinity revealed in biblical revelation? Alternatively put, what is the scriptural foundation for God's trinitarian self-revelation, especially for the identity of the Holy Spirit? The historical divine revelation given in the New Testament exhibits a triadic pattern—Father, Son, and Holy Spirit—affording insight into the being of God, that God is the Father, revealed by the Son, through the Spirit. For example, at his baptism in the Jordan, says John Paul II, Jesus is *"exalted before the eyes of Israel as the Messiah,* that is to say the 'One Anointed' with the Holy Spirit." A triadic pattern is exhibited here. John Paul II adds, "For when all the people were baptized and as Jesus, having received baptism, was praying, 'the heaven was opened, and the Holy Spirit descended upon him in bodily form, as dove'[22] [Luke 3:21f.; cf. Matt 3:16; Mark 1:10] and the same voice from heaven said 'This is my beloved Son, with whom I am well pleased' [Matt 3:17]."[23] The manifestation of the dove signifies the eternal rest of the Spirit on the Son, and, most significant, that the Messiah is the beloved Son of the Father. John Paul adds: "His solemn exaltation cannot be reduced to the messianic mission of the 'Servant of the Lord'. In the light of the theophany at the Jordan, this exaltation touches the mystery of the very person of the Messiah. He has been raised

---

21. I am closely following the order of questions on the Trinity in the *Catechism of the Catholic Church*, no. 235. For a theological analysis of the biblical data on the Trinity, I am indebted to Letham, *Holy Trinity,* 34–85. Helpful, too, was Weinandy, *Father's Spirit of Sonship,* 25–52, and Wainwright, *Trinity in the New Testament,* especially 199–234.

22. On the symbol of the Holy Spirit as a dove, the *Catechism* states: "At the end of the flood, whose symbolism refers to Baptism, a dove released by Noah returns with a fresh olive-tree branch in its beak as a sign that the earth was again habitable [Cf. Gen 8:8–12]. When Christ comes up from the water at his baptism, the Holy Spirit, in the form of a dove, comes down upon him and remains with him [Cf. Matt 3:16 and parallels]. The Spirit comes down and remains in the purified hearts of the baptized. In certain churches, the Eucharist is reserved in a metal receptacle in the form of a dove (*columbarium*) suspended above the altar. Christian iconography traditionally uses a dove to suggest the Spirit" (no. 701).

23. John Paul II, *Dominum et Vivificantem,* no. 19. Further references to this encyclical will be cited parenthetically in the text.

up because he is the beloved Son in whom God is well pleased. The voice from on high says: 'my son'" (*DV*, no. 19).

There are many other triadic statements in the New Testament linking the Holy Spirit with the Father and the Son (Rom 15:30; 1 Cor 12:4–6; 2 Cor 13:14; Gal 4:4–6; Eph 2:18; Col 1:3–8; 2 Thess 2:13–14; Titus 3:4–7). In writing of the gifts of the Spirit in 1 Corinthian 12, St. Paul refers to "the same Spirit," "the same Lord," and "the same God" (4–6). The Holy Spirit is called "the Spirit of Christ" (Rom 8:9; 1 Pet 1:11) and "the Spirit of [God's] Son" (Gal 4:6). In particular, the Holy Spirit is personally distinct from the Father and the Son (John 14:6, 26). As John Paul puts it, "In speaking of the Holy Spirit, Jesus frequently uses the personal pronoun 'he.'" "*He* will bear witness to me" (John 15:26). "*He* will convince the world of sin" (John 16:8). "When the Spirit of truth comes, *he* will guide you into all the truth" (John 16:13). "*He* will glorify me" (John 16:14). From these texts it is evident that the Holy Spirit is a Person, and not merely an impersonal power issuing from Christ (cf. e.g., Luke 6:19: "Power came forth from him . . ."). As a Person, he has his own proper activity of a personal character."[24] For instance, the Spirit is said to speak (Acts 1:16; 8:29; 10:19; 13:2), teach (John 14:26), witness (John 15:26), search (1 Cor 2:10), will (1 Cor 12:11), and intercede (Rom 8:26–27). Furthermore, the pope adds, "When speaking of the Holy Spirit, Jesus said to the apostles: "You know him, for he dwells in you, and will be in you" (John 14:7). "He will teach you all things, and bring to your remembrance all that I have said to you" (John 14:26). "He will bear witness to me" (John 15:26). "He will guide you into all the truth." "Whatever he hears he will speak" (John 16:13). He "will glorify" Christ (cf. John 16:14), and "he will convince the world of sin" (John 16:8). The Apostle Paul, on his part, states that the Spirit "cries in our hearts" (Gal 4:6); "he apportions" his gifts "to each one individually as he wills" (1 Cor 12:11); "he intercedes for the saints" (Rom 8:27). The Holy Spirit revealed by Jesus is therefore a personal being (the third Person of the Trinity) with his own personal activity."[25]

The triadic pattern is also revealed in benedictions (2 Cor 13:14; Rev 1:4–6), and in the formula of baptism (Matt 28:19). The Trinitarian

---

24. John Paul II, *Catechesis on the Creed*, 18. Another reason why the Holy Spirit is recognized as the third divine person is because to lie to him, said St. Peter not long after Pentecost, is to lie to God (Acts 5:3–4).

25. Ibid. On the personal characteristics attributed to the Holy Spirit throughout the NT, see also, Letham, *Holy Trinity*, 60–61.

formula of baptism—"baptizing them in the name of the Father and of the Son and of the Holy Spirit"—reflects, says John Paul, "the intimate mystery of God, of the divine life, which is the Father, the Son and the Holy Spirit, the divine unity of the Trinity" (*DV*, no. 9).

This triadic pattern is also exhibited in the bonds that unite the Father, the Son and the Holy Spirit to one another. Says John Paul, "Thus 'the Holy Spirit . . . proceeds from the Father' [John 15:26] and the Father 'gives' the Spirit [John 14:16]. The Father 'sends' the Spirit in the name of the Son [John 14:26], the Spirit 'bears witness' to the Son [John 15:26]. The Son asks the Father to send the Spirit-Counselor [John 14:16], but likewise affirms and promises, in relation to his own 'departure' through the Cross: 'If I go, I will send him to you' [John 16:7]. Thus, the Father sends the Holy Spirit in the power of his Fatherhood, as he sent the Son [cf. John 3:16f., 34; 6:57; 17:3, 18, 23]; but at the same time he sends him in the power of the Redemption accomplished by Christ—and in this sense the Holy Spirit is sent also by the Son: 'I will send him to you'" (*DV*, no. 8). In other words, the Spirit is sent both by the Father and the Son: by the Father in the name of the Son, and by the Son after his return to the Father (cf. John 14:26; 15:26; 16:14). What is more, "the sending of the person of the Spirit after Jesus' glorification [John 7:39] reveals in its fullness the mystery of the Holy Trinity."[26] Thus, the *Catechism* adds, "the eternal origin of the Holy Spirit is revealed in his mission in time."[27] This is because God as he reveals himself in salvation history corresponds to God as he is in himself. The Spirit has divine status himself because he reveals the Father and the Son and only God reveals God. Moreover, because the Spirit is linked expressly with the Father and the Son, we can conclude that this link entails identity of status and consequently of being.[28] Thus, the Spirit, a distinct divine Person, shares in the one being of God, being coequal with the Father and the Son.

Trinitarian insight into the life of God, into who God is in himself, is acquired from revelation in history. Clark Pinnock rightly notes, "The immanent Trinity (God in himself) is revealed by the economic Trinity (God in history), from which we learn that God is Father, Son and Spirit."[29]

26. *Catechism*, no. 244.
27. Ibid.
28. Letham, *Holy Trinity*, 57–58.
29. Pinnock, *Flame of Love*, 32. George, *Is the Father of Jesus the God of Muhammad?*, 76–77.

The first principle here, then, is that "through the *oikonomia* the *theologia* is revealed to us; but conversely, the *theologia* illuminates the whole *oikonomia*."[30] This principle needs some, albeit brief, explanation.

On the one hand, in speaking of the Trinity we are referring to the mystery of God's inmost life—the Trinity in itself, or the three persons as they relate to one another (works of the Trinity *ad intra*) without regard to creation, commonly called the ontological or immanent Trinity—and the Fathers of the Church used the term *theologia* (theology) to designate that life. In other words, God does not have to be related to a created order in order to be Father, Son, and Holy Spirit. For instance, he is eternally Father in relation to his only Son, who is eternally Son only in relation to his Father (cf. Matt 11:27). Still, "The mystery of his inmost being," namely, that there is one God, the almighty Father, his only Son, and Holy Spirit, "enlightens our understanding of all his works."[31] On the other hand, in speaking of the Trinity, we are also referring to all the works of God in the whole history of salvation by which God reveals himself and communicate his life. The same Fathers used *oikonomia* (economy) to designate the triune God's saving plan and its implementation in salvation history—works of the Trinity *ab extra*.[32] This is commonly called the economic Trinity, which is the Trinity as revealed in creation, providence, and salvation, acting in the world, in human history. In other words, salvation history reveals who God is in himself—being "identical with the history of the way and the means by which the one true God, Father, Son, and Holy Spirit, reveals himself to men 'and reconciles and unites with himself those who turn away from sin.'"[33] In short, salvation history is in truth the *self*-revelation of the triune God.

How has the Church articulated the doctrine of the Trinity? This is the second question I will briefly address. The Trinity is one in being and articulating the unity of the one God, or the identity in being of the three persons, is complex. The Trinity is not one person who plays three separate roles; this is the heresy of modalism; it erases the real, eternal, and irreducible distinctions among the three persons of the trinity. Modalism "can also surface where there is a pervasive stress on salvation

---

30. *Catechism*, no. 236.
31. Ibid., no. 234.
32. Dünzl, *Brief History of the Doctrine of the Trinity in the Early Church*, 16–17.
33. *Catechism*, no. 234.

history, so as to eliminate any reference to eternal realities. When that is so, God's self-revelation in human history as the Father, the Son, and the Holy Spirit is no longer held to reveal who he is eternally in himself."[34] Certainly the Church also rejects tritheism as heretical: the belief that there are three gods. Rather, there is but one God in three persons, the "consubstantial Trinity." As the *Catechism of the Catholic Church* teaches, "The divine persons do not share the one divinity among themselves but each of them is God whole and entire: 'The Father is that which the Son is, the Son that which the Father is, the Father and the Son that which the Holy Spirit is, i.e., by nature one God'. In the words of the Fourth Lateran Council (1215): 'Each of the persons is that supreme reality, viz., the divine substance, essence, or nature.'"[35]

Furthermore, the divine persons—the Father, the Son, and the Holy Spirit—are really distinct from one another. Doesn't the real distinction among the divine persons threaten to destroy God's unity? No, God is one but not alone; their distinction from one another lies in the relationship of each to the other: united without confusion and divided without separation.[36] The divine persons are relative to one another and thus relationality is at the heart of the Godhead. Timothy George explains, "The one true God does not exist in static isolation, the Alone with the Alone. He lives instead in the fulsome fellowship of three divine persons eternally united in being, relationship, and love." Indeed, the Church rejects Unitarianism, because the latter reduces the unity of God to a unit. Rather, George adds, "In the biblical view, relationship is *constitutive* for God himself: The Father *gives*, the Son obediently *receives*, and the Holy Spirit *proceeds* from both of them."[37] Thus, the divine unity is Triune. Moreover, this is fundamental to the Church's understanding of the triune God because it makes it possible for us to understand that the mystery of God's unity is a unity of love, and that what links the Spirit to the relationship of Father

---

34. Letham, *Holy Trinity*, 500, Glossary, entry on modalism.

35. *Catechism*, no. 253; cf. also nos. 251–52.

36. The Athanasian Creed states: "No this is the Catholic faith: We worship one God in the Trinity and the Trinity in unity, without either confusing the persons or dividing the substance; for the person of the Father is one, the Son's is another, the Holy Spirit's another; but the Godhead of the Father, Son, and Holy Spirit is one, their glory equal, their majesty coeternal" (as cited in the *Catechism*, no. 266). For the whole creed, see http://www.bible-researcher.com/ecumenical-creeds.html.

37. George, *Is the Father of Jesus the God of Muhammad?*, 82.

and Son is "the bond of love," as St. Augustine phrased it.[38] John Paul elaborates on the identity of the Spirit as the mutual and reciprocal love that flows between the communion of Father and Son:

> In his intimate life, God "is love" [cf. 1 John 4:8, 16], the essential love shared by the three divine Persons: personal love is the Holy Spirit as the Spirit of the Father and the Son. Therefore he "searches even the depths of God" [Cf. 1 Cor 2:10], as *uncreated Love-Gift*. It can be said that in the Holy Spirit the intimate life of the Triune God becomes totally gift, an exchange of mutual love between the divine Persons, and that through the Holy Spirit God exists in the mode of gift. It is the Holy Spirit who is *the personal expression* of this self-giving, of this being-love. He is Person-Love. He is Person-Gift. . . . At the same time, the Holy Spirit, being consubstantial with the Father and the Son in divinity, is love and uncreated gift from which derives as from its source (*fons vivus*) *all giving of gifts* vis-à-vis creatures (created gift): the gift of existence to all things through creation; the gift of grace to human beings through the whole economy of salvation. As the Apostle Paul writes: "God's love has been pored into our hearts through the Holy Spirit which has been given to us" [Rom 5:5]. . . . Already the "giving" of the Son, *the gift of the Son*, expresses the most profound essence of God who, as Love, is the inexhaustible source of the giving of gifts. The gift *made by the Son* completes the revelation and giving of the eternal love: *the Holy Spirit*, who in the inscrutable depths of the divinity is a Person-gift, through the work of the Son, that is to say by means of the Paschal mystery, is given to the Apostles and to the Church in a new way, and through them is given to humanity and the whole world (*DV*, nos. 10, 23).[39]

The triune God invites us to share in his intimate life of the communion of mutuality and self-giving love between the divine Persons. So the

---

38. St. Augustine, *On the Holy Trinity*, 15.17–19, as cited in Pinnock, *Flame of Love*, 38. See also, Ratzinger (Benedict XVI), *God of Jesus Christ, Meditations on the Triune God*, 35: "The Father and the Son do not become one in such a way that they dissolve into each other. They remain distinct from each other, since love has its basis in a 'vis-à-vis' that is not abolished. If each remains his own self, and they do not abrogate each other's existence, then their unity cannot exist in each one by himself: rather, their unity must be in the fruitfulness in which each one gives himself and in which each one is himself. They are one in virtue of the fact that their love is fruitful, that it goes beyond them. In the third Person in whom they give themselves to each other, in the Gift, they are themselves, and they are one."

39. See also, *Catechism*, nos. 253–57.

statement "God is love" is not merely a statement about God's generic nature. Rather, it tells us about the very heart of the Trinitarian life, namely, that within the Trinity, before the creation of anything, there was real love and real communication, and hence that personality and relationality are at the heart of the universe. But John Paul says more in the above passage and it especially pertains to the Holy Spirit, namely, that it is the Spirit that makes the life of God Love-Gift. "The Holy Spirit is revealed to us not only as a Gift to humanity, but also as Gift subsistent in the very inner life of God. 'God is love', as St. John told us (1 John 4:8), essential love which is common to all three Divine persons, according to the clarification by theologians. But that does not exclude that the Holy Spirit, as Spirit of the Father and the Son, is Love in a personal sense. . . . Therefore he 'scrutinizes even the deep things of God' (1 Cor 2:10) with the penetrating power that belongs to Love. Therefore he is also the uncreated and eternal Gift shared by the three divine Persons in the inner life of God, one and three. His existence as Love is identified with his existence as Gift."[40] The pope's conclusion brings us to the third point I will briefly address. The triune God eternally exists in himself as a transcendent reality of interpersonal gift. He opens himself to man, giving himself as a gift to man in the Holy Spirit through the work of Christ the Redeemer. How, then, does the Father fulfill his plan of salvation, of creation, fall into sin, redemption, and sanctification, in and through the divine mission of the Holy Spirit?

The brief answer here to this question must be that the entire salvific power of Jesus' redemptive work—his life, passion, death, and resurrection—is transmitted to the Holy Spirit, and whose mission it is to complete the work of the Son by bringing to fulfillment the history of creation and salvation. Jesus says, "He [the Spirit] will glorify me, for he will take what is mine and declare it to you" (John 16:14). The Holy Spirit comes after Christ's finished work, indeed, he is sent as a result of the redemption effected by Christ as well as by virtue of his departure. Hence, clearly there exists a relation causal interdependence between his departure and the coming of the Holy Spirit (cf. John 16:7f.). John Paul emphasizes this point: "The Holy Spirit will come insofar as Christ will depart through the Cross: he will come not only *afterwards*, but *because of* the Redemption accomplished by Christ, through the will and action

---

40. John Paul II, *Catechesis on the Creed*, 312; cf. also, 304–9.

of the Father" (*DV*, no. 11; cf. also, nos. 14, 24, 30). Thus, "according to the divine plan, Christ's 'departure' is an indispensable condition for the 'sending' and the coming of the Holy Spirit." What then is the mission of the Holy Spirit?

Well, the Incarnation is brought about by the power of the Holy Spirit and, what is more, the Incarnation achieves the fullness of its redemptive efficacy through the Holy Spirit. Says John Paul, "By departing from this world, Christ not only leaves his salvific message, but gives the Holy Spirit, and to that is linked the efficacy of the message and of redemption itself in all its fullness."[41] In particular, the pope adds, "The Holy Spirit, [is] *the giver of life*, the one *in whom* the inscrutable *Triune God communicates himself to human beings*, constituting in them the source of eternal life" (*DV*, no. 1). "What begins now," the pope adds, "is *the new salvific self-giving of God, in the Holy Spirit*" (*DV*, no. 11). John Paul elaborates:

> It is a new beginning, first of all because *between* the first beginning and the whole of human history—from the original fall onwards—*sin has intervened*, sin which is in contradiction to the presence of the Spirit of God in creation, and which is above all in *contradiction to God's salvific self-communication to man*. ... At the price of the Cross which brings about the Redemption, in the power of the whole Paschal mystery of Jesus Christ, the Holy Spirit comes in order to remain *from the day of Pentecost onwards* with the Apostles, to remain with the Church and in the Church, and through her in the world (*DV*, no. 13).

Christ teaches that central to the Spirit's mission is to "convince the world concerning sin and righteousness and judgment" (John 16:7f.) so as to bring about a conversion and hence a sharing in the life of the Triune God, in the power of the Holy Spirit. "*Repent*, and let every one of you be baptized in the name of Jesus Christ *for the forgiveness of your sins*; and you shall receive the gift of the Holy Spirit" (Acts 2:37f.). This verse raises a very important question that I will deal with in the next section of this chapter, namely, in which way, or by what means, does the Holy Spirit apply the saving benefits obtained through the passion, death, and resurrection of Christ.

John Paul answers this question by laying the link between the saving action of the Holy Spirit—"He gives life"—and the sacramental way: "For the sacraments signify grace and confer grace: *they signify life and*

41. Ibid., 17.

give life" (*DV*, no. 63). The pope adds: "The Church is the *visible dispenser* of the sacred signs, while the Holy Spirit acts in them as the *invisible dispenser* of the life which they signify. Together with the Spirit, Christ Jesus is present and acting" (Ibid.). Again, John Paul writes, "This new coming of Christ by the power of the Holy Spirit, and his constant presence and action in the spiritual life, are accomplished *in the sacramental reality*" (*DV*, no. 61). Elsewhere, the pope adds, "The Holy Spirit, who is at the origin of the Incarnation of the Word, is the living source of all the sacraments instituted by Christ and at work in the Church. *It is precisely through the sacraments that he gives people 'new life', associating the Church to himself as his co-worker in this saving action.*"[42] I will thus briefly reflect in the next section on the Holy Spirit's work, as the giver of new life, in calling, regeneration, and conversion. I will also briefly consider the meaning and effect of the sacraments in the divine work of salvation, particularly the Sacrament of Baptism. What does it signify and how does it operate in the order of salvation.

THE SPIRIT:
THE LIVING SOURCE OF SACRAMENTAL LIFE

John Paul II correctly remarks, "The Holy Spirit, especially through the 'means of salvation instituted by Jesus Christ', brings to fulfillment the mission entrusted to the Church to work for universal redemption."[43] In light of this claim, three questions will command my attention in this section. First, of what does the Holy Spirit, as the Spirit of truth, convince the world concerning sin and righteousness and judgment? Second, what is the relation between calling, regeneration, and conversion? Third, how must we conceive of the connection that exists between the work of the Holy Spirit and the function of the sacraments, especially, Baptism in bringing new life or sanctifying grace as a supernatural gift to man?[44]

Regarding the first question, we can say that the proper action of the Holy Spirit as the Spirit of truth is to convince man, in the first place, concerning his sin. The sin in question here is not only the specific sin of

---

42. Ibid., 351.

43. Ibid., 355.

44. Helpful in answering these questions is John Paul II, *Reconciliatio et Paenitentia*, nos. 18–22. Also, *Catechism of the Council of Trent*, Part II, The Sacraments, 141–60, and Baptism, 161–98. See also, Ott, *Fundamentals of Catholic Dogma*, 325–60.

rejecting Jesus and his redemptive work. Indeed, it is not limited to the knowledge of any specific sin, but rather it refers to the source of man's sinfulness on earth, namely, to "the sin that according to the revealed Word of God constitutes *the principle and root of all the others.*" That is, the pope adds, "We find ourselves faced with the original reality of sin in human history and at the same time in the whole of the economy of salvation. It can be said that in this sin the *'mysterium iniquitatis'* has its beginning" (*DV*, no. 33).[45] This original sin is an act of man's will, indeed the sin of Adam, his disobedience, opposing his will to the will of God, to his salvific will. This one man's "original disobedience *a rejection*, or at least *a turning away from the truth contained in the Word of God*, who creates the world" (*DV*, no. 33).[46]

Hence, whenever I sin against God, my sin is a reflection of the dynamics of sin, of the mystery of iniquity, indeed, of "the hereditary sinfulness of human nature," as the pope phrases it (*DV*, no. 44), which never ceases to be active in and through human actions. John Paul calls this original disobedience to God's Word the "anti-Word" or the "anti-truth."[47] Man falsifies the truth about himself, that is, his creaturely subjectivity depends on the Creator and the impassable limit for a created being that is the source of existence and freedom. But in falsifying the truth about himself, man also completely "falsifies the *truth about who God is.*" In other words, "God the Creator is placed in a state of suspicion, indeed of accusation, in the mind of the creature. For the first time in human history there appears the perverse 'genius of suspicion'. He seeks to *'falsify' Good itself, the absolute Good*, which precisely in the work of creation has manifested itself as the Good which gives in an exhaustible way: as *bonum*

---

45. John Paul writes: "When on the eve of the Passover Jesus speaks of the Holy Spirit as the one who 'will convince the world concerning sin', on the one hand this statement must be given *the widest possible meaning*, insofar as it includes all the sin in the history of humanity" (*DV*, no. 29).

46. The selfsame Word of God, that is, Jesus Christ, is not only the mediator of redemption but also the mediator of creation. "This Word is the same Word who was 'in the beginning with God', who 'was God', and without whom 'nothing was made that was made', since 'the world was made through him' [Jn. 1:1, 2, 3 10]. He is the Word who is also the eternal law, the source of every law which regulates the world and especially human acts" (*DV*, no. 33).

47. I give a more extensive account of John Paul's notion of original disobedience in my article, "Living Truth for a Post-Christian World: The Message of Francis Schaeffer and Karol Wojtyla."

diffusivum sui, as *creative love*. Who can completely 'convince concerning sin', or concerning this motivation of man's original disobedience, except the one who alone is the gift and the source of all giving of gifts, except the Spirit, who 'searches the depths of God' and is the love of the Father and the Son" (*DV*, no. 37).

The "Spirit of truth" convinces man of the truth concerning not only his sins, but also enables him "to know *the truth about that righteousness* which entered human history in Jesus Christ" (*DV*, no. 48). Being convinced of my sin is required by my conversion and response to the Gospel. Conversion of the human heart, which entails inner contrition and a sincere and firm purpose of amendment, is the indispensable condition for repentance and the forgiveness of sins: "the interior judgment of the conscience, and this, being a proof of the action of the Spirit of truth in man's inmost being, becomes at the same time a new beginning of the bestowal of grace and love: 'Receive the Holy Spirit' [John 20:22]" (*DV*, no. 31). The ultimate truth about my sins in respect of the saving work of Jesus Christ is not merely that I stand accused and judged, under the wrath of God (cf. Eph 2:3; Rom 5:9), but rather that my sins have been forgiven, that Christ died for me while I was a sinner, indeed God's enemy (Rom 5:8, 10), and yet that I have now been reconciled with the Father, by the redemptive power of Christ crucified and risen, in and through the power of the Holy Spirit. "The Holy Spirit, who takes from the Son the work of the Redemption of the world, by this very fact takes the task of the salvific 'convincing of sin'. This convincing is *in permanent reference to 'righteousness'*: that is to say to definitive salvation in God, to the fulfillment of the economy that has as its center the crucified and glorified Christ" (*DV*, no. 28). And in a clear allusion to the Pauline teaching that there is therefore now no condemnation to those who are in Christ Jesus (Rom 8:1), the pope adds, "this *salvific economy of God* in a certain sense removes man from '*judgment*', *that is from damnation.* . . . The Holy Spirit, by showing sin against the background of Christ's Cross in the economy of salvation (one could say 'sin saved'), enables us to understand how his mission is also 'to convince' [man] of the sin that has already been definitively judged ('sin condemned')" (*DV*, no. 28). Again, the pope says.

> Those who are converted, therefore, are led by the Holy Spirit out of the range of the '*judgment*', and *introduced into that righteousness which is in Christ Jesus*, and is in him precisely because he receives it from the Father, as a reflection of the holiness of the Trinity. This

is the righteousness of the Gospel and of the Redemption . . . It is the righteousness which *the Father gives to the Son and to all those united with him in truth and in love* (*DV*, no. 48).

In short, Christ came into the world to save sinners, and if the Spirit is to continue, in the world and in the human spirit, the salvific work that is rooted in the sacrifice of Christ's cross, then he must convince the world concerning, sin, judgment, and righteousness.

Now, there is a second question to consider: what is the relationship of calling, regeneration, and conversion, and how are we to understand that relationship? It will shortly become evident why this question is important in understanding the saving work of the Holy Spirit. Let me say something in the first place about the distinction I am drawing between regeneration and conversion. The sacraments of the Gospel of Jesus Christ are essentially sacraments of grace.[48] In this matter, quoting Dutch neo-Calvinist Abraham Kuyper, "The Reformed stand with Rome, Luther, and Calvin against Zwingli in their adherence to a divine working of grace in the sacrament."[49] Now, granted that the Reformed and Roman Catholics agree that baptism is a sacrament of grace, they nonetheless part ways over the position of baptismal regeneration. The Catholic Church teaches that the sacrament of Baptism effects regeneration and renewal. Aside from the objection that this teaching has no scriptural basis, Reformed theologians, such as Bavinck and Berkouwer, are convinced that the call to genuine faith, repentance, and conversion is shortchanged or ignored altogether if we suppose that a man is reborn through the sacrament of Baptism. I am theologically sensitive to this objection, and I'll respond to it in the following way.

---

48. Bavinck correctly notes, "The difference [between the Reformed, Roman Catholics and Lutherans] in the doctrine of the sacraments . . . does not concern the question whether God really imparts his grace but in what way he does this" (*GD* IV, 461 [483]). I think it also concerns the sort of grace that is imparted, with the Roman Catholic claiming that the sacrament imparts saving grace and the Reformed that it *only* imparts grace for the purpose of nourishing the weakness of our faith.

49. As cited in Berkouwer, *De Sacramenten*, 101–2; ET: *Sacraments*, 84. Both sources will be cited throughout this chapter, first the original as *GD*, followed by the pagination of the English translation in square brackets [ ]. The Swiss Reformer Zwingli (1484–1531) sees the sacraments as a mere or empty sign (*nudum signum*), implying the exclusion of grace from the sacrament. Bavinck says, regarding the position of the Zwinglians, "True, the sacraments visibly represent the benefits that believers have received from God, but they do this as confessions of our faith and do not impart grace" (*GD* IV, 448 [470]).

What grace of God does the sacrament of Baptism signify?[50] Well, the *Catechism of the Catholic Church* teaches that the sacrament of Baptism signifies union with Christ, the forgiveness of sins, the gift of the Holy Spirit, of regeneration and renewal, and incorporation into the Church, the Body of Christ, which is the new and reborn humanity in Christ.[51] Indeed, "Baptism not only purifies from all sins, but also makes the neophyte 'a new creature', an adopted son of God, who has become a 'partaker of the divine nature', member of Christ and co-heir with him, and a temple of the Holy Spirit." "The Most Holy Trinity gives the baptized sanctifying grace," the *Catechism* adds, "the grace of *justification*: [1] enabling them to believe in God, to hope in him, and to love him through the theological virtues; [2] giving them the power to live and act under the prompting of the Holy Spirit through the gifts of the Holy Spirit; [3] allowing them to grow in goodness through the moral virtues. Thus the whole organism of the Christian's supernatural life has its rooted in Baptism."[52] In short, the Church clearly teaches that justification is conferred in baptism, and hence man is reborn or regenerated through that sacrament.[53] The gracious act of God in the sacrament of baptism signifies that those who were dead in sin are now alive in Christ, giving rise to a new existence in Christ and his Body, the reborn humanity, of which conversion and faith is its first fruit.

But a question arises in light of the plain fact that all baptized persons do not bear the fruit of conversion and faith: Is that because the sacrament of baptism does not always accomplish what it signifies—always, inevitably and unconditionally? In other words, can baptism efficaciously communicate grace on the recipient of the sacrament but nevertheless be

---

50. I will return shortly to discuss how the sacrament of baptism operates, that is from what it signifies to its effect.

51. *Catechism*, nos. 1262–1269. On what baptism signifies, see also the *Catechism of the Council of Trent*, Part II, 182–91. See also, John Paul II, *Dominum et Vivificantem*, no. 40: The Letter to the Hebrews "shows how *humanity, subjected to sin* in the descendants of the first Adam, in Jesus Christ became *perfectly subjected to God* and united to him, and at the same time full of compassion towards men. Thus there is *a new humanity*, which in Jesus Christ through the suffering of the Cross has returned to the love which was betrayed by Adam through sin. This new humanity is discovered precisely in the divine source of the original outpouring of gifts: in the Spirit, who 'searches . . . the depths of God' and is himself love and gift."

52. *Catechism*, nos. 1265–66.

53. Ibid., no. 1992.

fruitless in his life? Yes it can because sacramental efficacy is *not* derived from the belief or disposition of that recipient; and hence we can hold on to the Church's understanding of the objectivity of the sacrament of baptism as the sacrament of rebirth, of the grace of regeneration, *without* negating the necessity of individual conversion, of faith, of a personal response to Gospel. Indeed, faith and conversion are the fruits of that sacrament "in those who receive them with the required disposition."[54] Let me make it clear: faith and conversion is not the mechanism, as it were, that triggers regeneration but rather is its evidence.[55] Thus, the objectivity of the sacrament of baptism as a sacrament of regeneration, of rebirth, can be maintained without inevitably robbing the Gospel of the power of calling people to repentance, conversion, and faith.

Of course, whether baptized as an infant or an adult, the Gospel makes the same demand: "For all the baptized, children or adults, faith must grow *after* Baptism."[56] Thus, "By its very nature infant Baptism requires a *post-baptismal catechumenate.* Not only is there a need for instruction after Baptism, but also for the necessary flowering of baptismal grace in personal growth."[57] Evidence then that the grace of baptism has unfolded in an individual's life at some point after his baptism is that he makes a public act of confession, of personally accepting the Good News of God's saving actions, and of confessing that Jesus is Lord, and of course that cannot be done "except by the Holy Spirit" (1 Cor 12:3). St. Paul tells us, "that if you confess with your mouth that Jesus is Lord and believe in your heart that God has raised him from the dead you will be saved" (Rom 10:9).

Failure to make the distinction between regeneration and conversion, with the latter being the fruit of the former, results in the tendency to cheapen grace because it undercuts Christ's call to interior repentance, or what the *Catechism* calls "the first and fundamental conversion," which "is a radical reorientation of our whole life, a return, a conversion to God with all our heart." We also lose sight of the continuing resounding of Christ's call to conversion in the lives of Christians, and which

---

54. Ibid., no. 1131; see also, no. 1128.

55. For this helpful formulation of the relation between regeneration and conversion, I am indebted to Harvey, "Baptism as a Means of Grace."

56. *Catechism*, no. 1254.

57. Ibid., no. 1231. "The whole ecclesial community bears some responsibility for the development and safeguarding of the grace given at Baptism" (no. 1255).

the *Catechism* calls, "*second conversion*," which is expressed in a life of faithful obedience.[58] In short, failure to make this distinction is vulnerable to promoting false assurance inasmuch as one is tempted to focus upon the sacrament of Baptism as a mere external rite, breeding a kind of formalism and blind ritualism, with the call to genuine faith, repentance, and conversion easily being shortchanged or ignored altogether, and this in turn encourages a nominal Catholicism, a cultural Christianity, that is spiritually superficial. We are all familiar by now with Dietrich Bonhoeffer's famous castigation of that tendency.

> The price we are having to pay today in the shape of the collapse of organized religion is only the inevitable consequence of our policy of making grace available at all too low a cost. We gave away the word and sacraments wholesale; we baptized, confirmed and absolved a whole nation without asking awkward questions, or insisting on strict conditions. Our humanitarian sentiment made us give that which was holy to the scornful and unbelieving. We poured forth unending streams of grace. But the call to follow Jesus was hardly ever heard. Where were those truths which impelled the early Church to institute the catechumenate, which enabled a strict watch to be kept over the frontier between the Church and the world, and afforded adequate protection for costly grace? . . . To baptized infants without bringing them up in the life of the Church is not only an abuse of the sacrament, it betokens a disgusting frivolity in dealing with the souls of the children themselves. For baptism can never be repeated.[59]

Bonhoeffer is right that many of us can say we never heard the call to follow Jesus when we were growing up, even if we went to Catholic schools for twelve years, as was the case for me. In short, we were never evangelized and hence the call of the gospel to faith and conversion, and the new life in Christ empowered by the Holy Spirit, is unknown to many baptized Catholics. To offset the phenomenon of "cheap grace," as Bonhoeffer describes it above, we need to understand that in the order of salvation God's calling precedes regeneration and conversion. This is so because if there were no gospel call we could not be saved. "How shall they believe in Him of whom they have not heard?" (Rom 10:14). This is

---

58. *Catechism*, nos. 1427–28, 1431.
59. Bonhoeffer, *Cost of Discipleship*, 47, 179.

why the *Catechism* is right, "*God calls man first.*"⁶⁰ Earlier in the *Catechism* we find, "Although man can forget God or reject him, He never *ceases to call every man to seek him*, so as to find life and happiness."⁶¹

Following the Augustinian Calvinist, Herman Bavinck, I think—as an Augustinian Catholic—that we must distinguish an external call from the internal call of the Holy Spirit.⁶² God's external call comes to all men, and it refers to his general call "through nature, history, environment, various leadings, and experiences." It has as its medium the law of creation, common grace, or general revelation, as expressed in "the family, society, and state, in religion and morality, in heart and conscience," obliging all men to live according to God's goodness and truth. This call is, however, insufficient for salvation, "because it knows nothing of Christ and his [saving] grace and therefore cannot lead anyone to the Father" (John 14:6; Acts 4:12; Rom 1:16). "Even with this call," adds Bavinck, "the world in its folly and darkness did not know God (John 1:5, 10; Rom 1:21ff.; 1 Cor 1:21; Eph 2:12). Still, it [this call] is a rich form of God's involvement with his creatures, a witness of the Logos, a working of the Spirit of God of great significance for humanity."⁶³

Yet there is more: there is an expression of God's external calling that comes to man in the form of the revealed law and especially in the form of the revealed gospel, and this is a general gospel calling that summons all men to faith in Christ and to dependency on the grace of God. This is a universal offer of grace that is "seriously and sincerely meant" inasmuch as the gospel is proclaimed to all men as sinners, all of whom need redemption, but not all of whom respond to that saving message. By contrast, the calling of God that actually brings about a free and personal response from the person who hears the saving message of the gospel is sometimes called internal calling.⁶⁴ "He came to His own, and His own did not receive Him. But as many as received Him, to them He gave the right to become children of God, to those who believe in His name" (John 1:11–12). In other words, internal calling has to do with the Lord Jesus in-

---

60. *Catechism*, no. 2566; italics original.
61. Ibid., no. 30; italics added.
62. On this distinction, see St. Augustine, *Predestination of the Saints*, chapter 8.
63. Bavinck, *GD* IV, 1–72, and for the quotes in this paragraph, 2–3 [29–95].
64. *Catechism*, no. 2002: "God's free initiative demands *man's free response*, for God has created man in his image by conferring on him, along with freedom, the power to know him and love him. The soul only enters freely into the communion of love."

vitation to respond personally to his call: "Behold, I stand at the door and knock. If anyone hears My voice and opens the door, I will come in to him and dine with him, and he with Me" (Rev 3:20). Again, we find another invitation from the Holy Spirit and the Church to come to Christ: "And the Spirit and the bride say, 'Come!' And let him who hears say, 'Come!' And let him who thirsts come. Whoever desires, let him take the water of life freely" (Rev 22:17). Furthermore, this external call is a "preparatory grace": "The *preparation of man* for the reception of grace is already a work of grace. This latter is needed to arouse and sustain our collaboration in justification through faith, and in sanctification through charity."[65] "God immediately touches," the *Catechism* adds, "and directly moves the heart of man."[66] Indeed, God works in the hearts of men to make effective, by grace, the preaching of the gospel, without which there would be no saving response. Jesus said, "No one can come to Me unless the Father who sent Me draws him" (John 6:44). For example, when Lydia heard the gospel message in St. Paul's first visit to Philippi, "The Lord opened her heart to heed the things spoken by Paul" (Acts 16:14).

Finally, I want to turn now to address the question of sacramental efficacy, especially the notion of *ex opere operato* ("by the very fact of the action's being performed"[67]), through which the Holy Spirit gives new life. John Paul writes, "The fullness of the salvific reality, which is Christ in history, *extends* in a sacramental way *in the power of the Spirit-Paraclete*" (*DV*, no. 64). As I noted earlier in the concluding paragraph of the last section, John Paul lays the connection between the saving action of the Holy Spirit—"He gives life"—and the sacramental way: "For the sacraments signify grace and confer grace: *they signify life and give life*" (*DV*, no. 63). The pope adds: "The Church is the *visible dispenser* of the sacred signs, while the Holy Spirit acts in them as the *invisible dispenser* of the life which they signify. Together with the Spirit, Christ Jesus is present and acting" (Ibid.). Again, John Paul writes, "This new coming of Christ by the power

---

65. *Catechism*, no. 2001.
66. Ibid., no. 2002.
67. Ibid., no. 1128. I am following the *Catechism*'s translation of "ex opere operato" in the text. The translation could be shortened to simply "through the act performed" as does the English translator of Bavinck's *GD IV*. Or it could be lengthened to "by the fact that the sacramental rite is [validly] performed"; thus, "by the power of rite" as does the English translator of Flemish Domincan theologian Schillebeeckx's *Christus, Sacrament van de Godsontmoeting*. ET: *Christ, Sacrament of the Encounter with God*.

of the Holy Spirit, and his constant presence and action in the spiritual life, are accomplished *in the sacramental reality*" (*DV*, no. 61).

At this point we should cut off any needless misunderstanding between the Reformed and Catholic traditions over the ultimate efficient cause of the efficacy of the sacraments. I can think of no better witness to pushing aside this misunderstanding that has caused needless division between them than Bavinck. He writes: "God alone can be the author, initiator, and 'efficient cause' of the sacraments. He alone is the possessor and distributor of all grace. He alone can determine to what means he will bind himself in the distribution of his grace."[68] John Paul II agrees with Bavinck. He says "The Holy Spirit, who is at the origin of the Incarnation of the Word, is the living source of all the sacraments instituted by Christ and at work in the Church." Yet, John Paul II, working with the notion that the sacraments not merely signify but actually cause grace, presupposes that there are "two kinds of efficient causes, principal and instrumental." Aquinas explains the latter: "An instrument cause . . . acts not in virtue of its own form, but solely in virtue of the impetus imparted to it by the principle agent. . . . And this is the way in which the sacraments of the New Law cause grace. For it is by divine institution that they are conferred upon man for the precise purpose of causing grace in and through them . . . now the term 'instrument' in its true sense is applied to that through which someone produces an effect. This is why we are told in Titus [3:5], *He saved us by the washing of regeneration*."[69] In light of the meaning that instrumental cause possesses, which Aquinas and hence the Catholic tradition, does not pit over against principal or ultimate efficient cause, John Paul II can say quite properly, "*It is precisely through the sacraments that he gives people 'new life', associating the Church to himself as his co-worker in this saving action*."[70] In sum, the pope adds, referring us back to the principal cause of the sacrament, "Justification has been *merited for us by the Passion of Christ* who offered himself on the cross as a living victim, holy and pleasing to God, and whose blood has become the instrument of atonement for the sins of all men. Justification is conferred in Baptism, the sacrament of faith." Again, "The grace of the Holy Spirit has the power

---

68. Bavinck, *GD* IV, 451 [474].

69. Aquinas, *Summa Theologiae*, III, 62, 1, Vol. 56. Berkouwer understands the Thomistic background to the two kinds of efficient causes, principal and instrumental. See his work, *De Sacramenten*, especially, 79–80 [65–66].

70. John Paul II, *A Catechesis on the Creed*, 351.

to justify us, that is, to cleanse us from our sins and to communicate to us 'the righteousness of God through faith in Jesus Christ," a righteousness that is mediated "through Baptism."[71] In short, "Baptism is the sacrament of regeneration through water and in the Word."[72]

This will suffice to describe the meaning of baptism, the grace that it signifies. We turn now to the question of the effect of this sacrament, that is, how it operates. Basically, I am interested here in the idea of sacramental causality, and the question: Do sacraments effect what they signify? Alternatively put, what is the connection between the sacramental sign and that which is signified? If sacraments actually accomplish what they signify, in what sense does, say, the sacrament of baptism signify grace and confer grace, not as if the two things are unrelated properties of a sacrament; rather in the sense that the sacraments *cause* by signifying. How, then, do they exert their efficacy?[73] According to Berkouwer, "From the reformed side, the issue [does] not involve [questioning] the efficacy of the sacraments at all, but rather a totally different understanding of what this efficacy is."[74] And Bavinck himself claims that the Reformed rejection of *ex opere operato* does not mean that the connection between the sign and the thing signified is any less "objective, real, and essential" in its view.[75] I agree with Berkouwer that in order to see this point clearly, "we must examine what is meant by *opus operantum*."[76]

Perhaps the best way to get at an answer to this question is by contrasting the Catholic view of sacramental causality—the sacraments confer grace *ex opere operato* (literally: "by the fact that the sacramental rite is validly performed, and thus by the power of the rite")—as it is typically (mis-)understood by some Protestants—and not as the Catholic Church teaches—from two other views.[77] A representative misunderstanding and

71. *Catechism*, nos. 1992, 1987, respectively.

72. Ibid., no. 1213.

73. Berkouwer argues that the Calvinist (Reformed) objection to the Catholic teaching of *ex opere operato* should *not* be posed in term of sacramental efficacy. The question is not whether the sacraments are efficacious but rather how they exercise their efficacy. For Berkouwer's defense of sacramental efficacy but not *ex opere operato*, see his work, *De Sacramenten*, especially, 11–28, 66–107 [13–26, 56–89].

74. Berkouwer, *De Sacramenten*, 74 [62].

75. Bavinck, *GD* IV, 461 [482].

76. Berkouwer, *De Sacramenten*, 74 [62].

77. Stott, "Evangelical Doctrine of Baptism," 47–49. In response to Stott's view, see Harvey, "Baptism as a Means of Grace," 103–112. See also, Bavinck, *Saved by Grace*.

criticism of the Roman Catholic *ex opere operato* view is that of the well-known evangelical Anglican, John Stott. On this view, Stott says, "the sign always conveys the gift, automatically, by itself, *ex opere operato*, so that all those who receive the sign willy-nilly also receive the thing signified."[78] His chief objection to this view, as he understands it, is that "it does not take into account the necessary relationship between regeneration and faith in Scripture."[79] Accordingly, Stott takes *ex opere operato*—that what is accomplished through the sacraments is accomplished in the doing of the sacrament—to mean that grace is conferred "automatically" or "magically," apart from the interior dispositions of the recipient.

Significantly, Stott seems entirely unaware of the Catholic Church's teaching that "to attribute the efficacy of prayers or of sacramental signs to their mere external performance, apart from the interior dispositions that they demand, is to fall into superstition."[80] The Church rejects this reproach of "magic" of its sacramental doctrine: it has never taught that the subjective disposition of the recipient is unimportant.[81] For instance, Canon 6 of the Council of Trent's Decree on the Sacraments condemns the teaching "that sacraments of the New Law do not contain the grace which they signify, or that they do not confer this grace to those who present no

---

Bavinck's book was originally published in Dutch as *Roeping en Wedergeboorte*. The Dutch edition is online: http://www.neocalvinisme.nl/tekstframes.html. Extremely helpful in understanding the crucial differences between the Catholic and Calvinist traditions on sacramental causality is Berkouwer, *De Sacramenten*, especially, 139–72 [110–34]. I have also profited from Schillebeeckx, OP, *Christ*, especially, 47–89.

78. Stott, "Evangelical Doctrine of Baptism," 47–49.

79. This is how Harvey correctly summarizes Stott's objection to the *ex opere operato* view.

80. *Catechism*, no. 2111. Superstition is a violation of the First Commandment: "Superstition is the deviation of religious feeling and of the practices this feeling imposes. It can even affect the worship we offer the true God, e.g., when one attributes an importance in some way magical to certain practices otherwise lawful or necessary." Stott's essay, "Evangelical Doctrine of Baptism," was originally published in 1964, but it was republished in 1998. In between the first and second time his essay was published, the *Catechism of the Catholic Church* appeared, but Stott gives no indication of having read the *Catechism* on the sacraments in general, sacraments like baptism in particular, let alone the Council of Trent or any other Catholic theologians.

81. Berkouwer understands that precisely for this reason "It is impossible, therefore, to speak simplistically of the Roman Catholic sacramental doctrine as 'magical' for then we must say that the core of this doctrine has not been understood" (*De Sacramenten*, [66], translation altered to give the nuances of the original Dutch missing from the English translation).

obstacle."[82] Trent defines the disposition negatively: placing no obstacle in the way. As long as we understand that Trent defends the gratuity of grace with *ex opere operato* and hence that this necessary disposition is neither causal nor meritorious, that is, that the grace of the sacrament is not given *ex opere operantis*, which is to say on the basis of any disposition of the believer, we are free to ask how exactly the "dispositions of the recipient of a sacrament relate to the conferring of grace, either as conditions for or obstacles to receiving that grace."[83]

The all-too-brief answer to this question here must be: the right disposition is not necessary for supernatural grace to be communicated in the sacrament—the sacrament of baptism actually conveys new life—but an obstacle placed in the way prevents the fruitfulness of the grace of the sacrament. Ludwig Ott writes, "Against frequent distortions and reproaches . . . it must be stressed that the Catholic teaching of the efficacy of the Sacraments *ex opere operato* must in no wise be interpreted in the sense of a mechanical or magical efficacy. The *opus operantis* is not excluded. On the contrary, in the case of the adult recipient it is expressly demanded . . . Nevertheless the subjective disposition of the recipient is not the cause of grace; it is merely an indispensable pre-condition of the communication of grace (*causa dispositive*, not *causa efficiens*)." In other words, adds Ott, "The measure of the grace effected *ex opere operato* even depends on the grade of the subjective disposition: we receive grace according to the measure given by the Holy Spirit as He wills and according to each one's own disposition and co-operation."[84] As I said above, baptism can efficaciously communicate grace on the recipient of the sacrament but nevertheless be fruitless in his life to a greater or lesser degree. Thus, faith and conversion is not the mechanism, as it were, that triggers regeneration—the sacrament of baptism does that—but rather is its evidence. This answer will have to suffice for now. Let's now look at the two other views.

First there is the view, as John Stott puts it, where the sign is taken to effect nothing. "It *signifies* the gift visibly, but in no sense or circumstance *conveys* it. It is a *bare token* or symbol, and that is all." On the *bare token* view of baptism, the sacrament's actual effect upon those who receive it is

82. Council of Trent, Canons on the Sacraments in General, Canon 6, in *Sources of Catholic Dogma*, 262.

83. Garver, "Ex Opere Operato."

84. Ott, *Fundamentals of Catholic Dogma*, 330.

nil; it is a mere symbol pointing to grace but it no way conveys it.[85] Critics of this view, such as Stott and Harvey, and of course the Catholic tradition, are correct, that this is, to quote Harvey, an "impoverished understanding of the rite . . . in that it neither does justice to the early church emphasis on the effect of the rite nor to the biblical language that unites baptism and salvation."[86] Indeed, baptism is clearly linked with regeneration and salvation in the New Testament.[87] Evidence of this link is found in biblical passages such as St. Paul's words about being baptized into Christ (Gal 3:27) and being buried with Christ through baptism into death (Rom 6:4). There are more: "But when the kindness and the love of God our Savior toward man appeared, not by the works of righteousness which we have done, but according to His mercy he saved us, through the washing of regeneration and renewing of the Holy Spirit, whom He poured out on us abundantly through Christ our Savior" (Titus 3:4–6). Acts records that when St. Peter is asked what is required for salvation, he replies, "Repent and be baptized, every one of you, in the name of Jesus Christ for the forgiveness of your sins" (22:16; cf. also, 1 Pet 3:21).

An early critic of the *bare token* view is St. Thomas Aquinas. He affirms the view that the "sacraments of the New Law, in some way, cause grace; for it is evident that through the sacraments of the New Law a person is incorporated into Christ" [Gal 3:27]. Aquinas adds:

> Some people, however, say that the sacraments are not the cause of grace by their own action, but insofar as God causes grace in the soul when the sacraments are employed. Such people give as an example someone who presents a lead coin and receives, by the king's command, a hundred [Euros]. It is not as though the metal coin, by any action of its own, caused this person to be given that sum of money; rather, this occurs only because of the will of the king. Therefore, Bernard says in the sermon *On the Lord's Supper*

---

85. The Swiss Reformer Zwingli (1484–1531) sees the sacraments as a mere sign. Calvinist Kuyper rightly holds, "The Reformed stand with Rome, Luther, and Calvin against Zwingli in their adherence to a divine working of grace in the sacraments" (as cited in Berkouwer, *De Sacramenten*, 101–2 [84]).

86. Harvey, "Baptism as a Means of Grace," 104.

87. Reformed theologian Berkouwer agrees with this judgment: "And it is clear that neglect or disdain of the baptismal sacrament flagrantly contradicts the message of the New Testament. There is evidently a very important relation between baptism and the salvation of Christ, and the question is raised *what the nature* of this relation could be" (*De Sacramenten*, 140 [111]).

(no. 2), "Just as a canon is invested by means of a book, an abbot by means of a crosier, a bishop by means of a ring, so by the various sacraments various kinds of grace are conferred." But if we examine the question properly, we shall see that according to this way of understanding them the sacraments are mere signs: for the lead coin is nothing but a sign of the king's command that this person should receive money. Similarly, the book is a sign of the conferring of the office of canon. Therefore, according to this opinion, the sacraments of the New Law would be mere signs of grace; yet we have it on the authority of many saints that the sacraments of the New Law not only signify but also cause grace.

On closer inspection, Aquinas isn't merely objecting to the *bare token view*, but also to a view, which is sometimes called "occasionalism." On this view, the sacraments are reduced to being mere occasions for God's action, and hence rather than the sacramental signs themselves having *causal power*[88] by which they effect what they signify, they are "mere signs," which deprives them of any intrinsic connection to the gift of grace, and hence any connection between sign and signified.[89] By contrast, for Aquinas, in particular, God effects what the sacrament signifies *by way of* the sacrament. Both Bavinck and Berkouwer disagree. They claim not only to reject occasionalism, but also that in rejecting *ex opere operato* they nonetheless uphold a connection between the sign and the thing signified such that the sacramental sign is still "objective, real and essential." Bavinck, in particular, writes: "The relationship that exists between the sign and the thing signified in the sacrament is . . . not a physical, local, corporeal, or substantial connection." Rather, the sacraments are signs *and confirmations, or seals, or pledges* of God's promise of our redemption in Jesus Christ, which was made once for all when he offered himself up in his passion and death on the cross (Heb 7:27), but which the

---

88. For Aquinas, the sacraments acquire an additional causal power in addition to its natural power. For instance, he states, "It is not because of the natural power of the water that any spiritual effect is caused in Baptism, but because of the power of the Spirit which is in the water. . . . But what the power of the Spirit is to the water of Baptism, that they very body of Christ is to the appearance of bread and wine. They are operative only because of the very body of Chris they contain" (*Summa Theologiae* III, q. 73, a.2, Vol. 58).

89. For more on Aquinas's critique of "occasionalism," see Bauerschmidt's short commentary on *Summa Theologiae* III, q. 62, a.1 in his book, *Holy Teaching*, 258–62. See also, Wolterstorff, "Sacrament as Action, not Presence," 103–22, for an attempt to show that both Aquinas *and* Calvin do not subscribe to occasionalism, but rather to what Wolterstorff calls "theistic instrumentalism" (107).

sacraments assure us remains in effect, valid. God is the worker of grace *in* the sacrament, Bavinck and Berkouwer insist, countering the theory of so-called empty sign, or a bare token view, and by his grace we receive assurance of our salvation and the strengthening of our faith. "Whether God communicates that grace in, with, and under the sign, using the sign as a channel, or whether he does it in connection with the sign, does not affect the reality of that communication itself."[90] Is this Bavinck's generous orthodoxy? Is he allowing for the *ex opera operato* view in which the grace of God is distributed *through* and *by way of* the sacramental signs and not only *with* them? Unfortunately not, Bavinck quickly reverses himself claiming that "the grace of God is distributed only *with* but not *through* the Word and sacrament."[91] In that light, we can easily understand why Bavinck and Berkouwer repeatedly return to answer the charge that their view—the Reformed view—does not actually maintain the objective and realistic character of the sacraments, robbing them of what Peter Leithart has called "objective, real-world efficacy," and hence that their view forces them into that doctrine of occasionalism.[92]

But for the Catholic tradition the sacraments are not only a sign of the grace of our redemption in Jesus Christ, or additionally, a seal or assurance of that grace, but also a cause inasmuch as "they effect what they signify."[93] Significantly, as I explained earlier, Aquinas explains, in

90. Bavinck, *GD* IV, 459, 461 [481, 483].

91. Ibid., 465 [486].

92. Ibid., 465 [486]. Berkouwer, *De Sacramenten*, especially, 95–107, 139–72 [79–89, 110–39]. Leithart, a Reformed theologian, criticizes an element of Reformed sacramental doctrine in his article, "Why Sacraments are not signs."

93. Aquinas, *Summa Theologiae*, III, q. 62, a. 1, Vol. 56. As the *Catechism of the Council of Trent* stated regarding the sacrament of Baptism: "the solemn ablution of the body not only signifies, but has the power to effect a sacred thing which is wrought interiorly by the operation of the Holy Ghost" (146). Aquinas explicitly rejects the idea that that the material element of the sacrament is itself a "cause" of grace. He says in *Summa Theologiae* 3.66.1, Vol. 58: "Therefore some people have thought that the sacrament is the water itself, which seems to be the meaning of the passage quoted from Hugh of St. Victor [objection 2], for in the general definition of a sacrament he says that it is 'a material element', and in defining baptism he says it is 'water'. But this is not true; for since the sacraments of the New Law bring about a certain sanctification, the sacrament takes place where the sanctification takes place. But the sanctification does not happen in the water; rather, a certain instrumental sanctifying power, which is not permanent but transient, flows from the water into the human person, who is the subject of true sanctification. Consequently, the sacrament does not occur in the water itself, but in applying the water to a human being, that is, in the washing." As Bauerschmidt remarks

this connection, that "an efficient cause can be of two types: principal and instrumental."[94] Thus, he stresses that God is the cause of grace, as *causa principalis*—on this major point the Reformed and Catholic tradition are in fundamental agreement—and hence that God is the principal cause *in* and *by way of* the sacraments as efficient *causa instrumentalis*.[95] What this means is easy to grasp and of fundamental importance, and Berkouwer states it clearly: "Ultimately God, as *causa principalis*, is the worker of grace. In themselves and apart from God, the sacraments would not be able to communicate grace.... But these [sacramental] signs derive their ability to communicate grace from God's standing behind them, and because he employs the sacraments as *causa instrumentalis* in such a manner that it really produces grace.... This [*instrumentalis*] *causalitas* is the basis for the *ex opere operato*, for against the background of the *causa principalis* (God), grace is infused through the corporeal sign."[96] Unfortunately, despite this clear understanding, Berkouwer (as does Bavinck) repeatedly (and wrongly) charges the Roman Catholic sacramental doctrine with deism—as if *ex opere operato* means that the sacraments communicates grace in themselves and apart from God.

Put differently, Berkouwer correctly states, "Anyone who strongly emphasizes the [instrumental] causality of baptism—and the other sacraments—must also continue to emphasize that the [principal] cause of salvation is the historical reality of the cross of reconciliation."[97] Otherwise there is the real danger that the principal cause of grace will be conflated with the instrumental cause, breeding a kind of formalism and blind ritualism, and hence to a deistic view of the sacraments. Aquinas agrees, "And it is in this way that the sacraments of the New Law cause grace, for they are instituted by God to be employed for the purpose of conferring grace. Therefore Augustine says in *Against Faustus the Manichean*

---

here, "In other words, the purpose of baptism is not to make holy water, but to make holy people." Furthermore, he says, Hugh [of St. Victor] compares sacraments to jars that contain medicine, an analogy that is quite alien to Thomas's way of thinking about sacraments. Here Thomas makes clear that sacraments 'contain' grace only inasmuch as they *confer* grace through the use of visible signs in a ritual context" (as cited in *Holy Teaching*, 276, notes 7, 6).

94. Aquinas, *Summa Theologiae*, III, 62, a. 1, Vol. 56.

95. The Council of Trent (Session VI, Decree on Justification, Chapter 7) defines baptism as *causa instrumentalis* of justification.

96. Berkouwer, *De Sacramenten*, 80 [66].

97. Ibid., 145 [115].

(bk. 19), 'All these things', that is, pertaining to the sacraments, 'are done and pass away, but the power', that is, of God, 'that works through them remains forever'. But something is properly called an instrument when someone works through it; there it is written in Titus 3:5, 'He saved us through the washing of regeneration.'"[98] For Aquinas, then, God uses the sacrament itself is an "efficient instrument" to produce grace; of course God in Christ by the Spirit is the principal cause of grace but such grace is effectively received through the sacrament as an instrument. Indeed, the sacraments in themselves possess efficacy, according to the teaching of the Church, "because Christ himself is at work: it is he who baptizes, he who acts in his sacraments in order to communicate the grace that each sacrament signifies."[99] His redeeming acts are the source and cause of grace, and therein is the core of the doctrine of the *ex opere operato*, and not some impersonal ritualism or sterile formalism. As Edward Schillebeeckx correctly remarks, "A sacrament is primarily and fundamentally a personal act of Christ himself, which reaches and involves us in the form of an institutional act performed by a person in the Church who, in virtue of a sacramental character, is empowered to do so by Christ himself: an act *ex officio*. . . . Put positively, *ex opere operato* efficacy means that this [sacramental] act is Christ's act. *Ex opere operato* [literally: by the fact that the sacramental rite is validly performed" and thus "by the power of rite"] and 'in the power of the mystery of Christ' mean the same thing."[100]

The second view to consider is the view that Harvey calls the Covenant Sign View, and he takes it to be Stott's view. On this view, says Stott, "the sign not only signifies the gift, but seals or pledges it, and pledges it in such a way as to convey not indeed the gift itself, but a title to the gift—the baptized person receiving the gift (thus pledged to him) by faith, which

---

98. Aquinas, *Summa Theologiae*, III, q. 62, a. 1, Vol. 56.

99. *Catechism*, no. 1127. That the sacraments in themselves possess efficacy because they are acts of Christ himself is also taught by Pius XII, *Mystici Corporis*, "Holiness begins from Christ; and Christ is its cause. For no act conducive to salvation can be performed unless it proceeds from Him as from its supernatural source. 'Without me', He says, 'you can do nothing' [John 15:5]. . . . When the sacraments of the Church are administered by external rite, it is He who produces their effect in souls. He nourishes the redeemed with His own flesh and blood . . . He gives increase of grace and prepares future glory for souls and bodies. . . . [I]t is He who through the Church baptizes, teaches, rules, losses, binds, offers, sacrifices" (nos. 51, 54).

100. Schillebeeckx, OP, *Christ, The Sacrament of the Encounter with God*, 53, 70.

may be before, during or after the administration of the sacrament."[101] This view fundamentally differs from Bavinck's and Berkouwer's because they claim that the connection between the sign and the signified is such that gift itself is given by God with the sacrament even if not through the sacrament. The Covenant Sign View, as I understand Stott, also comes under Aquinas's objection as a version of "occasionalism" because the sacraments are not means whereby grace is conferred but rather only—in the case of baptism—a mere title to regeneration and salvation. Stott explains, "[Baptism] is not only the sign of covenant membership, but a seal or pledge of covenant blessings. Baptism does not convey these blessings to us, but conveys to us a right or title to them, so that if and when we truly believe, we inherit the blessings to which baptism has entitled us." The chief problem with this view—and both Catholics and Reformed theologians like Bavinck and Berkouwer would have trouble with Stott's view—is that it diminishes baptism's profound significance and content which is derived from the necessary relation between baptism and the salvation of Christ. For instance, in 1 Corinthians 6:11 Paul admonishes the Church concerning baptism: "but you were washed, but you were sanctified, but you were justified in the name of the Lord Jesus Christ, and in the Spirit of our God." Clearly, St. Paul is referring to baptism here as that which affected and changed the Corinthians, marking their transition from what they "were" to what they "are," that is, as Berkouwer puts it, "as a transition in the indivisible harmony of faith, baptism, communion with God, and isolation from the world."[102]

Yet, the more immediate problem with this view is that it implies a subjectivizing of this sacrament, implying that faith makes me the author of my salvation, which contributes to a serious devaluation of the sacrament and its objectivity. Thomas Harvey correctly objects to Stott's view that "baptism is the symbolic linguistic crucible of regeneration and new birth which gives form to the substance of faith in Christ. Therein regeneration is signified by our being gathered to a people where the Holy Spirit works through our existence in the church to conform us to Christ. Through baptism we enter this mode of existence, either willingly as adults or unwillingly as infants. Nonetheless, this regeneration is not triggered by my faith, rather my faith in Christ is its culmination.... Our

---

101. Stott, "Evangelical Doctrine of Baptism," 47–49.

102. Berkouwer, *De Sacramenten*, 160 [125]. See also, "Sacramental Life," in Sokolowski, *God of Faith & Reason*, 144–53.

being gathered to the church is not the result of our choosing, rather we are called by God into relationship."[103]

I turn now to the final section of this chapter to consider the issue of the certainty of faith and the Holy Spirit's epistemological significance. Bavinck will help us to segue into this issue by describing what the Scripture means by the certainty of faith: "faith . . . consists in the soul's union with the person of Christ according to the Scriptures and with Scripture as the word of Christ. Saving faith was again religious through and through. Its object was the grace of God in Christ; its foundation the witness of God in his Word; its author the Holy Spirit." He elaborates:

> According to Scripture, this faith brings its own certainty with it. It is the assurance . . . of things hoped for and the conviction . . . of things not seen (Heb 11:1), not because it is inherently so solid and firm but because it is grounded in God's testimony and promise, as the sequel of Hebrews 11 clearly teaches. It makes the invisible goods of salvation utterly certain for us; indeed, even much more certain that one's own insight or given scientific proof could ever make it. For that reason Scripture speaks of the confidence (Heb 4:16), the confidence of access (Eph 3:12), the full assurance (Heb 6:11, 12; 10:22) of faith; attributed to it are such qualities as courage (Matt 9:2), rejoicing (Rom 5:11), and joy (1 Pet 1:18, etc.). It contrasts with doubt, anxiety, fear, distrust (Matt 6:31; 8:26; 10:31; 14:31; 21:21; Mark 4:20; Luke 8:25; John 14:1; Rom 4:20; John 1:6). Certainty is a characteristic of faith through Scripture. Even in the midst of the most severe trials, when everything is opposed to them, hoping against hope, believers stand firm as seeing the Invisible (Job 19:25; Ps 23; 32; 51; Rom 4:20, 21; 5:1; 8:38; Heb 11; etc.).[104]

THE *TESTIMONIUM SPIRITUS SANCTI INTERNUM* AND THE CERTAINTY OF FAITH

Divine faith consists not only in accepting the whole truth that God has revealed but is also, says John Paul II, "a response of the whole person, highlighting its 'existential' and 'personalistic' dimension." "In knowing by faith," the pope adds, "man accepts the whole supernatural and salvific content of revelation as true. But at the same time, this fact introduces him into a profound relationship with God who reveals himself. If the

---

103. Harvey, "Baptism as a Means of Grace," 111.
104. Bavinck, *GD* I, 542 [573].

very content of revelation is the saving 'self-communication' of God, then the response of faith is correct to the degree that man—accepting that salvific content as the truth—at the same time 'entrusts his whole self to God'. Only a complete 'abandonment to God' on man's part constitutes an adequate response."[105] Bavinck (writing in 1894) criticizes an earlier expression of the Roman Catholic view for its alleged reduction of faith to intellectual assent to revealed truth. But Vatican I (1870) teaches that the obedience of faith requires the engagement of the intellect *and* the will: "Since human beings are totally dependent on God as their creator and Lord, and created reason is completely subject to uncreated truth, we are obliged to yield through faith to God the revealer full submission of intellect and will" in order "to share in an interior communion with him."[106] And as I shall show below, Aquinas had a rich view of the act of faith and thus was not a reductionist as Bavinck also alleges.[107] In short, authentic faith, on the Catholic view, has a double reference: divine faith is a truly personal communion with God, involving the intellect and will, indeed, the whole man, but it involves at the same time, and inseparably, believing the truth of God as divinely revealed in his Word.[108]

Yet, of course, the sinful heart of fallen man—which exists in a fallen state and thus in enmity toward God[109]—is incapable, apart from the grace of the Holy Spirit, of that supreme act of entrusting itself to God. The Holy Spirit's internal testimony is, significantly, neither a source of new revelations nor a communication of unknown truths but rather

---

105. John Paul II, *Catechesis on the Creed,* Volume I, *God Father and Creator,* 44–45

106. Vatican I, *Dogmatic Constitution Concerning the Catholic Faith,* Chapter 3, Faith, 445. *Catechism,* no. 154.

107. Bavinck, *GD* I, 540 [571].

108. *Catechism,* no. 150.

109. John Paul II, *Fides et Ratio,* no. 22: "The blindness of pride deceived our first parents into thinking themselves sovereign and autonomous, and into thinking that they could ignore the knowledge which comes from God. All men and women were caught up in this primal disobedience, which so wounded reason that from then on its path to full truth would be strewn with obstacles. *From that time onwards the human capacity to know the truth was impaired by an aversion to the One who is the source and origin of truth.* It is again the Apostle who reveals just how far human thinking, because of sin, became 'empty', and human reasoning became distorted and inclined to falsehood (cf. Rom 1:21–22). The eyes of the mind were no longer able to see clearly: reason became more and more a prisoner to itself. The coming of Christ was the saving event which redeemed reason from its weakness, setting it free from the shackles in which it had imprisoned itself" (italics added).

his testimony establishes man in relation to the revealed truths of God manifested in the Word of God. In other words, as Bavinck rightly says, "the testimony of the Holy Spirit is not the final *ground* but the *means* of faith. The ground of faith is, and can only be, Scripture, or rather, the authority of God."[110] Why do we believe Scripture to be the authoritative Word of God? Bavinck replies: "The Spirit is 'efficient cause,' 'the principle by which,' of faith. We believe Scripture, not because of, but by means of the testimony of the Holy Spirit. Scripture and the testimony of the Holy Spirit relate to each other as objective truth and subjective assurance."[111]

Trusting testimony, in general, is an ordinary and rational means of knowing things, just like perception, intuition, memory, inference. Enlisting Kevin Vanhoozer's succinct definition of testimony, which holds also for our convictions grounded in divine authority, we can say: testimony is "a speech act in which the witness's very act of stating p is offered as evidence 'that p', it being assumed that the witness has the relevant competence or credentials to state truly 'that p.'"[112] On this account of testimony, we accept the truth of statements that we do not see directly for ourselves but which it is reasonable to accept on the trustworthy word of others. This epistemological account of trusting human testimony, adhering to the truth in virtue of the testimony of a trustworthy witness, as a necessary and inescapable dimension of human activity, sheds some light, by analogy, on the claim that divine faith is a mode of adherence to trustworthy testimony. Yet, Christian faith is never just a specific instance of trusting in the word of others; it is not merely trust in man's testimony, but is rather a uniquely Spirit-guided Christian activity of divine faith, of believing not only what God says but also that Scripture really is the Word of God, he who speaks.

Yet, "the natural man does not receive the things of the Spirit of God, for they are foolishness to him; nor can he know them, because they are spiritually discerned" (1 Cor 2:14). So man's inability to make that supreme act of faith is manifested in his resistance to the evidence of divine testimony. Indeed, the "sinful heart" has epistemological significance because it may stand in the way of properly responding to the evidence of divine testimony, that is, the testimony of the Holy Spirit to Scripture as

110. Bavinck, *GD* I, 568 [597].
111. Ibid., 568 [597–98].
112. Vanhoozer, "Hermeneutics of I-Witness Testimony," 269. See also, Ashley, O.P., *Living the Truth in Love*, 54–55.

God's Word, and which constitutes faith's ground, by the force of divine authority.

I intentionally say the "evidence of testimony" (to borrow a phrase from Warfield), in this case the testimony of God's Word, rather than philosophical proofs or the intellectual arguments of historical apologetics (which makes the case for the authenticity and historical credibility of the Scriptures, particularly the New Testament, especially making the case for the historicity of the resurrection). These proofs or arguments are *not the actual source* of our conviction that the whole supernatural and salvific content of revelation is true. Indeed, such proofs and arguments, though definitely available, with the aim of showing that divine revelation is manifestly credible, are *unnecessary* in order for believers to be rationally justified in holding their beliefs about God to be true. Furthermore, philosophical proofs and historical apologetics, all be they available, will of themselves not make a man a Christian. Indeed, as Bavinck correctly remarks, "For that reason faith in Scripture cannot and does not rest on intellectual arguments but has its deepest ground in the witness of the Holy Spirit [to Scripture as the Word of God]." Vatican Council I (1870), like Bavinck, also affirms the epistemological significance of the internal testimony of the Holy Spirit (*testimonium Spiritus Sancti internum*): "Although the assent of faith is by no means a blind movement of the mind, yet no one can accept the gospel preaching in the way that is necessary for achieving salvation without the inspiration and illumination of the Holy Spirit, who gives to all facility in accepting and believing the truth."[113]

Of course this point does not imply, according to Vatican I and Bavinck, that proofs and intellectual arguments are without value.[114] The divine faith that is a gift of God's Holy Spirit is in conformity with human reason. "Even though faith is above reason, there can never be any real disagreement between faith and reason, since it is the same God who reveals the mysteries and infuses faith, and who has endowed the human mind with the light of reason." The Council, clearly, rejects the idea of an act of faith that is not grounded, in some sense, in evidence. Faith is in "accordance with reason," and thus, it follows, that the Holy Spirit does not produce saving faith without grounds. Still, although "the individual, to be sure, does not need to become a trained apologist first, and only af-

---

113. Vatican I, *Dogmatic Constitution Concerning the Catholic Faith*, Chapter 3, Faith, 445. Bavinck, *GD* I, 549 [579].

114. Bavinck, *GD*, I, 549–50 [578–79].

ter and as a result of that a Christian," Warfield adds, "he does require that kind and amount of evidence which is requisite to convince him before he can really be convinced: and faith, in all its forms, is a conviction of truth, founded as such, of course, on evidence."[115] In short, the conviction of faith rests on the evidence of divine testimony. Thus, no authentic faith without evidence; but there may be evidence without the proper "subjective nature or condition to which the evidence is addressed." As Warfield correctly puts it, "This is the ground of responsibility for belief, faith; it is not merely a question of evidence but of subjectivity; and subjectivity is the other name for personality. Our action under evidence is the touchstone by which is determined what we are. If evidence which is objectively adequate is not subjectively adequate the fault is in us."[116] But from a Christian epistemological perspective, one of the characteristic effects of sin is that we resist acknowledging the evidence of testimony as submitted to us in the gospel. It is precisely, then, sin's noetic effect that renders us subjectively inadequate to respond to the evidence of divine testimony, resisting the witness of the Holy Spirit.[117]

But how do we know that it is really God who speaks in the Scripture? Yes, the Church teaches that the Scripture itself is the Word of God. But why believe the Church? Can her claims be tested? Vatican I replies to this question: "Nevertheless, in order that the submission of our faith to the evidence of testimony should be in accordance with reason, it was God's will that there should be linked to the internal assistance of the Holy Spirit external indications of his revelation, that is to say divine acts, and first and foremost miracles and prophecies, which clearly demonstrating as they do the omnipotence and infinite knowledge of God, are the most certain signs of revelation and are suited to *the understanding of all*."[118] Significantly, signs suited to the understanding of all men, Vatican

---

115. Warfield, "Review of [Herman Bavinck] *De Zekerheid des Geloofs*," 120.

116. Warfield, "On Faith in its Psychological Aspects," 397–98.

117. Aquinas affirms the noetic effects of sin on the human intellect. He argues that the knowing powers of human reason suffer the wound of ignorance and is deprived of its direction toward truth; additionally, that the disordered state of our intellectual powers also affects "man's desire to know the truth about creatures," for he may wrongly desire to know the truth by not "referring his knowledge to its due end, namely, the knowledge of God" (*Summa Theologiae*, I–II, q. 85, a. 3, Resp., Vol. 26; q. 109, a. 2; II–II, q. 167, a. 1).

118. Vatican I, *Dogmatic Constitution Concerning the Catholic Faith*, Chapter 3, Faith, in *Sources of Catholic Dogma*, 445.

I states, and not just to the trained apologist. For example, the fulfillment of Old Testament prophecies, especially in the death and resurrection of Jesus Christ of which the apostles were eyewitnesses; Jesus' miracles of healing, freeing from demons, multiplying the loaves and fishes, raising people from the dead, and so forth; the teaching of Jesus "with a wisdom so profound as to provide a consistent answer to the greatest mysteries of human life"; and last, Jesus "perfectly exemplified these teachings in his own life and sacrificial death."[119] These signs can recommend the credibility of the Christian faith to our human senses and intelligence, motivating us toward belief in divine revelation, especially that it really is God who speaks. One more thing: "The great sign most accessible to all here and now is the Catholic Church itself in its life and teaching. This Church works throughout the world, and is striving to reach even those parts of the globe which are still closed to its mission. It is the living presence of Christ in today's world and what it says of Christ is to believed for the very same reasons that he should have been believed in his own times."[120] But these indices of revelation are not "the true ground of faith in revelation."[121] "We are only fully persuaded of the truth of Christianity and the authority of Scriptures by the testimony of the Holy Spirit," adds Bavinck, "who illumines our intellect, opens our hearts, and assures us that 'the Spirit is the truth' (1 John 5:6)."[122]

Of course the Council is not suggesting that the evidence of testimony, on its own, can produce divine faith. Rather, "the Catholic Church professes that this faith, which is the beginning of human salvation, is a supernatural virtue by which we, with the aid and inspiration of the grace of God, believe that the things revealed by Him are true, not because the intrinsic truth of the revealed things has been perceived by the natural light of reason, but *because of the authority of God himself* who reveals them, [and] who can neither deceive nor be deceived."[123] This divine authority is the objective motive of Christian faith.[124] The testimony of the Holy Spirit just is "the grace that moves a man's intellect and will to

---

119. Ashley, OP, *Living the Truth in Love*, 57–58.

120. Ibid., 60.

121. Bavinck, *GD* I, 549 [579].

122. Ibid., 567–68 [596–97].

123. Vatican I, *Dogmatic Constitution Concerning the Catholic Faith*, Chapter 3, Faith, 445; italics added.

124. Bavinck, *GD* I, 550 [580]. See also, Ashley, OP, *Living the Truth in Love*, 60–61.

believe" that Scripture is God's authoritative Word.[125] I will develop the argument below that the witness of the Holy Spirit is the *means*, and not the *ground* of faith; the latter being the authoritative Scripture. As I understand this important passage of Vatican I, the emphasis is on the issue not only of reaching assurance as to one's own participation in the saving benefits accomplished by the work of Christ, but also of reaching certainty with regard to the objective truths of divine revelation. Reaching that assurance comes only by the operation of the Holy Spirit, which is called the *testimonium Spiritus Sancti internum.*

Faith's knowledge of God is, then, the gift of the Holy Spirit, illuminating the understanding, softening the heart, and moving it to a willing, resolute surrender to the Word of revelation, perceiving the force and yielding to the "compelling power of the evidence of the trustworthiness of Jesus Christ as Savior submitted to him in the gospel."[126] The Fathers of Vatican I assure us that the Holy Spirit does not work an intellectually blind faith in the heart or one ungrounded in the evidence of testimony. The question I discuss in what follows is, then, the relationship between the "grounds" of faith and the Holy Spirit, who is the giver of faith itself. I turn now to give an account of this relationship in the theological epistemology of St. Thomas Aquinas.

FAITH AS A WAY OF KNOWING

Faith is a kind of knowing, according to Sacred Scriptures. We read in the Old Testament: "I know that the Lord will maintain the cause of the afflicted, and justice for the poor" (Ps 140:12); "For I know that the Lord is great, and our Lord is above all gods" (Ps 135:5); "I know, O Lord, that your judgments are right, and that you have humbled me in faithfulness" (Ps 119:75). And in the New Testament we read: "We have come to believe and know that You are the Christ, the Son of the living God" (John 6:69); "If you abide in My word . . . you shall know the truth" (John 8:31); "that you may know what is the hope of His calling, what are the riches of the glory of His inheritance in the saints, and what is the exceeding greatness of His power toward us who believe" (Eph 1:18–19).[127]

---

125. Bavinck, *GD* I, 550 [580].

126. Warfield, "On Faith in its Psychological Aspects," 399.

127. There are other New Testament writers who speak of the objects of faith as *known*. Thus St. Paul says, "Now if we have died with Christ, we believe that we shall also

But what kind of knowing is faith? St. Thomas holds that faith's full knowledge of God in Christ, seeing God "face to face" (1 Cor 13:12) in beatific communion, is eternal life, but also that "we must have within us some initial participation of this supernatural knowledge."[128] This faith is knowledge, for it "is the beginning of eternal life in us," says St. Thomas, and, he adds, "as such can be called certain knowledge and sight. This appears in the first Epistle to the Corinthians (13:12): 'For now we see in a mirror, dimly.'"[129] Without doubt, the biblical passages above and others indicate that knowledge in faith unites us to the "God and Father of our Lord Jesus Christ" (Col 1:3). By faith, as St. Thomas rightly notes, we come to see, that is, know, the Truth, but for now we see it, as St. Paul says, "in part, imperfectly," or as he says elsewhere, "we walk by faith, not by sight" in the sense of understanding (2 Cor 5:7).

Nevertheless, St. Thomas unquestionably holds that "in so far as there is certainty of assent, faith is knowledge, and as such can be called certain knowledge and sight." Yes, faith possesses a certitude that exceeds the believer's understanding or comprehension, and in this sense it is distinct from the more precise sense of knowledge. But what is it, then, to see the Truth in faith, and how does it differ from other acts of the mind such as understanding (*nous*), reasoning (*episteme*), holding an opinion, or doubting?

Aristotle's epistemology is the background here for St. Thomas' analysis. First, the immediately evident knowledge of some truth or other is understanding; and second, intelligent reasoning, or mediate knowing, consists of the reasoned demonstration of any true proposition. In these cases, we have a firm assent of the mind and knowledge of necessary, universal, and eternal realities. In other cases, according to Aristotle, we have belief or opinion or doubt. The mind is unable to reach a firm assent to a truth in any of these mental acts. Where we have an opinion, we may think that p, and it may well be true, but we do not rule out $-p$. The state

---

live with Him, knowing that Christ, having been raised from the dead, dies no more" (Rom 6:8–9). And again, "we also believe and therefore speak, knowing that He who raised up the Lord Jesus will also raise us up with Jesus, and bring us with you into His presence" (II Cor 4:13–14). For an important discussion of these passages and others as they bear on the question of faith as a form of knowing, see Von Balthasar, *Glory of the Lord*, vol. I, especially, 131–40.

128. Aquinas, *Truth*, q. 14, a. 2.

129. Ibid., q. 14, a. 2, ad 15.

of doubting involves being unsure about either *p* or –*p* so that one leans toward neither. Aristotle regards belief to be a deficient form of human knowing, because knowing, strictly speaking, is seeing for oneself that *p* is true, either directly and without argument or indirectly and on the basis of argument.

St. Thomas agrees with Aristotle, but only partly. He agrees: "Now things are said to be seen when they themselves cause the mind or the senses to know them. Clearly, then, no belief or opinion can have as object things seen, whether by sense or by intellect."[130] As St. Thomas also explains:

> Any science is possessed by virtue of principles known immediately and therefore seen. Whatever, then, is an object of a science is in some sense seen. Since it is impossible that the same thing be seen and believed by the same person . . . it is also impossible that the same thing be an object of science and of belief for the same person. . . . Matters set before the whole human community for belief, however, are in no instance the object of any science, and these are the object of faith pure and simple. In these terms faith and science are not about the same object.[131]

Thus, according to St. Thomas, the mysteries of faith are truths that are neither immediately nor demonstrably known, because there intrinsic truth is not evident to the human mind.

Still, he radically departs from Aristotle's epistemology. He regards faith as a mode of adherence, or holding fast to what one professes, that essentially involves the firm assent of the mind to the truth of some proposition or other, as objectively true and real. The principal inward act of faith involves the act of believing assent. And as an act of the intellect, assent is ordered to knowing what is true. Thus, affirming the truth of a proposition like "Jesus Christ is true God and true man," or "conceived by the Holy Spirit, born of the Virgin Mary," entails excluding their denial as true, namely, that Christ is only one or the other, or that Mary conceived of a human father, respectively. In that case, according to St. Thomas, faith is like all three—knowledge (understanding and reasoning), doubt, and opinion. Like those with knowledge, faith involves certainty, for they are settled in their assent. And like those with doubt and opinion, believers continue to think or to ponder. As St. Thomas puts this point, "The act

---

130. Aquinas, *Summa theologiae* II–II q. 1, a. 4, Vol. 31.
131. Ibid., q. 1, a. 5, Vol. 31.

of believing . . . is firmly attached to one alternative and in this respect the believer is in the same state of mind as one who has science or understanding. Yet the believer's knowledge is not completed by a clear vision, and in this respect he is like one having a doubt, a suspicion, or an opinion."[132]

This point about the firmness of believing assent, that is, having a conviction, assurance, raises the following question: are there cases of belief, conviction, where an individual is justified in assenting to something, indeed, to *someone*, not because he sees for himself that what the other states as "that p" is to be taken as truly "that p," but rather because he believes what he is convinced of on the ground of the other's trustworthy testimony, and hence that he is rational in taking the word of another as evidence "that p"?

FAITH AND TESTIMONY

St. Thomas himself responded affirmatively to this question, as did Augustine before him and Thomas Reid, John Henry Newman, Benjamin B. Warfield, Abraham Kuyper, Herman Bavinck, and John Paul II after him.[133] Newman and Kuyper agree that faith is, on the purely human level,

---

132. Aquinas, *Summa theologiae* II–II q. 2, a. 1.

133. On St. Augustine, see my study "Augustine on Faith and Reason," in *Collectanea Augustinian II* (New York: Peter Lang Publishing, 1993), and the literature given there. On Newman, see *Fifteen Sermons*, particularly Sermons IX, X, XII. For an important defense of testimony as an ordinary and rational means of knowing things, just as perception, memory, and reasoning, see Newman, "Religious Faith Rational," in *Parochial and Plain Sermons*, a collection of sermons preached between 1825–1843, Volume I, Sermon 16, 190–202; online: http://www.newmanreader.org/works/parochial/volume1/sermon15.html. See also, Newman's later work, *Essay in Aid of A Grammar of Assent*. In this work, Cardinal Newman wrote: "Now let us review some of those assents, which men give on evidence short of intuition and demonstration, yet which are as unconditional as if they had that highest evidence. First of all, starting from intuition, of course we all believe, without any doubt, that we exist; that we have an individuality and identity all our own; that we think, feel, and act, in the home of our own minds; that we have a present sense of good and evil, of a right and a wrong, of a true and a false, of a beautiful and a hideous, however we analyze our ideas of them" (148). Last but not least, on Kuyper, see *Encyclopedia of Sacred Theology*, § 46, pp. 125–46. Bavinck, *Gereformeerde Dogmatiek*, I, 536–40 [566–69]; and his, *Certainty of Faith*, 23–28. See also, "Faith," in the Collected Philosophical Papers of G.E.M. Anscombe, vol. 3, *Ethics, Religion and Politics*, 113–20; Sosa, "Testimony and coherence," in his *Knowledge in Perspective*, 215–22; and especially Trigg's reflections on the notion of doxastic practices, which bear resemblance to what Kuyper and Newman developed along different lines, in his paper on "Is a Religious

a necessary and irreducible mode of gaining cognitive certainty, whether about one's own self-existence, the reliability of our senses, our reasoning powers, memory, and even the reality of the external world. Like St. Thomas, Kuyper, for example, does not oppose faith here to knowing, but to discursive demonstration. Faith is a way of knowing that goes beyond the believer's knowledge or understanding or the ability to produce grounds. Says Kuyper, yet "I *know* all those things the existence of which, together with some relations of this existence, is actual fact to me."[134] They all agree, however, that faith is especially fitting in the case of firm beliefs involving the human disposition to trust testimony. In Reid's own words, testimony has "a native and intrinsic authority," because "the wise Author of Nature hath implanted in the human mind a propensity to rely upon human testimony before we give a reason for doing so."[135]

So adherence to trustworthy testimony is necessary both intellectually and practically.[136] Most things we think we know about history, geography, science, everyday existence, in short, virtually all human knowledge and activity is accepted on human faith. As Kuyper says, "Let it be emphatically repeated here, that only because my mother revealed to me who my father was, do I know this as a fact; and in almost every case this all-important circumstance that affects my whole existence cannot be certified except by *faith* in the content of this revelation."[137] So we cannot see it for ourselves and hence we assent to another's word as true. St. Thomas agrees, "And because in human society one person must make use of another just as he does himself in matters in which he is not self-sufficient, he must take his stand on what another knows and is unknown to himself, just as he does on what he himself knows. As a consequence, faith is necessary in human society, one person believing what another says."[138]

John Paul, too, clearly affirms that it is rational to believe in God on the basis of testimony, or the word of another, without the support of natural theology, that is, without being able to establish independently

---

Epistemology Possible?," 113–33.

134. Kuyper, *Encyclopedia*, 129.

135. On Reid, see *Inquiry into the Human Mind*, VI, 24.

136. Bavinck, *GD* I, 534–36 [566–68].

137. Kuyper, *Encyclopedia*, 146.

138. St. Thomas's Commentary on the *De Trinitate* of Boethuis is from *Faith, Reason and Theology*, q. 3, a.1, reply, 65–66.

for oneself the natural truths about God. In fact, one of the purposes of divine revelation is to make this truth and others available to those who are not able to demonstrate them. "Such a truth—vital and necessary as it is for life—is attained not only by way of [demonstrative] reason but also through trusting acquiescence to other persons who can guarantee the authenticity and certainty of the truth itself."[139] In general, and not just in particular with respect to Christian beliefs, most of our beliefs depend on the testimony of others and not on our own experience; this is true of virtually all knowledge, scientific, historical, moral, theological, and many others.[140] In John Paul's own words, "there are in the life of a human being many more truths which are simply believed than truths which are acquired by way of personal verification."[141] So it is entirely reasonable for the great majority of people to believe in God, not by engaging in philosophical proofs, but by relying on testimony, by trusting the word of another.

What is the meaning here of belief? Says John Paul, "'To believe' means to accept and to acknowledge as true and corresponding to reality the content of what is said, that is, the content of the words of another person . . . by reason of his . . . credibility. This credibility determines in a given case the particular authority of the person—the authority of truth. So then by saying "I believe," we express at the same time a double reference: to the person and to the truth; to the truth in consideration of the person who *enjoys special claims* to credulity."[142] The special claims to credibility enjoyed by the witness's act of stating "that p" is that the witness has the relevant competence or credentials to state truly "that p." Believing, then, involves

---

139. John Paul II, *Fides et Ratio*, no. 33.

140. Ratzinger/Benedict XVI defends the rationality of human faith's assent to testimony in his book, *Yes of Jesus Christ*, 5–9. "This kind of faith is always directed towards someone who 'know' the matter in hand. It presupposes the genuine expertise of qualified and trustworthy people. The second element is the trust of the majority who in their daily use of things are able to build less on the substantial knowledge that should lie behind such use. And finally the third element is a certain verification of knowledge in everyday experience. I may not be able to demonstrate scientifically that the electric current is working okay, but this is shown me by the everyday functioning of my various pieces of electrical apparatus, so that even though I am not a scientific specialist in this field I am not operating in the field of pure 'faith' that is totally lacking in confirmation" (8–9).

141. John Paul II, *Fides et Ratio*, no. 31.

142. John Paul II, *Catechesis on The Creed*, Vol. I, *God Father and Creator*, 31; italics added. See also, *Catechism of the Catholic Church*, no. 177: "'To believe' has thus a twofold reference: to the person and to the truth, by trust in the person who bears witness to it."

not only believing that something is true but also believing in a person, the latter characteristically being thought of as trust. "'Faith' then emerges as the appropriate name of those acts of mental consent in which the element of trust is prominent." Warfield adds, "In what we call religious faith this prominent implication of trust reaches its height."[143]

In its higher applications (to borrow Warfield's way of phrasing it), faith, believing, says John Paul, "involves an interpersonal relationship and brings into play not only a person's capacity to know [the truth] but also the deeper capacity to entrust oneself to others, to enter into a relationship with them which is intimate and enduring."[144] Its highest application, then, is divine faith. The *Catechism of the Catholic Church* clearly makes this point: "Faith is first of all a personal adherence of man to God. At the same time, and inseparably, it is a *free assent to the whole truth that God has revealed*. As personal adherence to God and assent to His truth, Christian faith differs from our faith in any human person. It is right and just to entrust oneself wholly to God and to believe absolutely what He says."[145] Thus, "to believe in," "to have faith in," "to entrust yourself to," comes to mean, in the pope's view, particularly in the case of divine faith, not simply a knowledge of propositional truths, but also a personal commitment to God, both a propositional knowledge and an affective trust, indeed, an act of the whole man. As John Paul says, "In knowing by faith, man accepts the whole supernatural and salvific content of revelation as true. But at the same time, this fact introduces him into a profound personal relationship with God who reveals Himself."[146] In the pope's own words again,

> By the authority of His absolute transcendence, God who makes Himself known is also the source of the credibility of what He reveals. By faith, men and women give their assent to this divine testimony. This means that they acknowledge fully and integrally the truth of what is revealed, because it is God Himself who is the guarantor of that truth. They can make no claim upon this truth which come to them as gift and which, set within the context of

---

143. Warfield, "On Faith in its Psychological Aspects," 392.
144. John Paul II, *Fides et Ratio*, no. 13.
145. *Catechism*, no. 150.
146. John Paul II, *Catechesis on The Creed*, Vol. I, *God Father and Creator*, 44. Warfield and John Paul II hold remarkably similar position on this matter of testimony. See Warfield's essay, "On Faith in its Psychological Aspects," especially, 392–403.

interpersonal communication, urges reason to be open to it and to embrace its profound meaning. This is why the Church has always considered the act of entrusting oneself to God to be a moment of fundamental decision which engages the whole person. In that act, the intellect and the will display their spiritual nature.[147]

Furthermore, the knowledge of faith had by the believer is superior to the knowledge that is provided through philosophical proofs. As St. Thomas says, "anyone is far surer of what he hears from the infallible God than of what he sees with his own fallible reason."[148] Divine faith, too, is a mode of adherence to trustworthy testimony; though in this unique instance we do not assent to the testimony of a man but rather to divine testimony. As St. Thomas says, "There is what the Apostle [Paul] says, 'When you received the word of God which you heard from us, you welcomed it not as the word of men, but as it is in truth, the word of God' (1 Thess 2:13). But nothing is more certain than the word of God. Therefore knowledge is not more certain than faith, nor is anything else."[149] The difference this makes to the epistemological dynamics of divine faith will become apparent below. I now want to consider St. Thomas's claim that there are two ways in which a thing can be the object of belief.

MODES OF DIVINE TRUTH

First, some objects of belief, in this life, exceed the grasp of reason of all men in an absolute sense. These objects of belief refer to mysteries of faith, revealed truths in the strict sense, namely, they are knowable only because of divine revelation. The blessed Trinity, the Incarnation, the divinity of Christ, and others are examples of these truths. Says St. Thomas, "it is impossible for any man to have scientific knowledge of these. Rather every believer assents to such doctrines because of the testimony of God to whom these things are present and by whom they are known."[150]

Although the truths of the mysteries of faith cannot be discovered or proved by human reason with its own resources, St. Thomas undoubtedly holds that there are convincing arguments for the reasonableness of the Christian faith. Faith is not the product of rational argument, for faith's

---

147. John Paul II, *Fides et Ratio*, no. 13.
148. Aquinas, *Summa Theologiae* II–II q. 4, a. 8, ad 2, Vol. 31.
149. Ibid.
150. Aquinas, *Truth*, q. 14, a. 9.

knowledge of God is a gift of God's grace. Yet rational motives play a crucial role in the believer's assent. As St. Thomas puts it, "For he would not believe unless, on the evidence of signs, or of something similar, he saw that they ought to be believed."[151] It would seem that one has an epistemic obligation to believe where reasons or signs of credibility are available. In short, St. Thomas alludes here to what in centuries to follow the common doctrine of the Church will call "motives of credibility[,] which show that the assent of faith is by no means a blind impulse of the mind"[152]

Second, some objects of belief exceed the grasp of reason of some men, but not all. These objects of belief refer to truths that are able to be revealed, but in principle they are knowable through the capacity of natural reason. In St. Thomas's own words, "In this class are those things which we can know about God by means of a demonstration, as that God exists, or is one, or has no body, and so forth. There is nothing to prevent those who have scientific proofs of these things from knowing them scientifically, and others who do not understand the proofs from believing them. But it is impossible for the same person to know and believe them."[153] Yet some of us, who first believe these truths on the testimony of God's Word, can later come to see their truthfulness for ourselves. "However," as St. Thomas often urges, "there is nothing to stop an individual accepting on faith some truth he can't demonstrate, even if it be in itself something that demonstration can make evident."[154]

---

151. Aquinas, *Summa theologiae* II–II q. 1, a. 4, ad 2, Vol. 31.

152. *Catechism*, no. 156.

153. Aquinas, *Truth*, q. 14, a. 9, reply.

154. Aquinas, *Summa theologiae* I q. 2, a. 2, ad 1, Vol. 1. There has been much misunderstanding of the role of the proofs of God's existence in St. Thomas's religious epistemology. Helm briefly considers two possible interpretations in his essay on "The 'Faith seeking Understanding' Programme," "Is Thomas proceeding, in typical rationalist fashion, to ground the propositions of faith in matters which are obvious or evident to everyone? And is he saying that the proposition that God exists is not credible if not provable? . . . If so, he is making the convincingness of such arguments a necessary condition of reasonable belief. However, there must be some doubt that this is what Aquinas believes he is doing, for he goes on to state that 'there is nothing to stop a man accepting on faith some truth which he personally cannot demonstrate, even if that truth in itself is such that demonstration could make it evident'. He appears to allow that the propositions of faith may be taken for granted, and to employ the proofs both to seek greater understanding of the nature of God, and greater certitude in his existence" (*Faith & Understanding*, 4–5). I think a strong case can be made for the interpretation, as Helm's puts it, that "Aquinas thought the proofs sufficient, but not necessary, for rational belief in God" (203, note 14, and 183). On this, see Aquinas, *Summa Contra Gentiles*, Bk. I,

Furthermore, St. Thomas regards this category of truths that fall within the reach of reason but still are able to be revealed as the preambles or prerequisites of the mysteries of faith. God's existence is a presupposition of, is implied in, believing truths like the Trinity and the Incarnation. In other words, we believe by Christian revelation, not by reason from creation, that God is a trinity of divine persons, whose nature is self-communicating love, proceeding from Father, to Son, to Holy Spirit.[155] But if we jettison rational access to some conception of God, His creation, and providence, as the necessary rational underpinning of this mystery, what, if anything, or who, if anybody, is being revealed, must be in considerable doubt.[156] As St. Thomas says, "Faith cannot universally precede understanding; for man cannot assent to some proposed things through believing unless he understands them somewhat."[157] Ralph McInerny helps us grasp the important role of these truths as *praeambula fidei*. "This does not mean that my acceptance of the Trinity and Incarnation would follow from my fashioning a cogent proof of God's existence. It does mean that

---

translated, with an introduction and notes, by Pegis (Garden City, NY: Doubleday & Company, 1955), 4, 2, 3, 6. See also, St. Thomas's commentary on the *De Trinitate* of Boethuis, in *Faith, Reason and Theology*, q. 3, a. 1; *Summa Theologiae*, II–II q. 1, a. 5 ad 3, and q. 2, a. 4, Vol. 31; and *Truth*, q. 14, a. 9.

155. St. Thomas recognized the limits of reason: "To dare to prove the Trinity by natural reason is to commit a double fault. . . . First, one misapprehends the dignity of faith itself, which has invisible things as its object, which is to say, those that go beyond human reason. . . . Further, one compromises the means to lead certain men to the faith. In effect, to bring as a proof of the faith reasons that are not necessary is to expose *that faith to the scorn of the infidels*; they think that it is upon these reasons that we base ourselves, and it is on account of them that we believe" (*Summa theologiae* Ia q. 32, a. 1). When explaining and defending the truths of faith that exceed the grasp of reason, according to St. Thomas we have only probable reasons and not necessary reasons. As Torrell, O.P., describes St. Thomas's views in his study, *Saint Thomas Aquinas*, Vol. 1, *Person and His Work*, 110: "That reason cannot demonstrate faith does not mean that it is impotent when faced with the objections of adversaries. On the contrary, Thomas shows a robust confidence in the capabilities of reason in the believer. 'Since natural reason cannot go against the truth of the faith', it can at least show that the adversaries arguments are not true demonstrations but sophisms that can be 'dismantled'" (*Summa theologia* I q. 1, a.8). What, then, is the foundation of the truths of faith? Says St. Thomas, "That which passes human reason we believe only through the revelation of God."

156. Trigg, *Rationality and Religion*, 181–82, 190, and 212. Trigg writes (212), "If reason cannot create a space in which the possibility of divine revelation can be allowed, the ability of humans to recognize any revelation as divine even through 'faith' is put into question. Faith itself must involve a conception of what it is we have faith in."

157. Aquinas, *Summa theologiae* II–II q. 8, a. 8, ad 2, Vol. 32.

those truths of faith could not stand if it were definitely disproved that God exists. Is it not here that we find the source of the believer's interest, as believer, in proofs for the existence of God?"[158]

The upshot of St. Thomas's point is that the God of the philosophers and the God of the believer cannot be totally distinct.[159] In other words, the object of faith and what we reason about concern the same God. To be sure, God's self-revelation yields a much richer conception of Himself, to say the least, than the metaphysics of theism, which expresses, however inadequately, something determinate and true about God the creator.

THREE DIFFERENT ASPECTS OF FAITH

Most important, as I showed above, the root idea behind a mode of adherence to trustworthy testimony is accepting something *because of who says it*. And this is how St. Thomas thinks of faith: we believe God himself when we hold to truths about God. As St. Thomas puts it, "When we believe God by faith, we reach God Himself. This is why I have said [in IIa–IIae q. 1, a. 1] that God is the object of faith not simply in the sense that we believe in God (*credimus Deum*) but also that we believe God (*credimus Deo*)."[160]

To describe the rich understanding of faith's relationship to God envisaged here, it is necessary to consider the three distinct aspects to one and the same act of faith as it relates to God. There is believing *in* God (*credere Deum*), believing God (*credere Deo*), and believing *unto* God (*credere in Deum*). Correspondingly, theological faith has both a material and a formal aspect. The material object refers to the *fides quae creditur*, the objective content of the faith that God has revealed, supremely God Himself as self-revealed, and to which I assent as true. This yields *believing in God*. The material object is not vague or abstract, for there is an objective, historical revelation, that is, the deposit of faith. As Romanus Cessario, O.P., puts it, "In the grace and favor of the Incarnation, God allows His truth to be measured out in human words. Moreover, within the

---

158. McInerny, *Being and Predication*, "Philosophizing in Faith," 237–46, and here at 244. I take up the question of natural theology and faith in chapter 5.

159. This is a crucial point of difference between the Catholic tradition and the Dutch neo-Calvinist Herman Dooyeweerd. I examine this difference in chapter 5.

160. Aquinas, *Summa theologiae* II–II q. 81, a. 5, Vol. 32.

logic of the Incarnation, the meaning of these human words adequately represents the divine truth they signify."¹⁶¹

The formal object refers to the medium through which faith's material object is known. Some scholastic theologians have found it helpful here to distinguish between the terminative formal object (*objectum formale quod*) and the mediating formal object (*objectum formale quo*). The former designates God as First Truth-in-Being. It is crucial for the Christian to recognize the identity of *being* and *truth* in the divine Being. The practical benefit of this truth for the Christian believer is this: God is always true to His word, and hence faithfulness is a perfection of His being, grounding the believer's total confidence. As T.C. O'Brien puts it, "The 'first truth' is the true God, the faithful God; faith accepts the one who speaks in order to accept what He speaks."¹⁶² Faith is, firstly, then a *believing God*, God as First Truth-Speaking. In St. Thomas's own words, "With regard to faith, then, if we look to its [terminative] formal object, it is the first truth, nothing else, because the faith of which we speak assents to nothing except as it is revealed by God."¹⁶³ The mediating formal object represents, to quote Fr. Cessario, the "medium that enables the subject to reach the formal object. Since only the divine nature itself can serve as an adequate medium for communication of divine Truth, God Himself serves as the medium in which theological faith attains to the First Truth. [T]he mediating formal object of theological faith [is referred to] as the Truth-speaking of God."¹⁶⁴ This last sentence brings us back to the crux of faith: we believe God, First Truth in Being and Speaking, only when we believe something because God Himself says it. Quite simply, the one who trusts God believes what He says, which is the *fides quae creditur*. O'Brien explains the upshot of this point: "God has spoken a definite word out of limitless, possible words. But once that word is heard, once

---

161. Cessario, OP, *Christian Faith*, 62. The phrase "Theological life" in the title of this book does not refer to theological study and learning, but rather "directly signifies a life transformed by grace and animated by the virtues of faith, hope, and charity—in short, the godly life" (1). I am indebted to Fr. Cessario's work for helping me to understand Aquinas's religious epistemology.

162. O'Brien, "Faith and the Truth Who is God," appendix 2 of *Faith*, vol. 31 of the *Summa theologiae*, 192. There are two other appendices by O'Brien from which I have also profited immensely, "Faith and the Truth About God," Appendix 3, and "Belief," Appendix 4, 195–204, and 205–15, respectively.

163. *Summa theologiae* II–II q. 1, a. 1, reply, Vol. 31.

164. Cessario, OP, *Christian Faith*, 56–57.

matters of belief are proposed, then the believer believes them, assents to them only because of the formal object of faith. He believes *that* they are revealed, he believes *what* is revealed, because he believes God, because he adheres to the first truth."[165]

Furthermore, our adhering by faith to God as the First Truth means that we share in God's own knowing, which is to know God as He knows Himself. Aquinas insists on this: faith through believing assent really unites the human mind to the divine knowing. "Faith ... makes a person's mind adhere [cling] to the truth which consists in God's own knowing, and so to transcend the truth of man's own mind." And again St. Thomas insists: "Through its assent faith conjoins a person's mind to the divine knowledge."[166] As Fr. Cessario puts it,

> Because faith unites us to the One who is supreme and First Truth itself, the believer gains an unimpeachable certitude about God and the things related to God. First Truth rescues Christian belief from being a deficient form of human knowing (the lot of belief in the Aristotelian schema), and makes of the very human disposition to give credence to another person a means of attaining the highest and most necessary Truth that is God Himself.[167]

At this point we must raise the question as to how the human mind can achieve a real knowledge of the truths of faith when what faith is about cannot be directly apprehended by our intellect. For St. Thomas, indeed, for the Catholic tradition, the answer is clear: "The light of faith makes one see the things that are believed."[168] As the Psalmist says, "In

---

165. O'Brien, "Faith and the Truth Who is God," 194. According to O'Brien, St. Thomas holds the same view: "To acknowledge that God has in fact chosen to set before men a definite message of salvation is to acknowledge that the human expression, in life, in knowledge and in language, of His message has a positive reference to the intrinsic, divinely constituted being and evidence of the realities revealed" ("Faith and the Truth About God," 203).

166. Aquinas, *Truth*, q. 14, a. 8, reply.

167. Cessario, *Christian Faith*, 93.

168. *Summa theologiae* II–II q. 1, a. 4, ad 3, Vol. 31. On this, see St. Thomas's Commentary, *2 Corinthians*, ii, *lect.* 3, as cited in *St. Thomas Aquinas*, 184: "*Now thanks be unto God, who always causeth us to triumph in Christ, and maketh manifest the savour of his knowledge* (2 Corinthians 2:14). Between knowledge through science and knowledge through faith there is this difference: science shines only on the mind, showing that God is the cause of everything, that he is one and wise, and so forth. Faith enlightens the mind and also warms the affections, telling us not merely that God is first cause, but also that he is saviour, redeemer, loving, made flesh for us. Hence the phrase, *maketh manifest*

Your light we see the light" (Ps 36:9). This light is the grace-given power to know conferred upon us as a participation in divine knowledge. It occurs, as does all knowledge, in the dynamic presence to the knower of what is known. How, then, is God in reality present to the human knower in the way he knows, that is, according to the mode of the knower? Quite simply, the human knower makes judgments about reality, and these judgments are expressed in propositions. Thus, from the perspective of the knower, that which is known, that is, true objects of faith, are truth-bearing statements that follow upon the believing assent of faith in a particular act of judgment. Faith is indeed propositional.[169] Yes, Aquinas does say, "Actus autem credentis non terminator ad enuntiabile sed ad rem."[170] That is, it is true to say that, according to Aquinas, the *ultimate object of faith* is not

---

the savour of his knowledge; its fragrance is diffused far and wide. Behold, the smell of my son is as the smell of a field which the Lord hath blessed" (Gen 27:27).

169. Cardinal Newman exposes the false dilemma behind the denial of the claim that faith is propositional in a crucial paragraph of *Essay in Aid of A Grammar of Assent* (108–9): "Here we have the solution of the common mistake of supposing that there is a contrariety and antagonism between a dogmatic creed and vital religion. People urge that salvation consists, not in believing the propositions that there is a God, that there is a Saviour, that our Lord is God, that there is a Trinity, but in believing in God, in a Saviour, in a Sanctifier; and they object that such propositions are but a formal and human medium destroying all true reception of the Gospel, and making religion a matter of words or of logic, instead of its having its seat in the heart. They are right so far as this, that men can and sometimes do rest in the propositions themselves as expressing intellectual notions; they are wrong, when they maintain that men need do so or always do so. The propositions may and must be used, and can easily be used, as the expression of facts, not notions, and they are necessary to the mind in the same way that language is ever necessary for denoting facts, both for ourselves as individuals, and for our intercourse with others. Again, they are useful in their dogmatic aspect as ascertaining and making clear for us the truths on which the religious imagination has to rest. Knowledge must ever precede the exercise of the affections." For a sound defense of propositional revelation, see Lamont, "Nature of Revelation," 335–45. See also, Helm, *Faith & Understanding*, " 'Faith seeks Understanding' Programme," "Sometimes there is misunderstanding at this point. When a person, in, say, reciting the Apostles' Creed, confesses as part of his faith that he believes in the resurrection of the body, though the faith is confessed in words, the person who confesses the faith does not place his trust in the words, but rather he trusts what the words denote or express. What the words 'I believe in the resurrection of the body' express, as they are usually understood, is some state of affairs, in this case some state of affairs about the future, which the one who confesses the proposition takes to be true, and also takes to be a fit object of religious confidence. In exercising such faith, the person may even be said to trust God insofar as he also believes that God has revealed certain propositions and so has warranted belief in those propositions" (3–25, and for this quote at 9).

170. Aquinas, *Summa Theologiae* II–II, q. 1, a. 2, ad 2, Vol. 31.

a set of theological formulas that we confess, but rather God himself, but it is also the case that for Aquinas articles of faith are necessary for knowing God. In other words, one assents primarily to God himself but as mediated in and through determinate propositions. This is the case because faith involves belief, and to have a belief means that one is intellectually committed, or has mentally assented, to the truth of some proposition or other. Faith involves belief, says Aquinas, and "belief is called assent, and it can only be about a proposition, in which truth or falsity is found."[171] As Charles Cardinal Journet puts it, "The object of faith is both the statement so far as this touches reality, and reality so far as this is shown in the statement. It is both the statement to which faith assents, and reality which becomes open to it by its assent, towards which it tends, and in which it terminates."[172] Furthermore, that assent to some definite propositions is essential to faith is clear from the New Testament itself (cf. Acts 2:41; Rom 10:9–17; 1 Cor 15:1–8; 1 Tim 46; 2 Tim 3:14, 4:1–5, and many other places).[173]

So the judgment of faith finds its ultimate term in the divine reality and attains the very referent of theological faith. So the believing assent to the truth of the proposition does not differ from assenting to what the proposition means, which is the reality proposed and believed in. "The act of the believer has as its term not a proposition but a reality," in the oft-quoted adage of St. Thomas. In view of St. Thomas's realist epistemology, as O'Brien puts it, "The knower does not fix on the being that the known has in the knower but on the being the known is in itself. The existence of the known in the knower has as its meaning and purpose the

---

171. Aquinas, *Truth*, q. 14, art. 8, ad 12.

172. Journet, *What is Dogma?*, 11–12. The *Catechism of the Catholic Church* puts this point quite accurately: "We do not believe in formulas, but in those realities they express, which faith allows us to touch. 'The believer's act [of faith] does not terminate in the propositions, but in the realities [which they express]' [Aquinas, *STh* II-II, 1, 2, *ad* 2, Vol. 31]. All the same, we do approach these realities with the help of formulations of the faith which permit us to express the faith and to hand it on, to celebrate it in community, to assimilate and live on it more and more" (no. 170).

173. Of course, as Grisez rightly emphasizes, "Catholic faith is not simply belief in a system of general propositions, but in the flesh and blood reality of the revelation of God in the Lord Jesus. We cling to the Word Incarnate, to the intactness of his mother's virginity, to the bloody reality of his death, to his fleshly risen life, to his bodily presence in the Eucharist, to the death-dealing effect of our first parents' sin, to the life-giving power of our Lord's risen body for our dead bodies, and to the confident hope that we shall embrace him in the flesh. Catholic faith is not afraid of what is too concrete to be intelligible. We kneel before matter: the Word made flesh" (*Way of the Lord Jesus*, vol. 1, 502).

cognitional union with the reality of the known."[174] In other words, this means that faith's judgments about God and about His saving action in the world lay hold of the very realities that the truth-bearing statements express and mediate. As Cessario puts it, "when Christian believers assent to the truth that Jesus is their Savior, they are united at that moment to the very mystery of Christ's salvific life and glorious resurrection, not simply a notional account of them. For in addition to affirming the existential character of the predicate (*copula*), the judgment of faith affirms the *verum*, or the true."[175]

St. Thomas insists that theological faith really joins the human mind to the divine knowing. Yet the limitations of faith's knowledge do not escape his attention. He cautions that "by faith we do not gaze upon the first Truth as He is in Himself."[176] This statement is not in conflict with St. Thomas's realist epistemology, however. It means simply that faith does not see for itself the intrinsic truthfulness of the propositions to which it assents. Faith is *credere Deo*, or a believing God. Yet Christian belief "is inchoately what the beatific vision is in its fullness." As the author of the Letter to the Hebrews expresses it, "Now faith is the substance of things hoped for, the evidence of things not seen" (Heb 11:1).[177]

So there is a real conformation of our minds to divine Truth. "We have it through faith, which by reason of an infused light holds those

174. O'Brien, translator's note, *Summa theologiae* II–II q. 1, a. 2, reply.
175. Cessario, *Christian Faith*, 98.
176. Aquinas, *Summa theologiae* II–II q. 1, a. 2, ad 3, Vol. 31.
177. St. Thomas explicates this classical biblical text in a passage worth quoting in full: "The words, *faith is the substance of things hoped for*, then, refer to the relationship of the act of faith to the end, the object of the will. We use the word 'substance' for the very beginning of any reality, especially when all that follows is contained virtually in this fundamental beginning. So understood faith is the substance of things to be hoped for, since the very beginning of things hoped for exists in us through the assent of faith, which virtually contains all that we hoped for. For we hope to receive blessedness by seeing in clear vision the truth we now cling to by faith. The words, *the evidence of things not seen*, describe the relationship of the act of faith to the kind of thought object which the object of faith is. Evidence is understood here as the effect of the evidence, since it is the evidence that brings about the mind's adherence to any truth; thus in this text the mind's firm hold on the truths of faith that appear not is called *evidence*. In another version the term conviction is used as well, since the believer's mind is convinced by the divine authority to assent to the unseen. Anyone interested in reducing the text to definitional form can say that faith is that habit [a stable possession of the soul] of mind whereby eternal life begins in us and which brings the mind to assent to things that appear not" (*Summa theologiae* II–II q. 4, a. 1, reply, Vol. 31).

things that are beyond our natural knowledge."[178] But this cognitive union is not merely intellectual, for faith is at its core fiduciary, that is, trusting, in character. As O'Brien says, "that relationship to God's word, to God speaking, is itself *belief*, it is *credere Deo*, not vision. The assent is the act of the mind that does cleave to God's word, because it is the beloved Father who speaks."[179] Although we believe with firm assent, belief is an imperfect sharing in the divine knowledge. As St. Paul expresses it, "For now we see in a mirror, dimly, but then face to face" (1 Cor 13:12). Says St. Thomas, "We cannot perfectly possess this way of knowing in the present life, but there arises here and now in us a certain sharing in, and a likeness to, the divine knowledge, to the extent that through the faith implanted in us we firmly grasp the first Truth itself for its own sake."[180] Again St. Paul writes, "Now I know in part, but then I shall know just as I also am known" (1 Cor 13:12).

FIRMNESS AND CERTAINTY OF CHRISTIAN FAITH

Furthermore, the firmness and sureness of Christian belief in the Scripture as God's Word cannot be explained by the intellect alone. For, as Bavinck asks, "what ground does the intellect have for accepting Scripture as the word of God?" Yes, proofs for God's existence and intellectual arguments of historical apologetics, as I suggested earlier in this section, may be motives of credibility. But for believing acceptance of the truth that Scripture is God's Word, an affective, volitional force, itself bent by grace, as the mover of faith, is required. But is this now a sufficient answer to Bavinck's question regarding the intellect's ground for accepting Scripture as God's Word? Not even Bavinck thinks so. He writes, "Certainly, the will cannot persuade the intellect to accept something as true without [external] reasons or grounds, and the will on its own cannot determine whether something is believable or true. The intellect itself, after all, has to acknowledge that something is divine and therefore deserves to be believed. Otherwise faith is unreasonable and the believer brushes aside this difficulty by saying: 'This is what I wish; this is what I command; my will takes the place of

---

178. Aquinas, *Truth*, q. 14, a. 2, reply.

179. O'Brien, "Belief: Faith's Act," 214.

180. Aquinas, Commentary on the *De Trinitate* of Boethius in *Faith, Reason and Theology*, q. 2, a. 1, reply.

my reason.'"[181] St. Thomas unpacks for us with some specificity the manner in which the gospel proclamation of divine truth effectively elicits the movement of the will.[182] The will is influenced, or engaged, by the good contained in the divine promise of the gospel, and this explains, in part, the dynamic behind the volitional element in belief.[183] Fr. Cessario explains St. Thomas' meaning in a long paragraph that repays meditation:

> To put it differently, while belief remains formally an act of the intellect, a person must hear something in the preaching of the Good News that is attractive.... The preacher makes an offer.... [T]his offer is [then] apprehended by the intellect and presented to the will, though merely under the common aspect of the good. In other words, the hearer recognizes in the Church's preaching something desirable, but from a natural point of view. This [good] could mean the consolation involved in the forgiveness of sins, the sense of security that comes with the promise of a permanent rule of justice and peace, or the human affection aroused by the announcement that God exercises a paternal regard over His children.... Or, the woman philosopher [the 20th century Carmelite Saint Edith Stein] discovers a way to surpass the limitations of human thought and the fallibility present in all human judgments. Because the Gospel reflects the ultimate intelligibility that divine Truth possesses, the one who hears the Gospel preached can perceive in every article of faith something of a promised human good, though the actual reality of the supernatural mystery entirely surpasses this created good. Then follows the will's act of choosing the good of God's promises.[184]

St. Thomas calls this initial act of the will's choosing the good of God's promise, following the Second Council of Orange (529), the pious affect of credibility.[185] As described above by Cessario, effectively hearing God's word involves recognizing and responding to the draw, attraction, magnetism, as it were, of a good in the promises of the Gospel. Of course, the will interacts with reason, for God moves the will in the context of evidence, or signs of credibility, which indicate that it is, indeed, God who is speaking here. As Fr. Cessario puts it, "the will commands the

---

181. Bavinck, *GD* I, 551 [582].

182. Aquinas, *Truth*, q. 14, a. 2, reply.

183. O'Brien, "Belief," 211.

184. Cessario, *Christian Faith*, 155.

185. On this, see sections 1915–1920 of the entry on the Second Council of Orange in *Christian Faith in the Doctrinal Documents of the Catholic Church*, 742–44.

intellect to assent judgmentally to the truth of God's promises (precisely as they are revealed by God to be true)."[186] But the believer's firm assent, conviction, is motivated not just by that evidence but also, even primarily, by the *pius credulitatis affectus*, the religious affect of credence. I take this last phrase to refer to the subjectivity of the regenerated individual who is now transformed by the power of the Holy Spirit and is now in a position to respond rightly to the testimony of the gospel.[187]

So it seems that the cause of believing is "not the insight of our intellect, nor a decision of our will." Rather, says Bavinck, it is "a power that is superior to us, bends our will, illumines our mind, and without compulsion still effectively takes our thoughts and reflections captive to the obedience of Christ [2 Cor 10:5]."[188] Bavinck cites St. Augustine, St. Thomas, and Vatican I in support of his claim that it is the internal testimony of the Holy Spirit that is the *cause* or *means* of my believing that Scripture is the authoritative Word of God. For instance, St. Thomas says, "Believing itself is an act of understanding assenting to divine truth by command of the will, moved by God in grace."[189] Thus, in the case of faith, it is God who actually moves the will through the principal agency of divine grace. St. Thomas continues: "Since man, in assenting to the things that are of faith, is raised above his nature, this must happen in him by a supernatural principle moving inwardly, which is God. And so as regards assent, which is the principal act of faith, faith is from God moving inwardly by grace."[190] Put differently, it is the light of infused faith (*lumen fidei*), which is a supernatural gift of God's grace, of divine illumination, that leads us to assent to a revealed truth. Again he says, "So also in the faith by which we believe in God there is not only accepting the object of assent, but something moving us to the assent. This is a kind of light—the habit of

---

186. Cessario, *Christian Faith*, 156.

187. This, too, is the teaching of Newman: "The Word of Life is offered to a man; and on its being offered he has Faith in it. Why? On these two grounds, the word of its human messenger, and the likelihood of the message. And why does he feel the message to be probable? Because he has a love for it, his love being strong. . . . He has a keen sense of the intrinsic excellence of the message, of its desirableness, of its likeness to what it seems to him Divine Goodness would vouchsafe, did He vouchsafe any. . . . Thus Faith is the reasoning of a religious mind, or of what Scripture calls a right or renewed heart" (*Fifteen Sermons Preached at Oxford University*, 195).

188. Bavinck, *GD* I, 561 [591].

189. Aquinas, *Summa theologiae* II-II q. 2, a. 9, reply, Vol. 31.

190. Ibid., q. 6, a. 2, reply.

faith—divinely imparted to the human mind." But faith has an external source as well, for as St. Paul says, "faith comes from hearing, and hearing by the word of God" (Rom 10:17), or as St. Thomas also says, "by way of the realities that are proposed from without and that had as their source divine revelation."[191] Hence, he continues, "two things are required for faith: one is the willingness of the heart to believe, and this comes not by hearing, but by the gift of grace; the other is a determination of what is to be believed, and this comes by hearing."[192]

There remains to ask whether Bavinck (and by implication, Aquinas) avoid the charge of circular reasoning in the following line of reasoning.

> To the question "Why do you believe?" Christians reply, "Because God has spoken" (*Deus dixit*). They cannot indicate another, deeper ground. If you then ask them, "But why do you believe that God has spoken, say, in Scripture?" they can only answer that God so transformed them internally that they recognize Scripture as the word of God. But having said that, they [have] said it all. The witness of God is the ground, but God's grace, the will, is the cause of faith.[193]

The circular reasoning in this line of thought is evident: "Why do you believe that Scripture is the word of God?" "Because this is the testimony to me of the Holy Spirit." "And why do you believe that this is the testimony to you of the Holy Spirit?" "Because Scripture tells us that it is the Holy Spirit that testifies that Scripture is the word of God." In response to the charge of circularity, Nicholas Wolterstorff rightly appeals to Bavinck's distinction between *ground* and *means*, or *reason* and *cause* of the belief in

---

191. Aquinas, Commentary on the *De Trinitate* of Boethius in *Faith, Reason and Theology*, q. 3, a. 1, ad 4.

192. Aquinas, *Expositio in Romanos* lect. 10. No. 3, as cited by Fr. Cessario in *Christian Faith*, p. 76.

193. Bavinck, *GD* I, 551 [582]. Elsewhere Bavinck writes: "To the question 'Why do you believe Scripture?' the only answer is: 'Because it is the word of God'. But if the next question is 'Why do you believe that Holy Scripture is the word of God?' a Christian cannot answer. That Christian will admittedly appeal to the marks and criteria of Scripture, to the majesty of its style, the sublimity of its content, the depth of its ideas, the abundant fruit it has borne, etc. But these are not the grounds of his or her faith; they are merely the attributes and characteristics that the believing mind later discovers in Scripture, just as the proofs for God's existence do not precede and undergird faith but flow from it and are constructed by it. All the proofs for belief in Scripture derived from its marks and criteria show with utter clarity that no deeper ground can be indicated. '*God said it*' (*Deus dixit*) is the foundational principle (*primum principium*) to which all dogmas, including the dogma of Scripture can be traced" (*GD* I, 559 [588–90]).

order to avoid that charge. Says Bavinck, "the testimony of the Holy Spirit is not the final ground but the means of faith. The ground of faith is, and can only be, Scripture, or rather, the authority of God."[194] Wolterstorff explains the point of this set of distinctions in Bavinck's religious epistemology: "When I say that I believe that Scripture is the word of God because this is the testimony to me of the Holy Spirit, I am specifying the *cause* of my belief. When I say that I believe the Spirit caused the belief because Scripture attributes faith in Scripture as the word of God to the Spirit, I am specifying the *reason* for my belief."[195] Wolterstorff is right: "Bavinck's answer to the charge of circularity seems to me perceptive and decisive."

FAITH, HOPE, AND CHARITY

God communicates Himself and the mystery of His will to us, which St. Thomas suggests, reaches us in two ways. These two dimensions of the act of God in revelation are as follows. "There is first God's activity in history that is accomplished through intimately connected words and deeds, culminating in Jesus Christ, who is both the mediator and fullness of revelation. Second, there is the activity, also historical and also mediated by Jesus Christ, by which God moves and assists someone to believe, that is, commit himself or herself to God, yielding to and accepting the divine self-communication."[196] It should now be clear that revelation, according to St. Thomas, is the dynamic presence of the living, true God, enabling the believer through the grace of the light of faith to assent, which is to accept God's presence to him as the known to the knower, and the beloved in the lover.

Knowing God in Christ, indeed entering into the very life of the blessed Trinity is not merely assenting to a created good perceived in the preaching of the Gospel like security or self-worth or relief from guilt. The actual reality of the supernatural mystery entirely surpasses created goods, for it involves, says Fr. Cessario, "fully embrac[ing] in love the revealed mystery about God and the things that pertain to God." We embrace the full substance of supernatural truth through the infusion of divine charity, which St. Paul says is "the love of God [that] has been poured out in our hearts by the Holy Spirit who was given to us" (Rom 5:5).

194. Ibid., 568 [597].
195. Wolterstorff, "Herman Bavinck."
196. Fr. Martin, *Feminist Question*, 2.

This brings us, finally, to *believing unto God* or *believing for the sake of God*—this aspect designates the eschatological direction or dynamic of faith.[197] The judgment of faith is not merely an intellectual act. It is part of a complete personal relationship to God. God is First Truth in Being and Speaking, but He is also the one beatifying reality, to whom and to whose gracious self-revelation a man responds and commits himself in an act of love. As St. Thomas puts it in one place, "God is the end of faith in that He is the unique good, who by His eminence transcends the capacities of human beings, but by His liberality offers His own very good to be shared in."[198] Thus, God invites us to share in His own life, and He draws us through the grace of Christ into an ever-deeper penetration and experience of the living, divine mysteries. The key to this affective knowledge of God is the infusion of the theological virtue of charity. Aquinas put it this way: "Charity signifies not only the love of God, but also a certain friendship with Him; which implies, besides love, a certain mutual return of love, together with mutual communion. . . . That this belongs to charity is evident from 1 John 4:16: *He that abideth in charity, abideth in God, and God in him*, and from 1 Cor 1:9, where it is written: *God is faithful, by Whom you are called unto the fellowship of His Son*. Now this fellowship of man with God, which consists in a certain familiar colloquy with Him, is begun here, in this life, by grace but will be perfected in the future life, by glory; each of which things we hold by faith and hope."[199] With the divine charity that has been poured into my heart and mind, there is the affective knowledge of being in love with God, of the reality believed in. As O'Brien explains, "this in turn becomes a basis for a cognitive experience that sustains and deepens faith. Faith in its finished form is animated by love."[200]

---

197. In this chapter, I cannot discuss the complex matter of dogmatic development, that is, faith seeking deeper "understanding of the realities and the words" of the truths of faith.

198. *Scriptum super libros Sententiarum* 3. 23. 2. 1, as cited by Davies, OP, *Thought of Thomas Aquinas* 277. See also, Exposition, *de Divinis Nominibus*, I, *lect*. 1, as cited in Gilby, *Aquinas*: "God is so good that it would be out of character for him to keep his knowledge of himself to himself and never to give himself intimately, for goodness of itself is generous" (9).

199. Aquinas, *Summa theologiae* II–II q. 66, a. 5, Vol. 38. As Fr. Cessario also says, "There is a difference between what a person cognitively apprehends in the act of knowing and what he or she really possesses in the act of love. . . . But because divine Truth is infinitely more profound than its conceptual expressions, belief incessantly tugs the believer toward a deeper penetration of the divine mysteries. Only the act of love ultimately bridges the gap between concept and reality" (*Christian Faith*, 98).

200. O'Brien, "Faith and the Truth about God," 204.

This last point brings us directly to our conclusion. St. Thomas affirms the fundamental difference between God's creative presence in the world as agent-cause, as the cause existing in the effect, and "the *special mode of God's presence through grace and the special love of God* in giving grace."[201] As to the latter, St. Thomas speaks of the divine indwelling, of the beloved in the lover, clearly inspired by the biblical language of the Gospel of John, "If anyone loves Me, he will keep My word; and my Father will love him, and We will come to him and make Our home with him" (John 14:23). This understanding of faith's union with God through grace of the Spirit is found in many sources. In concluding, let me quote just one: "Since the rational creature by its operation of knowledge and love attains to God Himself, according to this special mode God is said not only to exist in the rational creature, but also to dwell therein as in His own temple. So no other effect can be put down as the reason why the divine person is in the rational creature in a new mode, except sanctifying grace. Hence, the divine person is sent, and proceeds temporally only according to sanctifying grace."[202] This brings us back to where we started this chapter on the Holy Spirit. "The love of God has been poured out in our hearts by the Holy Spirit who was given to us" (Rom 5:5). The Holy Spirit is the Lord and Giver of life, the one in whom the Triune God communicates himself to man, constituting in him the source of eternal life.

201. Ibid., 189.

202. Aquinas, *Summa theologiae* Ia q. 43, a.3, Vol. 26. On this, see also II *Sent.* 26, q. 1, a. 1, ad 2: "God is said to love all creatures in that he bestows on them the goodness of their natures. But there is love literally and completely, as being like friendship, when he loves a creature not as an artisan loves his work, but . . . as a friend loves a friend; a love by which God draws the creature into the fellowship of his own joy, so that the creature's glory and blessedness become those by which God himself is blessed. This is the love whereby he loves the righteous, and which is called love par excellence; in consequence of this the effect of this love is called grace par excellence (although all natural goods could be called graces in that they are freely given by God." See also, "By faith the Christian soul enters, as it were, into marriage with God: *I will espouse thee to me in faith* (Hos 2:20). Human virtue will disappoint us, even the noblest, unless we recognize eternal and immortal good. Before Christ's coming no philosopher by his entire sustained effort could have known as much about God and the truths necessary for salvation as can a humble old woman now that Christ has come. Were we able of ourselves to understand all things, visible and invisible, it might be foolish to believe what we do not see. But in fact our knowledge is so meager that no scientist can ever completely expose the nature of a midge—we read of one researcher who spent thirty years in solitude in order to learn all about bees" (Exposition, *Apostles Creed*, as cited in Gilby, *Aquinas*, 184). O'Brien gives many other sources in "Faith and the Truth Who is God."

5

The God of Philosophy and of the Holy Scriptures

The ultimate aim and purpose of the present book is to discuss certain conceptions of the relations of faith and reason which, were they to be accepted, would preclude the very possibility of the notion of a Christian philosophy by making it a contradiction in terms. Having tried elsewhere to establish the reality of Christian philosophy as a historically knowable fact, I am attempting here to discover, within the very essence of the Catholic faith, the roots of its theoretical possibility, or in other words, to establish that the notion of a Christian philosophy appears as consistent from the point of view of the Catholic truth taken in its entirety, and from no other one.[1]

CALVINISM AT THE CROSSROADS

IN 1939, THE DUTCH neo Calvinist philosopher, Herman Dooyeweerd (1894–1977) threw down the gauntlet to his fellow-Kuyperians. In his defining essay, "Kuyper's Wetenschapsleer,"[2] Dooyeweerd responds to their criticism that he had rejected the thought of Abraham Kuyper (1837–1920) in his philosophical writings. He argued, in response to them, that he was faithful to Kuyper's fundamental Scriptural and religious conception of Calvinist thought, but that his Kuyperian critics had to choose between two interpretations of Calvinism found in Kuyper himself, namely, reformational Calvinism, on the one hand, and a scholasticism on the other that had taken root in the Calvinist tradition and which had found expression in Kuyper's systematic theological writings, especially his three volume work, *Encyclopaedie der Heilige Godgeleerdheid*

---

1. Gilson, *Christianity and Philosophy*, viii.

2. Dooyeweerd, "Kuyper's Wetenschapsleer"; idem, "Wat de Wijsbegeerte der Wetsidee aan Dr. Kuyper te danken heeft," 63–65.

(1893-1894) [3] as well as in the theological writings of Herman Bavinck.[4] Put differently, Dooyeweerd argues, in particular, that Kuyper's thought is not an integral unity, but rather it is divisible into a "reformational" and "scholastic" line, and it is precisely the tension between these two directions in Kuyper's thought that has brought Dutch Calvinist thought into irreconcilable conflict with itself and hence to a crossroads, a fork in the road, in the first half of the twentieth century.

In its fundamental thrust, Dooyeweerd's essay is a passionate plea for Calvinist thought to return to its essential wellspring in the "schriftuurlijk-reformatorische en religieuze grond-conceptie" [biblically reformational and fundamental religious conception] of the Reformation. The commanding concern of Dooyeweerd is that not only Kuyper but also Bavinck had entangled the fundamental religious principle of the Reformation in a web of philosophical concepts, Aristotelian-Thomistic notions as well as a modern epistemological problematic (Hume-Locke-Kant) that served not to illuminate but only to obfuscate biblical truth. Of course, at stake here, for Dooyeweerd, is the issue of the "hellenization" of the Christian faith in patristic and medieval Christian thought. In Dooyeweerd's view, the truth of revelation has been adapted or accommodated to Greek philosophy by Christians in their attempts to come to a rational understanding of the faith. The result is, for example, the speculative ideas of a realistic metaphysics (logos doctrine, *analogia entis*), which, as Dooyeweerd puts it, in terms echoing Kant, attempts to transgress the boundaries within which alone meaningful thought and reasoning is possible.

What Dooyeweerd wants is to counteract the influence of Scholasticism in Kuyper's intellectual lineage. He, therefore, is calling for the *dehellenization* of Calvinist thought by urging his fellow-Kuyperians to turn back from scholasticism, namely, from a Christian accommodation to a foreign worldview, as Dooyeweerd understands it, which results in subordinating the truth of Christian Revelation to a priori philosophi-

---

3. Kuyper, *Encyclopedia of Sacred Theology*. The original Dutch edition, *Encyclopaedie der Heilige Godgeleerdheid*, was a three-volume work; this translation contains all of volume 2 and the first 53 pages of vol. 1.

4. Evidence that Dooyeweerd's view of Kuyper remained unchanged almost thirty years later is found in his farewell Valedictory Lecture ("Afscheidscollege") of 16 October, 1965, "Het Oecumenisch-Reformatorisch Grondmotief van de Wijsbegeerte der Wetsidee and de Grondslag der Vrije Universiteit," 3–15.

cal ideas. Clearly, Dooyeweerd thinks of scholasticism, not as a particular method in teaching or writing, such as one finds in St. Thomas's *Summa Theologiae*, but rather as a particular philosophy, with a particular set of presuppositions, which entail a particular philosophical or theological position. Traces of this scholasticism are found in the Calvinist thought of Kuyper and Bavinck, according to Dooyeweerd.

Now, I should make clear that this concluding chapter of my book is about neither Dooyeweerd's nor Kuyper's thought. Rather, my focus is on the thought of Herman Bavinck, that is, I want to examine some features of Bavinck's scholasticism, as I understand it, in the areas of his epistemology and metaphysics, particularly as it is expressed in Volumes I–II of his magnum opus, *Gereformeerde Dogmatiek*. I shall also bring Bavinck into critical conversation with the thought of another scholastic, the philosopher-pope John Paul II, particularly his thought in the 1998 Encyclical Letter, *Fides et Ratio*.

Let me say that I begin with Dooyeweerd because he sees correctly, not only that Bavinck is a scholastic on certain philosophical issues—Bavinck embraces a version of the logos doctrine and the *analogia entis*; but also Dooyeweerd understands that at the root of scholasticism is the encounter between the biblical message and the heritage of Hellenistic philosophical inquiry. I also begin with Dooyeweerd because he identifies four of the key issues of scholastic thought that I'll examine in this chapter, even if only briefly: the relation between nature and grace; the problem of Christian philosophy; the natural knowledge of God; and speech to and about God. Before turning to examine each of those issues in the context of the thought of Bavinck and John Paul II, I want to try my hand at answering the fundamental question: What is scholasticism?

WHAT IS SCHOLASTICISM?

What is scholasticism? The most characteristic feature of the project of scholasticism, I would say, is its attempt to understand systematically the relationship between Christian faith and human rationality, faith and human knowledge, as a matter of "conjunctive coherence."[5] John Paul II expresses succinctly the core idea here: "There is no reason . . . for any ri-

---

5. Guarino, "God of Philosophy and of the Bible," 120. I have profited from Guarino's article in formulating the idea of scholasticism. The idea of "conjunctive coherence" originates with Pieper, *Scholasticism*, 37–39, 44–45, 118, 157–58, and 162.

valry between faith and reason. Each is to be found in the other; [and yet] each has its own sphere of operation."[6] Intriguing, but still requires here some explanation. What does John Paul mean? How is faith to be found *in* reason, and vice versa, reason *in* faith? Significantly, there is no "split level thinking" here, as if faith and reason occupy different compartments with no intrinsic relation between them.

Rather, faith and reason provide a "mutual aid" to each other.[7] John Paul explains, "The Church remains profoundly convinced that faith and reason 'mutually support each other'; each influences the other, as they offer to each other a purifying critique and stimulus to pursue the search for deeper understanding."[8] Faith offers a purifying critique of reason, freeing it from the noetic effects of sin, that is, "gnoseological concupiscence" (see Eph 4:17–18; Col 2:18, "fleshly mind"). Reason offers a purifying critique of one-sided conceptions of faith, such as in fideism.[9] The latter undervalues reason's truth-attaining capacities to attain "something absolute, ultimate and foundational" (as John Paul phrases it) for one of the following causes: either sin has allegedly destroyed those capacities, or under the influence of empiricism or Kantianism, reason's range is limited to the phenomenal world.[10]

Put differently, faith *qua* faith demands reason, not in order to know that the Christian faith is true, since faith itself is a way of knowing reality;

---

6. John Paul II, *Fides et Ratio*, no. 17.

7. This is the phrase Gilson enlists (*Christianity and Philosophy*, 72) to describe the help that faith and reason bring each other, and its source is Leo XIII, the 1879 Encyclical Letter *Aeterni Patris*.

8. John Paul II, *Fides et Ratio*, no. 100.

9. Ibid., no. 55.

10. The phenomenal world is the world as we know it experientially. Phenomenalism is an anti-metaphysical philosophy because it claims that we cannot know the transcendent reality that grounds my experience. John Paul rightly insists that a Scripturally-directed philosophy (see *Fides et Ratio*, nos. 81–83) requires a "philosophy of *genuinely metaphysical range*" in order "to vindicate the human being's capacity to know this transcendent and metaphysical dimension [of reality] in a way that is true and certain, albeit imperfect and analogical." He adds: "Wherever men and women discover a call to the absolute and transcendent, the metaphysical dimension of reality opens up before them: in truth, in beauty, in moral values, in other persons, in being itself, in God. We face a great challenge at the end of [the second] millennium [now the beginning of the next millennium] to move from *phenomenon* to *foundation*, a step as necessary as it is urgent. We cannot stop short at experience alone.... Therefore, a philosophy which shuns metaphysics would be radically unsuited to the task of mediation in the understanding of revelation" (no. 83).

rather, the dynamism of faith ("faith seeking understanding") demands reason in order to show the reasonableness of holding Christian beliefs to be true: providing the intelligibility needed to substantiate the truth claims of Christian doctrine. *Vice versa*: human reason needs faith in order for its truth-oriented capacities to be freed from the noetic effects of sin. In other words, "faith purifies reason," says John Paul—especially from the presumption of the human mind's self-sufficiency,[11] its pretended autonomy, rescuing "reason from over self-confidence," as John Paul also says, and, in consequence, from abolishing human reason's own foundation in the Logos. "The fundamental conviction of the Christian faith is," says Ratzinger, "that in the beginning was Reason and, thus, Truth: it brings forth man and human reason in the first place as beings capable of the truth." "In the beginning was the Word, the Logos, Reason," he adds; the truth of this statement should be taken "as the point of departure for inquiring into the truth itself."[12] Thus, faith leads human reason by properly relating it to the truths of revelation and, in turn, helping man's reason to think faithfully in the light of these truths about God, man and the world. In short, reasonable faith on the one hand, faithful reason on the other (as George Weigel once phrased it). Later in *Fides et Ratio*, John Paul writes: "Reason, bereft of Revelation, runs into devious paths which deprive it of the ability of discovering its ultimate goal," namely truth. "Faith, bereft of reason," John Paul adds, "exalts the feeling and experience of the spirit, and so is in danger of being no longer a universal gift."[13] That is, the more an emphasis is placed on an inner, subjective faith, whether it is a gift of the Holy Spirit or not, the more we begin to slide to a subjective notion of truth; and hence we are unable to account for the Christian

---

11. Ibid., nos. 76, 75. According to Aquinas, divine revelation liberates reason from its presumption of self-sufficiency. On this, see Aquinas's *Summa Contra Gentiles, Book One: God*, Chapter 5, paragraph 4: "Another benefit that comes from the revelation to men of truths that exceed the reason is the curbing of presumption, which is the mother of error. For there are some who have such a presumptuous opinion of their own ability that they deem themselves able to measure the nature of everything; . . . in their estimation, everything is true that seems to them so, and everything is false that does not. So that the human mind, therefore, might be freed from this presumption and come to a humble inquiry after truth, it was necessary that some things should be proposed to man by God that would completely surpass his intellect."

12. Ratzinger (Benedict XVI), "Theology and Church Politics," 155, 152. See also, *Fides et Ratio*, nos. 56, 106.

13. John Paul II, *Fides et Ratio*, no. 48.

faith's insistent claims to objective truth and universality. In sum, writes Ratzinger, "In the Christian faith, *reason* comes to light; precisely as faith, it demands *reason*. Reason comes to light through the Christian *faith*; reason presupposes the *faith* as its living space."[14] Faith needs reason; and vice-versa: reason needs faith.

We can hear that understanding of the relationship between faith and reason in Benedict XVI's Regensburg Address of September 12, 2006, when he derides not only the kind of reason that proceeds without faith but also the kind of position that fails to grasp that faith is inextricably bound up with reason, and, yes, even with a certain kind of philosophical thinking, for example, some form of philosophical realism.[15] We can see this understanding at work in Bavinck's thought not only because he is persuaded that there exists a deep convergence between the best of philosophy and the Christian faith, between the God of the philosophers and the God of Abraham, Isaac and Jacob—as he says in his Rectoral Address, *Christelijke Wereldbeschouwing* ["Christian Worldview"], given at the Free University of Amsterdam, 20 October 1904.[16] It is also at work in his attempt to provide a revelationally appropriate philosophy of knowledge,

---

14. Ratzinger (Benedict XVI), "Theology and Church Politics," 148.

15. All the quotes in this paragraph by Benedict XVI are from his Regensburg Address, "Faith, Reason, and the University, Memories and Reflections."

16. Bavinck, Rectoral Address, *Christelijke Wereldbeschouwing*, given at the Free University of Amsterdam, 20 October 1904: "De philosophie, die aan haar eigen idée getrouw blijft en zich niet in ijdele speculatie verliest, leidt daarom op tot dienzelfden God, dien de Christelijke religie ons als een God van wijsheid en genade openbaart. En de Christelijke religie maakt ons door hare revelatie met datzelfde theisme bekend, dat bij onbevooroordeeld onderzoek de grondslag van all wetenschap en wijsbegeerte blijt te zijn. Het is dezelfde God, dien vrome en wijsgeer behoeven en die aan beide in Zijne werken zich kenbaar maakt. Het is hetzelfde Woord, dat alle dingen heft gemaakt en in de volheid des tijds vleesch is geworden. Het is dezelfde Geest, die het gelaat des aardrijks vernieut en het halt van den zondaar verandert. En daarom: verus philosophus amator Dei, en: Christianus verus philosophus." [Philosophy which remains true to its own idea, and does not lose itself in idle speculation, therefore leads to that same God which the Christian religion reveals to us as a God of wisdom and grace. And the Christian religion makes known to us through its revelation that same theism that to the unprejudiced inquirer turns out to be the foundation of all science and philosophy. It is the same God whom both the believer and the philosopher need, and who makes himself known to both in his works. It is the same Word who has made all things, and in the fullness of time became flesh. It is the same Spirit who renews the face of the earth, and changes the sinner's heart. Therefore: *verus philosophus amator Dei*, the true philosopher is a lover of God, and *Christianus verus philosophus*, the Christian is the true philosopher.] I am thankful to Al Wolters for his careful translation of this Bavinck passage.

and of reality, which is the fruit of the proper conjunction and transformation of philosophy by faith and revelation, and capable of sustaining Christian faith and teaching, offering rational support for revelation's own claims.[17]

Briefly, now, the conjunctive coherence of faith and reason is a position, the validity of which was thrown into question in the era of late scholasticism in the fourteenth and fifteenth century. Regarding late scholasticism, Benedict XVI states in his Regensburg Address: "God's transcendence and otherness are so exalted that our reason, our sense of the true and good, are no longer an authentic mirror of God, whose deepest possibilities remain eternally unattainable and hidden behind his actual decisions." The Protestant Reformers expressed this line of thought in their anti-metaphysical impulse. Says Benedict: "Metaphysics appeared as a premise derived from another source, from which faith had to be liberated in order to become once more fully itself." Furthermore, adds Benedict, "When Kant stated that he needed to set thinking aside in order to make room for faith, he carried this program forward with a radicalism that the Reformers could never have foreseen. He thus anchored faith exclusively in practical reason, denying it access to reality as a whole." The upshot of this Kantianism reductionism is twofold: on the one hand, Christianity is reduced to a pure moral religion, "liberating it, that is to say, from seemingly philosophical and theological elements, such as faith in Christ's divinity and the triune God"; on the other hand, Kant's conception of reason and science was further radicalized by the impact of positivism and scientism. The latter especially claims that science gives us the whole and ultimate truth about reality. Therefore, concludes Benedict,

> if science as a whole is this and this alone, then it is man himself who ends up being reduced, for the specifically human questions about our origin and destiny, the questions raised by religion and ethics, then have no place within the purview of collective reason as defined by "science", so understood, and must thus be relegated to the realm of the subjective. The subject then decides, on the basis of his experiences, what he considers tenable in matters of religion, and the subjective "conscience" becomes the sole arbiter of what is ethical. In this way, though, ethics and religion lose their power to create a community and become a completely personal matter. This is a dangerous state of affairs for humanity, as we see

---

17. Bavinck, *Gereformeerde Dogmatiek*, I, 186–207, 466–591 [207–82, 497–621].

from the disturbing pathologies of religion and reason which necessarily erupt when reason is so reduced that questions of religion and ethics no longer concern it.

In sum, the scope of human reason appears to have been extremely reduced, not only in itself, but particularly in its relationship to the truths of faith, such that it no longer made sense to think that reason can set out on the way to faith. Questioning the task of coordinating faith and reason then raised the larger question of what meaning the concept of "conjunction" could continue to have.[18]

Christians are called by the Word of God to oppose a Gospel dominated by an alien philosophical system (Col 2:8). On this point Catholics and neo-Calvinists agree. In doing so, they were simply carrying out a practice with deep roots in the Christian tradition, indeed, in the Word of God that urges us to "destroy arguments and every lofty opinion raised against the knowledge of God, and take every thought captive to obey Christ" (2 Cor 10:5). Throughout the last two millennia, Christian thinkers, starting with almost every Church Father as well as every later thinker committed to historic Christian orthodoxy, including, of course, Herman Bavinck, have insisted that all philosophy, whether of Greek, modern, or contemporary origin, must be "critically purified," that is, amplified, corrected, and transformed in light of the truth of the Christian revelation. As Aquinas urges, to take but one example, when one draws on philosophical truth in the service of Christian faith, "do not mix water with wine, but rather change water into wine."[19] To take another example, in Etienne Gilson's wonderfully apt phrase, Christian thinkers must put "these fragments of truth in the service of revelation."[20] This service is, as Hans Urs von Balthasar rightly urges, "no mechanical adoption of alien chains of thought with which one can adorn and garland the Christian

---

18. Pieper, *Scholasticism*, 142.

19. Aquinas, *De Trinitate*, q. 2, a.3 ad 5.

20. Gilson, *Philosopher and Theology*, 188. Gilson's approach stands in the line of the "spoils from Egypt" trope. For an important discussion of this trope, see Guarino, *Foundations of Systematic Theology*, 269–310. He explains this trope as one "that characterized the work of so many early Christian writers. Insofar as God had created the world, had communicated himself to humanity by a primordial act of grace and love inscribed in creation itself, wisdom and truth could be found in many places. All such wisdom, however, the traditional spoils metaphor insists, must ultimately be disciplined by, and incorporated into, the revelatory narrative. Athens, whatever its own insights into truth, must ultimately be chastened by Jerusalem" (269).

dimension externally."[21] Thus, the task implied in Gilson's phrase could be distinguished, says Balthasar, into the "art of *breaking open* all finite, philosophical truth in the direction of Christ, and the art of *clarifying transposition*."[22] Regarding the former, Christians are deeply committed to the "all-embracing authority of Christ" (cf. Matt 28:18) over all forms of creaturely truth, because in Christ are hid all the treasures of wisdom and knowledge (cf. Col 2:2–3), and hence Christians "cannot rest until they have brought all these forms of into the service of the one truth. 'Everything is yours; but you belong to Christ, and Christ to God'" (1 Cor 3:23).[23] Regarding the art of clarifying transposition, Balthasar writes,

> The fragment or stone that they pick up may come from the bed of a Christian stream, or of a pagan or heretical stream, but they know how to cleanse it and to polish it until that radiance shines forth which shows that it is a fragment of the total glorification of God. Such a methodology may appear dangerous, because the clear and sharp outlines of the evangelical decision threaten to become blurred in it. This is the form of thought which necessarily *had* to be confused by unbelieving criticism with the syncretism of late Antiquity, the form of thought which permitted Christianity to amalgamate itself with the elements of Hellenism which were alien to its own being. But everything depends here on the disposition in which the synthesis is made: if the knowledge of the absoluteness of the truth of Christ stands at the abiding origin of such thought, and if the decision for him has been made with the entire purity of a loving soul, then it is legitimate and safe to adopt the intellectual mission to go out into all the world and to take captive all truth for Christ. "Test *everything* and retain what is good!" (1 Thess 5:21). But "do not conform yourselves to the spirit of the world" (Rom 12:2).[24]

Against this background, we can begin to understand the encounter between the Gospel and Greek thought. Both John Paul II and the early Ratzinger make several claims about this encounter. First, many of the earliest Fathers of the Church responded positively to the attempts of the early philosophers from Xenophanes to Plato "to display the close link

---

21. Hans Urs von Balthasar, "On the tasks of Catholic philosophy in our time," 155–156.

22. Ibid., 156.

23. Ibid., 158.

24. Ibid., 159.

between reason and religion." "As they [philosophers] broadened their view to include universal principles," he adds, "they no longer acquiesced in the ancient myths, rather they desired to support their belief in divinity on rational grounds."[25] In short, many of these Fathers recognized that reason, *logos*, already said something true about God. This, too, is Bavinck's view. Given general revelation—that is, God's revelation of himself in and through the works of creation—especially expressed in the doctrine of common grace, the Reformed theologian could, he says, "recognize all the truth, beauty, and goodness that is present also in the pagan world."[26] Yet, and here too Bavinck agrees, this is a truth admixed with serious error, falsehoods, and, in consequence, yields a truncated understanding of God, man, and the world. Whatever, then, pagan thought said to be true needed to be amplified, corrected, and transformed by revelation. Notwithstanding that important qualification, the choice for the *logos* as against any kind of myth, for the God of the philosophers as against the gods of the various religions, meant the definitive demythologization of the world and of religion, as the younger Ratzinger says in his 1968 classic, *Introduction to Christianity*.[27] Consequently, says John Paul, "On this basis the Fathers of the Church carried on a fruitful dialogue with ancient philosophers, and so opened the way to the proclamation and knowledge of God in Christ Jesus."[28]

Second, there is a remarkable agreement in Bavinck, Ratzinger, and Gilson on the name of God revealed in Exodus 3:13 and its significance for understanding a unity of belief and thought, of philosophy and faith. The biblical name for God, "I am," is unified with a philosophical idea, the notion of existence and being, of the existing real, of being itself. Says Bavinck, "God is the real, the true being, the fullness of being, the sum total of all reality and perfection, the totality of being, from which all other being owes its existence. He is an immeasurable and unbounded ocean of being; the absolute being who alone has being in himself."[29] In this union, says the young Ratzinger, one finds that "belief is wedded to

25. John Paul II, *Fides et Ratio*, no. 36.
26. Bavinck, *GD* I, 290-91 [319].
27. Joseph Ratzinger, *Introduction to Christianity*, 137-38.
28. John Paul II, *Fides et Ratio*, no. 36.
29. Bavinck, *Gereformeerde Dogmatiek*, II, 93; ET: *Reformed Dogmatics*, Vol. Two, *God and Creation*, 123. Both sources will be cited throughout this chapter, first the original, followed by the pagination of the English translation in square brackets [ ].

ontology," being (*ontos*) and God (*theos*) converge. Gilson writes of the "laborious gropings" (alluding to Acts 17:27) of Plato and Aristotle, as they sought to say something about God. Compared with their efforts, he adds, "how straight forward is the method of the Biblical revelation, and how startling its results." And then, famously, Gilson adds: "In order to know what God is, Moses turns to God. He asks His name, and straightway comes the answer: *Ego sum qui sum, Ait: sic dices filiis Israel; qui est misit me ad vos* (Exod 3:14). No hint of metaphysics, but God speaks, *causa finite est*, and Exodus lays down the principle from which henceforth the whole of Christian philosophy will be suspended. From this moment it is understood once and for all that the proper name of God is Being and that, according to the word of St. Ephrem, taken up again later by St. Bonaventure, this name denotes His very essence."[30] Gilson assures us that he is not claiming that Exodus 3:14 is "a revealed metaphysical definition of God." Still, he concludes, "but if there is no metaphysic *in* Exodus there is nevertheless a metaphysic *of* Exodus," and this was "developed in due course by the Fathers of the Church, whose indications on this point the mediaeval philosophers merely follow up and exploit."[31]

Bavinck agrees with the point made by Gilson that Exodus 3:14 is not a revealed metaphysical definition of God, which refers to God's aseity: "God is the One who *is*, an eternal immutable being, over against the factual nonbeing . . . of idols and the nonabsolute being . . . of creatures."[32] But Bavinck does not argue that the metaphysical interpretation of this passage belongs to an unwarranted philosophical displacement of YHWH. Rather, he underscores the point that the metaphysical interpretation is either stated or implied throughout Scripture, and hence, argues Bavinck, it is foundational to Exodus 3:15, underscoring the true identity of the God of Abraham, Isaac, and Jacob, the creating and redeeming God. Bavinck writes in a passage worthy of being cited at some length:

> He is who he is, the same yesterday, today, and forever. This meaning is further explained in verse 15: YHWH—the God of your fathers, the God of Abraham, Isaac, and Jacob—sends Moses, and that is his name forever. God does not simply call himself "the One who is" and offer no explanation of his aseity, but states expressly what and how he is. Then how and what will he be? That is

---

30. Gilson, *The Spirit of Medieval Philosophy*, 50–51.
31. Ibid., 433–434, note 9.
32. Bavinck, *GD* II, 114–15 [143].

not something one can say in a word or describe in an additional phrase, but "he will be what he will be." That sums up everything. This addition is still general and indefinite, but for that reason also rich and full of deep meaning. He will be what he was for the patriarchs, what he is now and will remain: he will be everything to and for his people. It is not a new and strange God who comes to them by Moses, but the God of the fathers, the Unchangeable One, the Faithful One, the eternally Self-consistent One, who never leaves or forsakes his people but always again seeks out and saves his own. He is unchangeable in his grace, in his love, in his assistance, who will be what he is because he is always himself. So in Isaiah he calls himself: "I am he, the first and the last" (cf. 41:4; 43:10, 13, 25; 44:6; 48:12). And indeed, his aseity is the foundation of this view of God, but it is not in the foreground nor directly expressed in the name.[33]

Are Bavinck and Gilson right that the metaphysical interpretation of God's faithfulness underscores his true identity? Is God's goodness, grace, and love, indeed, his self-identity rooted in who He actually *is*, and hence of his self-identification as "I am who am?" If so, then one can understand, Ratzinger argues, integrating the philosophical insight into the primacy of the existing real, of being itself, of the fullness of existence groped at by the Greek inquiry, with the revelation of the Lord of the universe manifested in the history of salvation, in Israel and in Jesus Christ. The "I am" of Exodus and again, for example, of Isaiah 48:12, "I am He; I am the first and I am the last," and finally, the "I am" of the Gospel of John (John 8:24; 8:58) all converge. Of course the God of the patriarchs, of the God and Father of our Lord Jesus Christ, of Jesus Christ himself in whom the fullness of the Godhead dwells bodily (Col 2:9), surpasses anything that the philosophers could imagine. But, Ratzinger insists, the God of salvation history does not cease to be the God of the philosophers—as Bavinck also argued—the truth and ground of being. Christianity's task is to comprehend, surpass, and correct, indeed, transform by revelation the God of the philosophers.

33. Bavinck, *GD* II, 115 [143]. I have altered the translation slightly of the last sentence of this quotation because the English translation does not quite get the nuance. The original Dutch: "Natuurlijk ligt hier de aseitas wel aan ten *grondslag* [italics added], maar deze treedt toch niet op den voorgrond en wordt niet rechtstreeks in den naam uitgesproken." The English translation has rendered "grondslag" with "underlies" and that, in my mind, seems too weak a word to translate the Dutch; "foundation" or "foundational" seems more fitting.

Third, in choosing the way of the *logos*, Christianity embraced a realist view of truth, strongly insisting on the cognitive claims of revealed truth, against a view of religion that that was devoid of truth, of reality, leading to religion being regarded as mere custom, useful traditions, and an outward form of life. "The Christian position, as opposed to this situation," says Ratzinger, "is put emphatically by Tertullian when he says with splendid boldness: 'Christ called himself truth, not custom.'"[34] Ratzinger labels this insight of Tertullian one of the "great assertions" of the early Church. As Fr. Thomas Guarino remarks, "For in rejecting myth and custom for the truth of being the Church undertook the abiding task of insisting on uniqueness of her own claims . . . its insistent claims to transcultural and transgenerational truth and universality."[35]

Fourth, both the young Ratzinger and John Paul II—and yes, Bavinck, too—are persuaded that the encounter between the Gospel and Greek thought was providential. Bavinck writes, "Though Christian dogma cannot be explained in terms of Greek philosophy, it also did not come into being apart from it. There is as yet no dogma and theology, strictly speaking, in Scripture. . . . Gradually a need arose to think through the ideas of revelation, to link it with other knowledge and to defend it against various forms of attack. For this purpose people need philosophy. Scientific theology was born with its help. This did not, however, happen accidentally. The Church was not the victim of deception. In the formation and development of the dogmas, the church fathers made generous [albeit critical] use of philosophy . . . to help them think through and defend the truth of God."[36] In Ratzinger's case he asks us to consider the vision of St. Paul in Acts 16:6–10 wherein his path to Asia is blocked by a word of knowledge he received from the Holy Spirit, while a Macedonian pleads for his aid, "Come over to Macedonia and help us" (16:9). St. Paul concluded that God had called him to preach the gospel to them (16:10). St. Paul's vision, in fact, "might well represent something like a first attempt at a 'theology of history', intended to underline the crossing of the gospel to Europe, 'to the Greeks', as a divinely arranged necessity." Ratzinger adds, "I am convinced that at bottom it was no mere accident that the Christian message, in the period when it was taking shape, first entered the Greek world and

---

34. Ratzinger, *Introduction to Christianity*, 141.
35. Guarino, "The God of Philosophy and of the Bible," 124, 126.
36. Bavinck, *GD* I, 576 [607].

there merged with the inquiry into understanding, into truth."[37] Benedict makes the same point in his Regensburg address.

Someone might object to Benedict's claim that the encounter between the Gospel and Greek thought is providential by insisting that the Church's early synthesis of faith and Hellenistic thought—an initial inculturation—ought not to be binding on other cultures. "The latter are said to have the right to return to the simple message of the New Testament prior to that inculturation, in order to inculturate it anew in their own particular milieu." Benedict sharply responds: "This thesis is not simply false, but it is coarse and lacking in precision. The New Testament was written in Greek and bears the imprint of the Greek spirit, which had already come to maturity as the Old Testament developed." "True," he adds, "there are elements in the evolution of the early Church which do not have to be integrated into all cultures. Nonetheless, the fundamental decisions made about the relation between faith and the use of human reason is part of the faith itself; they are developments consonant with the nature of faith itself."[38]

Fifth, in this connection, I cannot fail to note that the pope's position on the rejection of dehellenization is fully consistent with the general hermeneutical principle stated by John XXIII and affirmed by Vatican II: "the deposit or the truths of faith, contained in our sacred teaching, are one thing, while the mode in which they are enunciated, keeping the same meaning and the same judgment, is another."[39] With this formulation the Council opened the way to a legitimate theological diversity that nonetheless maintains a fundamental unity of faith and doctrine.[40]

NATURE AND GRACE

Three quarters of a century past, Jacques Maritain significantly remarked regarding the question of the relation of nature and grace that it is erroneous to ignore both the distinction between nature and grace as well

---

37. Ratzinger, *Introduction to Christianity*, 78, and note 16.

38. Benedict XVI, "Faith, Reason, and the University, Memories and Reflections."

39. "Est enim aliud ipsum depositum Fidei, seu veritates, quae veneranda doctrina nostra continentur, aliud modus, quo eaedem enuntiantur, eodem tamen sensu eademque sentential," in Ioannes XXIII, "Allocutio habita d. 11 oct. 1962, in initio Concilii," 54 *Acta Apostolicae Sedis* (1962).

40. I addressed this position in chapter II of this book.

as their union.⁴¹ Although Maritain firmly maintains the distinction between nature and grace, he nonetheless rejects a dualism of both a "hard" and a "soft" sort.⁴² Hard dualism, which Maritain rejects, conceives of nature first in terms of its own end, to which is then "superadded" a second, supernatural end. Yet, Maritain also rejects a softer dualism in which a harmony between nature and grace is conceived, but there is still an *extrinsic* relation between them. This more subtle form of dualism accepts that there is only one ultimate end for nature, a supernatural one, but it nonetheless fails to consider that this end directs and orders nature and all its intermediate ends, *from within* rather than alongside of or above nature. By contrast to both forms of dualism, Maritain emphasizes that grace restores or transforms nature from within.

Pared down for my purposes here, then, I shall argue that the *leitmotif* regarding a truly Catholic theology of the relationship of nature and grace can be formulated in the phrase: "grace restores or transforms nature." Now, this way of formulating the relation between nature and grace will undoubtedly strike some neo-Calvinists, as it did Abraham Kuyper, Herman Bavinck, and Herman Dooyeweerd, namely, as decidedly un-Catholic.⁴³ For more than a century, neo-Calvinists have contrasted their own "organic way of relating nature and grace," as Bavinck puts it, with "the mechanical juxtaposition and dualistic worldview of the Catholic Church."⁴⁴ Briefly, the standard neo-Calvinist account, such as Bavinck's, claims that the relation between these orders is, according to Roman Catholicism, seen as a two-story system: nature being either the purely passive substratum for grace or a self-enclosed order with its own natural ends, to which is then added the freely given gift of grace (*donum superadditum*) essential to attaining man's supernatural end. These two orders of nature and grace are regarded as *parallel* levels having only an

---

41. Maritain states, "There is one error that consists in ignoring [the] distinction between nature and grace. There is another that consists in ignoring their union," *Clairvoyance de Rome* (Paris, 1929), 222, cited in de Lubac, "Apologetics and Theology," *Theological Fragments*, 103, n. 28. For an extensive discussion of Maritain's theology of nature and grace, see my essay, "Nature and Grace," 240–68.

42. For the conceptual distinction between "hard" and "soft" dualism, I am indebted to Schindler, "Christology, Public Theology, and Thomism," 247–64.

43. Kuyper, *Lectures on Calvinism*, 122–23.

44. Bavinck, *GD* I, [303–5; 353–61]. See also, Bavinck, "Common Grace," 60. "Common Grace" is a translation of Bavinck's rectorial address at Kampen Theological Seminary, Netherlands, in December 1894, entitled "De Algemeene Genade."

extrinsic, but non-contradictory relation to each other; or, alternatively, the relation between nature and grace is such that the latter is taken to be a "plus-factor" wherein sacramental grace is "added-on" to natural realm through an external connection to the institutional Church. Thus, rather than elevating and transfiguring, say, marriage, in its own order, that is sanctifying it from *within*, grace seizing nature from the inside and restoring the original order of creation disturbed by sin, marriage is hallowed extrinsically, that is, by being rendered a sacrament that "adds on" the plus-factor of supernatural grace, through an external connection to the institutional Church. On this "two-tier" relationship—whether in a "parallel" or "supplementary" sense—between nature and grace, neo-Calvinists say, the latter is merely added (the *donum superadditim*) to a nature that has not been integrally affected by sin, and hence human nature requires little or no internal healing or redemption.

The standard textbook account of this Catholic view—and it is found in Bavinck's *Gereformeerde Dogmatiek*—is that nature and grace existed in a harmonious relation in man's pre-lapsarian condition. The post-lapsarian state is such that nature is wounded by the fall into sin in the sense that it loses the extra-added gift of grace, the divinely given endowments of original holiness and righteousness. Man's nature is *wounded*, the neo-Calvinist insists, but not *corrupted*. Thus, redemption in Christ then means that nature regains that supernatural gift of grace. According to the neo-Calvinist critics of this view, however, this understanding of the relation that nature has to grace deprives sin as well as Christ's redemptive work of its radical character. Because the loss of grace only affects the second-story and not the lower first-story, then nature as such is not affected by the fall and hence does not need to be restored through God's work of redemption.

I want to say that I agree with those, such as Bavinck, who rightly state the core problem with this view to be that it fails to consider that grace directs, orders, and transforms nature *from within* rather than alongside of or above nature. Says Bavinck, on this view, "Christianity is that which transcends and approaches the natural, but it does not penetrate and sanctify it. . . . The catholicity of the Christian principle that purifies and sanctifies everything is exchanged for a dualism that separates the supernatural from the natural by considering it as transcendent above the natural."[45] But now because the lower order of nature and culture is left

---

45. Bavinck, "Catholicity of Christianity," 229.

untouched by sin and hence untransformed by the grace of redemption, this results in a kind of naturalism at that lower level: a nature and culture, indeed, the whole spectrum of life, without God's transforming presence, running their own course separately from any contact with grace, and hence a nature and culture not ordered from *within* their depth to God become increasingly independent and autonomous. Bavinck rightly judges here that in this dualism of nature and grace we have one of the sources of the secularization of culture, on the one hand, and the marginalization of Christianity on the other.

Furthermore, I agree with Dooyeweerd that the mechanical juxtaposition and dualistic relation of nature and grace is unquestionably found in both Protestant and Catholic traditions.[46] Of course Catholic criticisms of this dualism have not been in short supply in the twentieth century. Besides Jacques Maritain, Catholic critics of this construal of nature and grace may also be found in the works of Karl Rahner, Henri de Lubac, Etienne Gilson, and Hans Urs von Balthasar, to name just several of the most illustrious but very different Catholic thinkers of the twentieth century.[47] Not only Dooyeweerd but also G.C. Berkouwer recognize this point in their later writings on neo-Thomism and the *nouvelle théologie* of Henri de Lubac, et al.[48] Where I strongly disagree with Bavinck and,

---

46. Dooyeweerd, *Twilight of Western Thought*, 44.

47. Here is a sample of important criticisms of the nature/grace dualism from a Catholic standpoint. De Lubac, *Mystery of the Supernatural*. See also, de Lubac's *Brief Catechesis*; Rahner, *Nature and Grace*; von Balthasar, *Love Alone*; idem, *Theology of Karl Barth*; Maritain, *Integral Humanism*.

48. Dooyeweerd, "Het Gesprek tussen het Neo-Thomisme and de Wijsbegeerte der Wetsidee," 202–13. In fact, Dooyeweerd states in 1964, "En nu, nu die *nouvelle théologie* opkwam en in de wijsbegeerte van de Neo-Scholastiek heel nieuwe geluiden naar voren kwamen, waarin ook gesproken werd van het religieuze centrum van de mens, ja, daar verloor opens dat tweede deel van mijn boek *Reformatie en Scholastiek*, vorzover het de scholastische richting betrof, eigenlijk haar grondslag, want de Rooms-Katholieken zouden zeggen: 'Waar heeft u het over, we leven in een veranderde tijd en de neo-scholastiek is allang ontwassen aan dat oude standpunt. Ze nadert u in hoge mate'. . . . Maar dat was ook de redden waarom ik dat tweede deel in z'n geheel nooit gepubliceerd heb van *Reformatie en Scholastiek*. Het bevredigde me niet meer" ("Centrum en Omtrek: De Wijsbegeerte der Wetsidee in en Veranderende Wereld,"12. [But now, with the rise of the *nouvelle théologie*, and new directions in neo-Scholastic philosophy, in which people also speak of the religious center of man—why, now the second part of my book *Reformation and Scholasticism* in fact suddenly lost its basis, at least as regards its treatment of Scholasticism, because the Roman Catholics would say, "What are you talking about? We are living in different times, and neo-Scholasticism has long outgrown the

by implication with Dooyeweerd as well as Kuyper, is with the thesis that dualism is, in short, *the* defining view of the Catholic tradition over against the "ineluctable unity of nature, sin and grace" (in the words of the American neo-Calvinist Henry Stob)[49] posited in the Biblical revelation and as grasped by neo-Calvinism. Although I, too, reject a "two-story" relationship between nature and grace, I share the judgment of Henri de Lubac, Jacques Maritain, Louis Dupre, Alasdair MacIntyre, Arvin Vos, Dewey Hoitenga, and others that, to quote Calvinist Hoitenga, this view is "a later (sixteenth- and seventeenth-century) corruption within Catholic thought, which entered it under the spell of the new humanist, Cartesian, and later Enlightenment views of an autonomous conception of reason and will."[50] Although I cannot argue the point fully here, my thesis is that the teaching of the Catholic Church on the unity of nature, sin, and grace is remarkably similar to the teaching of the neo-Calvinist tradition. With all due respect to my neo-Calvinist friends of long-standing, their resistance to my thesis must give way—resistance is futile, as the Borg of Star Trek fame would say—if I am right that there is a point of convergence between Catholicism and neo-Calvinism on the relation between nature and grace, namely, as a result of the achievement of grace, as a result of grace penetrating and transforming and perfecting nature from within, nature is redeemed in its own domain.

In this connection, let me cite several key passages on the relation between nature and grace from a 1931 remarkable book by Etienne Gilson, *Christianity and Philosophy*: "The true Catholic position consists in maintaining that nature was created good, that it has been wounded, but that it can be at least partially healed by grace [here and now] if God so

---

old standpoint. It has come very close to you" . . . But that was also the reason why I never published that second part of *Reformation and Scholasticism* in its entirety. I was no longer satisfied with it."] My thanks to Al Wolters for his careful translation of this passage. For Berkouwer's more positive assessment of Roman Catholicism in light of the Second Vatican Council, see his *Vatikaans Concilie en Nieuwe Theologie*, and compare it with his earlier, more negative, assessments of Roman Catholicism, *Conflict met Rome* and *De Strijd Om Het Roomsch-Katholieke Dogma*.

49. Stob, "Calvin and Aquinas," 130. Stob shares the standard neo-Calvinist view that "Roman Catholic thinkers tend to regard created nature, both human and non-human, as integrally exempt from the ravages of sin, and to restrict the effect of sin to the loss of supernatural endowments (the *superadditum*) with which the human head of the created cosmos was originally engraced" ("Observations on the Concept of the Antithesis," 241–58).

50. Hoitenga, Jr., *John Calvin*, 113.

wishes. This *instauratio*, that is to say, this renewal, this re-establishment, this restoration of nature to its primitive goodness, is on this point the program of authentic Catholicism." As Gilson also says elsewhere, "To say that grace is necessary to restore nature is quite other than to suppress that nature to the profit of grace: it is to confirm it by grace. Grace presupposes nature, whether to restore or to enrich it. When grace restores nature, it does not substitute itself for it, but re-establishes it; when nature, thus re-established by grace, accomplishes its proper operations, they are indeed natural operations [now transformed] which it performs." Finally, as Gilson also says later in this book, "Catholicism teaches that before everything the restoration of wounded nature by the grace of Jesus Christ. The restoration of nature: so there must be a nature, and of what value, since it is the work of God, Who created it and re-created it by repurchasing it at the prince of His own Blood! Thus grace presupposes nature, and the excellence of nature which it comes to heal and transfigure."[51] Thus, grace restores and transforms nature from within its own domain.

Indeed, this is how the late philosopher-pope John Paul describes the Church's mission of evangelization and, in fact, "the purpose of the Gospel," namely, "'to transform humanity from within and to make it new'. Like the yeast which leavens the whole measure of dough (cf. *Mt* 13:33), the Gospel is meant to permeate all cultures and give them life from within, so that they may express the full truth about the human person and about human life."[52]

In sum, what this understanding of the nature/grace relation means is that the redemption accomplished through Jesus Christ's saving work—His life, passion, death, resurrection, and ascension, in short, the total Christ event—does not (a) stand opposed to, and hence replace altogether, created reality, because the latter is hopelessly corrupt as a consequence of the fall into sin and needs replacing altogether. But nor does it merely (b) supplement or (c) parallel that reality, which would leave nature untouched by grace, merely preserved, side by side with, but unaf-

---

51. Gilson, *Christianity and Philosophy*, 21, 24, and 111, respectively.

52. John Paul II, *Evangelium Vitae*, no. 95. The quote within this quote is from Paul VI, *Evangelii Nuntiandi*, no. 18. Paul VI adds, "The purpose of evangelization is therefore precisely this interior change, and if it had to be expressed in one sentence the best way of stating it would be to say that the Church evangelizes when she seeks to convert, solely through the divine power of the message she proclaims, both the personal and collective consciences of people, the activities in which they engage, and the lives and concrete milieu which are theirs."

fected by Christ's grace, and thus nature and grace would have only an *extrinsic* relation to each other. Furthermore, it does not merely involve (d) acceptance of created reality, of one's humanity, *as it is*, for that would deny created reality's fallen state, which would, as Fr. Thomas Guarino puts it, "overlook God's judgment on the world rendered dramatically in the cross of Christ."[53] Rather, reality stands in need of being reconsecrated to God the Father, in Christ's redemption and through the power of the Holy Spirit and (e) seeks to penetrate and restore *from within* the fallen order of creation,[54] bringing it to fullness of expression in accordance with the concrete norm that is Jesus Christ. As John Paul II puts this last point in his 1999 *Letter to Artists* (no. 14), "Jesus Christ not only reveals God, but 'fully reveals man to man'. In Christ, God has reconciled the world to himself. All believers are called to bear witness to this; but it is up to you, men and women who have given your lives to art, to declare with all the wealth of your ingenuity that *in Christ the world is redeemed*: the human person is redeemed, the human body is redeemed, and the whole creation which, according to Saint Paul, 'waits with eager longing for the revealing of the sons of God' (Rom. 8:19), is redeemed. The creation awaits the revelation of the children of God also through art and in art."

THE IDEA OF CHRISTIAN PHILOSOPHY

In his 1962 intellectual autobiography, *The Philosopher and Theology*, Catholic philosopher, neo-Thomist Étienne Gilson wrote regarding the future of Christian philosophy: "The necessary condition to insure the future of Christian philosophy is to maintain the primacy of the Word of God, *even in philosophical inquiry*." "I am tempted to say," adds Gilson, "above all in matters of philosophical speculation."[55] We find a similar accent on the primacy of God's Word *in* philosophical inquiry almost

---

53. Guarino, *Foundations of Systematic Theology*, 20.

54. I owe this succinct way of formulating the various possibilities of relating nature and grace to my colleague Wolters, "What is to be done? Toward a neo-Calvinist Agenda." Especially influential not only in my own thinking but also that of Wolter's on the relation between nature and grace are the writings of Dutch neo-Calvinist philosopher Dooyeweerd (1894–1977). For a brief introduction to his thinking, see *Twilight of Western Thought*. Also instructive is Gustafson's chapter on nature and grace in his work, *Protestant and Roman Catholic Ethics*, 95–137. On nature and grace in the early history of the Church, see Pelikan, *Christian Tradition*, Vol. 1, Chapter 6, "Nature and Grace," 278–331.

55. Gilson, *Philosopher and Theology*, 228–29.

four decades later in John Paul II's *Fides et Ratio*.⁵⁶ This philosopher-pope affirms the notion of Christian philosophy, which is, according to John Paul, "the art of philosophizing in a Christian manner; namely a philosophical reflection [and practice] that is vitally conjoined to faith."⁵⁷ In this connection, most significant is John Paul's commitment to, and call for, a scripturally based philosophy, a Christian philosophy, one consonant with the Word of God itself, which one may never neglect without impunity. "In refusing the truth offered by divine revelation, philosophy only does itself damage, since this is to cut off access to a deeper knowledge of the truth."⁵⁸ Christian philosophy must, argues the pope, first, rehabilitate philosophy's sapiential task in developing an integral Christian worldview; second, embrace a realist notion of truth (denouncing relativism), and an account of the actual capacity of human reason to transcend experience in attaining knowledge of truth (denouncing positivism, pragmatism, and phenomenalism), as well as, third, retrieve a philosophy possessing a genuinely metaphysical range in a theological understanding of faith and morals.

Although I cannot argue the point fully here, Bavinck is committed to the same three points. He too argues for the necessity of an integral Christian world- and lifeview ("'einheitliche' wereld- en levensbeschouwing") in opposition to the dualistic legacy of a Kantian worldview at the end of the nineteenth century, in epistemology, metaphysics, anthropology, and morality.⁵⁹ He also presupposes a realist definition of truth

---

56. John Paul II, *Fides et Ratio*, nos. 80–89.

57. John Paul II, *Fides et Ratio*, no. 76. John Paul's conception of Christian philosophy may be traced backed to Gilson's influence on his thought. Gilson himself claims to owe his conception of Christian philosophy to the "epoch-making document" of Pope Leo XIII, the 1879 Encyclical Letter *Aeterni Patris*. Catholic thinker Novak has argued that Karol Wojtyla (aka John Paul II) "was much taken with the argument on Christian philosophy launched by Gilson ("Christian Philosophy of John Paul II," 243–56).

58. Ibid., no. 75.

59. Bavinck, *Christelijke Wereldbeschouwing*, "Een wereld- en levensbeschouwing wordt door drie punten bepaald. . . . De problemen, waarvoor de menschelijke geest altijd weer te staan komt, zijn deze: wat is de verhouding van denken en zijn, van zijn en worden, van worden en handelen? Wat ben ik, wat is de wereld en wat is in die wereld mijne plaats en mijn taak? Het autonome denken vindt op die vragen geen bevredigend antwoord; het oscilleert tusschen materialisme en spiritualisme, tusschert atomisme en dynamisme, tusschen nomisme en antinomisme. Maar het Christendom bewaart het evenwicht en openbaart ons eene wijsheid, welke den mensch met God, maar daarin ook met zichzelven, met de wereld en met het leven verzoent." [A world and life view

and an epistemological realism throughout the *Gereformeerde Dogmatiek* and elsewhere.[60] Finally, regarding metaphysics, Bavinck wrote: "The split between the Christian religion on the one hand and metaphysics on the other can neither be cleanly conceived nor practically executed. History has repeatedly demonstrated this fact in the past and again shows it today. For to make such a split somewhat possible, [post-Kantian theology is] compelled to form a one-sided and incomplete picture of the gospel of Christ." In sum, bringing together these three points, Bavinck adds,

> Religion does not and cannot exist, therefore, without a certain specific idea of God; and this idea in turn includes others ideas concerning the world, humanity, the origin and destiny of things. To believers these religious ideas have transcendental significance; they are profoundly convinced of their objective reality and truth. The moment we begin to regard these ideas as products of our own imagination, as ideas without reality, or even despair of the knowability of the metaphysical, our religion is done for. . . . God must also be served with the mind, and when the mind notes that religious notions do not correspond to reality, it cases to be religious. While a religious and a theoretical worldview, theology and

---

is defined by three points. . . . The perennial problems which the human mind faces are the following: what is the relationship of thought and being, of being and becoming, of becoming and action? What am I, what is the world, and what is my place and my task within that world? Autonomous thought does not find a satisfactory answer to these questions. It oscillates between materialism and spiritualism, between atomism and dynamism, between nomism and anti-nomism. But Christianity preserves a balance here, and reveals to us a wisdom which reconciles man with God, and thereby also with himself, with the world, and with life."] My gratitude to Al Wolters for his careful translation of this Bavinck passage and the one in the following note.

60. Bavinck, *Christelijke Wereldbeschouwing*, "Nu is waarheid echter het onmisbaar goed voor ons kenvermogen en daarom het doel aller wetenschap. Indien er geen waarheid is, valt daarmede ook alle kennis en wetenschap. De Christelijke religie betoont daarom allereerst hierin hare wijsheid, dat zij de waarheid kennen doet en handhaaft als eene objectieve realiteit, die onafhankelijk van ons bewustzijn bestaat en die door God in zijne werken van natuur en genade voor ons is uitgestald. Daarmede in overeenstemming gaat ieder mensch spontaan van de overtuiging uit, dat de wereld objectief buiten hem bestaat en zoo bestaat, als hij bij zuivere waarneming ze kennen leert." [Now truth is the indispensable good for our cognitive faculty, and therefore the goal of all science. If there is no truth, all knowledge and science falls away. The Christian religion therefore shows its wisdom above all in making the truth known, and maintaining it as an objective reality which exists independently of our consciousness, and which is displayed for us by God in his works of nature and grace. In accordance with this, every man has the spontaneous conviction that the world exists objectively, apart from himself, and exists the way he comes to know it through uncontaminated perception.]

science, are not identical, they cannot possibly be at war with each other. Such a dualism is inevitably in conflict with the unity of the human mind.[61]

Furthermore, according to John Paul, the relation between philosophy and theology is no longer construed according to the "two-story" textbook view of nature and grace. Yes, natural theology is possible, but not as "first" philosophy, laying the rational foundation for divine revelation, for revealed and supernatural truths, *prior* to and *apart* from faith. A foundationalism of this sort sets up some standard external to revelation itself, according epistemic primacy to some criterion other than revelation itself.

Instead of treating natural theology, or metaphysical and transcendental foundations, as a "first" philosophy, prior to Christian faith, developed independently of that faith, John Paul incorporates "first philosophy" within the larger embrace of Christian faith. Christian theology must endorse natural theology and metaphysical inquiry, not only for the sake of its own intelligibility, philosophical arguments providing support for the rational structure of Christian faith, but also precisely within the prior normative claims made by special revelation. It is the very nature of the revealed Word of God, says John Paul, which "demands recourse to philosophical reflections."[62] For example, the pope adds, "The Word of God refers constantly to things which transcend human experience and even human thought."[63] Thus, without philosophy's contribution, that is, without a philosophy possessing a genuinely metaphysical range, we would be ill-equipped to render the theological totality of Catholic Christianity, which needs to speak about being as well as meaning and about eternity as well as time. "It would be impossible to clarify theological issues such as . . . language concerning God, the personal relations within the Trinity, God's creative activity in the world, the relationship between God and man, and the identity of Christ as true God and true man. The same applies in various assertions of moral theology, in which certain concepts recur, like the moral law, conscience, freedom, personal responsibility, guilt, and so forth, all of which are defined with reference

---

61. Bavinck, *GD* I, 229–230 [256–57].
62. John Paul II, *Fides et Ratio*, no. 64.
63. Ibid., no. 83.

to philosophical ethics."[64] What we have here in John Paul II's thought is an a posteriori use of first philosophy that is demanded by the *prior* claims of Christian faith itself. Moreover, given the epistemic priority of the normative Christian revelation, argues John Paul, "Christian revelation therefore becomes the true place where the philosophical and theological disciplines in their mutual relationships, are yoked together and interact." Or as John Paul puts it elsewhere: "The Truth, which is Christ, imposes itself with a universal authority, which rules, encourages and gives success to theology and philosophy alike."[65] Indeed, revealed truth that offers the fullness of light not only illuminates the theological task but also the path of philosophical inquiry. "It is to be hoped," adds John Paul, "that theologians and philosophers will let themselves be guided by the authority of truth alone so that there will emerge a philosophy consonant with the Word of God [*philosophia cum Dei Verbo*]."[66] The pope elaborates on the relationship of philosophy and theology in respect of God's Word in a passage worthy of being cited at some length.

> In the light of these considerations, the relationship between theology and philosophy is marked by a kind of circular progress. Theology's source and starting point must always be the Word of God revealed in history, while its final goal will be an understanding of that Word which increases with each passing generation. But since the Word of God is Truth (cf. Jn. 17:7) the human search for truth—the philosophical mind observing its own laws—can only help God's Word to be better explained. We are not dealing here with the simple adoption of this or that concept or element of a philosophical system in theological discourse; what is important above all is that the reason of the believer should employ his own capacity for reflection in the discovery of truth, in the course of the movement which, beginning by taking up the Word of God, tries to gain a fuller comprehension of it. It is very evident that, moving between these two poles—that is between the Word of God and its deeper comprehension—reason is offered guidance and is warned against paths which would lead it astray from revealed truth and stray in the end from the truth pure and simple: rather reason is in this way spurred on to exploring new paths which, left to itself, it could hardly imagine that it could find. From this circular

---

64. Ibid., no. 66.
65. Ibid., no. 92.
66. Ibid., no. 79.

movement philosophy emerges the richer from its contact with the Word of God in attainment of new and unexpected ends.[67]

Perhaps a *crux interpretum* for testing my thesis about the relation between nature and grace in the Catholic tradition is the question regarding the idea of Christian philosophy. I have argued that John Paul II is committed to that idea in *Fides et Ratio*. Yet, I can imagine G.C. Berkouwer replying to me, as he did to Fr. M.F.J. Marlet, S.J., in his 1956 review article of Marlet's study of Dooyeweerd's transcendental philosophy.[68] Fr. Marlet embraced the idea of Christian philosophy, that is, "dasz philosophisches Denken immer umgriffen ist von einem theologischen Apriori im Sinne eines Offenbarungsapriori." In short, all philosophical thought is rooted in "konkrete und übertheoretische Voraussetzungen"[69] Although Berkouwer had no problem recognizing Marlet's affinity with Dooyeweerd's thought on the supra-theoretical, religious roots of philosophy, he seriously questioned whether Marlet's position on Christian philosophy, that is, on the religious roots of philosophy, was consistent with the Church's teaching, especially with the "duplex ordo" of knowledge, of faith and natural reason, found in Vatican Council I of 1870, reaffirmed in Pius XII's 1950 Encyclical Letter, *Humani generis* as well as, I would add, John Paul II's *Fides et Ratio*. "There is a twofold order of knowledge, distinct not only as regards its source, but also as regards its object. With regard to the source, we know in one by natural reason, in the other by divine faith. With regard to the object, besides those things to which natural reason can attain, there are proposed for our belief mysteries hidden in God which, unless they are divinely revealed, are incapable of being known."[70] On one dominant interpretation of this teaching, the idea of Christian philosophy is a contradiction in terms. It maintains that philosophy is self-sufficient in the natural realm of reason, that it must not be influenced by faith in that realm, and that there is no such thing as Christian philosophy. Of course proponents of this interpretation hold that the philosophical reflection

---

67. Ibid., no. 73.

68. Berkouwer, "Identiteit of Conflict? Een poging tot analyse." Marlet, SJ., *Grundlinien der Kalvinistischen 'Philosophie der Gesetzesidee' als Christilicher Transzendentalphilosophie*.

69. Marlet, SJ, *Grundlinien der Kalvinistischen 'Philosophie der Gesetzesidee' als Christilicher Transzendentalphilosophie*, 96, 99.

70. Vatican Council 1, 1869–1870, *Dogmatic Constitution on the Church*, Chapter 4, *On Faith and Reason*, 445.

of Christians should be true and compatible with the Christian faith, but such reflection should stand on its own, being the exclusive work of autonomous reason in the natural realm, unaided by faith, and indebted to faith no more than their secular counterparts in philosophy. Indeed, the concept of "Christian philosophy" makes no more sense on this view than it does to Martin Heidegger.[71] He wrote famously, "A 'Christian philosophy' is a round square and a misunderstanding. There is, to be sure, a thinking and questioning elaboration of the world of Christian experience, i.e. of faith. That is theology." In line with Heidegger, well-known historian of philosophy Frederick Copleston, S.J., succinctly writes, "The most that the phrase 'Christian philosophy' can legitimately mean is a philosophy compatible with Christianity; if it means more than that, one is speaking of a philosophy which is not simply philosophy, but which is, partly at least, theology." Of course criticism of the view—call it neo-scholasticism—represented by Copleston abound.

Gilson, for one, charges the neo-scholastic with rationalism. He is sensitive to the difference between the pure rationalist on the one hand, who makes human wisdom, or the order of reason, the measure of all truth, and the interpreter of the "duplex ordo" on the other who holds that the philosophical reflection of Christians must be compatible with Christianity, and also that philosophy is subordinate to theology, making available the highest standard of Christian wisdom, which is systematically articulated by Christian theology. Nevertheless, Gilson asks critically, "While the pure rationalist puts philosophy in the highest place, and identifies it with wisdom, the neo-scholastic subordinates it to the theology which alone, as he holds, fully deserves that name; but why then do certain neo-scholastics imagine that even when thus subordinated to theology, *their philosophy remains precisely of the same nature as any other that recognizes no Wisdom higher than itself?* How is this attitude to be explained?"[72] In other words, Gilson argues that this interpretation of human reason is rationalistic, guilty of the presumption of self-sufficiency, which is, in the words of John Paul II, "the typical temptation of the philosopher."[73] This presumption is not simply a "philosophical pride" that "seeks to present [one] partial and imperfect [philosophical] view as the

---

71. Heidegger, *Introduction to Metaphysics*, 6.
72. Gilson, *Spirit of Medieval Philosophy*, 4, italics added.
73. John Paul II, *Fides et Ratio*, no. 76.

complete reading of all reality."[74] Rather, it is a view of philosophy inspired by the "illusion of autonomy [that] would deny the essential dependence on God of every creature—the human being included."[75] In other words, "different philosophical systems have lured people into believing that they are their own absolute master, able to decide their own destiny and future in complete autonomy, trusting only in themselves and their own powers." But John Paul II clearly rejects this position. "This can never be the grandeur of the human being, who can find fulfillment only in choosing to enter the truth, to make a home under the shade of Wisdom and dwell there." He adds, "Only within this horizon of truth will people understand their freedom in its fullness and their call to know and love God as the supreme realization of their true self."[76] The Wisdom John Paul refers to here, and Gilson agrees, is the Word of Wisdom, the wisdom of God revealed in Jesus Christ, who is the "criterion of both truth and salvation."[77] Jesus Christ is the Way, the Truth, and the Life (John 14:6). The cross of Jesus Christ is the truth that challenges every philosophy's pretended autonomy or self-sufficiency. "The crucified Son of God is the historic event upon which every attempt of the mind to construct an adequate explanation of the meaning of existence upon merely human argumentation comes to grief."[78] In sum, Gilson traces this rationalistic attitude back to a dualistic, that is, extrinsic, conception of faith's relation to reason. He rejects this dualistic conception, as does John Paul II: "Once reason, as regards its exercise, has been divorced from faith, all intrinsic relation between Christianity and philosophy becomes a contradiction." Adds Gilson, "for a Christian, reason is not to be divorced from faith in the sphere of its exercise. . . . There is no such thing as a Christian reason, but there may very well be a Christian exercise of reason."[79] Elsewhere, Gilson says, "nothing less than an intrinsic relation between revelation and reason will suffice to give [the very concept of Christian philosophy] meaning."[80]

74. Ibid., no. 4.
75. Ibid., no. 80.
76. Ibid., no. 107.
77. Ibid., no. 23.
78. Ibid., no. 23.
79. Gilson, *Spirit of Medieval Philosophy*, 12.
80. Ibid., 35. See also, Gilson, *Christianity and Philosophy*, "Christian philosophy is a philosophy which, though formally distinguishing the two orders [of faith and reason], considers Christian Revelation to be an indispensable guide to truth" (101). John Paul II

Bavinck's interpretation of the idea of the "duplex ordo" is typical of many neo-Calvinists to date. He repeats throughout his writings the charge that Rome affirms the claim of rationalism in the sphere of natural reason.[81] Given his dualistic construal of the nature/grace relation in Catholic thought, I can understand why he says, "If for a moment you abstract from the supernatural order which Catholicism has built up around the natural order, then you will have nothing left but pure rationalism, genuine Pelagianism, and unadulterated deism."[82]

Still, Bavinck's charge is so far off the mark for any of the great masters of scholastic theology, such as Anselm, Bonaventure, Aquinas, Albert the Great, Duns Scotus, Occam, not to mention three great nineteenth-century Catholic theologians, the Germans Matthias Scheeben and J.A. Möhler and the English Catholic John Henry Newman. I can't be too hard on Bavinck, however, because, in regard to the charge of pure rationalism, certain Catholics have expressed themselves as though philosophy, says Gilson, "under the pretext that it is essentially rational, is a religiously neutral domain, wherein Revelation exercises no positive and direct influence," and hence they have rejected the idea of Christian philosophy.[83] Given this interpretation of natural reason, we can easily understand

---

insists, "In refusing the truth offered by divine Revelation, philosophy only does itself damage, since this is to preclude access to a deeper knowledge of truth" (*Fides et Ratio*, no. 75).

81. Bavinck, *GD* I, 275, II, [304; 77].

82. Bavinck, "Common Grace," 47. This interpretation of Roman Catholicism is also at issue in the famous Brunner- Barth debate over the nature and significance of natural theology. On this debate, see *Natural Theology*. This book has both Brunner's initial essay on "Nature and Grace" and Barth's reply, "Nein." In Roman Catholicism, Brunner alleges, "there is a *system* of natural theology, a self-sufficient rational system, detachable from *theologia revelata* and capable of serving it for a solid foundation" (46). Barth rejects Brunner's interpretation "of the Roman Catholic conception of the nature and significance of natural theology [as] sadly distorted. No one who has even to a small extent studied St. Thomas or the formulations of the Vatican [I] Decree, or who has discussed these matters with a Roman Catholic theologian of any erudition, will be able to say that according to Roman Catholic doctrine there is an 'unrefracted *theologia naturalis*' with which sin 'has as it were nothing to do', a system of natural theology, a self-sufficient rational system, detachable from the *theologia revelata* and capable of serving it for a solid foundation. How can Brunner make this out to be Roman Catholic doctrine" (95)? For an excellent analysis of the Barth-Brunner debate, see Berkouwer, *De Algemene Openbaring*, 14–46. ET: *General Revelation*, 21–57. Both sources will be cited throughout this chapter, first the original, followed by the pagination of the English translation in square brackets [ ].

83. Gilson, *Christianity and Philosophy*, 59.

why Berkouwer writes, "De sprong van het Vaticaans concilie [I] en van Humani Generis naar een religieus-Christelijke wijsbegeerte—in verband met het openbarings-apriori—blijft een sprong."[84] In other words, the leap to the idea of a religious and Christian philosophy from the "duplex ordo" of knowledge, of faith, and natural reason, found in Vatican Council I of 1870 and reaffirmed in Pius XII's 1950 Encyclical Letter, *Humani generis*, remains just that—a leap. I want now to challenge that interpretation of so-called Catholic rationalism.[85]

Now the views that Vatican I opposed are those of theological rationalism on the one hand and fideism on the other. The Council rejected the former because it denied all knowledge that could not be arrived at by the natural powers of reason. It strongly insisted that knowledge could be had, proper to faith, but which is beyond all natural human reason to discover, comprehend, and to justify for itself; revelation is not only a source of knowledge but an independent ground of assent.

The Council also rejected fideism because the Church holds that natural reason can advance to the knowledge of God's existence, as "the source and end of all things." This natural knowledge of God is mediated by the works of creation; it is analogous, inadequate, and true.[86] Regarding natural reason's powers to know God, one misinterprets Vatican I if one holds it is speaking about, not only a *de jure* possibility, but also a *de facto* possibility. It affirmed the former, but left the latter open. The former pertains to conditions of possibility regarding natural reason's ability to know God; the latter to the conditions of actual occurrence, that is, in what proportions and under what actual conditions, *here and now*, is natural reason's power to attain knowledge of God realizable. The fideist had taken the position from the concrete condition of human nature, namely, fallen and crippled in its power and intellectual range such that natural reason is radically corrupt, unable to know God truly, and hence not likely to be of much service to the gospel apart from grace. As stated above, the Council rejects fideism. Nevertheless, as Gilson correctly remarks, "If experience proves that this natural knowledge of God, certain though limited in profundity, is possible, it also shows how difficult it is

---

84. Berkouwer, "Identiteit of Conflict?," 16–17.

85. For this alternative interpretation of Vatican I, I am heavily indebted to von Balthasar, *Theology of Karl Barth*, especially 302–25.

86. As Berkouwer correctly notes in his work, *De Algemene Openbaring*, 50 [64].

in practice to attain it when reason is left completely to itself."[87] Gilson's point requires some explanation.

Now, the Council expressly refused—and records of the discussions at the Council make that evident—to counter fideism with a statement about the conditions of actual occurrence—it left the question open of a *de facto* possibility: whether or not knowledge of God's existence could be directly attained by the "fallen" reason of all men, free of doubt and uncertainty, without the help of "healing grace." Yes, the Council did decide the *de jure* question: "The same holy mother Church holds and teaches that God, the source and end of all things, can be known with certainty from the consideration of created things, by the natural power of human reason."[88] Still, this teaching does not imply that human reason itself is unhampered in attaining knowledge of God. Indeed, as Aquinas notes, "Owing to the weakness of our mind, human inquiry is prone to error. This is evident from the philosophers themselves, who in their rational search for the goal of human life and the means to attain it fell into many shameful errors."[89] *Pace* Berkouwer, it is the knowing agent himself, his truth attaining powers, that is, human reason itself and not merely extrinsic factors like the activity of the senses and the imagination, and the evil passions arising from original sin, which hampers man in gaining knowledge of natural truths about God.[90] Yes, of course the Council insists that natural reason has the capacity to know God. Nevertheless, in light of the weakness of human reason, it did insist on the moral but not absolute *necessity* of divine revelation so that man can attain to knowledge of God in the fallen state directly, with firm certainty and without any admixture of error. In the words of Pius XII, "It is for this reason that divine revelation must be considered morally necessary so that those religious and moral truths which are not of their nature beyond the reach of reason in the present condition of the human race, may be known by all men directly, with a firm certainty and with freedom from all error."[91] Again,

---

87. *Christianity and Philosophy*, 60.

88. Vatican Council 1, 1869–1870, *Dogmatic Constitution on the Church*, Chapter 4, On Faith and Reason.

89. Thomas Aquinas, Commentary on the *De Trinitate* of Boethius, q. 3, art. 1, ad 3m.

90. Berkouwer, *De Algemene Openbaring*, 52 [60].

91. Pius XII, *Humani Generis*, no. 3. Aquinas agrees with Pius' point here: "It is necessary for man to accept by faith not only things which are above reason, but also those which can be known by reason: and this for three motives. First, in order that man

the Council could not deny natural reason's power as such to attain that knowledge, here and now, in the conditions of actual occurrence. For as one Council Father put it, "A faculty that is never realized concretely in any act ought rather to be called an *in*capacity; indeed this incapacity is not just moral but physical [ontic]."⁹²

I now want to close the question that the Council left open by arguing that the statements of Vatican I on natural reason's powers are reconcilable with the claim that all natural knowledge of God occurs *de facto* within the concrete condition of man, in the state of grace or of sin, as a covenant-keeper or a covenant-breaker; indeed, man himself within the actual history of salvation is always *de facto* the man who has either turned away from God in sin or turned toward God in the light of grace and faith.⁹³ This turn toward God always occurs with his prevenient grace, or, in the words of Vatican I: "For the most merciful Lord stirs up those who go astray and helps them by his grace so that they may come to the knowledge of the truth [see 1 Tim 2:4]; and also confirms by his grace those whom he has translated into his admirable light [cf. 1 Pet 2:9; Col 1:13], so that they may persevere in this light."⁹⁴ I advance this argument because not only do I wish to be sensitive to Bavinck's theological point that the natural knowledge of God should be incorporated in the totality of the Christian faith, rather than being treated prior to and apart from that faith, but also I want to be faithful to Vatican I.

---

may arrive more quickly at the knowledge of Divine truth. . . . The second reason is, in order that the knowledge of God may be more general. For many are unable to make progress in the study of science, either through dullness of mind or through having a number of occupations and temporal needs, or even through laziness in learning, all of whom would be altogether deprived of the knowledge of God, unless Divine things were brought to their knowledge under the guise of faith. The third reason is for the sake of certitude. For human is very deficient in things concerning God. A sign of this is that philosophers in their researches, by natural investigation, into human affairs, have fallen into many errors, and have disagreed among themselves. And consequently, in order that men might have knowledge of God, free of doubt and uncertainty, it was necessary for Divine matters to be delivered to them by way of faith, being told to them, as it were, by God Himself Who cannot lie" (*Summa Theologiae*, II–II, q. 2, a. 4).

92. Balthasar, *The Theology of Karl Barth*, 320.

93. Aquinas claims that the age of discretion, when man has the use of reason, "is the time when man is bound by God's affirmative precept, which the Lord expressed by saying (Zech 1:3): 'Turn ye to Me . . . and I will turn to you'" (*Summa Theologiae*, I–II q. 89 a. 6).

94. Vatican Council 1, 1869–1870, *Dogmatic Constitution on the Church*, Chapter 3, On Faith.

Let me begin by stating clearly what the Council decided: that *within* this concrete history of salvation, exaltation and transformation in Christ Jesus, human nature is not destroyed or turned into its opposite. After all human nature is to be redeemed, not annihilated; nor is it merely preserved, side by side with, but unaffected by, the redeeming work of Jesus Christ. In short, grace does not stand opposed to, and hence replace altogether, natural reason. The latter is not hopelessly corrupt, a miserable wreck, as a consequence of the fall into sin, unable to give man access in some degree to God, and left only to await divine intervention in order to be of any service to the gospel. Rather, the natural capacity of a human being in some degree to know God, reason as it actually functions in its fallen state, continues to function in some degree even though it is wounded and weakened by sin. Indeed, rather than replacing natural reason, grace seizes nature from the inside and, far from lowering it, lifts nature up to serve its own ends. Thus it is from the interior that faith transforms reason to fulfill the most natural, that is, creational—but fallen—aspects of its identity. Human reason is addressed and challenged to its very roots but nothing unnatural is required of it. This is the view of John Paul II (and of Gilson, de Lubac, Maritain, et al.) clearly expressed when he says that all men are caught up in the sin of Adam, "which so wounded reason that from then on its path to full truth would be strewn with obstacles. From that time onward the human capacity to know the truth was impaired by an aversion to the One who is the source and origin of truth. It is again the Apostle [Paul] who reveals just how far human thinking, because of sin, became 'empty', and human reasoning became distorted and inclined to falsehood (cf. Rom 1:21–22)." "The eyes of the mind were no longer able to see clearly," the pope adds, "reason became more and more a prisoner to itself. The coming of Christ was the saving event which redeemed reason from its weakness, setting it free from the shackles in which it had imprisoned itself."[95] Let me develop this point briefly by saying something about the place of general revelation in the Council's teaching, what reason must know of God in its actual fallen state, and, finally, the sense in which the natural knowledge of God remains, in the Augustinian and Thomistic sense, "off target," a "miscarried knowledge," in spite of all its correct moments, after the fall into sin.

---

95. John Paul II, *Fides et Ratio*, no. 22.

Now, then, both Bavinck and Berkouwer are right: the knowledge of God that is attained by natural theology is not the product of human reason but rather rests upon the revelatory nature of creation, that is, God's self-revelation in and through the works of creation, and hence knowability from creation. As Bavinck says, "natural theology presupposes, first of all, that *God* reveals himself in his handiwork."[96] In other words, the natural knowledge of God from the works of creation is a result of divine self-revelation. Similarly, Berkouwer explains: "Natural theology does not even pretend to be able to construct a system by means of human nature. It does not pretend to be an *autonomous* theology.... [For it] rests basically upon revelation. This revelation, which is the source of natural theology, is not the special revelation in Christ and the Holy Scriptures, but the general revelation in creation, in created reality. It is the foundation of natural knowledge. The products of this revelation are the 'natural' knowledge of God and 'natural' morality."[97] Thus a kind of self-revelation—God's revelation of himself in and through the works of creation—stands at the beginning of every possible knowledge of God. This first gift is accessible only through the mediation of created reality; indeed, as Hans Urs von Balthasar puts it, "creation reveals the Creator 'naturally' and 'necessarily' inasmuch as it *is* nature. As something created it cannot help praising the Creator.... Thus we may say that the 'inferential' ascent of thought to the Creator is always borne by the Creator's prior decision to reveal himself in this nature itself."[98] So although many things about God are known from the bottom up, as it were—says St. Paul, from the things that God has made we come to a knowledge of his eternal power and divinity (Rom 1:19–20)—they are not "grounded" in my knowledge, but in objective reality. That is, God's revelation of himself in and through the works of creation, God's universal revelatory action, and the corresponding natural knowledge of God is grounded in that revelation.[99]

---

96. Bavinck, *GD* II, 46 [74].

97. Berkouwer, *De Algemene Openbaring*, 47 [61–62].

98. Balthasar, *Theology of Karl Barth*, 310.

99. Regarding the natural knowledge of God, Catholic theologian Karl Adam writes that this is a "form of [God's] gracious self-revelation." He adds, "The fact that we can discover God in the essential form of the world is not due first of all to the world but to God's displaying himself in the world." This passage is cited in Berkouwer, *De Algemene Openbaring*, 66 [80–81].

Now what response is due that revelation in creation? Vatican I is clear: "Since human beings are totally dependent on God as their Creator and Lord, and created reason is completely subject to uncreated truth, we are obliged to yield to God the revealer full submission of intellect and will by faith."[100] The act of faith—involving total submission, a commitment of the will, indeed of the whole person—does not in any way call into question the intellectual character of this act or the clear evidence of God it perceives. In fact, in this act of faith it is also a question of the natural activity of human reason. St. Paul's famous passage from Romans 1 that Vatican I cites in its document refers to, summons and claims man's natural power. As Balthasar puts it, "It is precisely human reason that is summoned not only to come to know God but to acknowledge him in its logical thinking."[101] Of course the Romans passage is even clearer about "the revelation of God's wrath"—for the God with whom man relates in this world is *de facto* the God of wrath and the God of grace; or, as Balthasar adds,

> The revelation of a *judgment* that is completely coordinated to supernatural grace. And this judgment as rendered says that the pagans indeed knew God but did not *acknowledge* him. The punishment that overtook them is the same—supernatural—damnation and abandonment that have also been visited upon the recalcitrant Jews. In fact, what is demanded here of the pagans is a supernatural recognition of the God who is revealing himself to them but that they have not given precisely because of the 'wrath' of God.... The guilt of the pagans therefore consists in this: that they do not place their natural faculties in the serviced of a believing submission to God but refuse the act of obedience that is an essential aspect of reason. Instead of this, they 'absolutize' their natural understanding, its power and its results. And that is precisely why they put something in the place reserved for God.[102]

Significantly, St. Paul affirms judgment of those who 'having known God, do not glorify him as God' (Rom. 1:20-21). What man *de facto* knows is a fact of such importance that it cannot be denied without ruining St. Paul's whole doctrine. That is, man resists what he *de facto* knows

---

100. Vatican Council 1, 1869–1870, *Dogmatic Constitution on the Church*, Chapter 3, *On Faith*.
101. Balthasar, *Theology of Karl Barth*, 315.
102. Ibid., 314–15.

about God, and thus it is precisely because, *although they knew God, they did not honor him as God or give thanks to him, that men are inexcusable.* In other words, an authentic and lasting knowledge of God is required even after sin in order to hold men accountable for their failure to honor God.¹⁰³ Without the natural capacity of man for knowing God, a knowledge mediated through created things, without a genuine possibility in the conditions of actual occurrence, no matter how hindered that knowledge might be in the way it unfolds and takes shape, then there is neither responsibility in the true sense ("men are without excuse") nor sin nor redemption. Without the capacity to form the natural knowledge of God, man could by nature be an atheist and the act of faith could in itself be neither reasonable nor shown to be reasonable. This is exactly the point of Vatican I in stating that "God, the source and end of all things, can be known with certainty from the consideration of created things, by the natural power of human reason."

Berkouwer's reply to this theological exegesis of Romans 1 is to insist that the function of this natural knowledge of God is *completely* exhausted by its religious relation to the wrath of God. Thus, says Berkouwer, "This 'knowledge' can never be isolated from the prevailing theme of Romans 1—the wrath of God. The history of theology parades before us numerous attempts to isolate it from the context. It is only with such kidnapping of the phrase from its context that it can be used to support a natural theology."¹⁰⁴ The problem with this reading of Romans 1 is that nature must get effaced by grace, because God's wrath rests on all our natural endeavors to come to knowledge of God—albeit inadequate but nonetheless true for all that. But why can't we distinguish—not separate—this natural knowledge of God from its function in the biblical context where that

---

103. On this see Murray, *Epistle to the Romans*, 41: "The first part of verse 21 is causally related to the last clause in verse 20 and gives the reason why those concerned are without excuse—they are without excuse 'on this account that, knowing God, they glorified him not as God, neither gave thanks'. The knowledge of God must in this context be the knowledge derived from the manifestation given in the visible creation. It is of this manifestation the apostle is speaking and it is this manifestation that is stated in verse 20 to leave men without excuse. Therefore the cognitive perception elicited from the manifestation of God's glory in the visible creation is spoken of as 'knowing God'. The inexcusableness resides in the fact that being in possession of this knowledge they possessed ought to have constrained." Murray's exegesis is shared by more recent commentaries, Catholic and Protestant alike. For the former, see Byrne, SJ, *Romans*, 66–67. For the latter, see Schreiner, *Romans*, 85–86.

104. Berkouwer, *De Algemene Openbaring*, 120 [148].

knowledge is understood by St. Paul to be the presupposition for man's guilt, rendering him inexcusable?

Let us admit that St. Paul's own explicit concern is not with what the unbeliever knows apart from grace in Christ, but, as Berkouwer puts it, "with what man has done and does with the clear revelation that comes to him."[105] Let us also agree with Berkouwer, as both Gilson and John Paul II evidently do, that the "*sensus divinitatis* is not an organ of the knowledge of God which transcends the corruption of human nature."[106] In Gilson's own words, "He who wishes to think truly as a Catholic will do well never to forget the great saying of Saint Paul to the Ephesians: 'that henceforward you walk not as also the Gentiles walk in the vanity of their mind: having their understanding darkened' [Eph 4:17–18]. Saint Thomas applies this text, which he himself quotes in his *Summa Contra Gentiles*, precisely to the truths naturally knowable to man." "A Catholic natural theology," Gilson adds, "is possible for the intellect assisted by the divine Word that dispels the darkness and shields it from vanity."[107] Clearly, then, Gilson does not purport to make "human reason in its apostasy from God," as Herman Dooyeweerd implies about all natural theology, "the main stay of a '*philosophia et theologia naturalis*'."[108] Furthermore, let us also agree that this "knowledge of God" that is exchanged for a lie, whatever else it entails, does not have a spiritually and morally transforming effect on a person. Nevertheless, I think it is possible to distinguish a natural power of human reason that achieves a partial knowledge of God, fully acknowledging that the truth known is embraced within a false perspective. I think we need to distinguish here, as American neo-Calvinist philosopher Calvin Seerveld did some years ago in his contribution to the *Festschrift* for South African neo-Calvinist philosopher Hendrik Stoker, between knowledge that is correct and accurate in some sense, from knowledge that is the fruit of obedient thinking (as Seerveld phrases it), namely, "the act and product of knowing [that] is manifestly Holy Spirit filled and shows God's redeeming presence."[109]

105. Ibid. 152 [125].

106. Ibid.

107. Gilson, *Christianity and Philosophy*, 81.

108. Dooyeweerd, *De Wijsbegeerte der Wetsidee*, Boek I, 484. ET: *New Critique of Theoretical Thought*, Vol. I, *Necessary Presuppositions of Philosophy*, 516.

109. Seerveld, "The relation of the arts to the presentation of truth," 165. Admittedly, Seerveld would not agree with the use to which I put his distinctions. His 2003 Jellema

What is more, such knowledge is necessary in order to make sense of the unbeliever's accountability before God.

Human beings are blameworthy in their rejection of God for the very reason that God reveals himself in and by creation to them, and hence they know him without, however, giving thanks or glorifying him, which results in their hearts being darkened and their thinking being empty. What kind of knowledge renders human beings inexcusable in their rejection of revelation? Mustn't this knowledge of God attain, in some limited, minimal, and yes, inadequate sense, the true God, without which there wouldn't be a sufficient basis for divine wrath? One thing is certain about the function of this knowledge—without it men wouldn't be blameworthy, indeed, God's wrath would be unjustified because the chief accusation against them would be nullified.

But if we accept that human beings after the fall are able to achieve a partial, incomplete knowledge of God, so the reformed objector like Berkouwer insists, then don't we diminish the force of the radical antithesis between knowing God and not knowing God, and thus the call to radical conversion from ignorance of God, that is clearly taught throughout the New Testament? Although I cannot argue the point fully here, I think we must strenuously avoid thinking that all that separates the unbeliever, whether or not he is a theist, from Christian faith is the *addition* of some knowledge of faith to the knowledge that he already possesses by reason. This kind of *quantitative* view (as Berkouwer phrases it) neglects the nature of the unregenerate mind's suppression of the truth and the call to radical conversion to the revelation of God in Christ through the testimony of the Holy Spirit.[110] For now, let it suffice to hear Gilson on this important point.

Lectures ("Our Temptation of Philosophy & Troubadour Philosophy") at Calvin College make that point abundantly clear.

110. On this crucial point, see Berkouwer, *De Algemene Openbaring*, "This kind of quantitative analysis neglects the nature of the distortion carried on by false religion . . . With this we meet one of the most important questions in the relation between revelation and knowledge. To get an insight into the only proper solution, it is necessary to be convinced that Romans 1 does not sacrifice anything of the radical antithesis between *knowing* and *not knowing* as it is taught throughout Scripture . . . [Saint] Paul is concerned to say that there is no half-way stop between the idolatry, foolishness, and darkness of heathendom and the knowledge of God. A man can leave the one for the other only by way of conversion as by the passage from life to death. This, too, is the only way of escape from the wrath of God" (114, 117 [144, 147]).

It is true that reason can demonstrate there is a God, but when Aristotle for the first time demonstrated the existence of a First Unmoved Mover, he had not yet taken a single step on the path of salvation. All the philosophical demonstrations of God put together will never yield an atom of faith, and since 'without faith it is impossible to please God', no certitude coming from my own reason can replace my assent to the truth of revelation. When God tells me of His own existence and bids me to believe His word, He is offering me a share in the knowledge that He has of Himself. This [faith] is more than a matter of information [that is, it is not merely the assent of the intellect to a body of propositions held as true because revealed by God]; it is [also] an invitation [to participate in God's self-knowledge].[111]

So the dilemma is as follows. On the one hand, if we stress that men are inexcusable in their rejection of God because they know very well that they are suppressing the truth of creation, then it isn't possible that they are blameworthy without some true knowledge of God. What troubles some with this conclusion is that this knowledge is then distinguished from the role it plays in justifying the wrath of God and taken as a basis on which a natural theology can be built. On the other hand, if we stress that fallen human beings can't know God in any sense whatsoever, emphasizing the emptiness of mind, vanity, foolishness, ignorance, indeed the truth-twisting nature of human beings after the fall, then it is difficult to see how they can still be blameworthy in resisting the truth about God. As St. Paul puts it, "although *they knew God*, they did not glorify Him as God, nor were thankful" (Rom 1:21). Hence, we cannot eliminate this knowledge from human beings after the fall without ruining St. Paul's very point, because it is precisely those who *"having known God"* are inexcusable for their perversity of failing to glorify God and give him thanks.[112]

---

111. Gilson, *Philosopher and Theology*, 66–67, 213.

112. In his essay, "On Ethics," Lewis makes a similar point with respect to man's knowledge of the moral law in Romans 2:12–16. He writes, "Did Christian Ethics really enter the world as a novelty, a new, peculiar set of commands, to which a man could be in the strict sense *converted*? I say converted to the practical ethics: he could of course be converted to the Christian faith, he could accept, not only as a novelty, but as transcendent novelty, a mystery hidden from all eternity, the deity and resurrection of Jesus, the Atonement, the forgiveness of sins. But these novelties themselves set a rigid limit to the novelty we can assume in the ethical injunctions. The convert accepted forgiveness of sins. But of sins against what Law? Some new law promulgated by the Christians? But that is nonsensical. It would be the mockery of a tyrant to forgive a man for doing what had never been forbidden until the very moment at which the forgiveness was announced.

Clearly, then, the response to that knowledge that man *de facto* possesses is not merely a response to an abstract God of the philosophers, but much more exactly a response to the concrete God of the Bible, of the history of salvation and of revelation. It is also clear that the response of faith, although an act of the whole person, takes into account a full activity of the rational powers of man in his coming to know God. To quote Balthasar again: "Paul's text itself shows this most unambiguously. The invisible qualities of God are seen as 'befitting reason'. The activity of nature is incorporated into this knowledge intact. Nature is what must perform the act of believing acknowledgement. The same holds for Wisdom 13:5ff and Acts 17:22. Whenever in such passages Scripture discusses a 'natural' knowledge of God, it is referring to man's natural cognitive faculty, and the guilt of unbelief is attributed to the abuse of these natural faculties. This can only be harmonized when we realize that our natural capacity for knowing God is incorporated as an inserted moment in the ultimate, supernaturally relevant knowledge."[113] This brings me to my last point.

What then is the sense in which the natural knowledge of God remains, in the Augustinian and Thomistic sense, "off target," a "miscarried knowledge," in spite of all its correct moments, after the fall into sin? Let me give a couple of examples from Aquinas to show the sense in which this is true.[114] One example: good moral acts are possible to the covenant-breaker, or the one who turns away from God in sin, but only the grace of redemption, which heals and transforms from within the disorder caused by original sin, alone ensures, not only that he, now a covenant-keeper, can sustain a vigorous moral life, but also that he can direct his individual moral acts toward his true and final end, that is, man's chief end, which is to know God and to glorify him forever. Now, although good moral acts are possible to the covenant-breaker, he nonetheless remains "off target," or "miscarries," and this is because a moral act in the full, true and perfect

---

The idea (at least in its grossest and most popular form) that Christianity brought a new ethical code into the world is a grave error. If it had done so, then we should have to conclude that all who first preached it wholly misunderstood their own message: for all of them, its Founder, His precursor, His apostles, came demanding repentance and offering forgiveness, a demand and an offer both meaningless except on the assumption of a moral law already known and already broken" (62–63).

113. Balthasar, *Theology of Karl Barth*, 318.

114. The quotations in this paragraph and the next are from St. Thomas Aquinas, *Summa Theologiae*, I–II, q. 65, art. 2, Vol. 22; *Summa Theologiae*, I–II, q. 85, a. 3, Resp., q. 109, a. 2, Vol. 26; II–II, q. 167, a. 1, Vol. 44.

sense, even the natural moral act, says Thomas, includes a total and free decision of man to order his moral life, by grace, to his final end and salvation. Otherwise, the natural moral virtues of the covenant-breaker are virtues only "in a way" and not in the primary sense; indeed, Aquinas argues that from the viewpoint of man's chief end, good moral virtues that fail to serve that end somehow are not true virtues. *"He that fails to acknowledge the truth, has no true virtue, even if his conduct be good"* (St. Augustine).

Another example: An act of knowledge about creation, knowing the truth about created things, is possible to the covenant-breaker, but he is unable to refer this knowledge to its due end, namely, the knowledge of God. Says Thomas: "Man's good consists in the knowledge of truth; yet man's sovereign good consists, not in the knowledge of any truth, but in the perfect knowledge of the sovereign truth.... Hence there may be sin in the knowledge of certain truths, in so far as the desire of such knowledge is not directed in due manner to the knowledge of the sovereign truth, wherein supreme happiness consists." Thus, as long as man remains in sin, he cannot know God the way he should know him. His knowledge remains in its decisive meaning a "miscarried knowledge," says Thomas, in spite of all its correct moments. For it occurs in the basic response of man's refusing to obey, or, in the words of Vatican I, "rendering to God the revealer the full submission of intellect and will by faith."

Let me conclude this section with a passage from John Paul II: "Seen in this light, reason is valued without being overvalued. The results of reasoning [about God] may in fact be true, but these results acquire their true meaning only if they are set within the larger horizon of faith: 'All man's steps are ordered by the Lord: how then can man understand his own ways?' (Prov 20:24). For Old [and New] Testament, then, faith liberates reason in so far as it allows reason to attain correctly what it seeks to know and to place it within the ultimate order of things, in which everything acquires true meaning.... Rightly, therefore, the sacred author identifies the fear of God as the beginning of true knowledge: 'The fear of the Lord is the beginning of knowledge'" (Prov 1:7; cf. Sir 1:14).[115]

---

115. John Paul II, *Fides et Ratio*, no. 20.

THE NATURAL KNOWLEDGE OF GOD

Bavinck's religious epistemology on the natural knowledge of God presupposes an anti-Cartesian epistemological realism. A few words about his epistemology are necessary before looking at his religious epistemology. First, Bavinck rejects the epistemology of modernity that begins by isolating man from the rest of the world. Man is taken to be an enclosed consciousness over against the world, as it were. In addition, this epistemology has a representational picture of the mind in which the ideas in the mind of the isolated thinking subject are the direct object of our conscious awareness, for instance, representations of perceived external objects. These ideas serve as the basis for inferring what perceptual objects must be like. In short, for the epistemology of modernity the perceptual world is not directly given to us; it is only an inference from ideas in the mind and in this way we justify our knowledge of external objects. A long-standing criticism of this representative theory of perception is that it leaves the knower in the egocentric predicament: he is unable to know whether his ideas have any relationship at all to reality, because he cannot transcend the veil of ideas in an act of cognitive self-transcendence.

Second, rather than consciousness, for Bavinck, the epistemological starting point "ought to be ordinary daily experience, the universal and natural certainty of human beings concerning the objectivity and truth of their knowledge.... Prior to all reflection and reasoning, everyone is in fact fully assured of the real existence of the world."[116] Significantly, this natural certainty regarding the real existence of the world is not the product of a syllogism, nor is it supported by proof; it is a basic belief, immediately known, "originating spontaneously within us along with perception itself. It is not a product but the foundation and starting point of all other certainty."[117] Thus, the world is not only directly given to us, but perception produces basis beliefs in us immediately, automatically, unless we act to short-circuit the natural effects of the world upon us. For Bavinck, therefore, there is no question of an isolated subject without the world, which would have to find its way out of the isolated consciousness. He rejects what he calls an "untenable dualism between subject and object," which, he argues, "leads logically as well as historically to ... idealism."[118]

---

116. Bavinck, *GD* I, 195 [223].
117. Ibid.
118. Ibid., 197 [224].

Rather, adds Bavinck, "Every human, after all, accepts the reliability of the senses and the existence of the external world, not by a logical inference from the effect. . . . Prior to all reflection and reasoning, everyone is in fact fully assured of the real existence of the world." As Bavinck also says, "[natural] certainty is not a conclusion drawn from a process of reasoning but is immediately present in us and given along with the perception itself."[119] Perception, among others, is a source of basic beliefs (to use a term of Reformed epistemology).

What is Bavinck's biblical and theological response to the subject-object dichotomy introduced into our thinking by the epistemology of modernity? How does he explain that the mind of man is fit to grasp the reality of things as they really are? The brief answer to this question here must be Bavinck's doctrine of the *Logos* found throughout his writings. For example, in his 1904 Rector's Address, *Christelijke Wereldbeschouwing*: "De leer van de schepping aller dingen door het Woord Gods is de verklaring van alle kennen en weten, de onderstelling van de correspondentie tusschen subject en object." [The teaching that all things were created through the Word of God [Col 1:16] is the explanation for the correspondence of subject and object [knower and known] and hence it is the foundation of all knowledge.][120] That is, according to Bavinck, the correspondence or kinship between object and subject, as he also says earlier in *Gereformeerde Dogmatiek* "rests only in the belief that it is the same Logos who created both the reality outside of us and the laws of thought within us and who produced an organic connection and correspondence between the two."[121] The Logos confers and sustains the existence of both

---

119. Ibid.

120. Bavinck, Rectoral Address, *Christelijke Wereldbeschouwing*, given at the Free University of Amsterdam, 20 October 1904.

121. Bavinck, *Gereformeerde Dogmatiek*, I, 205 [231]. See also, his Rector's address, *Christelijke Wereldbeschouwing*, "Alleen dan is er kennis der waarheid mogelijk, as wij uitgaan van het feit, dat subject en object, dat kennen en zijn aan elkander beantwoorden. Dit feit staat in het onmiddellijke besef van alle menschen vast en wordt door allen, die nog aan waarheid en wetenschap gelooven, bewust of' onbewust aanvaard. Aan de wetenschap is de taak opgedragen, om dit feit te verklaren; maar zoo zij dit niet vermag, zal zij het toch, op straffe van zelfmoord, onverzwakt moeten laten staan. En tot verklaring zal zij alleen in staat zijn, als zij zich voorlichten laat door de wijsheid van het Goddelijk Woord, die ons de belijdenis op de lippen legt van God den Vader, den Almachtige, Schepper des hemels en der aarde. Deze belijdenis is niet alleen het eerste artikel van ons Christelijk geloof, maar ook de groudslag en hoeksteen van alle kennis en wetenschap. Bij deze belijdenis is alleen te verstaan en te handhaven de harmonie

knower and known. He adds, "Only in this way is science possible, i.e., knowledge not only of the changing appearances but of the universal, the logical connections inherent in things," that is of the intelligibility of the world. This, too, is the view of Benedict XVI who in the new preface to the 2000 edition of his classic work, *Introduction to Christianity*, writes: "Ever since the Prologue to the Gospel of John, the concept of *logos* has been at the very center of our Christian faith in God. . . . The God who is *Logos* guarantees the intelligibility of the world, the intelligibility of our existence, the aptitude of reason to know God [*die Gottgemässheit der Vernunft*] and the reasonableness of God [*die Vernunftgemässheit Gottes*], even though his understanding infinitely surpasses ours and to us may so often appear to be darkness. The world comes from reason, and this reason is a Person, is Love—this is what our biblical faith tells us about God."[122] "If is true that the term *logos*—the Word in the beginning, creative reason and love," adds Ratzinger—is decisive for the Christian image of God, and if the concept of *logos* simultaneously forms the core of Christology, of faith in Christ, then the indivisibility of faith in God and faith in his incarnate Son Jesus Christ is only confirmed once more."[123]

A second question we need to ask Bavinck is this: in what does he ground the power of the human mind enabling man, at the very moment of perceiving things, to form the basic concepts and principles that would guide him further in all perception and reflection? This question, too, is answered by Bavinck in terms of the Logos. "The Logos who shines in the world must also let his light shine in our consciousness. That is the light of reason, the intellect, which, itself originating in the Logos, discovers

---

van subject en object van denken en zijn." [Knowledge is possible only if we assume the fact that subject and object, knowing and being correspond to each other. This fact is rooted in the immediate consciousness of all men, and is accepted, consciously or unconsciously, by all who still believe in truth and science. It is incumbent upon science to explain this fact, but if it is unable to do so it must nevertheless maintain it fully, on pain of epistemological suicide. And it will be able to come to an explanation only if it is enlightened by the wisdom of God's Word, which puts on our lips the confession of God the Father, the Almighty, Maker of heaven and earth. This confession is not only the first article of our Christian faith, but also the foundation and cornerstone of all knowledge and science. It is only by making this confession that one is able to understand and maintain the harmony of subject and object, thought and being.] My thanks again to Al Wolters who carefully translated this passage.

122. Ratzinger, *Introduction to Christianity*, 26.
123. Ibid., 28.

and recognizes the Logos in things."[124] Bavinck makes an allusion here to St. Thomas's account of the "light that, originating in God, shines in our own intellect." "God is the light of reason in which, by which, and through which all things that shine so as to be intelligible, shine." Man's reason is that divine light, argues Bavinck, but "it is not itself the divine logos, but it participates in it." As St. Thomas puts it, the natural light of human reason "is nothing else than a participated likeness of the uncreated light."[125] Adds Bavinck, "To be (*esse*), to live (*vivere*), and to understand (*intelligere*) is the prerogative of God in respect of his being (*per essentiam*), ours in respect of participation (*per participationem*)."[126] Thus, for Bavinck, the intelligibility of the created world is an embodiment of the thoughts of God and is the external foundation of human knowledge (*principium cognoscendi externum*). The natural light of reason is intrinsic to the integrity of the created order, enabling us to discover and recognize the logos in things. This is what Bavinck calls the internal foundation of knowledge (*principium cognoscendi internum*). "So," concludes Bavinck, "in the final analysis, it is God alone who from his divine consciousness and by way of his creatures conveys the knowledge of truth to our mind— the Father who by the Son and in the Spirit reveals himself to us. 'There are many who[127] say, 'O that we might see some good!' Let the light of your face shine on us, O Lord! (Ps 4:6)." I turn now to Bavinck's religious epistemology.

Belief in God is not, necessarily, the conclusion of an argument—says Bavinck.[128] Now, in light of this claim, we can understand why, epistemologically speaking, Bavinck distinguishes two kinds of knowledge about God that human beings naturally attain, namely, the implanted knowledge of God on the one hand, as he calls it, and the acquired knowledge of God on the other. It is no more the case, therefore, that belief in God is the product of an argument devised by human reasoning than it is the case for, say, memory beliefs or perceptual beliefs. The latter are basic beliefs (to use the term of Reformed epistemology) and so too, argues Bavinck, is belief in God—theistic beliefs arising spontaneously and without coer-

---

124. Bavinck, *GD* I, 207 [233].
125. Aquinas, *Summa Theologiae* I, q. 79, a. 5, Vol. 11.
126. Bavinck, *GD* I, 205 [232].
127. Ibid., 207 [233].
128. Bavinck, *GD* I, 562, and II, 47 [592; 76].

cion, without argumentation and proof, says Bavinck, and that properly serve as ultimate starting points in our reasoning. Of course that doesn't make philosophical arguments about God, or memory and perception, for that matter, superfluous. If it did, Bavinck would not have devoted time to discuss and evaluate the standard proofs of God's existence, which he wants neither to overvalue nor undervalue.

Let us recall the point I made earlier that the knowledge of God can have its origin only in God's self-revelation: general and special revelation. Regarding general revelation—the self-revelation of God in and through the works of creation—it should be understood that the metaphysical order of things would be subverted if we thought that the knowledge of God is grounded in, rather than known by, human reason. Although many things about God are known from the bottom up, as it were—says St. Paul, from the things that God has made we come to a knowledge of his eternal power and divinity (Rom 1:19-20)—they are not "grounded" in my knowledge, but in objective reality. A "ground of knowledge" and a "ground of existence" are distinct; or alternatively put, we must avoid confusing the ontic and noetic aspects of knowledge. As Bavinck rightly explains: "Although in a syllogism the existence of God may be the *conclusion*—just as, generally speaking, one may infer the existence of a worker from the existence of a piece of work—that existence in reality is still in fact the *origin* and *ground* of the existence of all things; indeed, it is even posited as such in the conclusion."[129] Bavinck understands the philosophical difference between the *causa essendi* (ontic) and the *causa cognoscendi* (noetic) in the practice of natural theology, but Berkouwer, arguably, does not.[130] In regard to natural theology, Bavinck writes: "Dependence in a syllogism is something very different from dependence in reality. A 'ground of knowledge' is far from being a 'ground of existence.'" Still, Berkouwer rolls out the standard claim that the acceptance of natural theology implies that belief in God's existence is based on arguments and proofs and hence that God has no foundation apart from them. "The contrary," says Bavinck, "rather, is the case." "The so-called proofs may introduce greater distinctness and lucidity," he adds, "but they are no means the final ground on which our certainty regard-

---

129. *GD* II, 62 [89–90].

130. *De Algemene Openbaring*, 60–68; ET: 74–83. See Echeverria, "Reformed Objection to Natural Theology," in the forthcoming Festschrift, *Thriving in Babylon* (Eugene, OR: Pickwick Publications, 2010).

ing God's existence is ultimately based."¹³¹ Again, that is the import of the philosophical distinction between the *causa essendi* (ontic) and the *causa cognoscendi* (noetic) in the practice of natural theology. Bavinck recognizes that difference and hence he is still able, unlike Berkouwer, to value theistic arguments.

What does Bavinck mean by implanted knowledge? Does he mean that man has an innate idea of God? Consider René Descartes, innatist *par excellence*. Descartes discovers upon examining the contents of his mind that he has an idea of God—"a certain substance that is infinite, independent, supremely intelligent and supremely powerful, and that created me along with everything else that exists—if anything else exists."[132] For him the idea of God that man possesses means that he is fully-equipped with a ready-made knowledge of God, which is innate and hence acquired *apart* from the things that God has made. This is unacceptable to Bavinck. He sides with the Scholastics who in their entirety rejected the theory of innate ideas. In particular, Bavinck notes, "Although Christian theology universally assumed that there were truths known by nature and not by revelation, truths obtained spontaneously, as it were, and not by intentional study and reflection, it nevertheless firmly rejected the theory of innate ideas."[133] For Bavinck then the natural knowledge of God is always mediated by the things that God has made. Otherwise, it leads, as he puts it, to a "rationalism that constructs the entire universe of being itself from the immanent thought-processes of the human mind." Consequently, he adds, "the visible world would no longer be a creation and revelation of God, an embodiment of divine thoughts. From it no eternal truths or intellectual knowledge could be deduced. Humans could only arrive at these by way of self-reflection and recollection as they isolated themselves from the world and retreated into themselves."[134] In sum, then, I dare to say that the biblical reason for Bavinck's rejection of the theory of innate ideas is that this theory cannot do justice to St. Paul's teaching in Romans 1 that the natural knowledge in question is not immediate but mediated—by way of the things that God has made.

---

131. *GD* II, 62 [90].
132. Descartes, *Meditations on First Philosophy*, Meditation Three, 76.
133. Bavinck, *GD* II, 33 [63].
134. Ibid., [68–69].

Perhaps it is not yet clear what Bavinck means by "implanted knowledge of God," especially when he calls it an "innate disposition." "'Implanted knowledge of God' does not mean that all people are immediately endowed by God himself with sufficient knowledge so as to be able to dispense with [creation] revelation. The term does not say that we are able, all by ourselves, to deduce conscious, clear, and valid knowledge of God from the contents of our minds. What it does say is that we possess the *capacity* (aptitude, faculty) and the *inclination* (*habitus*, disposition) to arrive at some firm, certain, and unfailing knowledge of God. Human beings gain this knowledge in the normal course of development and in the [epistemic] environment in which God gave then the gift of life. It arises spontaneously and without coercion, without scientific argumentation and proof. The words 'implanted', 'natural', and 'innate', accordingly, are not meant to convey the 'wherewithal' with which a person is born but merely to indicate that knowledge of God arises naturally, aside from any scientific input, from the human mind."[135]

Bavinck's reflections on the natural knowledge of God are important because they attempt to justify the claim that belief in God is both natural and normal; it is unbelief that is unnatural, the exception, requiring enormous efforts. I presume this means for Bavinck that, not only are philosophical proofs *not the actual source*, for most believers, of their assent to God's existence and his natural attributes, but also that such proofs are *unnecessary* in order for believers to be rationally justified in their beliefs about God. Says Bavinck, "surely it would be a 'wretched faith that first had to prove God's existence before it prayed to him'. The contrary, rather, is the case. There is not a single thing whose existence is certain to us only on the basis of proofs. We are fully convinced—prior to any argumentation—of our own existence, the existence of the world around us, the laws of logic and morality, simply as a result of the indelible impressions all these things make on our consciousness. We accept that existence—without constraint or coercion—spontaneously and instinctively. And the same is true of God's existence."[136]

Let me make my view plain here: nothing prevents the Catholic thinker from maintaining—not only for the reasons Bavinck gives but also according to Vatican I—that this is exactly what the Council is

---

135. Ibid., 42 [71].
136. Bavinck, *GD*, 63 [90].

getting at in stating that "God, the source and end of all things, can be known with certainty from the consideration of created things, by the natural power of human reason." Indeed, the dogma of the Catholic faith, taught by Vatican Council I, and reiterated by Vatican II[137], is that the existence of God can be known with certainty by natural reason *from* created things; that is, the knowledge in question is mediated by creation. Whether the Council meant to teach that this natural knowledge of God can be *philosophically* demonstrated and also that such demonstrations have in fact been accomplished is open to question.[138] One thing is sure, Vatican I does not speak of proofs for God's existence here; his existence can be known by way of the works of his hand, but the Council does not deny that it can be demonstrated. As Balthasar rightly notes, "Nothing is said by this against the logical validity of conclusiveness of proofs for God's existence (of which, for example, the oath against Modernism will speak)." In my judgment, von Balthasar, de Lubac, and others like John Henry Newman,[139] Jacques Maritain,[140] and Aidan Nichols, OP, are right in distinguishing these two kinds of natural knowledge of God. Nichols correctly observes regarding this famous passage from Vatican I: "It has sometimes been supposed that the council committed Catholics to seek a proof of God's existence in strict logical form, a demonstration in a quasi-mathematical sense. Yet the key words of the text are ample, broad,

---

137. Vatican II, *Dei Verbum*, no. 6.

138. Berkouwer correctly notes: "It is true that the Vaticanum does not speak of the provability [Dutch: bewijsbaarheid] but of the certainty of knowing God. However, when the [anti-]modernistic-oath of 1910 referred back to the Vatican Council's declaration of the natural light of reason, to this was added that God, who is knowable by the natural light of reason, 'can certainly be known as the cause of all things, and therefore can also be proved'" (*De Algemene Openbaring*, 53 [66–67]). Idem., *Een Halve Eeuw Theologie, Motieven en Stromingen van 1920 tot Heden*, 206. On the anti-Modernist oath of St. Pius X, *Sacrorum antistitum*.

139. For Newman's mature statement of his religious epistemology, see *Essay in Aid of a Grammar of Assent* (Notre Dame, IN: University of Notre Dame Press, 1979 [1870]).

140. Jacques Maritain writes regarding Romans 1:19–20 that St. Paul "was thinking not only of scientifically elaborated or specifically philosophical ways of establishing the existence of God. He had in mind also and above all the natural knowledge of the existence of God to which the vision of created things leads the reason of every man, philosopher or not. It is this doubly *natural* knowledge of God I wish to take up here. It is natural not only in the sense that it belongs to the rational order rather than to the supernatural order of faith, but also in the sense that it is *prephilosophic* and proceeds by the natural or, so to speak, instinctive manner proper to the first apperceptions of the intellect prior to every philosophical or scientifically rationalized elaboration" (*Approaches to God*, 17–18).

capable of multiple interpretation: a knowledge 'through the creation' (through some, or perhaps each and every, aspect of finite being), 'by the natural light of human reason' (human reason *tout court*, with no attempt to lay down in advance what mode or style of human rationality that might be)."[141] Given this interpretation of Vatican I, we can easily see how Bavinck epistemological distinction between pre-philosophical (implanted) knowledge of God and the philosophical knowledge acquired through arguments is perfectly compatible with the decree that God can be known with certainty from creation through natural reason. This decree need not be construed philosophically. Philosophical arguments for God's existence are available, sufficient but not necessary.

Of course what is surely the case is that Vatican I speaks against the possibility of the sinner freeing himself by rational means alone from his rejection of God resulting in the failure to yield to him the revealer full submission of intellect and will by faith. The Council Fathers wrote: "Now, although the assent of faith is by no means a blind movement of the mind, yet no one can accept the gospel preaching in the way that is necessary for achieving salvation without the inspiration and illumination of the Holy Spirit who gives to all facility in accepting and believing the truth."[142]

Bavinck uses the phrase "acquired knowledge of God" to describe the proofs for God's existence, or, strictly speaking, natural theology. What is the relationship between the innate and acquired knowledge of God? Bavinck draws an analogy here: just as faith seeks understanding (*fides quaerens intellectum*), or, as he puts it, faith aspires to become theology, so too does the "innate knowledge of God seek to complete itself in the acquired knowledge of God."[143] Does Bavinck subscribe to that strand of medieval thought in which the central function of natural theology, the theistic proofs, is to transform faith into knowledge, *scientia*? He doesn't say. Alternatively, are philosophical proofs the *source* of religious certainty? Definitely not! Bavinck tells us that the "so-called proofs may introduce greater distinctness and lucidity, but they are by no means the final grounds on which our certainty regarding God's existence is ultimately based. This certainty is solely determined by faith, that is, the spontaneity with which our consciousness bears witness to the existence

---

141. Nichols, *Epiphany*, 16.

142. Vatican Council 1, 1869–1870, *Dogmatic Constitution on the Church*, Chapter 3, *On Faith and Reason*. I discussed this claim at length in chapter 4.

143. Bavinck, *GD* II, 46 [74].

of God that urges itself upon us from all directions. The proofs, as proofs, are not the grounds but rather the products of faith."[144] But in what sense are they product of faith?

Well, the normative power of God's creation revelation is such that "God does not leave himself without a witness, either in nature or history, in heart or conscience, in life or lot."[145] In response to this Witness of God in general revelation, Christians have fashioned arguments for God's existence and the existence of the moral law, accounting for their own religious and ethical consciousness in response to that revelation. Bavinck does not regard these arguments for God's existence as compelling evidence. And yet, he says, although they may be weak as proofs in the strict sense of demonstrations, they are nevertheless stronger than arguments advanced for the denial of God's existence. Ultimately, their aim—of course not bypassing intellectual rigor—is to evoke a response in the mind and heart of the unbeliever to God's general revelation and hence these arguments are better seen as testimonies to that revelation. As testimonies, then, we might think of them as, as Francis Martin pointedly says, "an invitation to yield to the evidence and follow its lead."[146] In other words, "But conceived as testimonies, and proclaimed as the revelation of the God of whose existence every human is by nature—and prior to any reasoning of study—assured in the very depths of his or her soul, *they are of no small value*." In other words, adds Bavinck,

> They furnish [believers] the weapons with which their opponents, who in any case are not better armed than they, can be repulsed. . . . Together they [the testimonies of God's general revelation that have been condensed in the arguments for God's existence] make him known to us as the divine being who must be conceived by us as necessary and necessarily as existing; who is the sole, first, and absolute cause of all creatures; who consciously and purposefully governs all things, and who above all reveals himself as the Holy One in the conscience of everyone who believes.[147]

This, too, is the view of John Paul II about theistic arguments. He writes:

144. Ibid., 63 [90].
145. Ibid.
146. Martin, "Revelation as Disclosure," 225.
147. Bavinck, *GD* II, 64 [91] (italics added).

> One clearly sees that *the response to the question 'An Deus sit?'* [Does God exist?] *is not only an issue that touches the intellect; it is, at the same time, an issue that has a strong impact on all of human existence.* It depends on a multitude of situations in which man searches for the significance and the meaning of his own existence. Questioning God's existence is intimately united *with the purpose of human existence.* Not only is it a question of intellect; it is also a question of the will, even *a question of the human heart* (the *raisons du coeur* of Blaise Pascal). I think it is wrong to maintain that Saint Thomas's position stands up only in the realm of the rational. One must, it is true, applaud Etienne Gilson when he agrees with Saint Thomas that the intellect is the most marvelous of God's creations, but that does not mean that we must give in to a unilateral rationalism. Saint Thomas celebrates all the richness and complexity of each created being, and especially of the human being.... In this context, his *quinque viae*—that is, his 'five ways' that lead toward a response to the question *'An Deus sit?'*—should be read.[148]

Furthermore, the pope agrees with Bavinck that the natural knowledge of God is not, necessarily, the fruit of theistic arguments. "The truth made known to us by revelation is neither the product nor the consummation of an argument devised by human reason." Yet, like Bavinck, the pope holds that being a gift of God's grace, faith's knowledge of God is not based on reason, but it "can certainly not dispense with [reason]."[149] "Faith therefore has no fear of reason, but seeks it out and has trust in it. Just as grace builds on nature and brings it to fulfillment, so faith builds upon and perfects reason. Illumined by faith, reason is set free from the fragility and limitations deriving from the disobedience of sin and finds the strength required to rise to the knowledge of the Triune God."[150] According to John Paul, then, theistic arguments establish certain philosophically knowable truths about God. These are truths that "reason in its independent journey of truth already perceives."

Reason's *independent* journey? For some neo-Calvinists, the specter of autonomous reason looms over this way of expressing oneself. Perhaps it is appropriate here to say a few words about the sense in which the pope thinks of reason's independence, or, as he also says, a "valid autonomy of thought." John Paul clearly distinguishes, in his own words, a "valid

---

148. John Paul II, *Crossing the Threshold of Hope*, 30–31.
149. John Paul II, *Fides et Ratio*, no. 67.
150. Ibid., no. 43.

autonomy" from a "self-sufficiency of thought," the latter being, he adds, "patently invalid."[151] When he uses the former phrase he sometimes means philosophy's disciplinary autonomy in distinction to theology's; philosophy has its own rules, criteria, modes of argumentation, and so forth. On other occasions he simply means that reason in itself is still capable of apprehending truth and so philosophy is too. In other words, what he is saying is that human reason, while remaining true to itself, can by its own principles advance to a point where God becomes visible as the fundamental basis and ultimate meaning of all reality. Yes, human nature has been savagely wounded by the Fall, and so its powers, and thus its activities have been seriously damaged by sin, but its deepest foundation is still what God made it. That is, as John Paul puts it elsewhere, "No darkness of error or sin can totally take away from man the light of God the Creator."[152] Significantly, this is the power of God's general revelation and common grace, and the pope is saying that no one escapes its light. This means, then, that human reason, although finite, fallible, and fallen, and hence "seriously handicapped,"[153] as he also puts it, can still gain access to reality, to truth, and so, ineluctably, in some degree to God. This, too, is Bavinck's view.

Significantly, the pope argues that the task of fundamental theology should be to show how, in the light of the knowledge of faith, or, as Bavinck also puts it, in light of a mind that has been sanctified and eyes that have been opened, "revelation endows these truths, independently acquired by reason, with their fullest meaning, directing them towards the richness of the revealed mystery in which they find their ultimate purpose." I dare to say that John Paul and Bavinck would agree that the fullest meaning of these truths is, as Bavinck says, "to see God, the true and living God, in his creatures." They also agree that these truths must be "critically purified," that is, amplified, corrected, and transformed in light of the truth of the Christian revelation. So the pope, like Bavinck, doesn't treat natural theology prior to and apart from God's special revelation, divesting himself of that revelation in Scripture and the illumination of the Holy Spirit, and apart from any Christian presuppositions. Rather, John Paul says, given that human reason is wounded and weakened by

---

151. Ibid., no. 75.
152. John Paul II, *Veritatis Splendor*, no. 1.
153. John Paul II, *Fides et Ratio*, no. 75.

sin, given its inherent and historical limitations, "it is difficult enough to recognize the inalienable powers proper to [reason]." "But," adds the pope, "it is still more difficult at times to discern in specific philosophical claims what is valid and fruitful from faith's point of view and what is mistaken or dangerous. Yet the Church knows that 'the treasures of wisdom and knowledge' are hidden in Christ (Col 2:3) and therefore intervenes in order to stimulate philosophical inquiry, lest it stray from the path which leads to recognition of the mystery."[154] Thus, Christian thinkers are called to put these fragments of philosophical truth in the service of revelation. This service is, as Balthasar rightly urges, "no mechanical adoption of alien chains of thought with which one can adorn and garland the Christian dimension externally."[155] Rather, it is, says Balthasar, the "art of *breaking open* all finite, philosophical truth in the direction of Christ, and the art of *clarifying transposition*."[156] Regarding the former, Christians are deeply committed to the "all-embracing authority of Christ" (cf. Matt 28:18) over all forms of creaturely truth, because in Christ are hid all the treasures of wisdom and knowledge (cf. Col 2:2–3), and hence Christians "cannot rest until they have brought all these forms of thought into the service of the one truth. 'Everything is yours; but you belong to Christ, and Christ to God' (1 Cor 3:23)."[157]

Now, it is probably true that John Paul is more confident and optimistic about what natural theology can accomplish. Regardless of that difference, for the pope, the affirmations of Catholic faith ultimately depend on no reasoning, fallible or otherwise, but on the Word of God. As John Paul states at the beginning of *Fides et Ratio*: "Underlying every meditation which the Church undertakes is the awareness that she is the bearer of a message which takes its origin from God himself (cf. 2 Cor 4:1–2). The knowledge that she offers to man is not a fruit of her own reflections, but derives from the Word of God received in faith (cf. 1 Thess 2:13)."[158] For John Paul II, the foundation of the Christian theological enterprise, the *intellectus fidei* (the understanding of faith), is the *actus fidei* (the act of faith) in the *auditus fidei* (the hearing of faith). What, then, is this act

---

154. Ibid., no. 51.
155. Balthasar, "On the tasks of Catholic philosophy in our time," 155–56.
156. Ibid., 156.
157. Ibid., 158.
158. John Paul II, *Fides et Ratio*, no. 7.

of faith that is so imperative for the theologian? It must be thought of in two ways: the *fides quae*, the faith which the Church believes, the articles of faith which, as a member of the Church, I regard as true, because they form the objective content of truth that is Catholic Christianity; and the *fides qua*, the faith by which I turn to God the Father, in Christ, by the Spirit's power through my acceptance of what the Church believes. Thus, Christian theology takes its starting point, not in natural reason with its principles, but indeed the mysteries of faith, and that toward which it tends is not an evacuation of the mystery, but the submission of the whole man to the mystery of Christ: "Bringing into captivity every understanding unto the obedience of Christ" (2 Cor 10:5). Bavinck's charge, then, that, according to Roman Catholic theology, natural theology is the rational foundation of "revealed theology," prior to and apart from faith, whatever its historical accuracy—Bavinck forgets that all medieval theology claims to be theology founded on the Word of God, and nothing else—simply does not touch John Paul II.

Yet, Bavinck and the pope are in agreement that the theistic arguments produce clarity. They also account, as testimonies in faith, when systematically ordered and arranged in the proofs, for the believer's own religious consciousness of wonder at the world's very existence, its transience and contingency, apparent order, and purposiveness, and of ourselves, our finitude, senses of moral obligation, the grandeur and poverty of man, and others. These theistic arguments, says Bavinck, "furnish [believers] the weapons with which their opponents, who in any case are not better, armed than they, can be repulsed."[159] Indeed, Bavinck rightly construes these proofs as theoretical expressions of man's response, prior to all reasoning and philosophical argument, to God's normative revelation of himself in and through the works of creation, either in the world, nature or history, or in the human person. "It is God himself who does not leave any person without a witness [cf. Acts 14:17]." We return here to Bavinck's view that the God of the philosophers and the God of Holy Scripture is one and the same God.

> For Christians these proofs signify that it is one and the same God who manifests himself in nature and in grace, therefore that creation and re-creation, the realm of nature and the world of ethics, do not exist side by side in Manichean and dualistic fashion, but

---

159. Bavinck, *GD* II, 64 [91].

constitute one cosmos: the perfections of God that shine out in the world are the same as those which sparkle in the kingdom of God. Collectively, the testimonies that God sends to us in the world and are condensed in the so-called proofs are nothing other than a revelation of the name of the Lord by means of which he makes himself known to his creatures and gives us the right to address. [160]

ON SPEAKING TRULY, IF INADEQUATELY, ABOUT GOD

"Mystery is the lifeblood of dogmatics," says Bavinck in his opening line to Volume 2 of the *Gereformeerde Dogmatiek*.[161] Christian theology regards God as an adorable mystery. Man does not and cannot possess comprehensive knowledge of God. "It is completely incomprehensible to us how God can reveal himself and to some extent make himself known in created beings: eternity in time, immensity in space, infinity in the finite, immutability in change, being in becoming, the all, as it were, in that which is nothing. This mystery cannot be comprehended: it can only be gratefully acknowledged."[162] Does the inexpressibility of the mystery necessarily imply the negative indeterminacy of the mystery in every respect, or even that we cannot say something determinate and true about it, even though it remains inexhaustibly beyond us? Both Bavinck and the two popes, John Paul and Benedict, respond in the negative to these questions: inadequacy of expression does not mean total inexpressibility. Yes, "Absolute, full adequate [exhaustive] knowledge of God is therefore impossible. . . . It is in every respect finite and limited, but not for that reason, impure or untrue."[163] If inadequacy of expression means total inexpressibility, then none of what is said affirmatively of God is true of him—as Bavinck argues—not even true of God that he reveals, or that he is one or many, person or thing, substance or process, good or evil, purposive or non-purposive.

Bavinck writes, "The moment we dare to speak about God the question arises: How can we? We are human and he is the Lord our God. Between him and us there seems to be no such kinship or communion as would enable us to name him truthfully. The distance between God and

---

160. Bavinck, *GD* II, 64 [91].
161. Ibid., 1 [29].
162. Ibid., 22 [49].
163. Ibid., 76, 74 [108, 106].

us is the gulf between the Infinite and the finite, between eternity and time, between being and becoming, between the All and the nothing." And yet, adds Bavinck, most importantly, "While Holy Scripture affirms this truth [regarding the distinction between God and the world] in the strongest terms, it nevertheless sets forth a doctrine of God that fully upholds his knowability.... In Scripture ... the knowability of God is never in doubt even for a moment."[164]

John Paul II makes this last point in connection with the language of faith but also with the revealed truth of the Word of God. Regarding the former, he says, "Faith clearly presupposes that human language is capable of expressing divine and transcendent reality in a universal way—analogically, it is true, but no less meaningfully for that." The consequence of denying this would be that none of what we said affirmatively of God is true of him. "Were this not so," adds the pope, "the Word of God, which is always a divine Word in human language, would not be capable of saying anything about God. The interpretation of this Word cannot merely keep referring us to one interpretation after another, without ever leading us to a statement which is simply true; otherwise there would be no revelation of God."[165] For John Paul, the revealed truth of the Word of God is "the truth about God which God himself communicates through the sacred text." "This means that the Word of God which communicates the truth is expressed in human language, by means of that amazing 'condescension' which reflects the logic of the Incarnation." Indeed, it is the logic of the Incarnation and all that it entails that provides the reason why we can and may speak of God in creaturely language. God himself became man, coming down to the level of his creatures and revealed his name in and through his creatures. "Therefore," adds John Paul, "in interpreting the sources of Revelation theologians must remind themselves of the depth and appropriateness of the truth that the passages of Scripture desire to open up, even within the limits imposed by human language."[166] So both for Bavinck and John Paul the question, in light of the distinction between God and the world, isn't whether God is knowable, or whether we can speak truly, if inadequately, about him—God is knowable and we do speak to and about him—but rather how do we know God, indeed, how

---

164. Ibid., 2 [30].
165. John Paul II, *Fides et Ratio*, no. 84.
166. Ibid., no. 94.

can we speak of him. For these two thinkers, if one is to speak of God at all, one must speak with a broken voice that is not without some truth but that yet falls infinitely short of the full truth. That brokenness, however we understand it, is neither mere univocity nor equivocity. This thesis brings us to the matter of an analogy of being—likeness-in-diversity, continuity-in-discontinuity, within analogous speech to and about God.

In his Regensburg address, Pope Benedict XVI expressed the presupposition undergirding both Bavinck's and John Paul's thought regarding our speaking truly, if inadequately, about God. "[T]he faith of the Church has always insisted that between God and us, between his eternal Creator Spirit and our created reason there exists a real analogy, in which—as the Fourth Lateran Council in 1215 stated—unlikeness remains infinitely greater than likeness, yet not to the point of abolishing analogy and its language. God does not become more divine when we push him away from us in a sheer, impenetrable voluntarism; rather, the truly divine God is the God who has revealed himself as *logos* and, as *logos*, has acted and continues to act lovingly on our behalf."[167] We may speak here of the *analogia entis* (*analogy of being*) because it protects the radical difference between Creator and creature—as Bavinck and both popes do.

For them, the *analogia entis*, the real analogies between the Creator and the creature, is founded upon the doctrine of creation. It has nothing to do with an essentialist analogy between them. Berkouwer correctly states that Roman Catholic theologians strongly oppose the idea of the analogy of being in which "there is one universal Being under which both God and man are subsumed." "Rather," Berkouwer adds, "it presupposes a *difference* between Creator and creature. There is a great difference, an 'infinite difference', between God, 'the source of being', and all created beings. But this infinite distance does not eliminate all analogy. There is also a 'line of similarity' which God has himself established. God is not a hidden God. The words with which we speak about God are not simply a groping in the darkness of an unapproachable light. There is analogy, in spite of the infinite diversity—and analogy of *being*. 'Being and existence are in God, just as well as in the creatures.'"[168] What is more, Bavinck also

---

167. Benedict XVI, "Faith, Reason, and the University, Memories and Reflections." See Fourth Lateran Ecumenical Council, *De Errore Abbatis Ioachim*, II: "For between creator and creature there can be noted no similarity so great that a greater dissimilarity cannot be seen between them."

168. Berkouwer, *De Algemene Openbaring*, 56–57 [70–71].

explicitly rejects an interpretation of the analogy of being which analogizes God and creatures under the more general category of being, or a univocal conception of being. Says Bavinck, "There is no genus to which he [God] belongs as a member, and there are no specific marks of distinction [*differentia specifica*] whereby we can distinguish him from other beings in this genus. Even the being he has, so to speak, in common with all creatures does not pertain to him in the same sense as it does to them (univocally), but only analogically and proportionally."[169] Rather, Bavinck and the two popes analogize being in terms of the difference between God and creatures. Their approach undermines the notion, not only of a general and univocal category of being, but also of ontological equivocity.

Because of the radical distinction between the Creator and the creature, being itself already differs. If we recall the words of the Fourth Lateran Council—"For between creator and creature there can be noted no similarity so great that a greater dissimilarity cannot be seen between them"—that is precisely what it says, namely, that the creature's dissimilarity to God is infinitely greater that the similarity to him. This means that the *analogia entis* doesn't obscure God's transcendence, or altogether banish negative theology. As Bavinck puts it, "The knowledge we have of God is altogether unique. This knowledge may be called positive insofar as by it we recognize a being infinite and distinct from all finite creatures. On the other hand, it is negative because we cannot ascribe a single predicate to God as we conceive that predicate in relation to creatures. It is therefore an *analogical* knowledge: knowledge of a being who is unknowable in himself, yet able to make something of himself known in the being he created."[170] Yet, it doesn't exaggerate the import of negative theology. Rather, the *analogia entis* safeguards us from the dangers of agnosticism and experiential, symbolic expressivism, which is a form of subjectivism. Bavinck has an argument against both views that I want now to give.

At the turn of the nineteenth century, pantheistic philosophy, argues Bavinck, had equated the absolute with the indefinite and called all determination of God a limitation and negation. In doing so, it was guilty of confusing concepts. There is a world of difference between the Absolute and the indefinite, the unbounded, the boundless, the indeterminate, and the infinite extension in all directions. Now, Bavinck argues that God is,

---

169. Bavinck, *GD* II, 91 [121].
170. Ibid., 21–22 [48].

in the absolute sense of the term, the source, the primary efficient cause of our knowledge of him, for he is absolutely free, self-conscious, and true. Says Bavinck, "His self-knowledge and self-consciousness is the source (*principium essendi*) of our knowledge of him. Without the divine self-consciousness, there is no knowledge of God in his creatures. *Pantheism is the death of theology*."[171] The latter is the case, argues Bavinck, because pantheism does not acknowledge that God has a life and consciousness of his own that is the source of our knowledge of him.

Significantly, Bavinck is arguing that equating the Absolute with the indeterminate and calling all determination—making true affirmative assertions about God—a limitation and negation and hence a violation of God's being, leads to the view held by many Gnostics that what is final is, not the word, but silence. Bavinck elaborates: "If all determination is negation, then God may not be called the One, the Existent One, or the Absolute either. In that case all thought and speech about God is prohibited. If as humans we may not speak of God in a human and analogical manner, we have no choice but to be silent. To think and speak divinely of God is beyond us. But then all religion implodes. If God cannot be known, neither can he be felt and, in that feeling, enjoyed. Feeling is as finite as the intellect and finitizes and humanizes God in the same way. No possibility then exists either of God revealing himself objectively in his creatures or of us subjectively perceiving him by an organ. All religion, then, is sacrilege and all theology blasphemy."[172] This is agnosticism, argues Bavinck, and it relapses into the error of Gnosticism—as Ratzinger also argues. "God is mere 'inexpressible depth' and 'eternal silence'. There is no communion or kinship between him and his creatures." "It confines him to himself, makes him into an unknown invisible power who has neither consciousness nor will, who can in no way communicate himself who is eternal silence." Adds Bavinck, "But then any name by which we might wish to refer to him is an act of defamation, and assault on God's majesty, blasphemy."[173] This view also cannot escape the implication that God *cannot* reveal himself. Yet, if agnosticism is to resist ending up in atheism, it must maintain the existence of the Unknowable. But, as Bavinck argues, "as soon as it adopts this position, however, it is caught up in an intolerable

---

171. Bavinck, *GD*, I, 183–184 [212; italics added].
172. Bavinck, *GD* II, 23–24 [50].
173. Ibid., 73 [105].

self-contradiction. Augustine already commented that the proposition that we know nothing of God already presupposes a lot of knowledge of God and therefore what we have here is a contradiction in terms. . . . It is already quite significant to know that God is in no way creaturely."

Furthermore, Bavinck argues that we can in fact formulate true affirmative assertions about God and so talk to and about God cannot be considered merely symbolic. "A symbol is always a sensible object or action to denote a spiritual truth, while theology as such has to do not with such symbols but with spiritual realities. When consciousness, will, holiness, and so forth are ascribed to God, no one takes this in a 'symbolic' sense." "On the contrary," adds, Bavinck, "religious persons view such religious representations as being objectively true, and their religion languishes and dies the moment they begin to doubt this fact. If, accordingly, they were products of the imagination, their objective truth could not be maintained. . . . This 'symbolic' character of theology turns the names of God into a reflex of one's own inner life, deprives them of all objective reality, and looks for their ground in ever-changing subjective reason. Humanity then becomes the standard of religion: as humans are, so is their God."[174] Bavinck's and the two popes' primary objection to this anthropological reduction is that revelation's forms of expression would thus fluctuate with the historical transformations of religious subjectivity, which stems from the initial anthropological determination of the criterion of revelation. This is why John Paul writes, "A theology without a metaphysical horizon could not move beyond an analysis of religious experience, nor would it allow the *intellectus fidei* to give a coherent account of the universal and transcendent value of revealed truth."[175]

In conclusion, then, Bavinck argues that we do have some imperfect and deficient but nonetheless proper knowledge of who God really is—even though any comprehensive knowledge of God necessarily escapes us. The Word of God and Christian doctrine is unmistakable in this regard: Christian faith is word-oriented. God has revealed himself uniquely in the history of Israel; Jesus of Nazareth is the Logos incarnate, consubstantial with the Father—in him God himself is revealed, the truth of all things. Jesus Christ is the fullness and mediator of all Revelation. The Holy Spirit, worshipped together with the Father and the Son, sancti-

---

174. Ibid., 78 [109].
175. John Paul II, *Fides et Ratio*, no. 83.

fies us and leads the Church into the fullness of truth. As John Paul II says, "The Bible, and the New Testament in particular, contains texts and statements which have a genuinely ontological content. The inspired authors intended to formulate true statement, capable, that is, of expressing objective reality. It cannot be said that the Catholic tradition erred when it took certain texts of St. John and St. Paul to be statements about the very being of Christ. In seeking to understand and explain these statements, theology needs, therefore, the contribution of a philosophy which does not disavow the possibility of a knowledge which is objectively true, even if not perfect."[176] This knowledge of God, then, shares in God's own self-knowledge, which Bavinck calls archetypal, but the knowledge we have of God is always on a creaturely level and in a creaturely way—"only a weak likeness, a finite, limited sketch, of the absolute self-consciousness of God accommodated to the capacities of the human or creaturely consciousness," and such knowledge Bavinck calls ectypal. This ectypal knowledge cannot diminish the infinity of God because it is grounded in God's own self-knowledge. "Similarly, our knowledge does not limit God because (1) it is grounded in him, (2) can only exist through him, and (3) especially has as its object and content God as the infinite One." Finally, argues Bavinck, all knowledge of God must be called ectypal or analogical, not symbolic. Implied in this is the following:

1. All our knowledge of God is from and through God, grounded in his revelation, that is, in objective reason.

2. In order to convey the knowledge of him to his creatures, God has to come down to the level of his creatures and accommodate himself to their powers of comprehension.

3. The possibility of this condescension cannot be denied since it is given with creation, that is, with the existence of finite being.

4. Our knowledge of God is always only analogical in character, that is, shaped by analogy to what can be discerned of God in his creatures, having as its object not God himself in his knowable essence, but God in his revelation, his relation to us, in the things that pertain to his nature, in his habitual disposition to his creatures. Accordingly, this knowledge is only a finite image, a faint likeness and creaturely impression of the perfect knowledge that God has of himself.

---

176. Ibid., no. 82.

5. Finally, our knowledge of God is nevertheless true, pure, and trustworthy because it has for its foundation God's self-consciousness, its archetype, and his self-revelation in the cosmos.[177]

Finally, and most importantly, let us return to one of the main claims of Benedict's Regensburg address, namely, that the selfsame Logos, Jesus Christ, is the Mediator of creation and redemption. Says John Paul, "He is the eternal Word, in whom all things were created, [and in whom all things hold together], and at the same time the incarnate Word, who in his entire person reveals the Father (John 1:14, 18)."[178] Similarly, Vatican II teaches in Gaudium et Spes (no. 45): "For God's Word, by whom all things were made, was himself made flesh so that as perfect man he might save all men and sum up all things in himself. The Lord is the goal of human history, the focal point of the longing of history and of civilization, the center of the human race, the joy of every heart, and the answer to all its yearnings." Therefore, at the center of the analogical relation between God and the world is, properly understood, Jesus Christ himself, the primum analogatum, who by virtue of the hypostatic union is the key to the interpretation not only of creation, but of God himself. And so, we are back to Jesus Christ, to whom Bavinck's and John Paul II's work as a whole is centrally oriented and whom to follow humbly was their deepest desire.

---

177. Bavinck, *GD* II, 78–79 [110].
178. John Paul II, *Fides et Ratio*, no. 34.

Afterword

> *Truth, in fact, is lógos which creates diá-logos, and hence communication and communion ... Truth opens and unites our minds in the lógos of love: this is the Christian proclamation and testimony of charity.*[1]

I HAVE ATTEMPTED IN this book to engage in a dialogue of love with the thought of representative thinkers of the Dutch neo-Calvinist tradition on a variety of topics with the aim of achieving essential clarification regarding traditional controversies between Catholics and Reformed concerning nature and grace, the Church and the world, the idea of Christian philosophy, faith and reason, scholasticism, the sacramental life, the epistemological significance of the Holy Spirit, and others. I hope I have succeeded in achieving this aim, or at least of exhibiting fraternal dialogue so that we may grow toward the goal of full communion in truth and charity. After returning to the Church, such dialogue with contemporary neo-Calvinist brethren has not always been easy. My interlocutors, in practice, not only lacked knowledge of their own theological tradition, especially that of the thought of Kuyper and Bavinck, but also were shut up within their own limiting perspective of the Catholic tradition. I hope that my book will be an encouragement to them for rediscovering their own theological tradition as well as to move beyond their perspective of Catholicism. Perhaps this book of mine can serve as a starting point for generating ecumenical conversation on the range of issues discussed here between contemporary neo-Calvinists and Roman Catholics like myself.

In an effort to attain genuine ecumenical conversation in this book, I have tried to heed the words of Vatican II regarding the aim of fostering unity among Christians. That is, to make "every effort to eliminate words, judgments, and actions which do not respond to the condition of separated brethren with truth and fairness." Furthermore, I have sought "joyfully [to] acknowledge and esteem the truly Christian endowments

---

1. Benedict XVI, *Caritas in Veritate*, June 29, 2009, Encyclical Letter, no. 4.

from our common heritage which are to be found among our separated brethren," especially in the Dutch neo-Calvinist tradition. It should be evident from my book that I am in full accord with the council's teaching: "Whatever is truly Christian never conflicts with the genuine interests of the faith; "indeed, it can always result in a more perfect realization of the very mystery of Christ . . ." and the Church."[2]

Now, I do not have a conclusion to this book because the dialogue of love that is ecumenical conversation and fellowship is ongoing. This dialogue is grounded in the love that never ends, namely, the love that exists eternally between the persons of the Trinity—the Father, the Son, and the Holy Spirit. "*Love is given to God* as the perfect source of communion—the unity of Father, Son and Holy Spirit—that we may draw from that source the strength to build communion between individuals and Communities, or to re-establish it between Christians still divided. Love is the great undercurrent which gives life and adds vigor to the movement toward unity."[3]

---

2. All the quotations in this paragraph are from Vatican II, *Unitatis Redintegratio*, no. 4.

3. John Paul II, *Ut Unum Sint*, no. 21.

Selected Bibliography

Anscombe, G. E. M. "Faith." In Anscombe: *Ethics, Religion and Politics, Collected Philosophical Papers*, Vol. 3. Minneapolis: University of Minnesota Press, 1981, 113–20.
Aquinas, Thomas. *Summa Theologiae*. Vol. 1, *Christian Theology*. Translated by Thomas Gilby, O.P. New York: McGraw-Hill Book Co., 1965.
——. *Summa Theologiae*. Vol. 11. *Man*. Translated by Timothy Suttor. New York: McGraw-Hill Book Co., 1970.
——. *Summa Theologiae*. Vol. 12. *Human Intelligence*. Translated by Paul T. Durbin. New York: McGraw-Hill Book Co., 1968.
——. *Summa Theologiae*. Vol. 26. *Original Sin*. Translated by T.C. O'Brien, O.P. New York: McGraw-Hill Book Co., 1965.
——. *Summa Theologiae*. Vol. 31. *Faith*. Translated by T.C. O'Brien. New York: McGraw-Hill, 1975.
——. *Summa Theologiae*. Vol. 32. *Consequences of Faith*. Translated by Thomas Gilby. New York: McGraw-Hill Book Co., 1964.
——. *Summa Theologiae*. Vol. 38. *Injustice*. Translated by Marcus Lefébure, O.P. New York: McGraw-Hill Book Co., 1975.
——. *Summa Theologiae*. Vol. 39. *Religion and Worship*. Translated by Kevin D. O'Rourke, O.P. New York: McGraw-Hill Book Co., 1964.
——. *Summa Theologiae*. Vol. 44. *Well-Tempered Passion*. Translated by Thomas Gilby, O.P. New York: McGraw-Hill Book Co., 1972.
——. *Summa Theologiae*. Vol. 56. *Sacraments*. Translated by David Bourke. New York: McGraw-Hill Book Co., 1975.
——. *Summa Theologiae*. Vol. 58. *The Eucharistic Presence*. Translated by William Barden, OP. New York: McGraw-Hill Book Co., 1965.
——. *Summa Contra Gentiles, Book One: God*. Translated with an Introduction by Anton C. Pegis, F.R.S.C. Notre Dame: University of Notre Dame Press, 1975.
——. *Faith, Reason and Theology: Questions I–IV of his Commentary on the De Trinitate of Boethius*, Medieval Sources in Translation, 32. Translated by A. Maurer. Toronto: Pontifical Institute of Medieval Studies, 1987.
——. *Truth*, Vol. 3. Translated by James V. McGlynn, SJ. Indianapolis: Hackett, 1995.
Ashley, O.P. Benedict M. *Living the Truth in Love, A Biblical Introduction to Moral Theology*. Staten Island, NY: Alba House, 1996.
Balthasar, H. U. von. *Razing the Bastions, On the Church in this Age*. Translated by Brian McNeil, C. R. V. San Francisco: Ignatius Press, 1993 [1952].
——. *Love Alone*. Translated by D.C. Schindler. New York: Sheed and Ward, 1969.
——. *The Theology of Karl Barth, Exposition and Interpretation*. Translated by Edward T. Oakes, S. J. San Francisco: Ignatius Press, 1992.

———. *The Glory of the Lord, A Theological Aesthetics*, vol. I, *Seeing the Form*. Translated by Erasmo Leiva-Merikakis and edited by Joseph Fessio, S. J. and John T. Riches. San Francisco: Ignatius Press, 1982.

———. "On the tasks of Catholic philosophy in our time." *Communio: International Catholic Review* 20 (Spring, 1993): 147–87.

Barth, Karl. *The Church and Churches*, Edinburgh Conference on Faith and Order. Grand Rapids, MI: Eerdmans, 2005 [1936].

———. "Nein." In: *Natural Theology*. Translated by Peter Fraenkel, with an Introduction by John Baillie. London: Centenary Press, 1946.

Bauerschmidt, Frederick Christian. *Holy Teaching, Introducing the Summa Theologiae of St. Thomas Aquinas*. Grand Rapids, MI: Brazos Press, 2005.

Bavinck, Herman. *De Katholiciteit van Christendom en Kerk*. Kampen: G.Ph. Zalsman, 1888. Translated by John Bolt as "The Catholicity of Christianity and the Church." In: *Calvin Theological Journal* 27 (1992): 220–51. Original version is online: http://www.neocalvinisme.nl/hb/broch/hbkath.html.

———. *De Algemeene Genade*. Kampen: G.Ph. Zalsman, 1894. Translated by R.C. van Leeuwen as "Common Grace." in Calvin Theological Journal, Vol. 24 (1989): 45–47. Original version is online: http://www.neocalvinisme.nl/tekstframes.html.

———. *Gereformeerde Dogmatiek* Vol. I. Kampen: J. H. Kok, 1895. Edited by John Bolt. Translated by John Vriend as *Reformed Dogmatics, Prolegomena*, Vol. 1 (Grand Rapids, MI: Baker Academic, 2003).

———. *Gereformeerde Dogmatiek*, Vol. II. Kampen: J.H. Kok, 1897. Edited by John Bolt. Translated by John Vriend as *Reformed Dogmatics*, Vol. Two, *God and Creation* (Grand Rapids, MI: Baker Academic, 2004).

———. *Gereformeerde Dogmatiek* Vol. IV. Kampen: J.H.Kok, 1901. Edited by John Bolt. Translated by John Vriend as *Reformed Dogmatics*, Vol. 4, *Holy Spirit, Church, and New Creation* (Grand Rapids, MI: Baker Academic, 2008).

———. *De Zekerheid des Geloofs*. Kampen: J.H. Kok, 1901. Translated by Harry der Nederlanden as *The Certainty of Faith* (St. Catherines, Ontario: Paideia Press, 1980). The Dutch version is online: http://www.neocalvinisme.nl/tekstframes.html

———. *Roeping en Wedergeboorte*. Kampen: G.Ph. Zalsman, 1903. Translated by Nelson D. Kloosterman, Edited, with an Introductory Essay by J. Mark Beach, as *Saved by Grace, The Holy Spirit's Work in Calling and Regeneration* (Grand Rapids, MI: Reformation Heritage Books, 2008). The Dutch version is online: http://www.neocalvinisme.nl/tekstframes.html.

———. *Christelijke Wereldbeschouwing*. Kampen: J. H. Bos, 1904. Online: http://www.neocalvinisme.nl/hb/broch/hbchrwbesch.html.

———. "Het Rijk Gods, Het Hoogste Goed." In Bavinck: *Kennis en Leven*. Kampen: J. H. Kok, 1922.

Beckwith, Francis J. *Return to Rome: Confessions of an Evangelical Catholic*. Grand Rapids, MI: Brazos Press, 2009.

Bellah, Robert N., et al. "Individualism." *Habits of the Heart: Individualism and Commitment in American Life*. New York: Harper & Row, 1985, 334.

Berkouwer, G.C. *De Strijd Om Het Roomsch-Katholieke Dogma*. Kampen: J.H.Kok, 1940.

———. *Conflict met Rome*. Kampen: J.H. Kok, 1949. Translated by David H. Freeman as *The Conflict with Rome* (Grand Rapids, MI: Baker Book House, 1958).

———. *De Algemene Openbaring*. Kampen: J. H. Kok, 1951. Translated as *General Revelation* (Grand Rapids, MI: Eerdmans, 1955).

———. *De Sacramenten*. Kampen: J.H.Kok, 1954. Translated by Hugo Bekker as *The Sacraments*. Grand Rapids, MI: Eerdmans, 1969.

———. "Identiteit of Conflict? Een poging tot analyse." In: *Philosophia Reformata*, Vol. 21, 1956, 1–45.

———. *Recent Developments in Roman Catholic Thought*. Translated by J. J. Lamberts. Grand Rapids, MI: Eerdmans, 1958.

———. *Vatikaans Concilie en de nieuwe theologie*. Kampen: J. H.Kok, 1964. Translated by Lewis B. Smedes as *The Second Vatican Council and the New Catholicism*. Grand Rapids, MI: Eerdmans, 1965.

———. *De Heilige Schrift*, Vol. I. Kampen: Kok, 1966.

———. *Een Halve Eeuw Theologie, Motieven and Stroningen van 1920 tot Heden* (Kampen: J. H. Kok, 1974).

Blosser, Philip. "Papa Ratzi on the 'ecumenism of return.'" Online: http://pblosser.com/2005/09/ papa-ratzi-on-ecumenism-of-return.html.

Bolt, John. "Evangelical Ecclesiology: No Longer an Oxymoron?: A Review Essay," *Calvin Theological Journal* 39/2 (November 2004); 400–411.

Bonhoeffer, Dietrich. *The Cost of Discipleship*. Translated by R.H. Fuller. New York: MacMillan, 1957.

Braaten, Carl E., ed. *In One Body through the Cross: The Princeton Proposal for Christian Unity*. Grand Rapids, MI: Eerdmans, 2003.

———. *Mother Church, Ecclesiology and Ecumenism*. Minneapolis: Fortress Press, 1998.

———. "The Problem of Authority in the Church." In: Braaten, Carl E., and Robert W. Jenson, eds. *The Catholicity of the Reformation*. Grand Rapids, MI: Eerdmans, 1996, 53–66.

Brunner, Emil. "Nature and Grace." In: *Natural Theology*. Translated by Peter Fraenkel, with an Introduction by John Baillie. London: Centenary Press, 1946.

Byrne, Brendan, S. J. *Romans*. Collegeville, Minnesota: The Liturgical Press, 1966.

Calvin, John. *Institutes of the Christian Religion*. Book IV, 1, § 2. Online: http://www.reformed.org/master/index.html?mainframe=/books/institutes/.

Catechism of the Catholic Church. Citta del Vaticano: Libreria Editrice Vaticana, 1993.

Catechism of the Council of Trent. Translated into English with Notes by John A. McHugh, O P. and Charles J. Callan, O. P. New York: Joseph F. Wagner, Inc., 1945, Part II, The Sacraments, 141–160, and Baptism, 161–198.

Cessario, O. P. Romanus. *Christian Faith & Theological Life*. Washington, D.C.: Catholic University of America Press, 1996.

Chapping, S. J. Marcel. "Pope and Journalist, On a Recent Biography of Pope John XXIII," *Gregorianum* 67, 3 (1986): 517–31.

Clement XI. "Errors of Paschasius Quesnel." In: *The Sources of Catholic Dogma*, Edited by Roy J. Deferrari from the Thirtieth Edition of Henry Denzinger's *Enchiridion Symbolorum*. St. Louis/London: B. Herder Book Co., 1957, 349, no. 1379.

Clouser, Roy A. *The Myth of Religious Neutrality, An Essay on the Hidden Role of Religious Belief in Theories*. Revised Edition. Notre Dame, IN: University of Notre Dame Press, 2005.

Congar, O. P., Yves M. J. *Lay People in the Church*. Translated by Donald Attwater. Westminster, Maryland: The Newman Press, 1965.

———. *Dialogue between Christians, Catholic Contributions to Ecumenism*. Translated by Philip Loretz, S. J. Westminster, Maryland: The Newman Press, 1966.

———. *Ecumenism and the Future of the Church*. Chicago, ILL.: The Priory Press, 1967.

Selected Bibliography

———. *Jesus Christ*. Translated by Luke O'Neill. New York: Herder and Herder, 1966.
———. *Diversity and Communion*. Translated by John Bowden. London: SCM Press Ltd., 1984.
———. "A Last Look at the Council." In *Vatican II Revisited*. Alberic Stacpoole, ed. 237–58. Minneapolis, Minnesota: Winston Press, 1986.
Council of Trent. In: *The Sources of Catholic Dogma*, Edited by Roy J. Deferrari from the Thirtieth Edition of Henry Denzinger's *Enchiridion Symbolorum*. St. Louis/London: B. Herder Book Co., 1957, 285–303.
Congregation for the Doctrine of the Faith. "On the 'Ecumenical Movement.'" December 20, 1949. Online: http://www.ewtn.com/library/CURIA/CDFECUM.HTM.
———. *Mysterium Ecclesia*. June 24, 1973.Online: http://www.saint-mike.org/library/Curia/Congregations/Faith/Mysterium_Ecclesiae.html.
———. "Notification on the Book 'Church, Charism and Powe' by Father Leonardo Boff." March 11, 1985. Online: http://www.ewtn.com/library/curia/cdfboff.htm.
———. *Dominus Iesus*. On the Unicity and Salvific Universality of Jesus Christ and the Church. August 6, 2000. Online: http://www.vatican.va/roman_curia/congregations/cfaith/documents/rc_con_cfaith_doc_20000806_dominus-iesus_en.html.
———. "Responses to Some Questions Regarding Certain Aspects of the Doctrine of the Church." June 29, 2007. Online: http://www.vatican.va/roman_curia/congregations/cfaith/documents/rc_con_cfaith_doc_20070629_commento-responsa_en.html.
———. "Doctrinal Note on Some Aspects of Evangelization." December 3, 2007. Online: http://www.vatican.va/roman_curia/congregations/cfaith/documents/rc_con_cfaith_doc_20071203_nota-evangelizzazione_en.html.
Cottingham, John. *The Spiritual Dimension, Religion, Philosophy and Human Value*. Cambridge: Cambridge University Press, 2005.
Davies, O. P. Brian. *The Thought of Thomas Aquinas*. Oxford: Clarendon Press, 1992.
Descartes, René. *Meditations on First Philosophy*. Fourth Edition. Translated by Donald A. Cress. Indianapolis: Hackett, 1998 [1641].
DiNoia, O. P. J. Augustine. "The Church in the Gospel: Catholics and Evangelicals in Conversation." *Pro Ecclesia* Vol. XIII, No. 1(2004): 58–69.
Dooyeweerd, Herman. *De Wijsbegeerte der Wetsidee*, Boek I, *De Wetsidee als Grondlegging der Wijsbegeerte*. Amsterdam: H.J. Paris, 1935. Translated by David H. Freeman and William S. Young as *A New Critique of Theoretical Thought*, Vol. I, *The Necessary Presuppositions of Philosophy*. Philadelphia: Presbyterian and Reformed Publishing Company, 1969.
———. *De Wijsbegeerte der Wetsidee*, Vol. III, *De Individualiteits-Structuren der Tijdelijke Werkelijkheid*. *De Individualiteits-Structuren der Tijdelijke Werkelijkheid*, Deel II, Hoofdstuk IV, Het Structuur-Principe van het Tidelijk Kerkverband. Amsterdam: H.J. Paris, 1936, 451–509. Translated by David H. Freeman and H. De Jongste as *A New Critique of Theoretical Thought*, Vol. III, *The Structures of Individuality of Temporal Reality*. Part II, Chapter IV, The Structural Principle of the Temporal Church-Institution. Philadelphia: The Presbyterian and Reformed Publishing Company, 1955, 509–61.
———. "Wat de Wijsbegeerte der Wetsidee aan Dr. Kuyper te danken heeft." In: *De Reformatie*, October 29 (1937): 63–65.
———. "Kuyper's Wetenschapsleer." In: *Philosophia Reformata*, Vol. 4, no. 4 (1939): 193–232.

———. *Vernieuwing en Bezinning om het reformatorische grondmotief.* Zutphen: J. B. van den Brink, 1959. Translated by John Kraay and edited by Mark VanderVennen and Bernard Zylstra as *Roots of Western Culture* (Toronto: Wedge Publishing Foundation, 1979).

———. Herman Dooyeweerd, "Het Gesprek tussen her Neo-Thomisme and de Wijsbegeerte der Wetsidee," In: *Bijdragen, Tijdschrift voor filosofie en theologie*, Vol. 72 (1966): 202–13.

———. "Het Oecumenisch-Reformatorisch Grondmotief van de Wijsbegeerte der Wetsidee and de Grondslag der Vrije Universiteit." In: *Philosophia Reformata* 31 (1966), 3–15.

———. *Twilight of Western Thought: Studies in the Pretended Autonomy of Philosophical Thought.* Nutley, N.J.: Craig Press, 1968.

———. "Centrum en Omtrek: De Wijsbegeerte der Wetsidee in en Veranderende Wereld." In: *Philosophia Reformata* (Edited by J. Glenn Friesen), 72 (2007), 1–20.

Douma, J. *Kritische Aaantekeningen bij de Wijsbegeerte der Wetsidee.* Groningen: Uitgeverij De Vuurbaak, 1976. Translated by J.M. Batteau as *Another Look at Dooyeweerd. Some Critical Notes Regarding the Philosophy of the Cosmonomic Idea.* Winnipeg, Manitoba, Canada: Premier Publishing, 1981.

Dulles, S.J. Avery Cardinal. *Models of the Church.* Expanded Edition. New York: Doubleday, 1987 [1978].

———. *The Craft of Theology.* New York: Crossroad, 1992.

———. "Vatican II: Myth and Reality." *America*, February 24, 2003. Online: http://www.americamagazine.org/content/article.cfm?article_id=2810.

Dünzl, Franz. *A Brief History of the Doctrine of the Trinity in the Early Church.* Translated by John Bowden. London: T&T Clark, 2007.

Dupuis, Jacque, ed. "Second Council of Orange." in *The Christian Faith in the Doctrinal Documents of the Catholic Church.* Sixth revised and enlarged edition. New York: Alba House, 1996, 742–744.

Echeverria, Eduardo J. "Augustine on Faith and Reason." in *Collectanea Augustinian II: Presbyter Factus Sum.* New York: Peter Lang Publishing, 1993.

———. "My Journey Home." *Homiletic & Pastoral Review* (June 1999): 24–30. Online: http://www.chnetwork.org/journals/nesschurch/ness_3.htm.

———. "Nature and Grace: The Theological Foundations of Jacques Maritain's Public Philosophy." *Journal of Markets and Morality* 4, No. 2 (2001): 240–268.

———. "Living Truth for a Post-Christian World: The Message of Francis Schaeffer and Karol Wojtyla," *Religion & Liberty*, November and December (2002): 8–11.

———. "The Christian Faith as a Way of Life: In Appreciation of Francis Schaeffer." *Evangelical Quarterly*, Vol. LXXIX, No. 3, July 2007: 241–252.

———. "Confessions of a Catholic Ecumenist." In: *Fellowship of Catholic Scholars Quarterly*, 31, Spring 2008, No. 2: 35–44.

———. "Eucharistic Personalism." In: *The Liturgical Subject, Subject, Subjectivity and the Human Person in Contemporary Liturgical Discussion and Critique.* Ed. James G. Leachman, O.S.B. London: SCM Press, 2008, 74–113.

———. *Slitting the Sycamore, Christ and Culture in the New Evangelization.* Grand Rapids, MI: Acton Institute, 2008.

Fernandez, C. "Metaphysica Generalis," in *Philosophiae Scholasticae Summa*, ed. L. Salcedo and C. Fernandez, Third ed., Vol. I. Madrid: Ed. Católica, 1964.

Frame, John. *The Amsterdam Philosophy, A Preliminary Critique* (1972). Online: http://www.frame-poythress.org/frame_books/1972Amsterdam.htm#background.

Garver, S. Joel. "Ex Opere Operato." Online: http://www.joelgarver.com/writ/sacr/exopere.htm.

George, Timothy. *Is the Father of Jesus the God of Muhammad?* Grand Rapids, MI: Zondervan, 2002.

Gilby, Thomas, ed. *St. Thomas Aquinas: Theological Texts*, selected and translated with notes and introduction by Thomas Gilby. Oxford: Oxford University Press, 1955.

Gilson, Etienne. *Christianity and Philosophy*. Translated by Ralph MacDonald, C.S.B. New York/London: Sheed & Ward, 1939.

———. *The Spirit of Medieval Philosophy*, Gifford Lectures 1931–1932. Translated by A.H.C. Downes. New York: Charles Scribner's Sons, 1940.

———. *The Philosopher and Theology*. Translated by Cecile Gilson. New York: Random House, 1962.

Giussani, Luigi Msgr. *Why the Church?* Translated by Viviane Hewitt. Montreal & Kingston: McGill-Queen's University Press, 2001.

Grillmeier, Aloys. "Dogmatic Constitution on the Church, Chapter 1, Mystery of the Church." In: *Commentary on the Documents of Vatican II*, Volume 1. Translated from the German by Lalit Adolphus, et al. New York: Herder and Herder, 1967.

Grisez, Germain. *The Way of the Lord Jesus, Christian Moral Principles*, Vol. 1. Chicago: Franciscan Herald Press, 1983.

Guardini, Romano. *Vom Sinn der Kirche*. Mainz: Matthias Grünewald Verlag, 1922. Translated by Ada Lane as
The Church and the Catholic (New York: Sheed & Ward, Inc., 1935).

———. *Die Kirche Des Herrn*. Translated by Stella Langerom *The Church of the Lord, On the Nature and Mission of the Church* (Chicago: Henry Regnery Company, 1966).

———. *The Spirit of the Liturgy*. Trans. Ada Lane. New York: Crossroad, 1998 (1930).

———. *The Essential Guardini*. Selected and with an introduction by Heinz R. Kuehn. Chicago: Liturgy Training Publications, 1997.

Guarino, Thomas. *Foundations of Systematic Theology*. New York/London: T&T Clark, 2005.

———. "Tradition and Doctrinal Development: Can Vincent of Lérins still teach the Church?" *Theological Studies* 67 (2006): 34–72.

———. "The God of Philosophy and of the Bible." *Logos* 10:4 (Fall 2007): 120–30.

Gustafson, James. *Protestant and Roman Catholic Ethics*. Chicago: University of Chicago Press, 1978.

Harvey, Thomas. "Baptism as a Means of Grace: A Response to John Stott's 'The Evangelical Doctrine of Baptism.'" *Churchman*, Vol. 113/2 (1999): 103–112.

Hebblethwaite, Peter. *Pope John XXIII, Shepherd of the Modern World*. Garden City, NY: Doubleday & Company, 1985.

Heim, Maximilian Heinrich. *Joseph Ratzinger, Life in the Church and Living Theology*. Translated by Michael J. Miller. San Francisco: Ignatius Press, 2007.

Helm, Paul. *Faith & Understanding*. Grand Rapids, MI: Eerdmans, 1997.

Hoitenga, Jr., Dewey J. *John Calvin and the Will: A Critique and Corrective*. Grand Rapids, MI: Baker Book House, 1997.

International Theological Commission. "Select Themes of Ecclesiology on the Occasion of the Eighth Anniversary of the Closing of the Second Vatican Council," in *International Theological Commission: Texts and Documents, 1969–1985*, Preface by Joseph Cardinal Ratzinger, Edited by Reverend Michael Sharkey (San Francisco: Ignatius Press, 1989), 267–304.

———."On the Interpretation of Dogmas." In: *Origins*. Vol. 20 (May 17) 1990:1–14.

John XXIII. *Humanae salutis*. "Pope John Convokes the Council." Christmas Day, 1961. Apostolic Constitution. In: *The Documents of Vatican II*, General Editor, Walter M. Abbott, S.J. New York: Guild Press, 1966, 703–709.

———. "Pope John's Opening Speech to the Council." In: *The Documents of Vatican II*, General Editor, Walter M. Abbott, S.J. New York: Guild Press, 1966, 710–19. Online: http://www.vatican.va/holy_father/john_xxiii/speeches/1962/documents/hf_j-xxiii_spe_19621011_opening-council_lt.html.

———. "Allocutio habita d. 11 oct. 1962, in initio Concilii." In: 54 *Acta Apostolicae Sedis* (1962).

John Paul II. "Letter instituting the Pontifical Culture for Culture." May 20, 1982, in *Acta Apostolicae Sedis* LXXIV (1982): 683–688.

———. *Reconciliatio et Paenitentia*. ["On Reconciliation and Penance in the Mission of the Church Today"] December 2, 1984Post-Synodal Apostolic Exhortation. Online: http://www.vatican.va/holy_father/john_paul_ii/apost_exhortations/documents/hf_jp-ii_exh_02121984_reconciliatio-et-paenitentia_en.html.

———. *Dominum et Vivificantem*. ["On the Holy Spirit in the Life of the Church and the World"] May 18, 1986 Encyclical Letter. Online: http://www.vatican.va/holy_father/john_paul_ii/encyclicals/documents/hf_jp-ii_enc_18051986_dominum-et-vivificantem_en.html.

———. *Christifideles Laici*. ["On the Vocation and the Mission of the Lay Faithful in the Church and in the World"] December 30, 1988 Post-Synodal Apostolic Exhortation. Online: http://www.vatican.va/holy_father/john_paul_ii/apost_exhortations/documents/hf_jp-ii_exh_30121988_christifideles-laici_en.html.

———. *Redemptoris Missio*. ["On the Permanent Validity of the Church's Missionary Mandate"] December 7, 1990 Encyclical Letter. Online: http://www.vatican.va/holy_father/john_paul_ii/encyclicals/documents/hf_jp-ii_enc_07121990_redemptoris-missio_en.html.

———. *Veritatis Splendor*. ["Splendor of Truth"] 6 August 1993Encyclical Letter. http://www.vatican.va/holy_father/john_paul_ii/encyclicals/documents/hf_jp-ii_enc_06081993_veritatis-splendor_en.html.

———. *Tertio Millennio Adveniente*. ["On Preparation for the Jubilee of the Year 2000"] November 10, 1994, Apostolic Letter. Online: http://www.vatican.va/holy_father/john_paul_ii/apost_letters/documents/hf_jp-ii_apl_10111994_tertio-millennio-adveniente_en.html.

———. *Crossing the Threshold of Hope*. New York: Alfred A. Knopf, 1994.

———. *Ut Unum Sint*. ["On Commitment to Ecumenism"] May 25, 1995 Encyclical Letter. Online: http://www.vatican.va/holy_father/john_paul_ii/encyclicals/documents/hf_jp-ii_enc_25051995_ut-unum-sint_en.html.

———. *Evangelium Vitae*. ["The Gospel of Life"] March 25, 1995 Encyclical Letter. Online: http://www.vatican.va/holy_father/john_paul_ii/encyclicals/documents/hf_jp-ii_enc_25031995_evangelium-vitae_en.html.

———. *A Catechesis on the Creed*, Vol. I. *God Father and Creator*. Boston: Pauline Books & Media, 1996.

———. *A Catechesis on the Creed*, Vol. III. *The Spirit, Giver of Life and Love*. Boston: Pauline Books & Media, 1996.

———. *A Catechesis on the Creed*, Vol. IV. *The Church, Mystery, Sacrament, Community*. Boston: Pauline Books & Media, 1998.

———. *Fides et Ratio*. ["On the Relationship between Faith and Reason"] September 14, 1998 Encyclical Letter. Online: http://www.vatican.va/holy_father/john_paul_ii/encyclicals/documents/hf_jp-ii_enc_15101998_fides-et-ratio_en.html.

———. *Springtime of Evangelization*, The Complete Texts of the Holy Father's 1998 ad Limina Addresses to the Bishops of the United States, Ed. and Introduced by Fr. Thomas D. Williams, L.C. San Francisco: Ignatius Press, 1999.

———. *Novo Millennio Ineunte*. ["At the Close of the Great Jubilee of the Year 2000"] January 6, 2001 Apostolic Letter. Online: http://www.vatican.va/holy_father/john_paul_ii/apost_letters/documents/hf_jp-ii_apl_20010106_novo-millennio-ineunte_en.html.

Journet, Charles Cardinal. *Theology of the Church*. Translated by Victor Szczurek, O. Praem. San Francisco: Ignatius Press, 2004 [1958].

———. *What is Dogma?* Translated by Marx Pontifex, OSB. New York: Hawthorn Books, 1964.

Kasper, Walter Cardinal. "The Church as the Place of Truth." In Kasper: *Theology and Church*. Translated by Margaret Kohl. New York: Crossroads, 1989, 129–47.

———. *The God of Jesus Christ*. Translated by Matthew J. O'connell. New York: Crossroad, 1986.

———. "Responses to Some Questions Regarding Certain Aspects of the Doctrine of the Church," July 11, 2007. Online: http://www.radiovaticana.org/en1/Articolo.asp?c=144460.

———. "Canon Law and Ecumenism." In: *The Jurist* 69 (2009): 171–89.

———. "The Timeliness of Speaking of God: Freedom and Communion as Basic Concepts of Theology." In: *Worship*, Vol. 83, No. 4, (July 2009): 293–311.

Ker, Ian. "The Radicalism of the Papacy: John Paul II and the New Ecclesial Movements." In *John Paul the Great, Maker of the Post-Conciliar Church*. William Oddie, ed. 49–68. London: Catholic Truth Society & The Catholic Herald, 2003.

Komonchak, Joseph. A. "Dealing with Diversity and Disagreement, Vatican II and Beyond." Annual Catholic Common Ground Initiative Lecture 2003; online: http://www.nplc.org/commonground/lecture/komonchak2003.htm.

Kuyper, Abraham. *Lectures on Calvinism*, Stone Lectures, Princeton University, 1898. Grand Rapids, MI: Eerdmans, 1931.

———. *Encyclopaedie der Heilige Godgeleerdheid*, Tweede Deel. Kampen: J. H. Kok, 1909. Translated by Hendrik J. De Vries, with an Introduction by B. B. Warfield as *Encyclopedia of Sacred Theology, Its Principles*. New York: Charles Scribner's Sons, 1898.

———. *The Work of the Holy Spirit*. Translated by Hendrik J. De Vries, with an Introduction by B. B. Warfield. Grand Rapids, MI: Eerdmans, 1956 [1888].

Lamont, John R.T. "The Nature of Revelation." *New Blackfriars* (July–August 1991), 335–45.

Lee, Philip J. *Against the Protestant Gnostics*, New York: Oxford University Press, 1987.

Leithart, Peter J. *Solomon among the Postmoderns*. Grand Rapids, MI: Brazos Press, 2008.

———. "Why Sacraments are not signs." Online: http://www.credenda.org/issues/15-2liturgia.php?type=print.

Leo XIII. *Aeterni Patris*. On the Restoration of Christian Philosophy. August 4, 1879. Encyclical Letter. Online: http://www.vatican.va/holy_father/leo_xiii/encyclicals/documents/hf_l-xiii_enc_04081879_aeterni-patris_en.html.

———. *Satis Cognitum*. On the Unity of the Church. June 29, 1896 Encyclical Letter. Online: http://www.vatican.va/holy_father/leo_xiii/encyclicals/documents/hf_l-xiii_enc_29061896_satis-cognitum_en.html.

Letham, Robert. *The Holy Trinity, In Scripture, History, Theology, and Worship*. Phillipsburg, NJ: Presbyterian & Reformed Publishing Co., 2004.

Lewis, C. S. "On Ethics." In Lewis: *The Seeing Eye and Other Selected Essays*, Ed., Walter Hooper. New York: Ballantine Books, 1967.

Lonergan, S.J. Bernard J.F. *Method in Theology*. New York: Herder and Herder, 1972.

———. "The Dehellenization of Dogma," in *A Second Collection*, William F.J. Ryan, SJ and Bernard J. Tyrrell, S.J., eds. 11–32. Philadelphia: The Westminster Press, 1974.

———. *The Way to Nicea*. Translated by Conn O'Donovan. Philadelphia: Westminster Press, 1976.

Lubac, de Henri. *A Brief Catechesis on Nature & Grace*. Translated by Brother Richard Arnandez, F.S.C. San Francisco: Ignatius Press, 1984.

———. *Theological Fragments*. Translated by Rebecca Howell Balinski. San Francisco: Ignatius Press, 1989.

———. *The Mystery of the Supernatural*. Translated by Rosemary Sheed. Introduction by David Schindler. New York: Crossroad, 1998.

Luther, Martin. *Luther's Works*, Vol. 33, Edited J. Pelikan, H. T. Lehman, *et al*. Philadelphia: Fortress Press, 1972.

Malloy, Christopher J. "*Subsistit In*: Nonexclusive Identity or Full Identity," *The Thomist* 72 (2008): 1–44.

Marlet, SJ, Michael J. *Grundlinien der Kalvinistischen 'Philosophie der Gesetzesidee' als Christilicher Transzendentalphilosophie*. München: Karl Zink Verlag, 1954.

Maritain, Jacques. *Clairvoyance de Rome*. Paris: Spes, 1929.

———. *Integral Humanism, Temporal and Spiritual Problems of a New Christendom*. Translated by Joseph W. Evans. Notre Dame, IN: University of Notre Dame Press, 1973 [1936].

———. *Approaches to God*. Translated by Peter O'Reilly. New York: Macmillan, 1954.

Marshall, Bruce D. "The Church in the Gospel." *Pro Ecclesia*, Vol. I, 1992–93, No. 1: 27–41.

———. The Disunity of the Church and the Credibility of the Gospel," *Theology Today*, Vol. 50, No. 1(April 1993). Online: http://theologytoday.ptsem.edu/apr1993/v50-1-article8.htm.

———. "Who Really Cares about Christian Unity?" *First Things*, January 2001. Online: http://www.firstthings.com/print.php?type=article&year=2007&month=01&title_link=who-really-cares-about-christian-unity-31.

Martin, Francis. *The Feminist Question: Feminist Theology in the Light of Christian Tradition*. Grand Rapids, MI: Eerdmans, 1994.

———. "Revelation as Disclosure: Creation," in Michael Dauphinais & Matthew Levering, eds. *Wisdom and Holiness, Science and Scholarship, Essays in Honor of Matthew L. Lamb*. Naples, FL: Sapientia Press, 2007, 205–47.

McInerny, Ralph. *Being and Predication*. Washington, DC: Catholic University of America Press, 1986.

Muller, Richard A. *Dictionary of Latin and Greek Theological Terms Drawn Principally from Protestant Scholastic Theology*. Grand Rapids, MI: Baker Books, 1985.

Murray, John. *The Epistle to the Romans*, The English Text with Introduction, Exposition and Notes, Volume 1, Chapters 1 to 8. Grand Rapids, MI: Eerdmans, 1959.

Neuhaus, Richard John. *Catholic Matters, Confusion, Controversy, and the Splendor of Truth*. New York: Basic Books, 2006.

———. "How I Became the Catholic I Was." *First Things*, April 2002, 14–22.

———. "The Catholic Difference," in Charles Colson and Richard John Neuhaus, eds. *Evangelical and Catholics Together: Toward a Common Mission*. Dallas: Word Publishing, 1995.

Newman, John Henry. *An Essay in Aid of A Grammar of Assent*. Notre Dame, IN: University of Notre Dame Press, 1979 [1870].

———. *Fifteen Sermons Preached at Oxford University between 1826 and 1843*. Notre Dame, IN: University of Notre Dame Press, 1997.

———. "Religious Faith Rational," in *Parochial and Plain Sermons*, a collection of sermons preached between 1825–1843, Volume I, Sermon 16, 190–202. Online: http://www.newmanreader.org/works/parochial/volume1/sermon15.html.

Nichols, O. P. Aidan. *The Splendor of Doctrine*. Edinburgh: T&T Clark, 1995.

———. *Epiphany, A Theological Introduction to Catholicism*. Collegeville, MN: The Liturgical Press, 1996).

———. "Relaunching Christian Philosophy." In Nichols: *Christendom Awake: On Reenergizing the Church in Culture*. Grand Rapids, MI: Eerdmans, 1999, 53–71.

———. "Integral Evangelization." *Josephinum Journal of Theology*, Vol. 13, No. 1, (2006): 66–80,

Norman, Edward. *Secularization, Sacred Values in a Godless World*. London/New York: Continuum, 2003.

Novak, Michael. *The Open Church*. London: Darton, Longman & Todd, 1964.

———. The Christian Philosophy of John Paul II." In Novak: *On Cultivating Liberty: Reflections on Moral Ecology*. Brian C. Anderson, ed. New York: Rowman & Littlefield Publishers, Inc., 1999, 243–256.

O'Brien, T.C. "Faith and the Truth Who is God," appendix 2 of *Faith*, vol. 31 of the *Summa theologiae*. Translated by T.C. O'Brien. New York: McGraw-Hill, 1975, 186–1\94, 195–204, and 205–15, respectively.

———. "Faith and the Truth about God." Appendix 3. *Faith*, vol. 31 of the *Summa theologiae*. Translated by T.C. O'Brien. New York: McGraw-Hill, 1975, 195–204.

———. "Belief: Faith's Act." Appendix 4. *Faith*, vol. 31 of the *Summa theologiae*. Translated by T. C. O'Brien. New York: McGraw-Hill, 1975, 205–15.

O'Connor, James T. "The Church of Christ and the Catholic Church" (1983), in *The Battle for the Catholic Mind, Catholic Faith and Catholic Intellect in the Work of the of the Fellowship of Catholic Scholars 1978–95*, Edited by W. E. May and K. D. Whitehead, 248–263. South Bend, Indiana: St. Augustine's Press, 2001.

Olsen, Glenn W. *Beginning at Jerusalem, Five Reflections on the History of the Church*. San Francisco: Ignatius Press, 2004.

Ott, Ludwig. *Fundamentals of Catholic Dogma*, Edited in English by James Canon Bastible, D.D., Translated by Patrick Lynch. Rockford, Illinois: Tan Books and Publishers, Inc., 1974 [1952].

Pannenberg, Wolfhart. "Ecumenical Tasks in Relationship to the Roman Catholic Church," *Pro Ecclesia*, Vol. XV, No. 2, (Spring 2006): 161–71.

Paul VI. *Evangelii Nuntiandi*. December 8, 1975. Apostolic Exhortation. Online: http://www.vatican.va/holy_father/paul_vi/apost_exhortations/documents/hf_p-vi_exh_19751208_evangelii-nuntiandi_en.html.

Pelikan, Jaroslav. *The Christian Tradition: A History of the Development of Doctrine*, Vol. 1, The Emergence of the Catholic Tradition (100–600). Chicago: University of Chicago Press, 1971.

Pieper, Josef. *Scholasticism*. Translated by Richard and Clara Winston. New York/Toronto: 1964.

Pinnock, Clark H. *Flame of Love, A Theology of the Holy Spirit*. Downers Grove, ILL.: IVP Academic, 1996.

Pius X. *Sacrorum antistitum*. The Oath against Modernism. September 1, 1910. *Motu Proprio*. Online: http://www.fordham.edu/halsall/mod/1910oathvmodernism.html.

Pius XI. *Mortalium Animos*. On Religious Unity. January 6, 1928. Encyclical Letter. Online: http://www.vatican.va/holy_father/pius_xi/encyclicals/documents/hf_p-xi_enc_19280106_mortalium-animos_en.html.

Pius XII. *Mystici Corporis Christi*. June 29, 1943. Encyclical Letter. Online: http://www.vatican.va/holy_father/pius_xii/encyclicals/documents/hf_p-xii_enc_29061943_mystici-corporis-christi_en.html.

———. *Humani generis*. August 12, 1950. Online: http://www.vatican.va/holy_father/pius_xii/encyclicals/documents/hf_p-xii_enc_12081950_humani-generis_en.html.

Pontifical Council for Culture. *Towards a Pastoral Approach to Culture*, May 23, 1999. Online: http://www.vatican.va/roman_curia/pontifical_councils/cultr/documents/rc_pc_pc-cultr_doc_03061999_pastoral_en.html.

Portier, William L. "Here Come the Evangelical Catholics." *Communio* Vol. XXXI, No. 1, (Spring 2004): 35–66.

Rahner, Karl. *Nature and Grace and other Essays*. Translated by Dinah Wharton. London and New York: Sheed and Ward, 1963.

———. "Church, Churches and Religions." In Rahner: *Theological Investigations*. Vol. X. Translated by David Bourke. New York: Herder and Herder, 1973, 30–49.

———. "On the Theology of the Ecumenical Discussion." In Rahner: *Theological Investigations*, Vol. XI. Translated by David Bourke. London/New York: Darton, Longman & Todd/Seabury Press, 1974, 24–67.

———. "Towards a Fundamental Theological Interpretation of Vatican II." In: *Vatican II: The Unfinished Agenda*. Ed. Lucien Richard, O.M.I., 9–21. Mahwah, NJ: Paulist Press, 1988.

Ratzinger, Joseph (Benedict XVI). *Theological Highlights of Vatican II*. Translated by Henry Traub, S. J., Gerard C. Thormann, and Werner Barzel. New York: Paulist Press, 1966.

———. "Catholicism after the Council." In: *The Furrow* 18 (1967): 3–23.

———. *Das neue Volk Gottes: Entwürfe zur Ekklesiologie*, Second edition (Düsseldorf: Patmos-Verlag, 1977).

———. *Principles of Catholic Theology*. Translated by Sister Mary Francis McCarthy, S.N.D. San Francisco: Ignatius Press, 1987 [1982].

———. *Introduction to Christianity*. Translated by J.R. Foster. San Francisco: Ignatius Press, 1990.

———. *The Yes of Jesus Christ*. Translated by Robert Nowell. New York: Crossroad, 1991.

———. "Relativism: The Central Problem for Faith Today." In: *Origins*, October 31, 1996, Vol. 26: No. 20.

———. "*Deus Locutus Est Nobis in Filio*: Some Reflections on Subjectivity, Christology and the Church." In: *Proclaiming the Truth of Jesus Christ*, Papers from the Vallombrosa Meeting. Washington, D.C.: USCC, 2000, 13–29.

———. "Cardinal Ratzinger answers the main objections raised against the Declaration *Dominus Iesus*." In: *L'Osservatore Romano*, 22 November, 29 November, 6 December 2000, respectively. Online: http://www.ewtn.com/library/Theology/obdomihs.htm.

———. *The Spirit of the Liturgy*. Translated by John Saward. San Francisco: Ignatius Press, 2000.

———. *Truth and Tolerance: Christian Belief and World Religions*. Translated by H. Taylor. San Francisco: Ignatius Press, 2004.

———. "On the Ecumenical Situation." In Ratzinger: *Pilgrim Fellowship of Faith, The Church as Communion*. Edited by Stephan Otto Horn and Vinzenz Pfnür. Translated by Henry Taylor. San Francisco: Ignatius Press, 2005 [2002], 253–269.

———. "The Ecclesiology of the Constitution *Lumen Gentium*." In Ratzinger: *Pilgrim Fellowship of Faith, The Church as Communion*. Edited by Stephan Otto Horn and Vinzenz Pfnür. Translated by Henry Taylor. San Francisco: Ignatius Press, 2005, 123–52.

———. "Church Movements and Their Place in Theology." In Ratzinger: *Pilgrim Fellowship of Faith, The Church as Communion*. Edited by Stephan Otto Horn and Vinzenz Pfnür. Translated by Henry Taylor. San Francisco: Ignatius Press, 2005, 176–208.

———. *God's Revolution, World Youth Day and Other Cologne Talks*. San Francisco: Ignatius Press, 2006.

———. "Faith, Reason, and the University, Memories and Reflections." Lecture of the Holy Father, Aula Magna of the University of Regensburg, Tuesday, 12 September, 2006. Online: http://www.vatican.va/holy_father/benedict_xvi/speeches/2006/september/documents/hf_ben-xvi_spe_20060912_university-regensburg_en.html.

———. *Jesus of Nazareth*. Translated by Adrian J. Walker. New York: Doubleday, 2007.

———. Angelus, St. Peter's Square, Sunday January 21, 2007. Online: http://www.vatican.va/holy_father/benedict_xvi/angelus/2007/documents/hf_ben-xvi_ang_20070121_en.html.

———. "Luther and the Unity of the Churches." In Ratzinger: *Church, Ecumenism & Politics*. Translated by Michael J. Miller, et al. San Francisco: Ignatius Press, 2008 [1983], 100–31.

———. "On the Progress of Ecumenism." In Ratzinger: *Church, Ecumenism & Politics*. Translated by Michael J. Miller, et al. San Francisco: Ignatius Press, 2008 [1986], 132–38.

———. "The Ecclesiology of the Second Vatican Council." In Ratzinger: *Church, Ecumenism & Politics*. Translated by Michael J. Miller, et al. San Francisco: Ignatius Press, 2008 [1986], 13–35.

———. "Theology and Church Politics." In Ratzinger: *Church, Ecumenism & Politics*. Translated by Michael J. Miller, et al. San Francisco: Ignatius Press, 2008 [1980], 148–59.

———. *The God of Jesus Christ, Meditations on the Triune God*. Translated by Brian McNeil. San Francisco: Ignatius Press, 2008 [1976].

———. Benedict XVI, *Caritas in Veritate*, June 29, 2009, Encyclical Letter.

Reid, Thomas. *Inquiry into the Human Mind*. Edinburgh: Maclachlan, Stewart, and Co., 1846.

Ridderbos, Herman. *The Coming of the Kingdom*, Translated by H. de Jongste. Raymond O. Zorn, ed. Philadelphia, PA: Presbyterian and Reformed Publishing Company, 1962 [1950].

Root, Michael. "Catholic and Evangelical Theology." *Pro Ecclesia* Vol. XV, No. 1, (Winter 2006): 9–16.

Schaeffer, Francis A. *The Mark of the Christian*. London: InterVarsity Press, 1970.
Schmitz, Kenneth L. "St. Thomas and the Appeal to Experience," *Catholic Theological Society of America Proceedings*, 47 (1992): 1-20.
Schindler, David L. "Christology, Public Theology, and Thomism: de Lubac, Balthasar, and Murray." In: *The Future of Thomism*. Deal W. Hudson and Dennis William Moran, eds. 247-67. American Maritain Association, 1992.
Schillebeeckx, O. P., E. *Christus, Sacrament van de Godsontmoeting*. Bilthoven: H. Nelissen, 1960. Translated by Paul Barrett, OP, et al. as *Christ, The Sacrament of the Encounter with God* (Kansas City: Sheed and Ward, Ltd., 1963).
Schlink, Edmund. "Themes of the Second Vatican Council from the Evangelical Viewpoint." In Schlink: *The Coming Christ and the Coming Church*. Edinburgh /London: Oliver & Boyd, 1967 [1961], 296-329.
Schreiner, Thomas R. *Romans*. Grand Rapids, MI: Baker Books, 1998.
Seerveld, Calvin. "The relation of the arts to the presentation of truth." In: *Truth and Reality: Philosophical Perspectives on Reality*. Braamfontein: De Jong, 1971, 161-75.
———. "Our Temptation of Philosophy & Troubadour Philosophy." 2003 Jellema Lectures, Calvin College.
Sokolowski, Robert Msgr. *The God of Faith & Reason*. Washington, D.C.: Catholic University of American Press, 1995 [1982].
Sosa, Ernest. "Testimony and coherence." In Sosa: *Knowledge in Perspective: Selected Essays in Epistemology*. Cambridge: Cambridge University Press, 1991, 215-22.
Stob, Henry. "Calvin and Aquinas." In Stob: *Theological Reflections: Essays on Related Themes*. Grand Rapids, MI: Eerdmans, 1981, 126-130.
———. "Observations on the Concept of the Antithesis." In *Perspectives on the Christian Reformed Church, Studies in its History, Theology, and Ecumenicity*. Peter De Klerk & Richard R. De Ridder, eds. 241-258. Grand Rapids, MI: Eerdmans, 1983.
Stott, John. "The Evangelical Doctrine of Baptism." *Churchman*, Vol. 112/1 (1998): 47-49
Taylor, Charles. *Varieties of Religion Today, William James Revisited*. Cambridge, MA: Harvard University Press, 2002.
———. "Clericalism." *The Downside Review*, Vol. 78, No. 252 (Summer 1960): 167-180.
Tjørhom, Ola. *Visible Church-Visible Unity, Ecumenical Ecclesiology and "The Great Tradition of the Church."* Collegeville, Minnesota: The Liturgical Press, 2004.
———. "A Question of Balance: Unity and Diversity in the Life of the Church." *Pro Ecclesia*, Vol. XV, No. 2, 186-204.
Torrell, O.P. Jean-Pierre. *Saint Thomas Aquinas*, Vol. 1, *The Person and His Work*. Translated by Robert Royal Washington, D.C.: Catholic University of America Press, 1996.
Trigg, Roger. *Rationality and Religion, Does Faith Need Reason?* Oxford: Blackwell, 1998.
Troeltsch, Ernst. *The Social Teaching of the Christian Churches*, Vols.1 and 2. Translated by Olive Wyon, with an Introduction by H. Richard Niebuhr. New York: Harper Torchbooks, 1960. Originally published as *Die Soziallehren der Christlichen Kirchen und Gruppen*, 1911.
Vanhoozer, K. J. "The Hermeneutics of I-Witness Testimony: John 21:20-24 and the Death of the Author." In Vanhoozer: *First Theology: God, Scriptures and Hermeneutics*. Downers Grove, IL: InterVarsity Press; Leicester: Apollos, 2002.
Vatican Council I. Dogmatic Constitution *Dei Filius* on the Catholic Faith (1870), Chapter IV, Faith and Reason," in *The Sources of Catholic Dogma*, Edited by Roy J. Deferrari from the Thirtieth Edition of Henry Denzinger's *Enchiridion Symbolorum*. St. Louis/ London: B. Herder Book Co., 1957, 442-57.

Vatican Council II. *Lumen Gentium*. November 21, 1964. Online: http://www.vatican.va/archive/hist_councils/ii_vatican_council/documents/vat-ii_const_19641121_lumen-gentium_en.html.

———. *Unitatis Redintegratio*. November 21, 1964. Online: http://www.vatican.va/archive/hist_councils/ii_vatican_council/documents/vat-ii_decree_19641121_unitatis-redintegratio_en.html.

———. *Orientalium Ecclesiarum*, November 21, 1964. Online: http://www.vatican.va/archive/hist_councils/ii_vatican_council/documents/vat-ii_decree_19641121_orientalium-ecclesiarum_en.html.

———. *Dei Verbum*. November 18, 1965. Online: http://www.vatican.va/archive/hist_councils/ii_vatican_council/documents/vat-ii_const_19651118_dei-verbum_en.html.

———. *Apostolicam Actuositatem*, Decree on the Apostolate of the Laity, November 18, 1965. Online: http://www.vatican.va/archive/hist_councils/ii_vatican_council/documents/vat-ii_decree_19651118_apostolicam-actuositatem_en.html.

———. *Dignitatis Humanae*. December 7, 1965. Online: http://www.vatican.va/archive/hist_councils/ii_vatican_council/documents/vat-ii_decl_19651207_dignitatis-humanae_en.html.

———. *Gaudium et Spes*. December 7, 1965. Online: http://www.vatican.va/archive/hist_councils/ii_vatican_council/documents/vat-ii_cons_19651207_gaudium-et-spes_en.html.

Wainwright, Arthur. *The Trinity in the New Testament*. London: SPCK, 1963.

Warfield, B.B. "A Review of [Herman Bavinck's] *De Zekerheid des Geloofs*." In: *Princeton Theological Review*, Jan. 1903, 138–148.

———. "On Faith in its Psychological Aspects." In Warfield: *Studies in Theology*. New York: Oxford University, 1932, 537–66.

———. "The Biblical Doctrine of the Trinity." In Warfield: *Biblical and Theological Studies*, S.G. Craig, ed. Philadelphia: Presbyterian & Reformed, 1952.

Weber, Max. *Die Protestantische Ethik und der 'Geist' des Kapitalismus*. Tübingen: Mohr, 1934.

———. "Objectivity in Social Science and Social Policy." In Weber: *The Methodology of the Social Sciences*, edited and translated by E. A. Shils and H. A. Finch. New York: Free Press, 1949 [1909].

Weigel, S.J. Gustav. *Catholic Theology in Dialogue*. New York: Harper, 1961.

Weinandy, O.F.M. Cap. Thomas G. *The Father's Spirit of Sonship*. Edinburgh: T&T Clark, 1995.

Whitehead, Kenneth D. *The New Ecumenism*. Staten Island, NY: St. Pauls, 2009.

Willebrands, Johannes Cardinal. "Vatican II's Ecclesiology of Communion." *Origins* 17 (1987): 32.

Wolters, Albert. "What is to be done? Toward a neo-Calvinist Agenda." Online: http://www.wrf.ca/comment/article.cfm?ID=142.

Wolterstorff, Nicholas. "Sacrament as Action, not Presence." In *Christ: The Sacramental Word*, David Brown and Ann Loades, eds., 103–122. London: SPCK, 1996.

———. "Herman Bavinck—Proto-Reformed Epistemology." Unpublished paper presented at Calvin Theological Seminary Conference, Bavinck for the Twenty-First Century, September 18–20, 2008.

Zwaanstra, Henry. *Catholicity and Secession: A Study of Ecumenicity in the Christian Reformed Church*. Grand Rapids, MI: Eerdmans, 1991.

Subject/Name Index

Aquinas, Thomas, 16, 92, 120 n. 10, 141, 145–50, 152, 155 n. 117, 165 n. 154, 169–71, 176, 178, 184 n. 11, 187, 209, 210 n. 93, 218–19
Ashley, Benedict, 153 n. 112, 156 n. 119
Balthasar, Hans Urs von, 16, 78–79, 94, 187–88, 196, 208 n. 85, 212–13, 218, 227, 232
Bare token view, 144–46
Barth, Karl, 3–4, 12, 207 n. 82
Bavinck, Herman, xvii, 5, 13, 24, 38 n. 58, 41, 42 n. 75, 67, 76–9, 89, 92–4, 96–7, 120, 122–23, 135, 139, 141–42, 146–48, 150–54, 156, 160, 173, 175–77, 181–82, 185, 187, 189–92, 194–96, 200–1, 207, 210, 212, 220–26, 228–31, 233–41, 243
Berkouwer, G.C., xvii, xviii n. 22, 13, 23–25, 29–30, 37–38, 40, 78, 89 n. 83, 97 n. 97, 123, 135, 141, n. 69, 142 n. 73, 143 n. 77, n. 81, 145 n. 87, 146–48, 150, 196, 197 n. 48, 204, 208–9, 212, 214–16, 224–25, 227 n. 138, 236
Catechism of the Catholic Church, 93, 119–20, 122, n. 13, 123 n. 17, 124 n. 21, 126, 127 n. 30, 128, 129 n. 39, 136–40, 142 n. 71, 143 n. 80, 162 n. 142, 149 n. 99, 152 n. 106, 162 n. 142, 163, 171 n. 172
Causality, Instrumental and Principal, 147–49
Calvinism, xvi, xviii, 143, 180, 197,
Certainty of Faith, 52, 122, 151
Cessario, Romanus, 168 n. 161, 169, 172, 174, 177
Christian Philosophy, 12, 31 n. 36, 52, 81 n. 57, 180, 182, 190, 199–200, 204–06, 206 n. 80, 207–08, 243
Clouser, Roy, 61 n. 14, 67, n. 21, 117 n. 124
Congar. Yves M.J., 14–15, 17, 18 n. 51, 35, 39 n. 63
Covenant Sign View, 146–47, 50
Dominum et Vivificantem, 123, 124 n. 23, 125–26, 129, 131–5, 136 n. 51, 140–41
Dooyeweerd, Herman, xi, xvii, 54, 63 n. 16, 68–81, 81 n. 57, 82, 85–89, 91–92, 94–95, 98–99, 180–82, 194, 196 n. 48, 197, 204, 215
Dulles, Avery, 27 n. 23, 47 n. 94, 55 n. 5, 75, 77
Duplex Ordo, Vatican I, 204–12
Ecumenism, xiii, xvii, 2, 6, 10–11, 13–15, 16 n. 47, 17, 24, 35–36, 38–39, 42–43, 48, 50–52
Ex opere operato, 140–44, 147, 149
Faith and Knowing, 157–60
Faith and Reason, xix, 12, 27, 33, 122, 154, 183, 183 n. 7, 185–87, 204 n. 70, 206 n. 80, 209 n. 88, 243
Faith and Testimony, 160–64
Fides et Ratio, x, 23 n. 7, 29 n. 27, 32 n. 39, 100, 111 n. 111, 152 n. 109, 162 n. 139, 182, 183 n. 10, 184, 189 n. 25, 200, 204, 232
Gilson, Etienne, 15, 180 n. 1, 187–88, 189–90, 196–99, 200 n. 57, 205–9, 211, 215–16, 230

Subject/Name Index

Grisez, Germain, 23 no. 8, 25 n. 19, 30 n. 34, 33, 171 n. 173
Guardini, Romano, xi, 34, 53 n. 1, 54–69, 71, 73–74, 77, 82–83, 94, 98–115, 117
Harvey, Thomas, 137 n. 55, 142 n. 77, 143 n. 79, 145, 149–50, 151 n. 103
Holy Spirit, xiv, xvi, xix, 3–5, 7–12, 17, 18 n. 51, 35, 36 n. 54, 37, 44–45, 47–48, 52, 64, 68, 72, 79, 82, 99, 105, 113, 116, 119–22, 123–32
Holy Trinity, 9, 119 n. 4, 123, 124 n. 21, 125 n. 25, 126, 128 n. 34, 136,
John XXIII, xvii, 19, 21–23, 26 n. 19, 28, 51 n. 107, 193
John Paul II, x, xiii n. 3, xv–xvi, xix, 2–3, 4 n. 15, 10–12, 15, 22, 23 n. 7, 28–29, 31, 32 n. 41, 52, 55, 65, 83, 88 n. 80, 96 n. 93, 100, 111–12, 114, 119, 122, 124, 132, 141, 151, 152 n. 109, 160, 163 n. 146, 182, 188, 192, 199–200, 203–6, 211, 215, 219, 229, 232–33, 235, 240–41
Kasper, Walter, 6 n. 23, 16 n. 47, 56 n. 9, 58, 65, 101, 123 n. 19
Kuyper, Abraham, xvi, 76 n. 38, 123 n. 17, 135, 145 n. 85, 160–61, 180–82, 194, 197, 243
Language about God, 234–41
Lonergan, Bernard J.F., 26 n. 20, 27–29, 70
Lubac, Henri de, xviii, 16, 23 n. 8, 85–87, 90–91, 93, 194 n. 41, 196–97, 211, 227
Lumen Gentium, x, xiv–xv, xix, 4–5, 7, 36 n. 54, 37, 42 n. 74, 43, 44 n. 81, 46 n. 89, 53 n. 1, 82, 82 n. 59, 84 n. 61, 88 n. 78, 89 n. 83, 90 n. 84
Malloy, Christopher J., 41, 42 n. 73, 46 n. 88, 47 n. 93
Marlet, Michael J., 204
Martin, Francis, 121 n. 10, 229
Natural Knowledge of God, 220–28
Natural Theology, 226–34
Nature and Grace, 194–96, 196 n. 47, 197, 199, 201 n. 60, 202, 204, 243
Nichols, Aidan, 8, 30, 31 n. 36, 90, 112, 115, 227
Occasionalism, 146–50
Ratzinger, Joseph (Benedict XVI), xiii n. 5, 3–4, 6, 7 n. 24, 20, 25, 30 n. 35, 33–37, 39–44, 46–52, 64, 100 n. 103, 162 n. 140, 184–85, 188–89, 191–93, 238
Sacraments, xi, 4, 7, 13, 36 n. 54, 43, 72, 76, 79–80, 81 n. 57, 131–32, 135, 138, 140–42, 142 n. 73, 143, 143 n. 80, 144–45, 145 n. 80, 146, 146 n. 88, 147–49, 149 n. 99, 150
Sacramental Efficacy, 11–12, 137, 140, 142 n. 73
Schlink, Edmund, 38–39, 50
Scholasticism, 182, 186, 196 n. 48, 205, 243
Stott, John, 143–45, 149–50
Theology of faith and reason in Aquinas, 157–73
Troeltsch, Ernst, 53–54, 54 n. 2, 63 n. 16, 69–71, 73–75, 78, 85, 91, 94–95, 98
Truth and its formulations, 19–34
Unitatis Redintegratio, 18, 36, 37 n. 56, 40 n. 67, 42–43, 45 n. 85, 46 n. 90, 47 n. 94, 51 n. 107, 244 n. 2
Unity in Legitimate Diversity, 15–18
Ut Unum Sint, x, xiii n. 3, xv n. 14, 1 n. 2, 2–5, 8, 10–14, 18, 29, 53 n. 110, 244 n. 3
Vatican Council I, 26 n. 20, 154, 204, 208, 227–28
Vatican Council II, xix, 51 n. 107, 227, 241, 243
Veritatis Splendor, 231 n. 152
Wolters, Albert, 185, n. 16, 199 n. 54
Wolterstorff, Nicholas, 146 n. 89, 176–77

www.ingramcontent.com/pod-product-compliance
Lightning Source LLC
Chambersburg PA
CBHW050342230426
43663CB00010B/1951